AN EXEGETICAL SUMMARY OF

JOEL

This book is dedicated to

The Rev. Mark R. Raddatz

Faithful pastor among Christ's flock

Beloved brother

וַיהוָה מִצִּיּוֹן יִשְׁאָג וּמִירוּשָׁלַם יִתֵּן קוֹלוֹ
וְרָעֲשׁוּ שָׁמַיִם וָאָרֶץ
וַיהוָה מַחֲסֶה לְעַמּוֹ וּמָעוֹז לִבְנֵי יִשְׂרָאֵל

Joel 4:16

AN EXEGETICAL SUMMARY OF

JOEL

James N. Pohlig

International

Library of Congress Control Number 2003106375
ISBN: 1-55671-144-1

Printed in the United States of America

Copies of this and other publications of SIL International may be obtained from

International Academic Bookstore
7500 West Camp Wisdom Road
Dallas, TX 75236, USA

Voice: 972-708-7404
Fax: 972-708-7363
E-mail: academic_books@sil.org
Internet: http://www.ethnologue.com

ABBREVIATIONS AND REFERENCES USED IN THIS WORK

Commentaries

Allen — Allen, Leslie C. *The Books of Joel, Obadiah, Jonah, and Micah*. The New International Commentary on the Old Testament. Grand Rapids: Eerdmans, 1976.

Bewer — Bewer, Julius A. "Joel." In *A Critical and Exegetical Commentary on Micah, Zephaniah, Nahum, Habakkuk, Obadiah and Joel*. 1911. Reprint. International Critical Commentary. Edinburgh: T. & T. Clark, 1985.

Cohen — Cohen, A. *The Twelve Prophets*. The Soncino Books of the Bible. New York: Soncino Press, 1994.

Crenshaw — Crenshaw, James L. *Joel*. Anchor Bible. New York: Doubleday, 1995.

Dillard — Dillard, Raymond. "Joel." In vol. 1 of *The Minor Prophets: An Exegetical and Expository Commentary*, ed. Thomas Edward McComiskey. Grand Rapids: Baker, 1992.

Keil — Keil, C. F., and F. Delitzsch. Minor Prophets. *Commentary on the Old Testament in Ten Volumes*, vol. 10. Tr. Rev. James Martin. Grand Rapids: Eerdmans, n.d.

Prinsloo — Prinsloo, Willem S. *The Theology of the Book of Joel*. New York: Walter de Gruyter, 1985.

Stuart — Stuart, Douglas. *Hosea–Joel*. Word Biblical Commentary, 31. Waco, Tex.: Word, 1987.

Wolff — Wolff, Hans Walter. *A Commentary on the Books of Joel and Amos*. Tr. Waldemar Janzen, S. Dean McBride, Jr., and Charles A. Muenchow. Philadelphia: Fortress Press, 1977.

Journal articles

Frankfort — Frankfort, Thérèse. "Le כִּי de Joël 1:12." *Vetus Testamentum* 10 (1960): 445–48.

Garrett — Garrett, Duane A. "The Structure of Joel." *Journal of the Evangelical Theological Society* 28:3 (Sep. 1985): 289–97.

Good — Good, Robert M. "The Just War in Ancient Israel." *Journal of Biblical Literature* 104 (1985): 385–400.

Mariottini — Mariottini, Claude F. "Joel 3:10 [H 4:10]: 'Beat Your Plowshares into Swords.' " *Perspectives in Religious Studies* 14 (1987): 125–30.

Schwarz — Schwarz, Frederic D. "Day of the Locusts." *American Heritage*, July-August 1999.

Simkins — Simkins, Ronald A. "'Return to Yahweh': Honor and Shame in Joel." *Semeia* 68 (1996): 41–54.

VanGemeren — VanGemeren, Willem A. "Spirit of Restoration." *Westminster Theological Journal* 50 (1988): 81–102.

Wolff (a) — Wolff, Hans Walter. "Swords into Plowshares: Misuse of a Word of Prophecy?" *Currents in Theology and Missions* 12 (1985):133–47. (Tr. by Gary Stansell.)

English Bible versions

KJV King James Version
NASB New American Standard Bible
NIV New International Version
NRSV New Revised Standard Version
REB Revised English Bible
TEV Today's English Version

Dictionaries, grammars, and other resources

BDB — Brown, Francis. *The New Brown-Driver-Briggs-Gesenius Hebrew and English Lexicon.* Peabody, Mass.: Hendrickson, 1979.

BHS — Elliger, Karl, and Wilhelm Rudolph, eds. *Biblia Hebraica Stuttgartensia.* Stuttgart: Deutsche Bibelgesellschaft, 1977.

Gesenius — E. Kautzsch, ed. *Gesenius' Hebrew Grammar.* Oxford: Clarendon Press, 1952.

Foll — Follingstad, Carl M. *Deictic Viewpoint in Biblical Hebrew Text: a Syntagmatic and Paradigmatic Analysis of the Particle* כִּי (*kî*). Dallas, Texas: SIL International: 2001.

Harrison — Harrison, R. K. *Introduction to the Old Testament.* Grand Rapids: Eerdmans, 1969.

Hol — Holladay, William L., ed. *A Concise Hebrew and Aramaic Lexicon of the Old Testament.* Grand Rapids: Eerdmans, 1988.

TWOT — Harris, R. Laird, Gleason L. Archer, Jr., and Bruce K. Waltke, eds. *Theological Wordbook of the Old Testament.* 2 vols. Chicago: Moody Press, 1980.

Waltke — Waltke, Bruce K., and M. O'Connor. *An Introduction to Biblical Hebrew Syntax.* Winona Lake, Ind.: Eisenbrauns, 1990.

Wendland — Wendland, Ernst R. *The Discourse Analysis of Hebrew Prophetic Literature: Determining the Larger Textual Units of Hosea and Joel.* Mellen Biblical Press Series, Vol. 40. Lampeter, Dyfed, Wales: Mellen Biblical Press, 1995.

Wolff (b) — *Anthropology of the Old Testament.* Philadelphia: Fortress, 1975.

Other abbreviations

adj.	adjective
adv.	adverb
BH	Biblical Hebrew
conj.	conjunction
constr.	construct relationship in BH
def. art.	definite article
ET	A reading resulting from an emendation to the Masoretic text
fem.	feminine
fut.	future
imper.	imperative
imperf.	imperfect tense (so-called) in BH
infin.	infinitve
LXX	the Septuagint
Masc.	masculine
MT	Masoretic Text
part.	participle
pass.	passive
perf.	perfect tense (so-called) in BH
pl. or, in the semiliteral renderings of Hebrew, (p)	plural
poss.	possessive
pron.	pronoun
sing. or, in the semiliteral renderings of Hebrew, (s)	singular

TRANSLITERATION KEY

Consonants

Letter	Heb	Tlit.	Pronunciation
Aleph	א	ʾ	glottal stop as in *uh'oh* or Cockney *bottle* [ʔ], but silent when word final
Beth	ב	ḇ	v as in *van* [v]
with dagesh lene	בּ	b	b as in *bell* [b]
with dagesh forte	בּ	bb	bb as in *job bill* [bˑ] (geminate)
Gimel	ג	ḡ	g as in *gate* (no distinction with g) [g]
with dagesh lene	גּ	g	g as in *gate* [g]
with dagesh forte	גּ	gg	gg as in *big gate* [gˑ] (geminate)
Daleth	ד	ḏ	th as in *the* [ð] (voiced interdental fricative)
with dagesh lene	דּ	d	d as in *door* [d]
with dagesh forte	דּ	dd	dd as in *sad dog* [dˑ] (geminate)
He	ה	h	h as in *heave*, but silent when it is the last letter in a word
with dagesh, word final form	הּ	ẖ	normally not pronounced (mappiq—a graphic distinction)
Waw	ו	w	w as in *well* (though quite possibly [β] voiced bilabial fricative)
Zayin	ז	z	z as in *zeal* [z]
with dagesh forte	זּ	zz	zz as in *whiz zoom* [zˑ] (geminate)
Heth	ח	ḥ	ch as in *loch* (a deep h back in throat) [ʜ] (voiceless pharyngeal fricative)
Teth	ט	ṭ	t as in *tip* [t̪] (though possibly [tˤ] (voiceless pharyngealized stop)
Yodh	י	y	y as in *yellow* [y]
Kaph	כ	ḵ	ch as in German *Bach* [x] (velar fricative)
word final form	ך	ḵ	
with dagesh lene	כּ	k	k as in *king* [k]
with dagesh forte	כּ	kk	kk as in *track car* [kˑ] (geminate)
Lamedh	ל	l	l as in *liner* [l]
Mem	מ	m	m as in *mail* [m]
word final form	ם		
Nun	נ	n	n as in *noose* [n]
word final form	ן	n	
Samekh	ס	s	s as in *sell* [s]
Ayin	ע	ʿ	as in *aah* said for a doctor, but with h sound [ʕ] (voiced pharyngeal fricative), but silent word final
Pe	פ	p̄	f as in *face* (though possibly [ɸ] voiceless bilabial fricative)
word final form	ף	p̄	
with dagesh lene	פּ	p	p as in *pet* [p]
with dagesh forte	פּ	pp	pp as in *scrap paper* [pˑ] (geminate)
Tsadhe	צ	ṣ	ts as in *cats* [ts] (though possibly [sˤ] voiceless pharyngealized velar fricative)
word final form	ץ	ṣ	

Letter	Heb	Tlit.	Pronunciation
Qoph	ק	q	k as in German *kohl* [q] (uvular stop)
Resh	ר	r	r as in *rain* [r]
Sin (dotless)	ש	s̄	graphic symbol: not pronounced
Sin	שׂ	ś	s as in *sell* [s]
Shin	שׁ	š	sh as in *shell* [ʃ]
Taw	ת	ṯ	th as in *myth* [θ] (voiceless inderdental fricative)
with dagesh lene	תּ	t	t as in *tall* [t]
with dagesh forte	תּ	tt	tt as in *great teacher* [tˑ] (geminate)

Vowels

Letter	Heb.	Tlit.	Pronunciation
Pathah	ַ	a	a as in *bat* [æ] (or sometimes as in *father* [a])
Pathah Hateph (reduced)	ֲ	ă	a said quickly as in *above* [ə]
Qamets	ָ	ā	a as the first a in *father* [a]
Qamets He	ָה	â	(consonant used with vowel) a as in *father*
Qamets Hatuph	ָ	o	o as in *bought* [ɔ]
Qamets Hateph (reduced)	ֳ	ŏ	a said quickly as in *above* [ə]
Shewa	ְ	ə	a said quickly as in *above* [ə]
Hireq	ִ	i	i as in *pit* [ɪ]
Hireq Yodh	ִי	î	(consonant used with a vowel) i as in *machine* [i]
Tsere	ֵ	ē	e as in *they* [e]
Tsere Yodh	ֵי	ê	(consonant used with a vowel) e as in *they* [e]
Tsere He	ֵה	ēh	(consonant used with a vowel) e as in *they* [e]
Seghol	ֶ	e	e as in *pet* [ɛ]
Seghol Yodh	ֶי	ệ	(consonant used with a vowel) e as in *they* [e]
Seghol He	ֶה	eh	(consonant used with a vowel) e as in *pet* [ɛ]
Seghol Hateph (reduced)	ֱ	ĕ	a said quickly as in *above* [ə]
Holem		ō	o as in *bowl* [o]
Holem *Waw*	וֹ	ô	(consonant used with a vowel) o as in *bowl* [o]
Holem He	ֹה	ōh	(consonant used as a vowel) o as in *bowl* [o]
Qibbuts	ֻ	u	u as in *book* [ʊ]
Sureq	וּ	û	u as in *mood* [u]

INTRODUCTION

The dating of the Book of Joel

Many commentators traditionally dated Joel as pre-exilic on the basis of the book's place among the Minor Prophets in the Hebrew canon (between Hosea and Amos). Although the book itself provides no overt dating, Keil places Joel in the first part of the reign of Joash in Judah (ca. 837–807 B.C.), and Stuart writes of the probability that Joel is pre-exilic. They adduce the following reasons:

1. Keil assumes that Amos and Isaiah quote from the Book of Joel. (Amos 1:2 is said to draw from Joel 3:16, and Isaiah 13 is considered to be reminiscent of Joel; for example, Isa. 13:6 is said to be a quotation from Joel 1:15.) Stuart sees so much resemblance between 2:1–11 and Isaiah 13 that he cannot discount the possibility that Joel may be as early as the seventh century B.C.
2. Keil cites Joel's lack of reference to the great imperial powers—Assyria and Babylon—as Israel's enemies, nor even to Syria, against whom Joash died in battle, as suggesting that Joel should be dated from the first part of Joash's reign.
3. Keil notes that Joel makes no mention of the idolatry which angered Hosea and Amos, and that he rather seems to imply that the worship of YHWH in Judah is well established and has no rival.
4. Keil sees Joel's lack of reference to the monarchy as arguing for a period of a weak king. This condition fits the first part of Joash's reign, during which the high priest Jehoiada dominated the monarchy. On the other hand, Stuart sees Joel's failure to refer to the monarchy as silence from which one cannot argue either for or against a pre-exilic date.

Most contemporary scholars, however, give definite or tentative support to placing Joel in postexilic times, perhaps in the fifth century B.C. [e.g., Crenshaw], or between 445 B.C. and 343 B.C. [e.g., Wolff], for the following reasons:

1. The time of the exile seems excluded by the fact that Joel depicts Temple worship as functioning in the period [Crenshaw, Dillard, Wolff]. If one views certain expressions in Joel 2:11 and 3:4 (2:31) as having been borrowed from Malachi, and if one regards Joel's complete silence about any deficiency in Temple order or in the people's worship as indicating a well-functioning Temple and sacrificial routine, then Joel may be assumed to postdate both Malachi's prophetic inveighings against insufficient and complacent worship life and also the successful interventions of Nehemiah and Ezra [Wolff].
2. Joel does not take the people to task for idolatry or syncretism, which were rife under most kings. Infertile fields and droughts would

probably have elicited the worship of Baal, the fertility god, in the time of the monarchy [Dillard].

3. The use of the expression 'my sacred mountain' (הַר קָדְשִׁי *har qodšî*) in 2:1 to refer to Jerusalem alone indicates a date subsequent to Josiah's reforms [Dillard].
4. Joel's co-referent use of 'Judah' and 'Israel' implies that the northern kingdom has long been defunct [Crenshaw, Dillard].
5. Joel's reference in 2:9 to a city wall probably excludes the time of exile and its aftermath when Jerusalem had no functioning wall (i.e., 586–445 B.C.) [Crenshaw, Wolff]. On the other hand, this reference is not conclusive: Although the Babylonians had greatly damaged the wall, they did not completely level it; rather, they had contented themselves with knocking down various segments of it. Otherwise, it would have taken far longer than fifty-two days (see Neh. 6:15) to reconstruct it [Dillard].
6. Joel's reference in 4:2 (3:2)[1] to a deportation of Jerusalem's inhabitants might well place his book after the fall of Jerusalem [Crenshaw]. On the other hand, as Dillard points out, deportation had been widely practiced in the Near East since the Assyrians, and so a reference to deportation need not necessarily imply the Babylonian exile.
7. A very small Jewish population is implied by Joel's exhortation in 1:14 that every last person come to the solemn assembly, a condition which held only in postexilic times [Crenshaw].
8. Joel seems to refer to the conquest of Jerusalem (4:17 (3:17)) [Crenshaw]. Moreover, he refers to it in a very matter-of-fact manner, as if it is now old history for him and his audience [Wolff].
9. Joel makes no reference to the monarchy, thus implying a period when the religious leaders were in political charge of the people, a post-restoration condition. These leaders have assumed the duty of summoning the people to fasts of repentance, a duty which had earlier come under the purvey of the monarchy [Crenshaw, Wolff]. On the other hand, one could argue that Joel omits reference to the monarchy because the monarchy was very weak, as during the minority of King Joash [Dillard].

---

[1] The Book of Joel was first divided into chapters in the thirteenth century with the translation of the Vulgate, in which it was divided into the three chapters. (This division is still used in most English versions.) In the next century, the three-chapter division was applied as well to the LXX and to the Hebrew Bible. But beginning in the sixteenth century the Book of Joel was divided into four chapters in the Hebrew Bible [Wolff]. This exegetical summary uses both chapter schemes. Wherever there is a difference of verse numbers, the reference in the Hebrew Bible scheme is given first, and the reference in the Vulgate–LXX–traditional English scheme follows it in parentheses.

10. Joel makes no reference to Israel's traditional enemies, the Assyrians and the Babylonians [Crenshaw, Dillard]. While one might date the book on this basis from before the rise of the Assyrian Empire [Dillard], one might equally well date it during the Persian Empire [Dillard], which brought about relative political security [Crenshaw].
11. Joel's threat against Edom (4:19 (3:19)) is likely to have been in response to the Edomites' having brought Jewish fugitives to the Babylonian conquerors after the fall of Jerusalem [Crenshaw].
12. The reference to the slave-trading Phoenicians, who sold captured Jews to Sabeans, who in turn resold them to the Greeks, accords well with the seventh to fifth centuries B.C.[Crenshaw]. Tyre and Sidon were two important commercial centers condemned also by Ezekiel (Ezek. 27:13), as they had sought to profit from the Babylonian conquest of Judah [Dillard]. Since Sidon was destroyed by the Persian ruler Artaxerxes III Ochus in 343 B.C., the Book of Joel should most likely be dated before then [Wolff]. In addition, the Greeks are spoken of in 3:6 (4:6) as being far off and as providing a market for slaves only through Phoenician middlemen, which presumably would not have been the case after Alexander the Great's conquest of Tyre and Gaza in 332 B.C. Finally, the cities of Tyre and Sidon are associated with Philistia in 4:4 (3:4); there is extrabiblical evidence that in the later Persian Empire, these elements did indeed form one community [Wolff].
13. The Book of Joel has few genuine apocalyptic features, but it does appear to move in the direction of apocalyptic literature, featuring as it does a very simple eschatology—final defeat of Israel's enemies, restoration for Jerusalem, and the triumph of YHWH [Crenshaw]. Among the apocalyptic marks is an emphasis on periods of time, as shown in time formulas (2:23b, 2:25, 3:1, 3:2, 3:4b). The book also moves far beyond a simple, materialistic emphasis on national well-being to a developed concept of divine salvation. For example, Joel moves beyond the goal of having harvests sufficient enough to ensure Temple sacrifices (2:14b) to the goal of having God's Spirit create whole generations of prophets (3:1) [Wolff]. The day of YHWH, a familiar concept in earlier prophetic literature, is given universal effects in Joel, as he proclaims that YHWH's judgment will come upon all nations [Mariottini]. These are concerns not evident in the epoch of Ezra, Nehemiah, or Malachi, and not really datable before 400 B.C. [Wolff].
14. Joel uses words which apparently appear only late in BH. Some examples are שֶׁלַח *šelaḥ* 'weapon, missile', צַחֲנָה *ṣaḥănâ* 'stench', and סוֹף *sôp̄* 'rear' [Crenshaw, Wolff]. Another example, מְשָׁרְתֵי *məšārəṯê*, a plural term meaning 'servants of ... , ministers of ...', occurs only in postexilic literature; and the form מִן־בְּנֵי *min bənê* 'from the children' is typical of postexilic literature, while מִבְּנֵי *mibbənê* is common in pre-exilic [Dillard]. Other expressions in Joel

which occur nowhere else in the OT are probably of late BH origin: אלה *ʾlh* 'to lament', עבשׁ *ʿḇš* 'to shrivel', פְּרֻדֹת *pərudôṯ* 'seed grains', מֶגְרְפוֹת *meḡrəp̄ôṯ* 'clods', and עבט *ʿḇṭ* 'to change course' [Wolff]. Multiple references in Joel to meal offerings and libations indicate postexilic worship practices [Wolff].

15. Joel's striking ability to draw on earlier Biblical passages argues for a fairly late date [Crenshaw, Wolff], although some of his allusions might have been drawn from current prophetic language instead [Dillard]. Joel demonstrates an ability to reinterpret or reapply passages of earlier prophets [Mariottini]. Moroever, his citation of Obad. 17a in 3:5 (2:32) allows Joel to be dated after the mid–fifth century B.C., for Obadiah cannot date from before that time [Wolff].
16. The LXX (the Greek version of the Hebrew and Aramaic OT) appears to have considered Joel to be undated, for within its corpus Joel is grouped with Obadiah and Jonah, which are likewise without date. The basis for Joel's position in the LXX seems to be a similarity of message, particularly with Amos, which it precedes in the LXX: elements of 3:16 (4:16) and 3:18 (4:18) correspond to Amos 1:2 and 9:13. Moreover, Joel echoes Amos' judgment against various nations, especially Tyre, Philistia, and Edom. Thus, the placement of Joel in the LXX constitutes a literary device common in the assembly of OT books, that of preceding various documents with more recent texts, the aim being to guide the reader to a proper interpretation of the older texts [Wolff].

Two approaches to evaluating the unity of the Book of Joel

Interpreting Joel as a highly redacted text. Many commentators have been unable to reconcile a description of the historical locust plague in Joel 1 and perhaps Joel 2 with the apocalyptic theme of Joel 3–4. Bernhard Duhm (1875), the most influential of the redactionist exegetes of Joel, accepted Joel's authorship of most of chapters 1–2 but attributed the descriptions of locust invasions in Joel 1–2 to a poet, and the eschatology of Joel 3–4 to a preacher from the time of the Maccabees; in more recent times, Ernst Sellin (1929) and Theodore Robinson (1964), under Duhm's influence, have also argued against the book's unity [Harrison, Wolff]. Julius A. Bewer (1911), another of Duhm's followers, accepted Joel's authorship of most of chapters 1–2 and also of 3:1–4a (2:28–31a), and of 3:9–14a (4:9–14a), based on what he considered to be the real Joel's "superior" literary style. Like others, he assigned the motif of the day of YHWH in Joel 2 to a later author and editor, as he considered Joel's original work to feature only the locust plague, with no cosmic or eschatological implications.

Interpreting Joel as a unity. In contrast to the view beginning around 1875 of Joel as a highly redacted text, the twentieth century saw some scholars strongly defend the single authorship of Joel—at least of the book's major portions, if not of its entirety. Leslie C. Allen (1976) and H. W. Wolff (1975), for example, argue for Joel's essential unity. Wolff in particular has adduced literary features of the book as support for his position; he holds only 3:3–8 (4:4–8) to have been added later by another author, and 2:26b and 3:18–21 (4:18–21) to likely be later additions, perhaps by Joel himself.The textlinguist Ernst Wendland (1995) also approaches Joel as an organic unity, as, indeed, any textlinguist must. This is so, because if one has already dismembered the book by ascribing its parts to various sources or authors, the textlinguist has nothing left to analyze. Wendland offers a systematic analysis of the forms and functions of recursion in Joel, adducing from them patterns of textual binding, bounding, and prominence. A fair demonstration on these bases of the organic unity of a text can be very convincing.

The literary character of the Book of Joel

There are various views as to the literary genre of the Book of Joel:

1. Crenshaw views Joel as an address of the prophet to the people of Israel on the occasion of a national emergency.
2. Both Dillard and Wolff see Joel as probably a liturgical text meant for use in times of national lament, as were several psalms as well; it was used when the people gathered for fasting and prayer during emergencies. Although the text may have originated during a specific emergency in Israel, its historical details were probably excised in order for the text to serve on other occasions also. This explains the lack of such detail in Joel, but allows liturgical elaboration. Others as well (e.g., Théophane Chary) see Joel as a lament for a certain national disaster [Théophane Chary, *Les prophètes et la culte à partir de l'exil autour du Second Temple: L'idéal cultuel des prophètes exiliens et postexiliens*, Bibliothèque de Théologie 3/3 (Tournai: Desclée, 1955), cited by Dillard].
3. Ahlström considers Joel not as an actual lament, for there is no introduction, but as rather an exhortation to the priests to lament [Gosta W. Ahlström, *Joel and the Temple Cult of Jerusalem,* Supplement to *Vetus Testamentum* 21 (Leiden: E. J. Brill, 1971), cited by Crenshaw].

As to the book's literary features, Joel draws on many themes present in earlier Hebrew tradition, both written and oral; his use of the Pentateuch and the earlier literary prophets is inexhaustibly rich. Using these themes, Joel is able to explain the present agricultural calamities in the light of the blessings and strictures of YHWH's covenant with Israel, and also of the long tradition of YHWH's prophets' dealing with the nation of Israel. However, Joel often reverses the traditional prophetic use of images, giving them unexpected applications, among which irony is heavily featured. Corresponding to these reversals are reversals of national situations in the book. For example, the disasters brought to Israel by locust and plague in Joel 1–2 are reversed into untold blessings in Joel 3–4; and the army of locusts depicted in Joel 1 turns out to be in Joel 2—at least figuratively if not in reality—an army sent by YHWH himself [Crenshaw, Wendland].

Theories concerning the background for Joel's message to Judah

Theories that posit national sins in the background of this book. While Joel mentions no particular sin as lying behind the original national emergency that he depicts, commentators who base their view on the covenantal model have traditionally assumed that there was such a sin. Keil, for example, presumes that some sin prevented rapport between God and Judah because in Joel 2:13 the prophet exhorts the nation to 'return' (שׁוּב *šûḇ*) to God. Bewer assumes that the national calamity awakened in the people a sense of general sinfulness in their relationship to YHWH. Wolff considers that Judah's sin was her unwillingness to accept the prophetic tradition embodied in the concept of the day of YHWH as Ezekiel, and now Joel building upon that earlier prophet,[2] applied it to Judah herself.

In Joel's day, the priests had reason from their point of view to be satisfied: the Temple worship routine in restoration Judah had at last been re-established and was functioning properly, and indeed Joel found no fault in it. But Joel stood in the vigorous prophetic tradition of Israel, which carried him beyond the strictly priestly concerns. Joel saw YHWH doing something new in his dealings with his covenant people—something to which Isaiah and Amos had witnessed earlier, but which the community and the priestly circles now found convenient to ignore. That new thing was what Joel described as the coming day of YHWH, the subject of which Joel introduced in his book by means of an apparently historical locust plague that had recently devastated Judah. When Joel in 2:12 tells the nation to "return" to YHWH, he is not thinking of any traditional sin which would have been immediately recognizable in the light of Deuteronomy or of the longstanding Yahwistic covenant traditions. He is rather thinking of Judah's failure to be alert to the meaning of YHWH's current actions and his far-flung program for the future in relation to Israel and the other nations of the world. This program he sums up under the rubric "the day of YHWH." Ironically, Joel means "return to YHWH" in the old Deuteronomistic sense of "pay heed to YHWH," more so than in the sense of "repent from your sins of idolatry, etc.," (which is the sense of "return" in Hosea, Jeremiah, and Ezekiel). We may infer that Joel was implicitly criticizing the complacency created by the political and religious management of the covenant community of his day (for there was no monarchy in his day).

Theories that posit no national sin in the background of this book. Stuart observes that Joel's failure to rebuke the people for any particular sin makes this book unusual in comparison to most of the other literary prophets, although neither do Nahum and Habakkuk single out a sin. Crenshaw

---

[2] See especially Ezek. 33:1–20; 18:21–32; and 3:20–21.

considers that to impute to Israel a specific sin when Joel does not would be to ignore the complexities of human existence in which apparently undeserved calamities do indeed occur; even the use of שׁוּב *šûḇ* 'to return' in 2:13 is not conclusive proof that Joel is calling the people to repentance, for *šûḇ* can have senses other than 'to repent'. Stuart believes that the strong eschatological nature of the book makes any rebuke of the people's sin unsuitable: The calamities which have occurred and which portend the even more cataclysmic events associated with the day of YHWH seem to take all of Joel's attention.

In the view of Dillard, Wendland, and Wolff, the reason for the absence of reference to any specific sin is the liturgical function in Temple worship acquired by this book. Liturgies must be kept general so as to be applicable to many different situations. Certainly it is common for psalms of lamentation not to refer to particular sins.

The theory that this book concerns shame and honor rather than sin and judgment. Simkins proposes that Joel's message is not best read in the light of YHWH's ancient covenant with Israel, but instead in the light of the honor-shame anthropological model adduced by many for most ancient Mediterranean societies. Simkins presents the following key points:

1. Any effort to identify a national sin for which Joel rebukes the people is only speculative. Consequently, the traditional interpretation of the book within the Mosaic covenantal model of sin–threatened punishment–repentance–restoration–blessing is forced.
2. The honor-shame model, which characterizes much current anthropology of ancient and modern Mediterranean cultures, suggests itself as an alternative basis for interpreting Joel. This model comprises the following elements: (a) An individual identifies and evaluates himself in terms of the honor he enjoys in his society and which his society awards him according to his reputation and social standing; that is, one's claim to honor is validated only by its public acknowledgement.[3] (b) The individual usually acquires honor by competing for it against his peers. Often the competition occurs along family or clan lines, according to which the gains and losses in social deference and precedence are carefully tallied, out of the assumption that one's gain in honor necessitates another's loss. Such loss is termed shame and results when one is unsuccessful in maintaining his honor or when the society declines to substantiate his claim to a certain deference or precedence. (c) Being the arena in which these conflicts are played out, the society itself suffers fragmentation from underlying tension, but

---

[3] See Bruce J. Malina, *The New Testament World: Insights from Cultural Anthropology* (Atlanta: John Knox, 1981]. See also Bruce J. Malina and Jerome H. Neyrey, "Honor and Shame in Luke-Acts: Pivotal Values of the Mediterranean World," in *The Social World of Luke-Acts: Models for Interpretation,* ed. J. H. Neyrey (Peabody, Mass.: Hendrickson, 1991], 25–65. These sources are cited by Simkins.

attempts to compensate by maintaining a veneer of courtesy and obligations mutual to its members. (d) But since it is the arena of conflict, the society also is the key to the individual's own identity and self-evaluation: He sees himself through the collective's opinion of himself. Thus the individual assumes a grave responsibility to uphold the collective's corporate honor, whether the collective be his family, clan, or village; for while he can bask in the collective's honor, there is also the danger that any ill-considered action of his own might ruin it.

3. In the OT, the honor-shame model can be applied on many various levels of Israel's society. For the purposes of Joel, however, the model is seen as operating between Judah and the surrounding nations. A prosperous Judah is evidence of YHWH's faithfulness to her and is the source of her pride in the community of nations. Evidence of YHWH's continued presence with Judah (e.g., her victories in warfare) is another source of her honor. On the other hand, if Judah should suffer disaster that is unmerited on her part by any unfaithfulness to YHWH, then her claim before the other nations to be the object par excellence of YHWH's love and loyalty is likely to be mocked. Thus in 2:17, Joel sees his nation as having become a target of scorn. Thus again, the book ends with YHWH's promising honor to Judah, in 4:17 (3:17).
4. In applying the honor-shame model to Joel, one should appreciate that in the cultures of Israel and the surrounding nations, the notion of joy was conceived less as an emotion and more as pleasures arising from engagement in certain rituals, such as the Temple sacrificial and worship routines, the festivals, and marital relations with one's wife. Similarly, the notion of sadness was linked to ritual activities such as fasting, the tearing of one's clothes, and sitting in ashes. In other words, an emotion depended on actions by which it was elicited as much as the actions depended on the emotion. It was always appropriate for Israel to celebrate YHWH's presence by engaging in ritual actions of joy; conversely, YHWH's withdrawal from Israel would be marked by ritual mourning.[4]
5. Within an honor-shame interpretation of Joel, the prophet is seen as proposing a remedy: that the people should—not repent, strictly speaking, for there has been no prior sin to repent of, but rather—resume the public or Temple worship, not by resuming the full sacrificial routine (for the famine made that impossible according to 1:9), but by performing the public rituals of mourning before YHWH,

---

[4] See Gary Anderson, "Celibacy or Consummation in the Garden? Reflections on Early Jewish and Christian Interpretations of the Garden of Eden," *Harvard Theological Review* 82 (1989): 121–48. See also Gary Anderson, *A Time to Mourn, a Time to Dance: The Expression of Grief and Joy in Israelite Religion* (Philadelphia: University of Pennsylvania Press, 1991]. These sources are cited by Simkins.

as Joel enjoins in 1:13–14. Such mourning will bring honor to YHWH, and he will then restore Israel's honor.

The calamities in Joel

The calamities depicted in Joel have been the object of much debate, especially the first (1:2–12) and the third (2:1–17). Are the descriptions of these two calamities to be taken literally? Should either one be taken so—and which one? Are the two calamities identical? One's view of the first and third calamities greatly affects the answers to these three questions: (1) What are the book's parts? (2) What relationship do the book's parts have to each other? (3) What is the book's ultimate meaning? The following chart summarizes various ideas on the nature of the calamities. Also displayed are salient references in Joel under which these views are expressed.

Commentators	**1:2–12** Literally, a locust invasion.	**1:15–20** Literally, a drought.	**2:1–17** Literally, some kind of devastating invasion.
Allen, Bewer, Keil	A real locust invasion, identical to what is described in 2:1–17.	A real drought.	Another description of the same locust invasion depicted in 1:2–12, or perhaps a succeeding wave of locusts. Allen and Keil regard Joel as identifying the locust plague with the approach of YHWH's judgment day. Bewer, however, regards the connection between the plague and the day of YHWH as the work of an editor, rather than of Joel. He also regards 2:1–17 as describing the coming of the first of the many waves of locusts named in 1:2–12.
Simkins	A real locust invasion.	A metaphor for the same locust invasion.	Another locust invasion in the next agricultural season.
Crenshaw, Dillard, Wolff	A real locust invasion, functioning as a harbinger of the coming day of YHWH.	A real drought.	YHWH's divine army, described in terms of locusts and human armies, comes to judge Israel and to war against evil.
Stuart, Garrett	An invasion of a foreign enemy.	A real drought.	Invasion by the Assyrians or Babylonians.
Soncino	A real locust invasion.	A real drought.	A real locust invasion.
VanGemeren	A real locust invasion, representative of the day of YHWH.		

The structure of the Book of Joel

Dividing the book in two parts: 1:2–2:17 and 2:18 to the end. Many commentators see the Book of Joel as divided into two great halves, 1:2–2:17 and from 2:18 to the book's end. In this view, the first half is characterized by the theme of judgment upon Judah and the necessity to repent, and the second half presents YHWH's response to the repentance. Wendland's analysis shows just how these two halves are balanced:

1. They are balanced in the number of words. Part 1 (1:2–2:17) has 424 word units (counting equally separate words and words joined together with a *maqqeph*, or hyphen in BH), and Part 2 (2:18–4:21) has 425.
2. They are balanced in the subdivisions. Each half consists of two "oracles," and each oracle consists of two "stanzas." Of each pair of stanzas in any oracle, the first stanza is longer than the second. Each stanza consists of three to five strophes.
3. They are balanced in the nature of the stanzas. In each pair of stanzas, the second stanza presents some kind of thematic progression vis-à-vis the first stanza, or some kind of response to it. For example, Stanza B presents the people's reaction to the disaster portrayed in Stanza A. Stanza D presents the prophet's challenge to the people to respond as they should to the invasion depicted in Stanza C. Moreoever, each stanza has a peak, which usually occurs near the end of the stanza. Stanza D (2:12–17) is a summons to the people to turn to YHWH, and it fulfills a double second duty: It is the climax to Part 1 of the book and also a transitional element leading to Part 2. (See Appendix 2 for details of Wendland's organization of Joel.)

Dividing the book in two parts: 1:2–2:27 and 3:1 (2:28) to the end. Some commentators, such as Bewer, have made the bipartite division of Joel after 2:27. In this view, the first half deals with the plagues (however they are interpreted), the summons to Judah to repent, and YHWH's promise of mercy and dignity for his people and renewal of the land. The second half then deals with the day of YHWH and what it will mean: spiritual blessing for Judah and judgment upon her enemies together with cosmological signs signaling the defeat of all YHWH's foes and his never-ending presence among his people.

Combining the first two views of how to divide the book. Garrett proposes that Joel has in fact what might be called two epicenters, 2:17/18 and 2:27/3:1 (2:27/28). These epicenters are structurally defined by two introverted structures which are interlocking and which span the entire book. These introverted structures are as follows:

A	judgment: *locust* plague	chapter 1		
B	judgment: *apocalyptic army*	2:1–11		
C	transition and lead into the response of YHWH	2:12–19		
B´	grace: destruction of *apocalyptic army*	2:20	A	*judgment*
A´	grace: defeat of locusts and renewal of the land	2:21–27	B	*grace*: renewal of the land
			B´	*grace*: gift of Spirit
			A´	*judgment*: hostile nations' defeat

Note that the first introverted structure ends at 2:27, which is the second epicenter of the book. The second introverted structure begins at 2:20, which is after the first epicenter of the book.

Conventions used in presenting the text of Joel in this exegetical summary

Cola. The semiliteral translation is presented in imitation of the presentation of the Masoretic Hebrew text in BHS, which usually presents one bicolon per line (sometimes a tricolon per line) with a space between each colon, as in Joel 2:1 below:

תִּקְעוּ שׁוֹפָר בְּצִיּוֹן   וְהָרִיעוּ בְּהַר קָדְשִׁי
יִרְגְּזוּ כֹּל יֹשְׁבֵי הָאָרֶץ   כִּי־בָא יוֹם־יְהוָה כִּי קָרוֹב׃

The semiliteral translation is presented similarly, with spaces separating the parts of a bicolon or a tricolon. A bicolon of English text is presented on one line, running over to a second line if its length so demands. In the following example, Joel 2:1, the second bicolon appears at first glance to be very long, but note that a translation choice is presented here by means of a slash (/).

Blow[a] (a-)ram's-horn[b] on[c]-Zion,[d] (colon α) **and-sound-an-alarm[e] on[f]-(the-)** (colon β)

mountain(-of)[g] my-holiness.[h]

Let- all (the-)inhabitants(-of)[i] the-land[j] -tremble[k] / All (the-) (colon γ)

inhabitants(-of)[i] the-land[j] will-tremble,[k] for[l] (the-)day(-of)[m] (colon δ)

YHWH is-coming,[n] for[o] (it is) near.[p]

The cola will be referred to with Greek letters as shown in the example above.

The Masoretic division of some verses departs from the regular bicolon per line, in that some lines in the BHS are divided by secondary Masoretic accents. In these cases, no effort has been made in the semiliteral translation to distinguish these smaller units from regular cola. For example, Joel 4:13 appears as follows in BHS:

שִׁלְח֣וּ מַגָּ֔ל כִּ֥י בָשַׁ֖ל קָצִ֑יר
בֹּ֤אוּ רְדוּ֙ כִּֽי־מָ֣לְאָה גַּ֔ת
הֵשִׁ֙יקוּ֙ הַיְקָבִ֔ים כִּ֥י רַבָּ֖ה רָעָתָֽם׃

Here the athnach, marking the foremost division in the verse, occurs at the end of the first line. Secondary and tertiary accents divide the following lines, but the semiliteral translation takes no notice of the differences among these accents:

Swing(p)[a] (the-)sickle,[b] for[c] (the-)harvest[d] is-ripe[e];
go(p)[f] tread(p)(grapes in the winepress),[g-1] / go(p) descend,[g-2] for[h] (the-) winepress[i] is-full,[j]
(the-)wine-vats[k] have-overflowed,[l] for[m] great[n] (is) their-wickedness.[o]

Parentheses and slashes. Parentheses are employed in the semiliteral translation to signal English words or other morphemes whose semantic values are judged to be implied in the Hebrew text. An example is in the first bicolon of Joel 2:1:

Blow[a] (a-)ram's-horn[b] on[c]-Zion,[d] and-sound-an-alarm[e] on[f]-(the-)
(colon α) (colon β)
mountain(-of)[g] my-holiness[h]

The expression *ram's-horn*, being unqualified by an article in Hebrew, is judged to denote any representative of that class of musical instrument; hence, the English indefinite article *a* is inserted between parentheses before it. In the same bicolon, the English definite article *the* is noted parenthetically as implied before *mountain*. This article reflects the definiteness of *mountain* provided by the Hebrew construct relationship between *mountain* and *my-holiness*. Again, the English preposition *of* is inserted in order to signal the same Hebrew construct relationship.

Parentheses are also used to enclose *s* or *p* when they are inserted after the 2nd person English pronoun in order to denote the singular or plural pronoun; thus,

you(s) you(p)

The slash (/) is employed to indicate two viable literal translations of a portion of the Hebrew text or two different Hebrew textual readings. In the following bicolon from Joel 2:1, the slash separates two understandings of the Hebrew verb 'tremble'—the first translation sees the verb as a jussive, and the second as an imperfect:

Let- all (the-)inhabitants(-of)[i] the-land[j] -tremble[k] / All (the-)

inhabitants(-of)[i] the-land[j] will-tremble[k]

The hyphen. Hyphens indicate the combination of separate Hebrew morphemes in one Hebrew word. But a partial English viewpoint is represented also in the hyphenation. For example, in Joel 1:12, the expression

and-the-fig-tree(s)

represents the combination of the *waw* connective 'and', the definite article *ha* 'the', and the lexical item *təʾēnâ* 'fig tree'. Because in this context the singular noun indicates a collective generality, *s* appears in parentheses after *tree* to signal a plural English concept, but *tree* is also hyphenated to *fig* because of the English convention that spells this species of tree as two words. Any potential confusion over the dual Hebrew and English use of the hyphen is dispelled in the lexicon field following.

A very common employment of the English viewpoint occurs in the representation of Hebrew verbs, e.g., in Joel 1:19:

for fire has-burned

where the expression *has-burned* indicates that a single Hebrew word is represented as by two English words. Again, the lexicon field specifies that this is indeed one Hebrew word.

The discontinuous use of hyphens signals a skewing between the Hebrew word order and fairly conventional English word order used in the semiliteral translation. For example, in Joel 2:19, the hyphenation in the expression

and- I-will- -not -make you(p)

is meant to show that the Hebrew word order and morpheme combinations are thus:

and-not I-will-make you

Tagging of the lines of the semiliteral translation. Where there is need, the lines of the semiliteral translation are tagged. MT in parentheses designates a reading conforming to the Masoretic text. Where an expression or a line in the MT can be read in more than one way, multiple "(MT)" tags are employed, as in the following example, Joel 1:12:

The-vines have-dried-up and-the-fig-trees are-ready-to-fall,
(the-)pomegranates, even (the-)date-palms and-(the-)apple-trees, all (the-)trees(-of) the-field have-dried-up;
(MT$_1$) surely joy has-dried-up away-from (the-)sons(-of) men.
(MT$_2$) surely joy has-been-put-to-shame by (the-)sons(-of) men.

The above display implies that two different verbs, as well as two different prepositions following the verbs, can be understood from the MT.

If the MT in more than one portion of a verse is open to different understandings, renderings of the first Hebrew portion are tagged as MT_1, MT_2, etc., while renderings of the second portion are tagged as MTT_1, MTT_2, etc., as below, in Joel 2:8:

> **And-one[a] does- not -crowd[b] another[c]; everyone[d] goes[e] in-his-(own-) way[f];**
> **(MT_1) and-through[g] the-weapons[h-1] they-burst[i];**
> > **(MTT_1) they-do- not -stop[j]**
> > **(MTT_2) they-are- not -hurt.[j]**
>
> **(MT_2) and-through[g] the-water-channel[h-2] they-descend[i]; they-do-not -stop.[j]**

A reading resulting from a proposed change (generally called an emendation) to the Masoretic text is tagged "ET," as below in Joel 2:2:

> **(A-)day(-of)[a] darkness[b] and-gloom,[c] (a-)day(-of) cloud-masses[d] and-gloom;[e]**
> **(MT) like[f] dawn[g-] being-spread[h] over[i]-the-mountains,[j]**
> **(ET) like[f] blackness[g-2] being-spread[h] over[i]-the-mountains,[j]**
> **(is/comes[k])(a-)people[l] numerous[m] and-vast,[n]**

In such cases, the MT reading is usually given first. More than one emended reading is shown with subscripted numerals: "(ET_1)," "(ET_2)."

The presention of the various fields

Intertextual references. The Book of Joel is filled with references to other biblical documents. These references range from clear citations to vague allusions. The intertextual reference field has been devised to signal clearly to the reader some of the more obvious references. The great quantity of references which have been noted testify that Joel worked mainly in the context of the Pentateuch and the Mosaic covenant of YHWH with Israel. He also worked within a great prophetic tradition, which upheld and interpreted that covenantal relationship, and which provided an entire vocabulary and repertoire of expressions. It would appear that genuine prophets were indeed expected to use this stock of traditions, and Joel certainly does not disappoint.

Text. This field presents textual difficulties and various opinions concerning them. Occasionally this field presents a significantly altered understanding of the MT found in other ancient versions, even though the MT itself may not be in doubt. On other occasions, this field presents various understandings among modern commentators and versions of the MT itself, even in the absence of any proposed emendation.

Syntax. This field presents various difficulties and exegetical views arising from ambiguity in the syntax of the MT.

Lexicon. This field presents Hebrew lexical items in both Hebrew script and transliteration. An English translation of the relevant phrase, with the item in question underlined in the English, precedes the Hebrew presentation, as in the following example, Joel 1:18. The English phrase allows the reader to situate the Hebrew lexical item in its immediate context. Normally three reference works are cited for the lexical item: *The New Brown-Driver-Briggs-Gesenius Hebrew and English Lexicon* [BDB], *A Concise Hebrew and Aramaic Lexicon of the Old Testament* [Hol], and *Theological Wordbook of the Old Testament* [TWOT]. The relevant pages in the print editions of the first two works are given, as well as the reference number of the lexical item in the last work.

> **how (the-)cattle groan** בְּהֵמָה *bəhēmâ* [BDB p. 96], [Hol p. 34], [TWOT 208a]

Here follows a discussion of the presentation of nouns and noun-like forms in their construct state. Often the construct state is noted in the semiliteral translation, as in Joel 1:1:

> **(the-)message(-of) YHWH** constr. of דָּבָר *dāḇār*

The sequence of *construct noun + genitive noun* can encode any of a very wide range of semantic relationships, and the lexicon field does not attempt to explicitly identify these relations. However, the citation of various English renderings often makes clear the relation that the versions and commentators judge to be in play. In some cases the semantics of the construct-genitive relationship are specifically discussed, as in Joel 1:20:

> **(the-)beasts(-of) (the-)fields** שָׂדֶה *śāḏeh* [BDB p. 961], [Hol p. 349], [TWOT 2236b]: 'field' [BDB, Hol; Crenshaw, Keil; KJV, NASB, REB]. *Śāḏeh* can denote either a cultivated field or uncultivated, uninhabited space [BDB]. The construct relationship between בַּהֲמוֹת *bahămôṯ* 'beasts' and שָׂדֶה *śāḏeh* 'field' is generally translated as "beasts of the field." Crenshaw and REB have "beasts in the field."

Sometimes the semiliteral translation identifies the construct semantics by adding parenthetical material, as in Joel 1:4; in this case the lexicon field clearly states that *(the-)remainder(-left by)* represents *yeṯer* in its construct state:

> **(the-)remainder(-left by) the-shearer(s)** constr. of יֶתֶר *yeṯer*

Here the lexical item translated as "remainder" is presented, by means of the parenthetical implied material, as the object of "shearers" in some sense.

For the sake of completeness, the construct state is also noted in the case of nouns bearing pronominal suffixes, as in Joel 1:2:

> **your(p)-forefathers** constr. pl. of אָב *ʾāḇ*

In these cases, of course, it must be recognized that *construct noun + pronominal suffix* can indicate a wide range of semantic relations, and these are often commented on as well.

The presentations in this field of a certain Hebrew prefix and and a certain particle merit comments. The *waw* prefix, attached usually to nouns and verbs and most often glossed in the semiliteral translation as 'and', is noted in this field when translations and commentators differ significantly in their view about which temporal or logical relation is being encoded by the prefix. The *waw* prefix will be termed "*waw* connective."

On occasion, what was traditionally interpreted as the same *waw* prefix appears as a frozen part of the wayyiqtol verb form (marking the mainline in narrative discourse) and weqatal verb form (marking the mainline in predictive, procedural, and instructional discourse). Although one cannot in these cases truly speak of a *waw* prefix, traditional Hebrew grammar has considered this *waw* as the same prefix and has linked it to the variety of temporal and logical relationships in which the verb stands with the preceding material; about these relationships opinions often differ, just as with the *waw* connective. When the *waw* appears as a frozen part of a verb form, it will be noted as "*waw* of the attached weqatal verb form" or "*waw* of the attached wayyiqtol verb form."

The particle כִּי *kî* appears in the lexicon field even more often than the *waw* particle. This particle is traditionally viewed as capable of expressing a very large range of temporal and logical relations, and it is very common to find much difference of opinion about its semantic value in any given instance. The lexicon field will present these various opinions, mostly in the form of glosses, e.g., "because" or "surely," or in the form of a stated function, e.g., as introducing a relative clause.

The presentation of recursion in Appendix 1

Appendix 1, which is, for the most part, based on Ernst Wendland's analysis, presents the varieties of repetition—morphological, syntactic, and lexical—that permeate the Book of Joel and characterize the tight structure of Joel's poetry. Besides being intrinsically interesting, these recursive structures give important clues to the analyst who seeks patterns of thematic cohesion, textual constituent bounding, and textual prominence in Joel.

Recursive textual structures give important clues to prominence: (1) Recurring textual material or conceptual material (the latter being identical in concepts or ideas but expressed by varying vocabulary), as it recurs across a varying textual background, may acquire prominence.[5] (2) Recurring textual material or conceptual material may become a constant backdrop against

[5] See an example in Appendix 1 under Joel 1:2, "(4) RECURSION."

which other varied material shows up prominently.[6] (3) An abrupt variation in the recursive structure may signal prominence.[7]

A recursive structure can signal various sorts of prominence. Recursion can imply an idea of completeness[8] or of abundance[9] or of intensity in a quality or event.[10] There is sometimes implied an emphasis of contrast or unexpectedness with regard to another object, quality, or event.[11] On the other hand, a peak or high point may be signaled by recursion, as the climax in a narrative, whether past or predictive,[12] or as in an emotive passage.[13] Finally, a recursive structure might signal thematic importance.[14]

---

[6] See an example in Appendix 1 under Joel 1:2, "(2) RECURSION." Regarding the inclusio involving that verse and 1:14, the material *not* covered within the inclusio (i.e., cola ε–ζ of 1:14) is very prominent.

[7] See an example in Appendix 1 under Joel 4:1–3, "RECURSION."

[8] See an example in Appendix 1 under Joel 1:13–14, "(2) RECURSION."

[9] See an example in Appendix 1 under Joel 2:13, "RECURSION."

[10] See an example in Appendix 1 under Joel 1:6, "RECURSION"; and under Joel 1:19 "(2) RECURSION"; and under Joel 2:2 "(1) RECURSION."

[11] See an example in Appendix 1 under Joel 2:2, "(2) RECURSION."

[12] See, for example, the recurring actions in Joel 2:9.

[13] See Joel 4:12–14 (3:12–14).

[14] See Joel 3:5 (2:32); 4:16–17 (3:16–17); and 4:20–21 (3:20–21].

EXEGETICAL SUMMARY OF JOEL

Part 1 of Joel

It is widely held that the first half of Joel (1:2–2:17) comprises Part 1 of the book. Here are presented the judgment of YHWH against Judah and a call for Judah to respond. Thus Crenshaw, for example, entitles Part 1 "divine judgment against Judah and its response." Similarly, Keil entitles Part 1 "the judgment of God, and the prophet's call to repentance." Less helpfully, Allen entitles it "Judah, locusts, and God."

Wendland points out that Part 1 contains 424 "word-units" (i.e., single words or words joined by a *maqqeph*, a sort of Hebrew hyphen), while Part 2 has 425 word-units. Thus even a kind of lexical balance is present in the book, a balance which corresponds to the thematic balance between the two parts.

Joel clearly reflects the primacy of the Sinaitic covenant. Part 1, particularly, recapitulates the covenantal blessings and curses of Deuteronomy 32 [Stuart]:

	Deuteronomy 32	**Joel 1:1–2:17**
Call to attention	32:1–2	1:2–3
Justness of YHWH	32:3–4	2:13–14
Appeal to remember the past	32:7	1:2
Israel: YHWH's special people	32:8–12	1:17
Past agricultural bounty	32:13–14	1:5–20; 2:3
YHWH's rejection	32:19–21	1:15; 2:11, 17
Destructive fire	32:22	2:3, 5
Harm	32:23	2:13
Arrows	32:23	2:8
Famine	32:24	1:4–20
Harmful animals	32:24	1:4, 6
Invasion	32:25	1:6; 2:1–11
Taunt of the enemy	32:27	2:17
YHWH's rejection	32:26–30	1:15; 2:11, 17
Judgment day	32:34–35	1:15; 2:1, 2, 11
Rescue and forgiveness	32:36–38	2:12–14, 17
Deliverance from Israel's enemies	32:39–43	2:20–27
Recompense from the land	32:43	2:18–27

DISCOURSE UNIT: 1:1–20 [Wolff]. The topic is "Locusts as forerunners of the Day of Yahweh."

Comments on this discourse unit: The portion 1:5–14 comprises in general a "call to communal lamentation," a recognized literary form in the OT, in which a king, a prophet, or some other authority summons the people to pray for or seek God's help in a crisis. This form usually includes the following elements: the summons itself, the explicit reference to the addressees, and the reason for the summons, which is generally introduced by the particle כִּי *kî* or by the preposition עַל *ʿal.* (See 2 Sam. 3:31, Jer. 4:8, Zeph. 1:11, and Ezek. 21:17 for other examples of the use of *kî* and *ʿal* in this genre.) While 1:5–14 also includes fragments of lamentations in 1:16–18, 19b–20, these cannot be called complete lamentations, because they lack the usual elements of petition, vow, and statement of confidence in YHWH.

One reaches the center of the discourse unit only at 1:15, in which is revealed for the first time Joel's true theme, the day of YHWH [Wolff].

DISCOURSE UNIT: 1:1–13 [NASB]. The topic is "the devastation of locusts."

DISCOURSE UNIT: 1:1 [Cohen, Crenshaw]. The topic is "the superscription" [Cohen, Crenshaw].

1:1

(The-)message(-of)[a] YHWH[b] which was[c] to[d] Joel (the-)son(-of)[e] Pethuel.

LEXICON—a. **(the-)<u>message(-of)</u> YHWH** constr. of דָּבָר *dāḇār* [BDB p. 182], [Hol p. 67], [TWOT 399a]: 'word' [BDB, Hol; Crenshaw, Dillard, Wolff; KJV, NASB, NIV, NRSV, REB], 'message' [Allen; TEV].

b. **(the-)message(-of) <u>YHWH</u>** יהוה *yhwh* [BDB p. 217], [Hol p. 130], [TWOT 484a]: 'Lord' [Dillard; KJV, NASB, NIV, NRSV, REB, TEV], 'YHWH' [Crenshaw, Allen, Wolff].

c. **which <u>was</u> to** 3rd masc. sing. Qal perf. of היה *hyh* [BDB p. 224], [Hol p. 78], [TWOT 491]: 'to come' [Dillard; KJV, NASB, NIV, NRSV, REB, Wolff]. *Hyh*, the principal verb 'to be' in Hebrew, has a large variety of functions; besides providing linkage, it can also denote incipient existence, 'to become' [BDB, Hol]. Crenshaw translates the phrase 'which was to Joel' as 'entrusted to Joel', since the verb *hyh* bears this sense in the context of God's word coming to a prophet; Allen has 'received by Joel'.

d. **which was <u>to</u>** אֶל *ʾel* [BDB p. 39], [Hol p. 16], [TWOT 91]: 'to' [Crenshaw, Dillard, Wolff; KJV, NASB, NIV, NRSV, REB, TEV]. The primary function of the preposition *ʾel* is to indicate motion or direction to or towards something [BDB, Hol].

e. **(the-)son(-of)** constr. of בֵּן *bēn* [BDB p. 119], [Hol p. 42], [TWOT 254]: 'son' [BDB, Hol; Crenshaw, Allen, Dillard, Wolff; KJV, NASB, NIV, NRSV, REB, TEV].

QUESTION—Who was Joel?

He is called "son of Pethuel," but is otherwise unknown to us [Keil, Dillard]. One rabbinic tradition said that he was a son of Samuel and a Levite. Others have him as living in the time of King Jeroboam or of King Manasseh [Cohen].

QUESTION—What can be noted about Joel's name?

The name יוֹאֵל *yôʾēl* means 'whose God is Jehovah' [Keil], 'YHWH is God' [Allen, Crenshaw, Dillard], but this meaning does not appear to play a role in the book's exegesis [Dillard]. It has been suggested that 'Joel' is a symbolic name, the reversal of 'Elijah', and that his father's name, Pethuel, signifies 'seduced by God'. It is certainly true that one incontestably symbolic name appears in the book, namely, the Valley of Jehoshaphat, meaning 'YHWH has rendered judgment'. "Joel," however, was a common name in various Israelite tribes, occurring in many genealogical lists in 1 and 2 Chronicles [Crenshaw, Wolff].

QUESTION—Where did the prophet Joel carry out his ministry?

He probably lived in Judah [Allen, Keil] and apparently carried out his ministry in and around Jerusalem, for it was there that his prophecy had its thematic focus [Dillard, Keil]. Because of his way of talking about priests, one may probably conclude that he himself was not a priest [Wolff], although he was very knowledgeable about the priests' roles [Allen]. A rabbinic tradition held that he was a Levite [Cohen]. This tradition could be correct, as Joel may have been a prophet associated with the institutionalized worship at Jerusalem; certainly the work of other such prophets appears in various psalms [Allen].

QUESTION—What role does this verse play?

The formula "the word of YHWH came to ..." is used more than two hundred times in the OT to introduce oracles and collections of oracles, and it does the same here [Dillard].

QUESTION—What is unusual about this superscription?

It is one of two prophetic superscriptions (the other is that of Jonah) that gives the least amount of information: only the names of the prophet and the prophet's father [Crenshaw]. Moreover, this "message" of YHWH includes, in fact, pronouncements about him and entreaties made to him, especially in the first half of the book; the second half is almost entirely composed of first person speech attributed to him [Wolff].

DISCOURSE UNIT: 1:2–2:17 [Keil; REB]. The topic is "the judgment of God, and the prophet's call to repentance" [Keil], "the day of the Lord" [REB].

DISCOURSE UNIT: 1:2–20 [Crenshaw, Dillard; TEV]. The topic is "a summons to lament and return to YHWH" [Crenshaw], "the locust plague: the immediate disaster" [Dillard], "the people mourn the destruction of the crops" [TEV].

Comments on this discourse unit: Strophe 1 (1:2–4) is a summons to the people in general to hear the prophet; strophe 2 (1:5–7) summons perhaps heavy drinkers, or perhaps all the nation from its preferred life of relaxation, to consider the crisis which is upon them; strophe 3 (1:8–10) directs the despair over the crisis to the priests and invests it with religious significance; strophe 4 (1:11–12) invokes the farmers to despair as well; strophe 5 (1:13–14) urges a course of action upon the priests and the whole nation; strophe 6 (1:15–18) links the present catastrophe with the coming day of YHWH; and strophe 7 (1:19–20) enlarges the disaster to include even the animals, who cry to YHWH in distress [Crenshaw]. Verses 1:15–20 may be said as well to constitute a liturgy of lamentation [Dillard]. In contrast to this view, it has been noted that the eschatological theme of the second half of Joel does not suggest that the book was meant to constitute a liturgy. Very possibly, however, Joel looked to Temple liturgy as a source for many of the forms that appear in the book [Allen].

DISCOURSE UNIT: 1:2–14 [Wendland]. This discourse unit is comprised of Stanza A. The topic is a "call to lament over a national disaster."

DISCOURSE UNIT: 1:2–12 [NIV, NRSV]. The topic is "an invasion of locusts" [NIV], "lament over the ruin of the country" [NRSV].

DISCOURSE UNIT: 1:2–7 [Cohen]. The topic is "the unprecedented plague."

1:2

Listen-to[a] this[b], (you(p)) the-elders,[c] and-hear[d] (this), all (you(p)) dwellers(-in)[e] the-land.[f]

Did- this[g] –happen[h] in-your(p)-days[i] or[j] in-(the-)days(-of) your(p)-forefathers?[k]

LEXICON—a. **<u>listen-to</u> this** masc. pl. Qal imper. of שׁמע *šmᶜ* [BDB p. 1033], [Hol p. 376], [TWOT 2412]: 'to listen to' [Hol], 'to hear' [BDB; Keil, Allen, Dillard, Wolff; KJV, NASB, NIV, NRSV, REB], 'to pay attention' [TEV], 'to take heed to' [Crenshaw].

b. **listen-to <u>this</u>** fem sing. demonstr. of זֶה *zeh* [BDB p. 260], [Hol p. 86], [TWOT 528]: 'this' [BDB, Hol; Crenshaw, Keil, Allen, Dillard, Wolff; KJV, NASB, NIV, NRSV, REB]. The demonstrative pronoun *zeh* functions here cataphorically, referring to what follows [Hol] in a neutral way (e.g., 'this' [BDB]). Both occurrences of this pronoun in this verse and the feminine pronoun in the next refer ahead to the plague of locusts, which the prophet begins to specify only in 1:4.

c. **(you) the-elders** pl. of זָקֵן *zāqēn* [BDB p. 278], [Hol p. 91], [TWOT 574b]: 'elder' [BDB, Hol; Allen, Dillard, Wolff; NASB, NIV, NRSV, REB], 'old man' [Keil; KJV], 'older people' [TEV], 'old-timers' [Crenshaw].

d. **and-hear (this)** masc. pl. Hiphil imper. of אזן *ʾzn* [BDB p. 24], [Hol p. 8], [TWOT 57]: 'to hear' [BDB], 'to listen' [BDB, Hol; Allen; NASB, NIV, REB, TEV], 'to pay attention' [Dillard], 'to give ear' [KJV, NRSV], 'to attend' [Keil, Wolff], 'to listen' [Crenshaw].

e. **all (you) dwellers(-in) the-land** constr. pl. masc. Qal part. of ישב *yšḇ* [BDB p. 442], [Hol p. 146], [TWOT 922]: 'to dwell' [BDB, Hol], 'to live' [Hol; Dillard; NIV]. This participle is also translated as a noun: 'inhabitants' [Keil, Wolff; KJV, NASB, NRSV, REB]. TEV translates it as a pronoun: 'everyone'. Crenshaw translates the phrase כֹּל יוֹשְׁבֵי הָאָרֶץ *kōl yôšəḇê hāʾāreṣ* 'all dwellers in the land' as "every local resident"; Allen has "all the country's population."

f. **all (you) dwellers(-in) the-land** אֶרֶץ *ʾereṣ* [BDB p. 76], [Hol p. 28], [TWOT 167]: 'land' [BDB, Hol; Keil, Dillard, Wolff; KJV, NIV, NASB, NRSV, REB], 'territory' [Hol], 'Judah' [TEV], 'country' [Allen].

g. **did- this -happen** fem sing. demonstr. of זֶה *zeh* [BDB p. 260], [Hol p. 86], [TWOT 528]: 'this' [BDB, Hol; Dillard; KJV, NIV], 'such a thing' [Keil, Allen, Wolff; NRSV], 'the like of this' [REB], 'anything like this' [NASB], 'anything comparable' [Crenshaw], not explicit [TEV]. The demonstrative pronoun *zeh* functions here cataphorically, referring to what follows [Hol] in a neutral way.

h. **did- this -happen** 3rd fem. sing. Qal perf. of היה *hyh* [BDB p. 224], [Hol p. 78], [TWOT 491]: 'to happen' [BDB, Hol; Crenshaw, Keil, Allen, Dillard, Wolff; NASB, NIV, NRSV, REB, TEV], 'to be' [KJV]. *Hyh*, the principal verb 'to be' in Hebrew, has many different functions; besides providing linkage, it can also convey an event idea [BDB, Hol].

i. **in-your(p)-days** constr. pl. of יוֹם *yôm* [BDB p. 398], [Hol p. 130], [TWOT 852]: 'day' [BDB, Hol; Keil, Wolff; KJV, NASB, NIV, NRSV, REB], 'lifetime' [Hol; Allen, Dillard], 'time' [Crenshaw; TEV].

j. **in-your(p)-days or in-(the-)days(-of) your(p)-forefathers** וְאִם *wəʾim* [BDB p. 49], [Hol p. 19]: 'or' [Hol; Crenshaw, Keil, Dillard, Wolff; NASB, NIV, NRSV, REB, TEV], 'or even' [KJV]. *Wəʾim* often occurs in coordinate questions [Hol]. *Wəʾim* is a composite conjunction.

k. **your(p)-forefathers** constr. pl. of אָב *ʾāḇ* [BDB p. 3], [Hol p. 1], [TWOT 4a]: 'forefather' [BDB; Allen; NIV, REB], 'ancestor' [Hol; NRSV, TEV], 'father' [Keil, Dillard, Wolff; KJV, NASB], 'parent' [Crenshaw].

QUESTION—What literary form does this verse have?

It has the form of a call to receive instruction, much used in ancient wisdom literature. It was meant to call attention to the material it introduced [Wolff].

QUESTION—What role is played by the combination of שִׁמְעוּ־זֹאת *šimᶜû -zōʾṯ* 'listen to this' and וְהַאֲזִינוּ *wəhaʾăzînû* 'hear this'?

The combination of שׁמע *šmᶜ* and אזן *ʾzn*, both denoting 'to hear, listen', marks the start of many oracles [Dillard].

QUESTION—What is the meaning of הַזְּקֵנִים *hazzəqēnîm* 'elders'?

1. This term refers here to elderly people in general, those who can remember back the furthest [Cohen, Crenshaw].
2. This term refers to the elders as the effective leaders in Joel's time. The elders had played a crucial role in local government during the time of the judges, but had been eclipsed during the monarchy. Now their importance can be seen, not only by Joel's references to them, but by their appearance in the Book of Ezra [Wolff].

QUESTION—What role is played by the combination of הַזְּקֵנִים *hazzəqēnîm* 'you elders' and כֹּל יוֹשְׁבֵי הָאָרֶץ *kōl yôšəḇê hāʾāreṣ* 'all you inhabitants of the land'?

This parallelism serves to mark off the unit 1:2–14 [Dillard].

QUESTION—What land is meant by הָאָרֶץ *hāʾāreṣ* 'the land'?

The land of Judah is meant [Keil, Wolff].

QUESTION—What is the nature of the question in this verse?

This question is rhetorical: it and its context imply an obvious negative answer. Wendland considers that this question stands in a reason relation to the command which precedes it: "hear what I have to say, for you have never seen such a disaster before."

QUESTION—What is the larger significance of the question in this verse?

It is to introduce Joel's concern, which is evident throughout the book, for understanding the sweep of history in order to recognize unique events when they occur, and especially in order to recognize that the day of YHWH is near. The result of this recognition is to see reality from YHWH's point of view [Wolff].

1:3

Relate[a] it to[b]-your(p)-children,[c] and-your(p)-children to-their-children,

and-their-children to-(the-)generation[d] following.[e]

INTERTEXTUAL REFERENCE—This verse evokes the OT concern that parents in the covenant community of YHWH pass down to their children the knowledge of what he has done for their people, as in Exod. 10:1–2 and in Ps. 71:18 [Wendland].

LEXICON—a. **relate it** masc. pl. Piel imper. of ספר *spr* [BDB p. 707], [Hol p. 259], [TWOT 1540]: 'to relate' [BDB, Hol], 'to recount' [BDB], 'to tell' [Hol; Crenshaw, Keil, Allen, Dillard, Wolff; KJV,

NASB, NIV, NRSV, REB, TEV]. *Spr* often carries a nuance of formal recitation, which could well fit a liturgical text [Dillard].

b. **to-your(p)-children** -לְ *lə-* [BDB p. 510], [Hol p. 167], [TWOT 1063]: 'to' [Crenshaw, Wolff; NIV, REB]. *Lə-*, a proclitic, here signals addressee [BDB, Hol].

c. **to-your(p)-children** pl. constr. of בֵּן *bēn* [BDB p. 119], [Hol p. 42], [TWOT 254]: 'child' [BDB, Hol; Crenshaw, Allen, Dillard; KJV, NIV, NRSV, REB, TEV], 'son' [Keil, Wolff; NASB]. *Bānîm*, which may be restricted in sense to male children, is here to be taken in its unrestricted sense to fit the context of family as a whole [Crenshaw].

d. **and-their-children to-(the-)generation following** דּוֹר *dôr* [BDB p. 189], [Hol p. 69], [TWOT 418b]: 'generation' [Hol; Crenshaw, Keil, Allen, Dillard, Wolff; KJV, NASB, NIV, NRSV, REB, TEV].

e. **to-(the-)generation following** אַחֵר *ʾaḥar* [BDB p. 29], [Hol p. 10], [TWOT 68b]: 'following' [Hol; Wolff], 'afterwards' [BDB], 'next' [Crenshaw, Keil, Allen; NASB, NIV, TEV], 'another' [Dillard; KJV, NRSV, REB].

QUESTION—What is this verse reminiscent of?

The phrase עָלֶיהָ לִבְנֵיכֶם סַפֵּרוּ *ʿālêhā libnêkem sappērû* alludes to Exod. 10:2, 6; Joel sees the present locust invasion in the same light as the plague of locusts God had sent upon the Egyptians—and also in the light of Moses' warnings of punishment to the Israelites in the case of their infidelity to YHWH (Deut. 28:38–42) [Keil]. The command to pass on to later generations what Joel is about to recount fits Israel's long tradition of remembering YHWH's mighty deeds in ancient times [Crenshaw]. Such knowledge is not knowledge for its own sake, but rather for the sake of present events that will affect future generations because YHWH's word is connected to these events. The concern that a long succession of generations receive knowledge is characteristic of wisdom literature in general. Moreover, with 1:2–4, Joel points ahead with an apocalyptic nuance to the day of YHWH, a theme he will develop in the second half of the book [Wolff].

1:4

(The-)remainder[a](-left by) the-shearer(s)[b] the-swarmer(s)[c] (have-)eaten,[d]
and-(the-)remainder(-left by) the-swarmer(s) the-creeping-locust(s)[e] (have-)eaten,
and-(the-)remainder(-left by) the-creeping-locust(s) the-leaping-locust(s)[f] (have-)eaten.

LEXICON—a. **(the-)remainder(-left by) the-shearer(s)** constr. of יֶתֶר *yeter* [BDB p. 451], [Hol p. 148], [TWOT 936a]: 'remainder' [BDB, Hol], 'leavings' [Keil, Allen]. This noun is also translated with a verb phase: 'what ... (has) left' [Crenshaw, Dillard, Wolff; KJV, NASB, NIV, NRSV, REB].

b. <u>shearer(s)</u> גָּזָם *gāzām* [BDB p. 160], [Hol p. 58], [TWOT 338a]: 'shearer' [Allen], traditionally 'locust' (just become mature, ready for flight); 'caterpillar' (possibly better than 'locust') [Hol]; 'locust swarm' [NIV], 'locusts' [BDB; REB], 'flying locusts' [Dillard], 'cutting locust' [NRSV], 'gnawer' [Keil], 'gnawing locust' [NASB], 'palmerworm' [Cohen; KJV], 'chewer' [Crenshaw], 'biter' [Wolff]. The Hebrew singular of this noun is understood as a generic and so allows for a plural translation. The same is true of the following "swarmers" and "locusts."

c. **the-<u>swarmer(s)</u> (have-)eaten** אַרְבֶּה *ʾarbeh* [BDB p. 916], [Hol p. 26], [TWOT 2103a]: 'swarmer' [REB], 'locust' [BDB, Hol; Wolff; KJV]; 'great locusts' [NIV], 'adult locusts' [Dillard], 'swarming locust' [Crenshaw; NASB, NRSV], 'swarmer locust' [Allen], 'multiplier' [Keil]. The word *ʾarbeh* denotes a certain species of "migratory or desert locust, *Schistocera gregaria*, in winging stage" [Hol]. It is usually regarded as appearing in uncountable numbers [BDB]. Cohen takes *ʾarbeh* to mean literally 'a swarm'.

d. **the-swarmer(s) <u>(have-)eaten</u>** 3rd masc. sing. Qal perf. of אכל *ʾkl* [BDB p. 37], [Hol p. 14], [TWOT 85]: 'to eat' [Hol; Keil, Allen, Dillard; KJV, NASB, NIV, NRSV], 'to devour' [Wolff; REB], 'to consume' [Crenshaw].

e. **the-<u>creeping-locust(s)</u> (have-)eaten** יֶלֶק *yeleq* [BDB p. 410], [Hol p. 135], [TWOT 870a]: 'creeping locust' [NASB], 'locust' [Hol]; 'young locusts' [NIV], 'hopper' [Allen, Dillard, Wolff; REB], 'hopping locust' [NRSV], 'licker' [Keil], 'cankerworm' [Coh; KJV], 'jumper' [Crenshaw]. *Yeleq* denotes the locust's 'creeping, unwinged stage' [Hol]. The twelfth-century Jewish commentator Kimchi regarded this noun as derived from ילך *ylk̲* 'to lap up' [Cohen].

f. **the-<u>leaping-locust(s)</u> (have-)eaten** חָסִיל *ḥāsîl* [BDB p. 340], [Hol p. 111], [TWOT 701a]: 'leaping locust' [Dillard], 'specific stage of the locust or cockroach' [Hol]; 'a kind of locust' [BDB], 'other locusts' [NIV], 'destroying locust' [NRSV], 'devourer' [Keil], 'caterpiller' [Cohen; KJV], 'stripping locust' [NASB], 'jumper' [Wolff], 'grub' [REB], 'finisher' [Crenshaw], 'destroyer' [Allen]. In Joel *ḥāsîl* denotes the young locust [TWOT].

QUESTION—To what does יֶתֶר *yet̲er* 'remainder' refer?

It refers to unconsumed vegetables and plants [Keil], which would probably be nothing more than the remaining shoots of plants otherwise eaten [Crenshaw].

QUESTION—How are the various terms for locusts used in this passage to be distinguished?

1. These are terms for the locust in its various developmental stages, all of which are destructive of crops.
   a. גָּזָם *gāzām* 'flying locust' refers to the stage before the mature adult; it has well-developed wings. The locust in this stage is sometimes

translated as 'the biter', since the root of *gāzām* in Aramaic means 'to cut'. The Jewish commentator Ibn Ezra cited Jepheth b. Ali's derivation of *gāzām* from גזז *gzz* 'to shear' [Cohen]. *Gāzām* might refer to a solitary locust, as distinct from *ʾarbeh*, locusts in swarm [Wolff].

b. אַרְבֶּה *ʾarbeh* the generic term for 'locust' in the OT, but referring here to the sexually mature locust. This term is perhaps derived from the adjective רַב *raḇ* 'numerous'. The mature insect can reach almost 6 cm. in length [Wolff].

c. יֶלֶק *yeleq* refers to the 'hopper', a stage of the locust larva. Presumably, it hops about, as its wings are not yet functional [Wolff].

d. חָסִיל *ḥāsîl* (the 'leaping locust') refers to a middle stage, in which the locust is bigger than before, but possessing its wings encased within a membrane. *Ḥāsîl* is derived from חסל *ḥsl* 'to finish off, consume' [BDB, Dillard]. The insect in this stage is 2–3 cm. long [Wolff].

2. These terms, drawn from a repertory of nine locust terms in the OT, have probably lost their original meanings and have been amassed to emphasize the disaster [Cohen, Crenshaw]—certainly these four terms were already quite early viewed as apocalyptic language denoting completeness [Wolff];[15] they are for practical purposes now synonymous and are, in fact, found only in poetic or poetry-like passages in the OT [Keil]. The number four indicates universality and completeness (see Jer. 15:2–3 and Ezek. 14:21 for four kinds of destruction) [Crenshaw]. Thus TEV has in effect translated with this viewpoint: "swarm after swarm of locusts settled on the crops; what one swarm left, the next swarm devoured." It is true that some commentators understand this list of locust terms as representing four distinct stages of development of the creature; this is, however, unlikely, given that 2:25 employs a different order of the same terms [Crenshaw].

3. They are terms for four different species of locust. For example, אַרְבֶּה *ʾarbeh* denotes the most common species [the Jewish commentator Kimchi, cited by Cohen].

QUESTION—What was the nature of the locust invasion described here?

1. Joel is describing successive invasions of locusts during one season of cultivation [Keil].

---

[15] The uncertainty surrounding the four terms in this passage is heightened by several other possibilities: (1] dialectal variation may be involved; (2) succeeding swarms of invading locusts might have been given various names; (3) the adult locusts differ in color among themselves, depending upon whether they are solitary or in swarms [Wolff]. This uncertainty has perhaps contributed to the feeling that apocalyptic language is involved here.

2. Simkins believes, as others have also, that Joel is describing invasions of locusts during two successive seasons of cultivation. But Keil objects that if this were the case, the phrase "what is left" would be meaningless.
3. Wolff offers the following possible scenario: Solitary locusts (גָּזָם *gāzām)* appear first, without doing much crop damage; but then large swarms (אַרְבֶּה *ʾarbeh)* arrive and wreak havoc in the fields; these give birth one or two months later to countless young locusts, which, first in an early developmental stage (יֶלֶק *yeleq*), and then in a later stage (חָסִיל *ḥāsîl*), eat everything that is left before being compelled by lack of sustenance to seek food farther afield. The entire destruction covers more than one year of cultivation (see 2:25).

QUESTION—What translation difficulties may be present in this verse?

1. The various terms for the locusts might pose a problem. The translator might choose to adopt TEV's solution and translate on the order of "swarm after swarm of locusts."
2. A less obvious difficulty is the implicit information (three times) in this verse: "what the shearers have left the swarmers have eaten" implies that the "shearers" have indeed left behind something to eat. This implicit information might have to be presented explicitly in translation.

QUESTION—What is the significance of Joel's speaking of four locust types?

The number four indicates universality, as in Jer. 15:3 and in Ezek. 14:21: all of Judah has been affected by the locust invasions [Keil] and the destruction is complete [Cohen, Crenshaw].

QUESTION—What is the significance of Joel's account of a locust plague in the light of what is known of life in the ancient Middle East and in modern times?

There is extensive ancient literature on locusts from Egypt, Canaan, and Mesopotamia. It emphasizes the invincibility of locust attacks and the overwhelming numbers of the insects. Some refer to attacks over three-year periods [Crenshaw, Wolff].

As Joel 1 develops, the growing suspicion that the prophet is describing the locust plague in terms of the well-known day-of-YHWH theme finds confirmation in 1:15: *alas for-the-day, for near (is) (the-)day(-of) YHWH, and-as-violence from Shaddai it-will-come*. Such a devastating plague would be particularly threatening to a small and weak postexilic Judean community, for the result would be not only general economic disaster, famine, and the disruption of the sacrificial routine of Temple worship (see 1:8–9), but also very possibly the complete destruction of the community. Thus YHWH, whose "day" had in the past threatened Israel's enemies, now seemed prepared to wreak his vengeance on the faithless among his own people [Allen].

For us who have never witnessed a locust attack, the following account by Frederic D. Schwarz describing such an event in the American Great Plains during the 1870s, may prove informative:

The [locusts] typically descended without warning in a ravenous horde out of a bright summer sky. As they got nearer, their faint buzzing built up to a terrifying cyclonelike roar. (One German farmer, hearing a swarm approach, fell to his knees and shouted, “Der jüngste Tag! [Judgment Day!]”). In the space of a few minutes, they blocked out the sun, noticeably lowering the temperature. Grasshopper swarms resembled snowstorms, with insects seeming to fall out of the sky as far upward as the eye could see. When they began to feed, the crunching of millions upon millions of tiny jaws sounded like a prairie fire. A crawling layer several inches thick carpeted the ground and covered every growing thing. When the hoppers moved on, the area they left behind looked as if it had been burned to the ground.

Grasshoppers liked grain and garden produce best, but they would eat any sort of vegetation, from grass to weeds to buried roots and bulbs to the bark, leaves, and branches of trees, which they sometimes broke off by their sheer weight. Nor did they stop with living plants; straw hats, the binding on shocks of grain, and tobacco all were devoured, as were wooden items (tool handles, window frames, fence planks, even paper) and fabrics (clothing, curtains, bedclothes, mosquito netting, canvas). Leather, too, was considered tasty: harnesses, the sweatband of a hat, a wallet (along with the currency inside it), old boots. One settler saw a swarm eating wool off the back of a live sheep. And when everything else had been consumed, the grasshoppers ate each other.

1:5

Wake-up,[a] (you(p)) drunkards,[b] and-weep,[c] and-howl,[d] all (you(p)) drinkers (-of)[e] wine,[f]
because-of[g] (the-)new-wine[h] for[i] it-has-been-cut-off[j] from[k]-your(p)-mouth.[l]

SYNTAX—The two imperatives וּבְכוּ *ûḇəḵû* ‘weep’ and וְהֵילִלוּ *wəhêlilû* ‘and howl’ are both served by the introductory imperative הָקִיצוּ *haqîṣû* ‘wake up’. The effect, then, is: “wake up, you drunkards, and weep; wake up, all you who drink wine, and howl” [Crenshaw].

LEXICON—a. **wake-up** masc. pl. Hiphil imper. of קיץ *qyṣ* [BDB p. 884], [Hol p. 318], [TWOT 2019]: ‘to wake up’ [Crenshaw, Allen, Dillard; NIV, NRSV, REB, TEV], ‘to awake’ [BDB, Hol; Keil, Wolff; KJV, NASB]. *Qyṣ* is ‘to awake out of the reeling of intoxication’ [Keil]; most often it is ‘to wake from sleep’ [Dillard]. Crenshaw understands this imperative as introducing both ‘weep’ and ‘howl’: “wake up and weep; wake up and howl.” LXX adds ἐξ οἴνου αὐτῶν ‘from their wine’ to explain the kind of sleep the drunkards are in [Wolff], and this device may be appropriate in other languages as well. The call to wake up is actually a call to face the reality of the catastrophe brought on by the locusts [Wolff].

b. **(you) drunkards** masc. pl. of שִׁכּוֹר *šikkôr* [BDB p. 1016], [Hol p. 369], [TWOT 2388b]: ‘drunk(en)’ [BDB, Hol; Keil], ‘drunkard’

[Allen, Dillard, Wolff; KJV, NASB, NIV, NRSV, REB, TEV], 'imbiber' [Crenshaw]. Crenshaw prefers a more neutral translation: Joel refers in the parallel line to all those who drink wine (כָּל־שֹׁתֵי יָיִן *kol-šōṯê yāyin*), not merely the alcoholics. In addition, Joel refers further in this verse to sweet or new wine (עָסִיס *ʿāsîs*), which, although alcoholic, was far less intoxicating than older wine, and which was associated with the simple pleasures of relaxing under a shade tree at home (cf. Amos 9:13).

c. **and-weep** masc. pl. Qal imper. of בכה *bḵh* [BDB p. 113], [Hol p. 39], [TWOT 243]: 'to weep' [Hol; Crenshaw, Keil, Allen, Dillard, Wolff; KJV, NASB, NIV, NRSV, REB, TEV].

d. **and-howl** masc. pl. Hiphil imper. of ילל *yll* [BDB p. 410], [Hol p. 135], [TWOT 868]: 'to howl' [BDB, Hol; Keil; KJV], 'to wail' [Hol; Allen, Dillard, Wolff; NASB, NIV, NRSV], 'to cry' [TEV], 'to mourn' [REB], 'to sob' [Crenshaw].

e. **all (you) drinkers (-of) wine** constr. masc. pl. Qal part. of שׁתה *štẖ* [BDB p. 1059], [Hol p. 385], [TWOT 2477]: 'to drink' [BDB, Hol; Crenshaw, Keil, Dillard, Wolff; KJV, NASB, NIV, NRSV, REB].

f. **all (you) drinkers (-of) wine** יַיִן *yayin* [BDB p. 406], [Hol p. 134], [TWOT 864]: 'wine' [BDB, Hol; Crenshaw, Keil, Dillard, Wolff; KJV, NASB, NIV, NRSV, TEV]. Allen, NASB, REB, and TEV translate the phrase שֹׁתֵי יָיִן *šōṯê yāyin* as "wine drinkers."

g. **because-of (the-)new-wine** עַל *ʿal* [BDB p. 752], [Hol p. 273], [TWOT 1624p]: 'because of' [Hol; KJV, NIV], 'on account of' [BDB; NASB], 'because' [Dillard], 'because of' [Crenshaw, Wolff], 'over' [NRSV], 'at' [Keil], 'for' [Allen], not explicit [TEV].

h. **because-of (the-)new-wine** עָסִיס *ʿāsîs* [BDB p. 779], [Hol p. 279], [TWOT 1660a]: 'new wine' [Keil; KJV, NIV, REB], 'grape juice (freshly pressed, unfermented)' [Hol], 'sweet wine' [BDB; Crenshaw, Allen; NASB, NRSV], 'must' [Dillard], 'juice' [Wolff]. TEV translates this word with a phrase: "the grapes for making new wine." The twelfth-century Jewish commentator Kimchi regarded *ʿāsîs* as denoting the juice pressed from any fruit, including grapes [Cohen]. Dillard considers that *ʿāsîs*, being derived from עסס *ʿss* 'to tread on', refers to wine that is sweet because it has not yet fermented to the point of its natural sugar being consumed. This is not to say that such wine could not intoxicate (see Isa. 49:26 and Hos. 4:11). Although *ʿāsîs* could sometimes refer to very alcoholic or fortified wine (see 1:5 in LXX: οἱ πίνοντες οινον εἷς μέθηv), in 3:18 (4:18) the referent seems to be fresh wine, only slightly alcoholic or not at all. Another viewpoint is given by TWOT, which claims that the gloss 'sweet wine' can be misleading, since it implies today only partially fermented wine, whereas in ancient times a literally corresponding term γλεῦκος (see Acts 2:13) denoted very strong wine, perhaps made from very sweet juice in which the fermentation had been a lengthy process. In this case, Joel would be referring here to quite intoxicating wine.

i. **<u>for</u> it-has-been-cut-off** כִּי *kî* particle [BDB p. 471], [Hol p. 155], [TWOT 976]: 'for' [Keil, Wolff; KJV, NIV, NRSV, REB], not explicit [Crenshaw; TEV]. Allen, as well as NASB, translates *kî* as introducing a relative clause: "that is cut off from your mouth."

j. **for <u>it-has-been-cut-off</u>** 3rd sing. masc. Niphal perf. of כרת *krt̲* [BDB p. 503], [Hol p. 165], [TWOT 1048]: 'to be cut off' [BDB, Hol; Keil, Wolff; KJV, NASB, NRSV], 'to be snatched' [Allen; NIV], 'to be kept from' [Dillard], 'to be denied' [Crenshaw; REB]. TEV translates the phrase נִכְרַת מִפִּיכֶם *nik̲rat̲ mippîk̲em* 'has been cut off from your mouth' as "has been destroyed." The use of *krt̲* here suggests the physical action of a knife or sword, cutting away a person's cup of wine, just as he is raising it to his lips. This image is semantically linked to the manner in which locusts destroy plants, by cutting instead of licking [Crenshaw].

k. **<u>from</u>-your(p)-mouth** מִן *min* [BDB p. 577], [Hol p. 200], [TWOT 1212]: 'away from' [Hol], 'from' [BDB; Keil, Allen, Wolff; KJV, NASB, NIV, NRSV]. The preposition *min* here indicates separation from something [BDB].

l. **from-your(p)-<u>mouth</u>** constr. of פֶּה *peh* [BDB p. 804], [Hol p. 289], [TWOT 1738]: 'mouth' [BDB, Hol; Keil, Allen, Dillard, Wolff; KJV, NASB, NRSV], 'lip' [NIV], not explicit [REB]. *Peh* 'mouth' constitutes a synecdoche (part for a whole); Crenshaw and REB translate it concretely as "you."

QUESTION—What is the significance of Joel's reference to שִׁכּוֹרִים *šikkôrîm* 'drunkards'?

1. It is that heavy drinkers do not normally care for faithfulness to God. Their lack of drink signals an end to prosperity (see Ps. 104:15, Song of Sol. 5:1) [Dillard].
2. It may be that *šikkôrîm* refers to drunkards, those who abuse alcohol, or that *šikkôrîm* refers to wine drinkers, those who enjoy taking their ease at home while drinking. In either case, Joel uses this reference as a metaphor for a nation oblivious to God's actions and designs [Crenshaw].

1:6

For[a] (a-)nation[b] has-come[c] against[d] my-land,[e] powerful[f] and-not numbered,[g]
its-teeth[h] (the-)teeth(-of) (a-)lion[i] and-(the-)fangs(-of)[j] (a-)lioness[k] (are) to-it.

LEXICON— a. **<u>for</u>** כִּי *kî* particle [BDB p. 471], [Hol p. 155], [TWOT 976]: 'for' [Crenshaw, Keil, Dillard, Wolff; KJV, NASB, NRSV], 'because' [Allen], not explicit [NIV, REB, TEV].

b. **(a-)<u>nation</u> has-come** גּוֹי *gôy* [BDB p. 156], [Hol p. 57], [TWOT 326e]: 'nation' [BDB, Hol; Crenshaw, Dillard, Wolff; KJV, NASB, NIV, NRSV], 'people' [BDB; Keil], 'army of locusts' [TEV], 'horde' [Allen; REB].

c. **<u>has-come</u> against my-land** 3rd masc. sing. Qal perf. of עלה *ʿlh* [BDB p. 748], [Hol p. 273], [TWOT 1624]: 'to come' [Dillard], 'go up' (of war) [BDB, Hol], 'to come up' [Keil, Wolff; KJV], 'to invade' [Allen; NASB, NIV, NRSV, REB], 'to attack' [Crenshaw; TEV]. The primary sense of *ʿlh* is 'to go up, to ascend' [BDB], but עָלָה עַל *ʿālâ ʿal* (literally, 'to go up against') is normally used for an attack or invasion [Cohen, Dillard].

d. **<u>against</u> my-land** עַל *ʿal* [BDB p. 752], [Hol p. 273], [TWOT 1624p]: 'against' [BDB, Hol; Dillard, Wolff], 'over' [Keil], 'upon' [KJV], not explicit [Crenshaw, Allen; NIV, NRSV].

e. **against my-<u>land</u>** אֶרֶץ *ʾereṣ* [BDB p. 76], [Hol p. 28], [TWOT 167]: 'land' [BDB, Hol; Crenshaw, Keil, Dillard, Wolff; KJV, NASB, NIV, NRSV, REB, TEV], 'territory' [Hol], 'country' [Allen].

f. **<u>powerful</u> and-not numbered** עָצוּם *ʿāṣûm* [BDB p. 783], [Hol p. 280], [TWOT 1673d]: 'powerful' [Crenshaw, Wolff; NIV, NRSV, TEV], 'vast' [REB], 'mighty' [BDB, Hol; Dillard; NASB], 'strong' [Keil; KJV], 'massive' [Allen]. The word connotes great numbers or quantity [Hol] and therefore great strength [BDB], often in a military sense [Dillard].

g. **powerful and-not <u>numbered</u>** מִסְפָּר *mispār* [BDB p. 708], [Hol p. 204], [TWOT 1540f]: 'number' [BDB, Hol]; (with negation, as in this verse) 'innumerable' [BDB; Crenshaw, Keil; NRSV], 'infinite' [Hol], 'without number' [Dillard; KJV, NASB, NIV], 'too many to count' [TEV], 'past counting' [Allen; REB], 'beyond numbering' [Wolff].

h. **its-<u>teeth</u> (the-)<u>teeth</u>(-of) (a-)lion** pl. constr. of שֵׁן *šēn* [BDB p. 1042], [Hol p. 378], [TWOT 2422a]: 'tooth' [BDB, Hol; Crenshaw, Keil, Allen, Dillard, Wolff; KJV, NASB, NIV, NRSV, REB, TEV]. Crenshaw conflates *its-teeth (the-)teeth(-of) (a-)lion and-(the-)fangs(-of) (a-)lioness (are) to-it* and translates it as "with leonine teeth and fangs."

i. **its-teeth (the-)teeth(-of) (a-)<u>lion</u>** אַרְיֵה *ʾaryēh* [BDB p. 71], [Hol p. 27], [TWOT 158a]: 'lion' [BDB, Hol; Keil, Allen, Dillard, Wolff; KJV, NASB, NIV, NRSV, REB, TEV]. Lions have, of course, very powerful teeth and jaws [Crenshaw].

j. **and-(the-)<u>fangs</u>(-of) (a-)lioness** constr. of מְתַלְּעוֹת *mətalləʿōṯ* [BDB p. 1069], [Hol p. 222], [TWOT 2516d]: 'fangs' [Crenshaw, Allen, Wolff; NASB, NIV, NRSV, REB], 'jawbone' [Hol], 'teeth' [BDB], 'incisor' [Dillard], 'bite' [Keil], 'cheek teeth' [KJV]. *Mətalləʿōṯ* appears in the OT only as parallel with *šēn* 'tooth' [Wolff].

k. **and-(the-)fangs(-of) (a-)<u>lioness</u>** לָבִיא *lāḇîʾ* [BDB p. 522], [Hol p. 172], [TWOT 1070c]: 'lioness' [BDB, Hol; Cohen, Keil, Dillard,

Wolff; NASB, NIV, NRSV, REB], 'lion' [Allen; TEV], 'great lion' [KJV]. *Lāḇî'* may denote either 'lion' or 'lioness', but in proximity to אַרְיֵה *ʾaryēh* 'lion', as in this passage, it probably denotes 'lioness' [Dillard]. *Lāḇîʾ* is found only in OT poetry [Crenshaw].

QUESTION—What is the significance of the כִּי *kî* particle at the beginning of this verse?

It introduces the real reason for alarm over the locust plague. The crisis goes far beyond simply being deprived of wine; it calls into question Israel's continued existence, certainly on the physical level, due to the devastation of the agriculture (1:6–7, 10–12), but, more profoundly, also on the spiritual level, since the daily sacrifices at the Temple can no longer be performed (1:9, 13) [Crenshaw].

QUESTION—How is גּוֹי *gôy* 'nation' used in this passage?

It is used metaphorically for a swarm of locusts. *Gôy* often connotes hostility in a people and often functions synonymously with עַם *ʿam* 'a people', as in Joel 2:2. The word *ʿam* is used to describe both locusts and ants in Prov. 30:25–26 [Cohen, Crenshaw, Keil]; it describes locusts in Prov. 30:27 as being kingless, but still marching in order like an army [Crenshaw, Wolff]. Joel here reverses a literary theme found in the OT (e.g., Judges 6:5) and in ancient extrabiblical literature, in which invading armies are compared to locust plagues. The following example is from a Sumerian text [T. Jacobsen, *The Harps That Once...: Sumerian Poetry in Translation* (New Haven and London: Yale University Press, 1987), cited by Crenshaw]:

> Numerous like locusts
> they came striding,
> stretched out their arms in the desert for him
> like gazelle and wild ass snares,
> nothing escaped their arms,
> nobody did their arms leave.

QUESTION—Who is the referent of the possessive pronoun in אַרְצִי *ʾarṣî* 'my land' (and of גַּפְנִי *gap̄nî* 'my vine' and תְּאֵנָתִי *təʾēnātî* 'my fig tree' in 1:7)?

1. The referent is the prophet; the expression is tantamount to saying "the land of God's people" (see the comments on lexicon under 1:7) [Keil, Kimchi (cited by Cohen)].
2. The referent is probably YHWH; Joel's language becomes ambiguous at times, as he appears to alternate between a prophet's speech on behalf of YHWH and speech of YHWH himself. This phenomenon is not unusual in other OT prophets as well [Crenshaw].

QUESTION—What is the figure of speech concerning the teeth of a lion?

It is a metaphor; its point of similarity is that the locusts cut the vegetation with as much power as lions exert when tearing their prey with their teeth [Cohen, Wolff].

1:7

(They-)have-transformed[a] my-vine(s)[b] into-(a-)horror[c] and-my-fig-tree(s)[d] into-splinter(s);[e]

stripping,[f] (they-)have-stripped-the-bark-from[g]-it and-have-thrown(-it)-away[h], its-branches[i] have-become-white.[j]

INTERTEXTUAL REFERENCE—This verse evokes Mic. 4:4 וְיָשְׁבוּ אִישׁ תַּחַת גַּפְנוֹ וְתַחַת תְּאֵנָתוֹ *wəyāšəḇû ʾîš taḥat gap̄nô wəṯaḥat təʾēnāṯô* 'and each shall sit under his own vine and under his own fig tree'. As elsewhere, Joel here reverses the imagery, creating irony for a people who had presumed to always have YHWH's blessings [Wendland].

LEXICON—a. **(they)-have-transformed** 3rd masc. sing. Qal perf. of שׂים *sym* [BDB p. 962], [Hol p. 351], [TWOT 2243]: 'to transform into' [BDB], 'to make (into)' [Hol; Crenshaw, Keil; NASB], 'to reduce to' [Dillard]. Allen translates the phrase שָׂם גַּפְנִי לְשַׁמָּה *śām gap̄nî ləšammâ* 'they have turned my vine into a horror' as "they have wrought havoc among my vines." The implied grammatical subject of this verb is גּוֹי *gôy* 'nation' of 1:6 [Cohen].

b. **(they)-have-transformed my-vine(s) into-(a-)horror** constr. of גֶּפֶן *gep̄en* [BDB p. 172], [Hol p. 63], [TWOT 372a]: '(grape)vine' [Hol], 'vine' [BDB; Keil, Allen, Dillard, Wolff; KJV, NASB, NIV, NRSV, REB], 'grapevine' [TEV], 'vineyard' [Crenshaw]. *Gep̄en* almost always denotes a grape-bearing vine [BDB]. The Hebrew singular is understood here as a generic and so allows for a plural translation. The same is true of 'fig tree' and 'splinter/stump' in this verse.

c. **(they)-have-transformed my-vine(s) into-(a-)horror** שַׁמָּה *šammâ* [BDB p. 1031], [Hol p. 375], [TWOT 2409d]: 'horror' [BDB, Hol], 'waste of land' [BDB], 'desolation' [Crenshaw, Dillard], 'wilderness' [Keil], 'waste' [NASB]. *Šammâ* denotes ruin brought by judgment [Hol]. For the phrase שָׂם גַּפְנִי לְשַׁמָּה *śām gap̄nî ləšammâ* 'they have transformed my vine into a horror' Wolff; KJV, NIV, NRSV, and REB have "it has laid waste" or "they have laid waste"; TEV has "they have destroyed our grapevines"; Allen has "they have wrought havoc among my vines."

d. **and-my-fig-tree(s) into-splinter(s)** תְּאֵנָה *təʾēnâ* [BDB p. 1061], [Hol p. 386], [TWOT 2490]: 'fig tree' [BDB, Hol; Crenshaw, Keil, Allen, Dillard, Wolff; KJV, NASB, NIV, NRSV, REB, TEV]. *Təʾēnâ* denotes the *Ficus Carica L.* [Hol].

e. **and-my-fig-trees into-splinters** קְצָפָה *qəṣāp̄â* [BDB p. 893], [Hol p. 322], [TWOT 2059a]: 'splinters' [Crenshaw, Allen; NASB], 'stump' [Hol], 'snapping' [BDB], 'splintering' [BDB], 'stump' [Hol], 'collapse' [Dillard], 'sticks' [Keil]. For the phrase שָׂם ... וּתְאֵנָתִי לִקְצָפָה *śām ... ûtəʾēnāṯî liqṣāp̄â* NIV has "it has ruined my fig trees"; NRSV has "it has splintered my fig trees"; TEV, "they have chewed up our fig trees"; Allen, "and smashed my fig trees to splinters"; REB, "they have left my fig trees broken"; Wolff, "it has broken down my fig tree." (By this

Wolff means that the branches have been broken off.) Keil considers *qəṣāp̄â* to be a verbal infinitive with a feminine pronominal suffix attached, referring overtly to גַּפְנִי *gap̄nî* 'my vines' and also by implication to תְּאֵנָתִי *tə'ēnāṯî* 'my fig trees'.

f. **stripping, (they)-have-stripped-the-bark-from-it** Qal infinitive of חשׂף *ḥśp̄* [BDB p. 362], [Hol p. 118], [TWOT 766]: 'to peel' [Keil], 'to pluck bare' [REB]. Most versions do not translate this infinitive separately from the conjugated form of *ḥśp̄* below.

g. **stripping, (they)-have-stripped-the-bark-from-it** 3rd masc. sing. Qal perf. of חשׂף *ḥśp̄* (see *f* above): 'to strip the bark from' [Hol], 'to strip off' [BDB], 'to strip off bark' [Crenshaw; NIV, NRSV, TEV], 'to strip bare' [Dillard, Wolff; NASB], 'to peel' [Keil], 'to bark' [KJV], 'to make clean bare' [KJV], 'to strip of bark' [REB], 'to denude' [Allen].

h. **and-have-thrown(-it)-away** 3rd masc. sing. Hiphil perf. of שׁלך *šlḵ* [BDB p. 1020], [Hol p. 372], [TWOT 2398]: 'to throw away' [Hol; NIV], 'to throw' [BDB; NRSV], 'to fling' [BDB], 'to discard' [Dillard], 'to cast away' [Keil, Wolff; KJV, NASB], 'to hurl aside' [Crenshaw], not explicit [TEV]. Allen translates the expression as "littering the ground."

i. **its-branches have-become-white** pl. constr. of שָׂרִיג *śārîg* [BDB p. 974], [Hol p. 355], [TWOT 2284a]: 'branch (of vine)' [Hol; Allen; Dillard; KJV, NASB, NIV, NRSV, REB, TEV], 'tendril' [BDB], 'shoot' [Keil], 'cutting' [Crenshaw], 'twig' [Wolff].

j. **its-branches have-become-white** 3rd pl. Hiphil perf. of לבן *lḇn* [BDB p. 526], [Hol p. 172], [TWOT 1074b]: 'to become white' [Hol; NASB], 'to be white' [TEV], 'to grow white' [Keil], 'to turn white' [Allen; NRSV], 'to make white' [BDB], 'to be left white' [Dillard], 'to be made white' [KJV], 'to whiten' [Crenshaw], 'to be blanched white' [Wolff]. In the NIV and REB this verb is translated as transitive with "branches" as the object: "leaving the branches white." The whiteness apparently indicates that the branches are completely bare, having been stripped of their bark by the locusts.

QUESTION—What is the referent of the pronouns in חֲשָׂפָהּ *ḥăśāp̄āh̲* 'they have stripped the bark from it' and in שָׂרִיגֶיהָ *śārîḡẹhā* 'its branches'?

The referent is both vines and fig trees, as their association together was very strong for the Israelites [Crenshaw].

QUESTION—What is the referent of the implied pronoun "it" in the phrase וְהִשְׁלִיךְ *wəhišliḵ and-have-thrown(-it)-away*?

1. It is the vine itself, and not merely its bark [Keil].
2. It is both vine and fig tree [Crenshaw].

QUESTION—What is the significance of the references to גַּפְנִי *gap̄nî* 'my vine' and תְּאֵנָתִי *tə'ēnāṯî* 'my fig trees'?

1. Joel uses these images to express God's intimate relation to Israel, which is his vineyard, his garden. God's judgment threatens this paradise [Dillard].

2. The association of vineyards and fig trees evoked for the Israelites full, satisfying, and peaceful life (1 Kings 4:25; 2 Kings 18:31; Mic. 4:4; Zech. 3:10) [Crenshaw]; vineyards and fig trees were symbols of YHWH's security for Israel and of the prosperity promised in the divine covenant with Israel [Wolff]. (See the comments under 1:9–10 for another use of similar images.)

DISCOURSE UNIT: 1:8–12 [Cohen]. The topic is "a call to mourning."

1:8

Lament[a] like-(a-)virgin[b] clothed-in[c] sackcloth[d] for[e] (the-)husband (-of)[f] her-youth.[g]

LEXICON—a. **lament** fem. sing. Qal imper. of אלה *ʾlh* [BDB p. 46], [Hol p. 16], [TWOT 95]: 'to lament' [Hol; Keil, Allen, Wolff; KJV, NRSV], 'to wail' [BDB; NASB, REB], 'to mourn' [Dillard; NIV], 'to cry' [TEV], 'to cry aloud' [Crenshaw].

b. **lament like-(a-)virgin** בְּתוּלָה *bəṯûlâ* [BDB p. 143], [Hol p. 52], [TWOT 295a]: 'virgin' [BDB; Hol; Keil, Dillard, Wolff; KJV, NASB, NIV, NRSV, REB], 'young woman' [Crenshaw; TEV], 'girl' [Allen].

c. **clothed-in sackcloth** fem. sing. constr. Qal pass. part. of חגר *ḥgr* [BDB p. 291], [Hol p. 95], [TWOT 604]: 'to be clothed' [Crenshaw], 'to put on' [Hol], 'to gird on' [BDB], 'girded with' [Keil, Wolff; KJV, NASB], 'to be wrapped in' [Dillard], 'to be dressed in' [NRSV]. Allen, NIV, and REB avoid translating this verb by using a phrase such as "like a virgin in sackcloth."

d. **clothed-in sackcloth** שַׂק *śaq* [BDB p. 974], [Hol p. 354], [TWOT 2282a]: 'sackcloth' [BDB, Hol; Crenshaw, Keil, Dillard, Wolff; KJV, NASB, NIV, NRSV, REB]. Allen translates this noun by an explanatory noun phrase: "funereal sackcloth." *Śaq* denotes poorly woven cloth of goat hair. It was usually black [Dillard] and was worn in mourning [Hol].

e. **for (the-)husband(-of) her-youth** עַל *ʿal* [BDB p. 752], [Hol p. 273], [TWOT 1624p]: 'for' [Keil, Dillard; KJV, NASB, NRSV], 'because of' [BDB, Hol; Wolff], 'over' [Crenshaw; REB]. This preposition is translated as a verb by Allen ("mourn") and by NIV ("grieving for").

f. **for (the-)husband(-of) her-youth** constr. of בַּעַל *baʿal* [BDB p. 127], [Hol p. 43], [TWOT 262a]: 'husband' [BDB, Hol; Crenshaw, Dillard, Keil, Wolff; KJV, NIV, NRSV], 'young man' [TEV], 'bridegroom' [NASB], 'betrothed' [REB].

g. **for (the-)husband(-of) her-youth** constr. of נְעוּרִים *nəʿûrîm* [BDB p. 655], [Hol p. 240], [TWOT 1389d]: 'youth' [BDB, Hol; Crenshaw, Keil, Dillard, Wolff; KJV, NASB, NIV, NRSV, REB]. *Nəʿûrîm* denotes one's youth [BDB, Hol] and includes the time of engagement, terminating only with one's wedding [Dillard, Wolff]. Allen translates the phrase בַּעַל נְעוּרֶיהָ *baᶜal nəᶜûrêhâ* as "her young fiancé"; TEV, "the young man she was going to marry."

QUESTION—To whom is the imperative אֱלִי *ʾĕlî* 'lament' addressed?

1. The addressee is probably either the city of Jerusalem or Judah, since the addressee is compared to a virgin [Cohen, Crenshaw, Dillard]. Both Jerusalem and Judah were often personified as women in the OT [Crenshaw].
2. There is no readily understandable addressee of *ʾĕlî* 'lament', suggesting that the text here has been corrupted. The LXX reads θρήνησον πρός με 'wail to me'. In view of πρός με 'to me' here, the MT אֱלִי *ʾĕlî* 'lament' may well have read אֵלַי *ʾēlay* 'to me' originally, and θρήνησον suggests that the word הֵילִיל *hêlîl* 'wail' appeared here as well as in 1:5 [Wolff].

QUESTION—What does בְּתוּלָה *bətûlă* mean?

1. It means a virgin. The context here is of a virgin betrothed to a man; the bridewealth has been paid, but before the couple will have come together, the man dies [Frank Zimmerman, "Some Textual Studies in Genesis," *Journal of Biblical Literature* 73:97–101, cited by Crenshaw; Dillard]. The expression בַּעַל נְעוּרֶיהָ *baᶜal nəᶜûrêhā* must denote the young man who has contracted to marry her [Wolff].
2. *Bətûlâ* means only 'young woman' [G. J. Wenham, "*Betûlāh*: A Girl of Marriageable Age," *Vetus Testamentum* 22, cited by Crenshaw]. The situation envisaged in this verse could therefore be between engagement and marriage, or it could—and more probably would—be in the early years of marriage [Crenshaw; Cohen regards either state of engagement or marriage as possible here]. It could also possibly be one of a young wife deserted by her husband [Crenshaw, Dillard]. The LXX has ἐπὶ τὸν ἄνδρα αὐτῆς τὸν παρθενικόν 'for the husband of her maidenhood', signifying her first husband [Wolff].

QUESTION—What is the point of similarity in the simile in this verse?

It is that Joel is calling for lamentation as intense as that which is given the death of an intended husband, which is naturally very intense [Wolff].

1:9

(Grain-)offering(s)[a] and-drink-offering(s)[b] have-been-cut-off[c] from[d]-(the-) house(-of)[e] YHWH,
the-priests[f] have-mourned,[g] (the-)ministers(-of)[h] YHWH.

INTERTEXTUAL REFERENCE—This verse ironically evokes Deut. 7:12–13: "if you obey these ordinances, and you keep them and do them, YHWH your God will keep with you the covenant and the loyalty which he swore to your fathers. And he will love you and bless you, and he will make you increase and will bless the fruit of your womb and the produce of the ground, *your grain and your wine and your oil* ...." As in 1:7, longstanding symbols of YHWH's covenantal blessing upon Israel are featured in 1:9, but in a context of malediction instead of blessing.

TEXT—The LXX reads θυσιαστηρίῳ 'to the altar', which suggests a BH reading of מִזְבֵּחַ *mizbēaḥ* 'altar'. Finding this reading more appropriate to the passage's context than the MT, Wolff accordingly translates "the ministers of the altar."

LEXICON—a. **(grain-)<u>offerings</u>** מִנְחָה *minḥâ* [BDB p. 585], [Hol p. 202], [TWOT 1214a]: 'grain offering' [Dillard; NASB, NIV, NRSV, REB], 'cereal offering' [Crenshaw, Allen], 'meat offering' [Keil; KJV], 'meal offering' [Wolff], 'offering' [BDB, Hol], 'sacrifice' [Hol]. The noun is singular and is understood here as a generic reference. (The same is true of 'drink offering'.) In a cultic context, *minḥâ* usually refers to offerings of grain [Hol]. Ground grain, moistened with wine or oil (the drink offering), was offered along with the lamb each morning and evening (Exod. 29:38–40; Num. 28:3–8) [Dillard]. For the phrase הָכְרַת מִנְחָה וָנֶסֶךְ *hāḵraṯ minḥâ wānesek̠* 'grain offerings and drink offerings have been cut off', TEV has "there is no grain or wine to offer."

b. **and-<u>drink-offering(s)</u>** נֶסֶךְ *nesek̠* [BDB p. 651], [Hol p. 239], [TWOT 1375a]: 'drink offering' [BDB, Hol; Keil; KJV, NIV, NRSV, REB], 'libation' [Hol; Crenshaw, Allen, Dillard, Wolff; NASB].

c. **<u>have-been-cut-off</u> from-(the-) house(-of) YHWH** 3rd masc. sing. Huphal perf. of כרת *krṯ* [BDB p. 503], [Hol p. 165], [TWOT 1048]: 'to be cut off' [Dillard, Wolff; KJV, NASB, NIV, NRSV, REB], 'to be eliminated' [Hol], 'to be lacking' [Hol], 'to be withheld' [Crenshaw], 'to be destroyed' [Keil], 'not to be' [TEV], 'to disappear' [Allen].

d. **have-been-cut-off <u>from</u>-(the-) house(-of) YHWH** מִן *min* [BDB p. 577], [Hol p. 200], [TWOT 1212]: 'away from' [Hol], 'from' [BDB; Crenshaw, Keil, Allen, Dillard, Wolff; KJV, NASB, NIV, NRSV, REB].

e. **have-been-cut-off from-(the-) <u>house(-of)</u> YHWH** constr. of בַּיִת *bayiṯ* [BDB p. 108], [Hol p. 38], [TWOT 241]: 'house' [BDB, Hol; Crenshaw, Keil, Wolff; KJV, NASB, NIV, NRSV, REB], 'Temple' [Allen, Dillard; TEV].

f. **the-<u>priests</u> have-mourned** pl. of כֹּהֵן *kōhēn* [BDB p. 463], [Hol p. 152], [TWOT 959]: 'priest' [BDB, Hol; Crenshaw, Keil, Allen, Dillard, Wolff; KJV, NASB, NIV, NRSV, REB, TEV].

g. **the-priests <u>have-mourned</u>** 3rd masc. pl. Qal perf. of אבל *ʾb̠l* [BDB p. 5], [Hol p. 2], [TWOT 6]: 'to mourn' [BDB, Hol; Crenshaw, Keil, Wolff; KJV, NASB, NRSV, REB, TEV], 'to be in mourning' [NIV], 'to grieve' [Dillard], 'to grieve aloud' [Allen].

h. **(the-)<u>ministers(-of)</u> YHWH** masc. pl. constr. Piel part. of שׁרת *šrṯ* [BDB p. 1058], [Hol p. 384], [TWOT 2472]: 'to minister' [BDB, Hol; Dillard, Wolff; NIV, NRSV, REB], 'to serve' [BDB, Hol; Keil]. *Šrṯ* denotes service in the cult at a sanctuary [Hol], but also service done for a king or another in authority [BDB]. The construct relationship between 'servants of' and YHWH is translated by some with more elaborate phrases: "those who minister before the Lord" [NIV], "those who minister to the Lord" [Dillard; REB]. Others employ a possessive expression: 'the ministers of the Lord' [Keil; NASB, NRSV], 'the Lord's ministers' [KJV], 'YHWH's officials' [Crenshaw], 'YHWH's ministers' [Allen]. TEV seems to assume a relationship of more than just apposition between הַכֹּהֲנִים *hakkōhănîm* 'priests' and מְשָׁרְתֵי יהוה *məšārəṯê yhwh* 'the ministers of YHWH' when it translates "the priests mourn because they have no offerings for the Lord." The expression *məšārəṯê yhwh* 'the ministers of YHWH' directs attention to the priests, not as immediate servants of YHWH, but rather as those who tend to his house, for the LXX translates here 'ministers to the altar', and even the MT of 1:13 the same way. Joel speaks mostly of the offerings as going to the house of YHWH, instead of to YHWH himself (2:14 is an exception to this generality) [Wolff].

QUESTION—What is meant by grain offerings and drink offerings?

The grain offering was the offering of flour, salt, and olive oil; it was made along with the lamb and, after the Temple's restoration, was made twice daily. The drink offering—an offering of wine—was made in addition to the grain offering [Crenshaw, Wolff]. The expression מִנְחָה וָנֶסֶךְ *minḥâ wānesek̲* 'grain offerings and drink offerings' occurs only in late texts of the postexilic era. These offerings were called the '*tāmîd̲*-offerings' (תָּמִיד *tāmîd̲* the regular or daily offerings) [Wolff].

QUESTION—What is the implication of the cessation of grain offerings and drink offerings in the Temple?

It is that the daily morning and evening sacrifices ceased because of the failure of the grain, oil, and wine. The cessation of the daily sacrifices, the most regular sign of YHWH's covenant with Israel, implies that YHWH has suspended his covenant [Keil], and that his blessing is no longer effectual [Wolff]. The abundance of the staples of grain, oil, and wine had been in better times a sign of YHWH's covenantal presence in Israel. The priests themselves suffered from the loss of food, for they ate a portion of the sacrifices [Crenshaw].

Wolff sees a farther-reaching implication of the suspension of the daily sacrifices: that YHWH's ultimate salvation plan transcends a faithful Jewish covenant community with a well-functioning *cultus* or worship routine.

1:10

(The-)field(s)[a] have-been-devastated[b], (the-)ground[c] has-dried-up[d-1] /mourns,[d-2]

for[e] (the-)grain[f] has-been-devastated, (the-)new-wine[g] has-dried-up[h] (the-)olive-oil[i] (is) about-to-fail.[j]

INTERTEXTUAL REFERENCE—Joel 1:10 evokes Deut. 7:12–13:

And it shall be, because you obey these commands and have kept them and carried them out, YHWH your God will keep for you the covenant and the faithfulness which he swore to your fathers. And he will love you and bless you and will cause you to multiply and will bless the fruit of your womb and the fruit of your ground, your grain and your wine and your oil, the offspring of your cattle, the increase of your flocks in the land which he swore to your fathers to give you."

These three items, grain, wine, and oil, become symbols of YHWH's blessing upon Israel and occur as such again in Num. 18:12 and Hos. 2:8 as well as here in Joel [Wendland].

LEXICON—a. **(the-)field(s) have-been-devastated** שָׂדֶה *śāḏeh* [BDB p. 961], [Hol p. 349], [TWOT 2236b]: 'field' [BDB, Hol; Crenshaw, Keil, Dillard, Wolff; KJV, NASB, NIV, NRSV, REB, TEV], 'countryside' [Allen]. The singular noun is understood here as a generic reference.

b. **(the-)field(s) have-been-devastated** 3rd masc. sing. Pual perf. of שׁדד *šḏḏ* [BDB p. 994], [Hol p. 361], [TWOT 2331]: 'to be devastated' [BDB, Hol; Crenshaw; NRSV], 'to be laid waste' [Hol; Keil, Wolff], 'to be ruined' [Allen; NASB, NIV, REB], 'to be destroyed' [Dillard], 'to be wasted' [KJV], 'to be bare' [TEV].

c. **(the-)ground has-dried-up/mourns** אֲדָמָה *ʾăḏāmâ* [BDB p. 9], [Hol p. 4], [TWOT 25b]: 'ground' BDB, Hol; Crenshaw, Keil, Allen; NIV, NRSV, REB, TEV], 'land' [BDB; Dillard, Wolff; KJV, NASB]. *ʾăḏāmâ* denotes arable ground or soil [BDB, Hol].

d-1. **(the-)ground has-dried-up** אבל *ʾḇl* [Hol p. 2]: 'to dry up' [Hol; NIV], 'to be wilted' [Wolff]. The idea of the ground drying out might look ahead to Joel's explicit report of a drought in 1:20, or it might apply to the plants which could not survive the heat, having been irreparably damaged by the locusts [Crenshaw]. On the other hand, Simkins sees in this verb a metaphor for the locusts' destruction.

d-2. **(the-)ground mourns** 3rd fem. sing. Qal perf. of אבל *ʾḇl* [BDB p. 5], [Hol p. 2], [TWOT 6]: 'to mourn' [BDB; Keil; KJV, NASB, NRSV, REB, TEV], 'to grieve' [Dillard]; 'to groan' [Crenshaw], 'to be grief-stricken' [Allen]. The ground is personified [Crenshaw].

e. **for (the-)grain has-been-devastated** כִּי *kî* particle [BDB p. 471], [Hol p. 155], [TWOT 976]: 'for' [Keil, Dillard; KJV, NASB, NRSV, REB], 'because' [Allen; TEV], 'indeed' [Crenshaw, Wolff], not explicit [NIV].

f. **for (the-)grain has-been-devastated** דָּגָן *dāḡān* [BDB p. 186], [Hol p. 68], [TWOT 403a]: 'grain' [BDB, Hol; Crenshaw, Allen, Dillard, Wolff; NASB, NIV, NRSV, REB, TEV], 'corn' [BDB; Keil; KJV] (but this might be British English usage for 'wheat'). *Dāḡān* is the generic term for grains and cereals, which in Israel are essentially wheat and barley [Dillard].

g. **(the-)new-wine has-dried-up** תִּירוֹשׁ *tîrôš* [BDB p. 440], [Hol p. 389], [TWOT 2505]: 'new wine' [BDB; Keil, Dillard, Wolff; KJV, NASB, NIV, REB], 'wine' [Hol; Crenshaw; Allen; NRSV], 'grapes'

[TEV]. *Tîrôš* is an archaic word, used chiefly in old and poetic passages [Hol]. *Tîrôš* denotes new wine [BDB; Dillard] and must be about equivalent to עָסִיס *ʿāsîs* 'new wine' of 1:5, although some regard it as equivalent to יַיִן *yayin* 'wine' of 1:5 [Dillard].

h. **(the-)new-wine <u>has-dried-up</u>** 3rd masc. sing. Hiphil perf. of יבשׁ *ybš* [BDB p. 386], [Hol p. 127], [TWOT 837]: 'to dry up' [BDB, Hol; Dillard, Wolff; KJV, NASB, NIV, NRSV, TEV], 'to be dried up' [Crenshaw], 'to make dry' [BDB], 'to be spoiled' [Keil], 'to come to naught' [REB], 'to be in a sorry state' [Allen].

i. **(the-)<u>olive-oil</u> (is) about-to-fail** יִצְהָר *yiṣhār* [BDB p. 844], [Hol p. 140], [TWOT 1883c]: 'olive oil' [BDB, Hol; Wolff], 'oil' [Crenshaw, Keil, Allen; KJV, NIV, NRSV, REB], 'fresh oil' [Dillard; NASB], 'olive trees' [TEV]. *Yiṣhār* denotes unprocessed olive oil [BDB].

j. **(the-)olive-oil (is) <u>about-to-fail</u>** 3rd masc. sing. Pual perf. of אמל *ʾml* [BDB p. 51]: 'to fail' [Dillard; NASB, NIV, NRSV, REB], 'to be feeble' [BDB], 'to feebly fail' [Allen], 'to be depleted' [Crenshaw], 'to be abated' [Wolff]. אֻמְלַל *ʾumlal* [Hol p. 20], [TWOT 114b]: 'ready to fall' [Hol], 'frail' [Hol], 'to decay' [Keil], 'to languish' [KJV], 'to be withered' [TEV].

QUESTION—What is the significance of Joel's choosing to mention these three products of the land?

Grain, wine, and oil often represent together in the OT all major classes of agricultural products [Dillard] and thus also the fecundity of the covenant-awarded land [Wolff]; also, they were necessary in the Temple worship [Cohen, Crenshaw, Wolff].

QUESTION—What is the disaster implied in this verse?

1. A drought is implied, and with this end of the second strophe a climax is reached, signaled especially by alliteration in this verse [Wolff].
2. This verse appears to imply a drought, but this implication is a metaphor for the destruction caused by the locusts [Simkins].

1:11

Be-ashamed[a-1]/wilt[a-2] (you(p)) serfs;[b] howl,[c] (you(p)) wine-growers,[d] over[e]-(the-)wheat[f] and-over[e]-(the-)barley,[g] for[h] (the-)grain-harvest(-of)[i] (the-)field(s)[j] is-ruined.[k]

LEXICON—a-1. **<u>be-ashamed</u>** masc. pl. 2nd Hiphil imper. of בּוֹשׁ *bûš* [BDB p. 101], [Hol p. 36], [TWOT 222]: 'to be ashamed' [BDB, Hol; Crenshaw, Wolff; KJV, NASB], 'to despair' [NIV, REB], 'to abase oneself' [Dillard], 'to be dismayed' [NRSV], 'to turn pale' [Keil], 'to grieve' [TEV], 'to express sorrow' [Allen]. The LXX treats הֹבִישׁוּ *hōḇîšû* as a perfect verb form ('the serfs have been ashamed'), but the presence of other imperatives lead most to consider this word to be an imperative also [Dillard]. *Hōḇîšû* 'be ashamed' is a clear word play on הוֹבִישׁ *hôḇîš* 'has dried up' of the previous verse. The Israelites associated shame with disaster [Crenshaw, Wolff]. The Jewish commentator Abarbanel saw in this verse an expression of the allegorical use of vines and fig trees, which together symbolized the nation of Israel [cited by Cohen].

a-2. <u>wilt</u> masc. pl. 2nd Hiphil imper. of יבשׁ *yḇš* [BDB p. 386], [Hol p. 127], [TWOT 837]: 'to wilt' [Stuart], 'to dry up' [BDB, Hol]. This verb is used in 2 Sam. 19:6 and Hos. 2:7 in the sense of 'despair', and is so used here as well [Stuart].

b. **(you-)<u>serfs</u>** pl. of אִכָּר *ʾikkār* [BDB p. 38], [Hol p. 15], [TWOT 88a]: 'serf' [Hol], 'farmer' [Crenshaw, Allen, Dillard; NASB, NIV, NRSV, REB, TEV], 'ploughman' [BDB], 'husbandman' [Keil; KJV], 'tiller of the soil' [Wolff]. The word *ʾikkārîm* denotes a peasant who works the land of another [Hol; Dillard]; it is a loan word from Akkadian [Crenshaw].

c. **<u>howl</u>, (you-)wine-growers** masc. pl. Hiphil imper. of ילל *yll* [BDB p. 410, [Hol p. 135], [TWOT 868]: 'to howl' [BDB, Hol; Keil; KJV], 'to wail' [Hol; Allen, Dillard, Wolff; NASB, NIV, NRSV], 'to cry' [TEV], 'to lament' [REB], 'to sob' [Crenshaw].

d. **howl, (you-)<u>wine-growers</u>** pl. of כֹּרֵם *kōrēm* [BDB p. 501], [Hol p. 164], [TWOT 1040]: 'wine-grower' [Hol], 'vintner' [Crenshaw], 'vine grower' [NIV], 'vinedresser' [BDB; Keil, Allen, Wolff; KJV, NASB, NRSV, REB], 'to tend vines' [Dillard], 'ones who take care of vineyards' [TEV]. *Kōrēm* is the masc. pl. Qal part. of כרם *krm* 'to tend vineyards' [BDB], and denotes one who works the vineyards of another [Dillard]. Joel might be enlarging the sense of *kōrēm* to include grower of fruit trees (see the following verse) [Crenshaw].

e. **<u>over</u>-(the-)wheat and-<u>over</u>-(the-)barley** עַל *ʿal* [BDB p. 757], [Hol p. 273], [TWOT 1624p): 'over' [Keil; NRSV, REB], 'about' [Dillard], 'for' [Allen; KJV, NASB, NIV], 'on account of' [Crenshaw], 'because of [Wolff]. The word *ʿal* introduces the object of an emotion [BDB].

f. **over-(the-)<u>wheat</u>** חִטָּה *ḥiṭâ* [BDB p. 334], [Hol p. 101], [TWOT 691b]: 'wheat' [BDB, Hol; Crenshaw, Keil, Allen, Dillard, Wolff; KJV, NASB, NIV, NRSV, REB, TEV]. Wheat was more highly valued than was barley, which was the staple of the poor [Crenshaw].

g. **and-over-(the-)<u>barley</u>** שְׂעֹרָה *śəʿōrâ* [BDB p. 972], [Hol p. 354], [TWOT 2274f]: 'barley' [BDB, Hol; Crenshaw, Keil, Allen, Dillard, Wolff; KJV, NASB, NIV, NRSV, REB, TEV].

h. **<u>for</u> (the-)grain-harvest(-of) (the-)field(s) is-ruined** כִּי *kî* particle [BDB p. 471], [Hol p. 155], [TWOT 976]: 'because' [Allen, Dillard; KJV, NASB, NIV], 'for' [Crenshaw, Keil, Wolff; NRSV]. TEV sees *kî* as an intensifier: 'yes, all the crops are destroyed'. In REB it is not explicit.

i. **for (the-)<u>grain-harvest(-of)</u> (the-)field(s) is-ruined** constr. of קָצִיר *qāṣîr* [BDB p. 894], [Hol p. 322], [TWOT 2062a]: 'yield of grain harvest' [Hol], 'harvest' [BDB; Crenshaw, Keil, Allen, Dillard, Wolff;

KJV, NASB, NIV, REB], 'crops' [NRSV, TEV]. *Qāṣîr* can also denote the activity of harvesting grain [BDB, Hol].

j. **for (the-)grain-harvest(-of) (the-)field(s) is-ruined** שָׂדֶה *śāḏeh* [BDB p. 961], [Hol p. 349], [TWOT 2236b]: 'field' [BDB, Hol; Keil, Allen, Dillard, Wolff; KJV, NASB, NIV, NRSV, REB]. *Śāḏeh* denotes either a cultivated field or uncultivated, uninhabited space [BDB]. The singular is here understood as a generic reference, hence the plural translation. The construct relationship between *qāṣîr* 'harvest' and *śāḏeh* 'field' is expressed by a preposition, as in "the harvest in the field" [Allen, Dillard] or "the crops of the field" [Keil; NRSV], or it is not explicit [Crenshaw; TEV].

k. **(the-)grain-harvest(-of) (the-)field(s) is-ruined** 3rd masc. sing. Qal perf. of אבד *ʾbḏ* [BDB p. 1], [Hol p. 1], [TWOT 2]: 'to be ruined' [Hol; Crenshaw; NRSV], 'to perish' [BDB; Keil; KJV], 'to be destroyed' [Dillard; NASB, NIV, TEV], 'to be lost' [Allen, Wolff; REB].

QUESTION—Why are the serfs and the vinedressers addressed in these terms in 1:11–12?

These are probably tenant farmers and workers [Wolff], who suffer along with the rest of the population from the plague of locusts; they will lack both food and the wherewithal to pay for their fields' rent [Dillard]. They are facing the ruin of their staple crops, the wheat and the barley. The vineyards and the fruit trees. In fact, all trees, fruit-bearing or not, are destroyed by the locusts [Keil].

1:12

The-vine(s)[a] have-dried-up[b] and-the-fig-tree(s)[c] are-ready-to-fall[d], (the-)pomegranate(s),[e] even[f] (the-)date-palm(s)[g] and-(the-)apple-tree(s)[h],

all (the-)trees(-of)[i] the-field have-dried-up;[j]

(MT1) surely[k] joy[l] has-dried-up[m-1] away-from[n] (the-)sons(-of)[o] men.[p]

(MT2) surely[k] joy[l] has-been-put-to-shame[m-2] by[n] (the-)sons(-of)[o] men.[p]

LEXICON—a. **the-vine(s) have-dried-up** גֶּפֶן *gep̄en* [BDB p. 172], [Hol p. 63], [TWOT 372a]: '(grape) vine' [Hol; TEV], 'vine' [BDB; Crenshaw, Keil, Allen, Dillard, Wolff; KJV, NASB, NIV, NRSV, REB]. The singular is here understood as a generic reference, as is the case also with 'fig tree', 'pomegranate', 'date palm', and 'apple tree' in this verse.

b. **the-vine(s) (have-)dried-up** 3rd fem. sing. Hiphil perf. of יבשׁ *yḇš* [BDB p. 386], [Hol p. 127], [TWOT 837]: 'to dry up' [BDB, Hol; Dillard; KJV, NASB, NIV], 'to make dry' [BDB], 'to wither' [Crenshaw; NRSV, TEV], 'to be spoiled' [Keil], 'to come to naught' [REB], 'to be wilted' [Wolff], 'to be in a sorry state' [Allen]. Another word play on בּוֹשׁ *bûš* 'to be ashamed' occurs here: הוֹבִישָׁה *hôḇîšâ* can be read as 'is ashamed', but it is better read 'has withered' because of the parallelism with the next phrase [Crenshaw].

c. **and-the-<u>fig-tree(s)</u> (are-)ready-to-fall** תְּאֵנָה *təʾēnâ* [BDB p. 1061], [Hol p. 386], [TWOT 2490]: 'fig tree' [BDB, Hol; Keil, Allen, Dillard, Wolff; KJV, NASB, NIV, NRSV, REB, TEV], 'fig' [Crenshaw]. *Təʾēn â* denotes the *Ficus Carica L.* [Hol].

d. **and-the-fig-tree<u>(s)</u> <u>(are-)ready-to-fall</u>** fem. sing. of אֻמְלַל *ʾumlal* [Hol p. 20], [TWOT 114b]: 'ready to fall' [Hol], 'frail' [Hol], 'withered' [Wolff; NIV], 'to fail' [Dillard; NASB, REB], 'to feebly fail' [Allen], 'to droop' [NRSV], 'to be faded' [Keil], 'to languish' [KJV], 'to wither and die' [TEV], 'to be scorched' [Crenshaw]. BDB (p. 51) regards this form as 3rd fem. sing. Pual perf. of אמל *ʾml*: 'to be feeble'.

e. **(the-)<u>pomegranate(s)</u>** רִמּוֹן *rimmon* [BDB p. 941], [Hol p. 340], [TWOT 2170]: 'pomegranate (*Punica granatum L.*)'—the fruit and the tree [BDB, Hol; Crenshaw, Keil, Allen, Dillard, Wolff; KJV, NASB, NIV, NRSV, REB]. The pomegranate was a symbol of fertility; its fruit and its juice could be consumed in various ways; its leaves could be woven into such things as baskets and mats. [Dillard].

f. **<u>even</u> (the-)date-palm(s)** גַּם *gam* [BDB p. 168], [Hol p. 61], [TWOT 361a]: 'also' [KJV, NASB], 'even' [Wolff], not explicit [Crenshaw, Allen; REB].

g. **even (the-)<u>date-palm(s)</u>** תָּמָר *tāmār* [BDB p. 1071], [Hol p. 392], [TWOT 2523b]: 'date-palm' [BDB; Wolff] (*Phoenix dactylifera*)'—the fruit and the tree [Hol], 'palm' [Keil, Allen, Dillard; NASB, NIV, NRSV, REB], 'palm tree' [KJV], 'date' [Crenshaw].

h. **(the-)<u>apple-tree(s)</u>** תַּפּוּחַ *tappûaḥ* [BDB p. 656], [Hol p. 393], [TWOT 1390c]: 'apple'—the fruit and the tree [BDB, Hol; Crenshaw, Keil, Wolff; KJV, NASB, NIV, NRSV, REB], 'apricot' [Allen, Dillard]. The identification of *tappûaḥ* is not certain, although it has traditionally been considered 'apple' [Dillard]; other possibilities are 'quince', 'citron', and 'apricot' [Crenshaw].

i. **all (the-)<u>trees(-of)</u> the-field (have-)dried-up** pl. constr. of עֵץ *ʿēṣ* [BDB p. 781], [Hol p. 279], [TWOT 1670a]: 'tree' [BDB, Hol; Crenshaw, Keil, Allen, Dillard, Wolff; KJV, NASB, NIV, NRSV, REB]. In TEV the sense of the phrase רִמּוֹן גַּם־תָּמָר וְתַפּוּחַ *rimmon ḡam-tāmār wəṯappûaḥ* 'the pomegranate trees and even the date palms and apple trees' is subsumed under the following phrase, כָּל־עֲצֵי הַשָּׂדֶה *kol-ʿăṣê haśśāḏeh* 'all the trees of the field'. Crenshaw translates the phrase *kol-ʿăṣê haśśāḏeh* as "every tree in the orchard."

j. **all (the-)trees(-of) the-field <u>have-dried-up</u>** 3rd common pl. Qal perf. of יבשׁ *yḇš* (see above): 'to dry up' [Dillard; NASB, NIV], 'to be dried up' [NRSV, REB], 'to wither away' [Keil, Wolff], 'to wither' [Allen; KJV], 'to wilt and die' [TEV], 'to wilt' [Crenshaw].

k. <u>surely</u> **joy has-dried-up** כִּי *kî* particle [BDB p. 471], [Hol p. 155], [TWOT 976]: 'surely' [NIV, NRSV], 'yea' [Keil], 'even' [Dillard], 'indeed' [Crenshaw, Wolff; NASB], 'and' [REB], not explicit [Allen; TEV], 'because' [Frankfort; KJV].

l. **surely <u>joy</u> has-dried-up** שָׂשׂוֹן *śāśôn* [BDB p. 965], [Hol p. 355], [TWOT 2246a]: 'joy' [Hol; Crenshaw, Keil, Allen, Dillard, Wolff; KJV, NIV, REB, TEV], 'rejoicing' [BDB; NASB], 'exultation' [BDB, Hol]. For Stuart, *śāśôn* 'joy' is pictured here as wilting on mankind (בְּנֵי אָדָם *bənê ʾādām*), as fruit may wilt on its tree. Simkins also regards *śāśôn* as figurative, but in a different way: he points out that (1) in the cultures of Israel and the surrounding nations, the notion of joy was conceived less as an emotion and more as pleasures arising from one's engagement in certain rituals; and that therefore (2) one should probably regard *śāśôn* here as a figure of speech standing for the people who have the privilege of worshiping YHWH. Adding this view to his positions on the verb בוש *bûš* 'to be ashamed', the preposition מִן *min*, and the phrase בְּנֵי אָדָם *bənê ʾādām* 'mankind', Simkins then gives the following sense to the final bicolon of this verse: "The worshippers of YHWH have been put to shame by the nations."

m-1. **surely joy <u>has-dried-up</u>** 3rd masc. sing. Hiphil perf. of יבשׁ *ybš* (see *j* above): 'to dry up' [Dillard, Wolff; NASB], 'to wither away' [KJV, NIV, NRSV], 'to expire' [Keil], 'to be gone' [TEV], 'to come to an end' [REB], 'to utterly vanish' [Crenshaw], 'to turn in sorrow away' [Allen], 'to wilt' [Stuart].

m-2. **surely joy <u>has-been-put-to-shame</u>** 3rd masc. sing. Hiphil perf. of בושׁ *bûš* [BDB p. 101], [Hol p. 36], [TWOT 222]: 'to be put to shame' [Simkins], 'to be abashed' [Bewer], 'to stand ashamed' [Hol]. Simkins argues for the reading of *bûš* 'to be ashamed' rather than *ybš* 'to dry up' on the following grounds: (1) the preposition מִן *min* never unambiguously appears in the OT as complementing the Hiphil of the verb *ybš* 'to dry up'. *Min* does, however, introduce an agent or instrument in association with *bûš* 'to be ashamed', as in Isa. 1:29, Jer. 2:36, and Jer. 10:14.

n. **surely joy has-dried-up <u>away-from</u> (the-)sons(-of) men** מִן *min* [BDB p. 577], [Hol p. 200], [TWOT 1212]: 'away from' [Hol; Allen], 'among' [Dillard, Wolff], 'from' [BDB; Crenshaw, Keil, Stuart; KJV, NASB, NIV]. Most view the preposition *min* here as indicating separation from something [BDB]. Simkins, however, understands *min* here to indicate agency: "exultation has been put to shame by the sons of men."

o. **(the-)<u>sons(-of)</u> men** pl. constr. of בֵּן *bēn* [BDB p. 119], [Hol p. 42], [TWOT 254]: 'son' [BDB, Hol; Wolff; KJV, NASB], 'child' [Keil, Dillard].

p. **(the-)sons(-of) <u>men</u>** אָדָם *ʾādām* [BDB p. 9], [Hol p. 4], [TWOT 25a]: 'man' [Dillard, Wolff; KJV, NASB], 'people' [Hol], 'mankind'

[BDB], 'human being' [Stuart]. The expression בֶּן אָדָם *bēn ᵓādām* denotes a single man [Hol]. For the phrase בְּנֵי אָדָם *bənê ᵓādām* NIV has "mankind"; NRSV, REB, and TEV have "the people"; Keil, "the children of men" (also Dillard); Crenshaw, "the populace"; Allen, "men's company." Simkins, on the other hand, understands this phrase as "the nations," as distinguished from the expression בְּנֵי צִיּוֹן *bənê ṣiyyôn* 'sons of Zion', which refers to YHWH's covenant people.

QUESTION—What function does the particle כִּי *kî* have in this verse?

1. It has an emphasizing function [most commentators and versions]. *Kî* cannot signify 'because' here, for the loss of joy must be a result of the agricultural failure, not the cause [Crenshaw, Wolff].
2. It expresses causation, in that *kî* looks back to the imperatives הֹבִישׁוּ *hōḇîšû* 'be ashamed' and הֵילִילוּ *haylîlû* 'howl' of 1:11; the serfs and vinedressers are in effect told to lament *because* there is no more joy for mankind [Keil].
3. It expresses causation, as is understood by both the LXX (reading ὅτι) and the Vulgate (reading *quia*). Certainly all the other instances of *kî* in Joel 1 express causality, and it would be anomalous for this instance not to do the same. Instead, however, of looking back to the imperatives of 1:11 as explained in 2 above, *kî* does indeed look back to the two preceding bicola of 1:12. It should be understood by virtue of the following: (1) The trees mentioned are all fruit trees, which depended mostly upon the practice of irrigation in Israel (unlike the grain crops). (2) The maintenance of the irrigation systems demanded unrelenting effort on the part of the cultivators. (3) Because of the locust attacks, the cultivators had become demoralized ("joy has wilted") to the point of neglecting their fruit trees. These trees are therefore said to have dried up, not only because of the locust attacks, but also from their subsequent neglect. Joel thus implies the following chain of thought: the locusts wreak devastation in the land; the grain, olives, and vinyards are destroyed; the priests and populace, including the cultivators of the fruit trees, are completely demoralized; finally the fruit trees wilt from the lack of watering [Frankfort].

QUESTION—How should the expression בֶּן אָדָם *bēn ᵓādām* be interpreted?

1. Many translate this in a universal manner: 'men', 'mankind', or 'the children of men'.
2. Some translate it in a more restricted manner to denote the Jewish population: 'the people', 'the populace'. Crenshaw defends this by implying that the context shows that joy has left those who have been adversely affected by the agricultural disaster, such as the serfs, the vinederess, and the priests. The expression *bēn ᵓādām* evokes a reminder of the ground's (*ᵓadāmâ*) suffering.
3. Although generally denoting 'mankind', Simkins understands this phrase to denote in Joel the nations surrounding Israel. He sees *bēn ᵓādām* in

contrast, then, to the phrase בְּנֵי צִיּוֹן *bənê ṣiyyôn* 'sons of Zion' (2:23), which denotes YHWH's covenant people.

DISCOURSE UNIT: 1:13–2:17 [NRSV]. The topic is "a call to repentance and prayer" [NRSV].

DISCOURSE UNIT: 1:13–20 [Cohen; NIV]. The topic is "a call to repentance" [Cohen, NIV].
Comments on this discourse unit: The lamentation to which the prophet has called Judah in the preceding section will effect no change in the situation; only sincere repentance and humble cries for help to YHWH, which the prophet now enjoins, may do so. To the plague of locusts is added in this section a drought as well [Keil].

1:13
Put-on-sackcloth[a] and-lament[b], (you(p)) the-priests,[c] wail,[d] (you(p)) servants(-of)[e] (the-)altar.[f]
Go-in(p)[g] spend-the-night[h] in[i]-sackcloth[j], servants(-of)[k] my-God,[l]
for[m] withheld[n] from[o]-(the-)house(-of)[p] your(p)-God[q] (have-been) offer-ing(s)[r] and-drink-offering(s).[s]

TEXT—Wolff follows the LXX's reading, λειτουργοῦντες θεῷ 'ministers of God', instead of 'ministers of my God', מְשָׁרְתֵי אֱלֹהָי *məšārt̲ê ʾĕlōhāy*, saying that the expression in the following phrase כִּי נִמְנַע מִבֵּית אֱלֹהֵיכֶם *kî nimnaʿ mibbêt̲ ʾĕlōhêk̲em* 'for there have been withheld from your house of God' favors the idea of "ministers of God" instead of "ministers of my God."

LEXICON—a. **put-on-sackcloth** masc. pl. Qal imper. of חגר *ḥgr* [BDB p. 291], [Hol p. 95], [TWOT 604]: 'to put on sackcloth' [Hol; Dillard; NIV, NRSV, REB, TEV], 'to tie on sackcloth' [Allen], 'to gird oneself' [Keil, Wolff; KJV] 'to gird on' [BDB], 'to gird oneself with sackcloth' [NASB], 'to don mourning garments' [Crenshaw]. The noun שַׂק *śaq* sackcloth is here omitted [Hol] and must be understood [Keil, Wolff]. Sackcloth was worn while fasting and sorrowing [Crenshaw].

b. **and-lament** masc. pl. Qal imper. of ספד *spd̲* [BDB p. 704], [Hol p. 258], [TWOT 1530]: 'to lament' [BDB; Crenshaw, Keil, Allen, Dillard, Wolff; KJV, NASB, NRSV], 'to sound a lament' [Hol], 'to wail' [BDB], 'to beat the breast as sign of mourning' [Hol], 'to weep' [TEV], 'to mourn' [REB]. Lamentation in this sense was accompanied by gestures, such as beating the breast [Dillard].

c. **(you(p)) the-priests, wail** pl. of כֹּהֵן *kōhēn* [BDB p. 463], [Hol p. 152], [TWOT 959]: 'priest' [BDB, Hol; Crenshaw, Keil, Allen, Dillard, Wolff; KJV, NASB, NIV, NRSV, REB, TEV].

d. **(you(p)) the-priests, wail** masc. pl. Hiphil imper. of ילל *yll* [BDB p. 410], [Hol p. 135], [TWOT 868]: 'to wail' [Hol; Allen, Dillard,

Wolff; NASB, NRSV], 'to howl' [BDB, Hol; Keil; KJV], 'to mourn' [NIV], 'to lament' [REB], 'to sob' [Crenshaw], not explicit [TEV].

e. **(you(p)) servants(-of) (the-)altar** masc. pl. constr. Piel part. of שׁרת *šrṯ* [BDB p. 1058], [Hol p. 384], [TWOT 2472]: 'to serve' [BDB; Keil; TEV] (in cult at sanctuary) [Hol], 'to minister' [BDB, Hol; Allen, Dillard, Wolff; KJV, NASB, NIV, NRSV, REB], 'to preside' [Crenshaw].

f. **(you(p)) servants(-of) (the-)altar** מִזְבֵּחַ *mizbēaḥ* [BDB p. 258], [Hol p. 188], [TWOT 525b]: 'altar' [BDB, Hol; Keil; Dillard, Wolff; KJV, NASB, NIV, NRSV, REB, TEV]. The construct relationship between מְשָׁרְתֵי *məšārəṯê* 'ministers' and *mizbēaḥ* 'altar' is expressed by a prepositional phrase: 'before the altar' [NIV], 'of the altar' [Keil, Allen; KJV, NASB, NRSV, REB], 'at the altar' [TEV], 'over the altar' [Crenshaw]. Note that Joel alters his designation of the priests from his earlier מְשָׁרְתֵי יְהוָה *məšārəṯê yhwh* 'ministers of YHWH' [Crenshaw].

g. **go-in(p) and-spend-the-night in-sackcloth** masc. pl. Qal imper. of בּוֹא *bôʾ* [BDB p. 97], [Hol p. 34], [TWOT 212]: 'to go in' [Allen], 'to come' [Hol; Crenshaw, Keil, Dillard, Wolff; KJV, NASB, NIV, NRSV, REB], 'to come in' [BDB], 'to go' [TEV]. This verb here may imply a solemn procession of the faithful to the Temple [Dillard], but at least seems to imply that the priests should go there [Crenshaw].

h. **go-in(p) (and) spend-the-night in-sackcloth** masc. pl. Qal imper. of לון *lwn* [BDB p. 533], [TWOT 1096]: 'to pass the night' [BDB; Keil, Wolff; NRSV], 'to spend the night' [Hol; Crenshaw, Allen, Dillard; NASB, NIV], 'to lie all night' [KJV], 'to lie all night long' [REB]. TEV translates this verb as duration of time: "all night." Holladay (p. 176) considers that the verb root is לִין *lyn* 'to spend the night'.

i. **in-sackcloth** -בְּ *bə-* [BDB p. 88], [Hol p. 32], [TWOT 193]: 'in' [Crenshaw, Keil, Allen, Dillard, Wolff; KJV, NASB, NIV, NRSV, REB].

j. **in-sackcloth** pl. of שַׂק *śaq* [BDB p. 974], [Hol p. 354], [TWOT 2282a]: 'sackcloth' [BDB, Hol; Crenshaw, Keil, Allen, Dillard, Wolff; KJV, NASB, NIV, NRSV, REB]. The word *śaq* denotes poor quality material of goat hair, which was worn in mourning [Hol]. TEV translates the expression בַּשַּׂקִּים *ḇaśaqqîm* 'in sackcloth' functionally: "mourns."

k. **servants(-of) my-God** masc. pl. constr. Piel part. of שׁרת *šrṯ* (see *e* above): 'servants' [Keil], 'to minister' [Crenshaw, Allen, Dillard, Wolff; KJV, NASB, NIV, NRSV, REB].

l. **servants(-of) my-God** constr. of אֱלֹהִים *ʾĕlōhîm* [BDB p. 43], [Hol p. 17], [TWOT 93c]: 'God' [BDB, Hol; Keil, Dillard, Wolff; KJV, NIV, NRSV, REB]. The construct relationship between מְשָׁרְתֵי *məšārṯê* 'ministers' and אֱלֹהָי *ʾĕlōhāy* 'my God' is expressed by a prepositional phrase: 'before my God' [NIV], 'of my God' [Crenshaw, Keil, Allen; KJV, NASB, NRSV, REB]. The phrase מְשָׁרְתֵי אֱלֹהֵי *məšārṯē ʾĕlohê* 'ministers of my God' is not translated explicitly by TEV. Joel might be using the possessive suffix of *ʾĕlōhāy* 'my God' to stress the religious unity that he and his addressees have [Crenshaw].

m. **<u>for</u> withheld- from (the-)house(-of) your(p)-God** כִּי *kî* particle [BDB p. 471], [Hol p. 155], [TWOT 976]: 'for' [Crenshaw, Keil, Dillard, Wolff; KJV, NASB, NIV, REB], 'because' [Allen], not explicit [NRSV, TEV].

n. **<u>withheld-</u> from (the-)house(-of) your(p)-God** 3rd masc. sing. Niphal perf. of מנע *mnᶜ* [BDB p. 586], [Hol p. 202], [TWOT 1216]: 'to be withheld' [BDB, Hol; Crenshaw, Dillard, Wolff; KJV, NASB, NIV, NRSV, REB], 'to be withdrawn' [Keil], 'to be denied' [Allen]. TEV translates this verb as "there is no."

o. **withheld- <u>from</u> (the-)house(-of) your(p)-God** מִן *min* [BDB p. 577], [Hol p. 200], [TWOT 1212]: 'from' [Crenshaw, Keil, Dillard, Wolff; KJV, NASB, NIV, NRSV, REB], not explicit [Allen]. The preposition *min* here indicates separation from something [BDB]. Because of its position immediately following the verb, the expression מִבֵּית אֱלֹהֵיכֶם *mibbêṯ ʾĕlōhêḵem* 'from the house of your God' is more prominent than the following expression, מִנְחָה וָנָסֶךְ *minḥâ wānāseḵ* 'grain offerings and libations' [Crenshaw].

p. **withheld- from (the-)<u>house(-of)</u> your(p)-God** constr. of בַּיִת *bayiṯ* [BDB p. 108], [Hol p. 38], [TWOT 241]: 'house' [BDB, Hol; Crenshaw, Keil, Wolff; KJV, NASB, NIV, NRSV, REB], 'temple' [Allen, Dillard], not explicit [TEV].

q. **withheld- from (the-)house(-of) your(p)-<u>God</u>** constr. of אֱלֹהִים *ʾĕlōhîm* (see *l* above): 'God' [Crenshaw, Keil, Allen, Dillard, Wolff; KJV, NASB, NIV, NRSV, REB].

r. **<u>offering(s)</u> and-drink-offering(s)** מִנְחָה *minḥâ* [BDB p. 585], [Hol p. 202], [TWOT 1214a]: 'grain offering' [Dillard; NASB, NIV, NRSV, REB], 'cereal offering' [Crenshaw], 'meal offering' [Wolff], 'offering' [BDB, Hol; Allen], 'sacrifice' [Hol], 'meat offering' [Keil; KJV], 'grain to offer' [TEV]. The singular is here understood as a generic reference, which allows for a plural translation.

s. **offerings and-<u>drink-offering(s)</u>** נֶסֶךְ *neseḵ* [BDB p. 651], [Hol p. 239], [TWOT 1375a]: 'drink offering' [BDB, Hol; Keil; KJV, NIV, NRSV, REB], 'libation' [Hol; Crenshaw, Allen, Dillard, Wolff; NASB], 'wine to offer' [TEV]. The singular is here understood as a generic reference, which allows for a plural translation.

QUESTION—Who is the referent of the personal pronoun 'my' in the expression אֱלֹהָי *ʾĕlōhāy* 'my God'?

The referent is the prophet [Keil].

QUESTION—What is the discourse status of 1:13–14?

These verses are tied to 1:2–12 as shown by thematic vocabulary and the repetition in v. 14 of address to the elders and all the inhabitants of the land. At the same time, vv. 13–14 appear to constitute a transition to 1:15–

20 in that they provide detailed instructions for lamentation. In short, they are a call to lamentation, perhaps a separate call or perhaps part of the call constituted by 1:2–12 [Dillard].

QUESTION—What is the implication of the cessation of daily offerings at the Temple?

It is that the daily fellowship with YHWH is also interrupted [Wolff].

DISCOURSE UNIT: 1:14–20 [NASB]. The topic is "starvation and drought."

1:14

Announce (a-)holy[a] fast,[b] call[c] (a-)solemn-assembly,[d]
gather[e] (the-)elders,[f] all inhabitants(-of)[g] the-land,[h]
(to) (the-)house(-of)[i] YHWH your(p)-God,[j] and-call-for-help[k] to YHWH.

SYNTAX—The syntax of אִסְפוּ זְקֵנִים כֹּל יֹשְׁבֵי הָאָרֶץ *ʾispû zəqēnîm kol yōšəḇê hāʾāreṣ* is disputed.

Phrase	*ʾispû*	*zəqēnîm*	*kol yōšəḇê hāʾāreṣ*	
Gloss	gather	elders	all inhabitants of the land	
				Followed by
Viewed as	imperative	obj. of verb	vocative	Keil
Viewed as	imperative	vocative	obj. of verb	Cohen; REB
Viewed as	imperative	obj. of verb	obj. of verb	NIV

LEXICON—a. **announce-a-holy fast** masc. pl. Piel imper. of קדשׁ *qḏš* [BDB p. 873], [Hol p. 313], [TWOT 1990]: 'to announce' [Wolff], 'to appoint a holy day' [Hol], 'to observe as holy' [BDB], 'to declare' [NIV], 'to proclaim' [Dillard], 'to sanctify' [Keil; KJV, NRSV], 'to give orders for' [TEV], 'to consecrate' [NASB], 'to appoint something solemn' [REB], 'to arrange something sacred' [Crenshaw], 'to order something sacred' [Allen].

b. **announce-a-holy fast** צוֹם *ṣôm* [BDB p. 847], [Hol p. 304], [TWOT 1890a]: 'a fast' [BDB, Hol; Crenshaw, Keil, Allen, Dillard; KJV, NASB, NRSV,TEV], 'holy fast' [Wolff; NIV], 'solemn fast' [REB].

c. **call (a-)solemn-assembly** masc. pl. Qal imper. of קרא *qrʾ* [BDB p. 894], [Hol p. 323], [TWOT 2063]: 'to call' [Hol; Dillard; KJV, NIV, NRSV, TEV], 'to call out' [Keil], 'to summon' [BDB; Hol], 'to proclaim' [Allen, Wolff; NASB, REB], 'to announce' [Crenshaw]. This word implies the proclamation of a solemn assembly and a ban of work on that day [Gösta W. Ahlström, *Joel and the Temple Cult of Jerusalem*, Supplement to *Vetus Testamentum* 21 (Leiden: Brill, 1971), cited by Dillard].

d. **call (a-)solemn-assembly** עֲצָרָה *ʿăṣārâ* [BDB p. 783], [Hol p. 281], [TWOT 1675c]: 'solemn assembly' [KJV, NASB, NRSV], 'festive assembly' [Hol], 'sacred assembly' [BDB; NIV], 'assembly' [Keil, Dillard; TEV], 'day of abstinence' [REB], 'religious assembly' [Crenshaw], 'solemn holiday' [Wolff], 'special service' [Allen]. The word *ʿăṣārâ*denotes a meeting for the purposes of worship [Keil], but originally denoted merely the stopping of work for a period [Crenshaw]. Wolff believes that even in Joel's time, *ʿăṣārâ* had not yet come to denote a religious assembly, but only the stopping of work.

e. **gather (the-)elders** masc. pl. Qal imper. of אסף *ʾsp̄* [BDB p. 62], [Hol p. 23], [TWOT 140]: 'to gather' [BDB, Hol; Crenshaw, Dillard, Wolff; KJV, NASB, NRSV, REB, TEV], 'to summon' [NIV], 'to assemble' [Keil, Allen].

f. **gather (the-)elders** pl. of זָקֵן *zāqēn* [BDB p. 278], [Hol p. 91], [TWOT 574b]: 'elder' [BDB, Hol; Keil, Allen, Dillard, Wolff; KJV, NASB, NIV, NRSV, REB], 'leader' [TEV], 'the elderly' [Crenshaw]. Crenshaw argues that זְקֵנִים *zəqēnîm* here denotes, as in 1:2, the old people of the land, not the elders as a class of leaders. Bewer, on the other hand, considers *zəqēnîm* to be a title.

g. **all inhabitants(-of) the-land** constr. pl. masc. part. of ישׁב *yšḇ* [BDB p. 442], [Hol p. 146], [TWOT 922]: 'to dwell' [BDB, Hol; Dillard], 'to live' [Hol; NIV, REB]. Keil, Wolff, KJV, NASB, and NRSV translate this verb as a noun, "inhabitant." TEV has "people"; Crenshaw has "resident"; Allen has "population."

h. **all inhabitants(-of) the-land** אֶרֶץ *ʾereṣ* [BDB p. 76], [Hol p. 28], [TWOT 167]: 'land' [BDB, Hol; Keil, Dillard, Wolff; KJV, NASB, NIV, NRSV, REB], 'country' [BDB; Allen], 'territory' [BDB], 'Judah' [TEV], 'area' [Crenshaw].

i. **(to) (the-)house(-of) YHWH your(p)-God** constr. of בַּיִת *bayiṯ* [BDB p. 108], [Hol p. 38], [TWOT 241]: 'house' [BDB, Hol; Crenshaw, Keil, Wolff; KJV, NASB, NIV, NRSV, REB], 'temple' [Allen, Dillard], not explicit [TEV]. The phrase בֵּית יְהוָה אֱלֹהֵיכֶם *bêṯ yhwh ĕlōhêḵem* functions as an accusative of location and must be understood as 'to the house of YHWH your God', according to Keil. Crenshaw, on the other hand, argues that *bêṯ* represents a contraction of the preposition -בְּ *bə-* 'to' plus the noun בַּיִת *bayiṯ* 'house'. In either case the sense is the same.

j. **(to) (the-)house(-of) YHWH your(p)-God** constr. of אֱלֹהִים *ʾĕlōhîm* [BDB p. 43], [Hol p. 17], [TWOT 93c]: 'God' [BDB, Hol; Crenshaw, Keil, Allen, Dillard, Wolff; KJV, NASB, NIV, NRSV, REB, TEV].

k. **and-call-for-help to YHWH** masc. pl. Qal imper. of זעק *zʿq* [BDB p. 277], [Hol p. 91], [TWOT 570]: 'to call for help' [Hol], 'to cry out' [BDB; Dillard, Wolff; NASB, NIV, NRSV, REB], 'to cry to/unto' [Crenshaw, Keil, Allen; KJV, TEV]. *Zʿq* denotes vociferous and persistent prayer [Keil].

QUESTION—What Temple activities are implied by this passage?

The lack of means to conduct the daily sacrifices and the summons to formal national lamentation imply that although the Temple routine has been disrupted, there is or should still be activity in the Temple. The new order of the day is the ritual of mourning, with all-night priestly vigils, roughly garbed priests in sackcloth, and a liturgy of lamentation [Dillard]. Such fasts lasted usually for one day [Wolff].

QUESTION—What is Joel's real concern in issuing this call to national mourning?

1. Joel does not take the priests or people to task for the empty-hearted performance of rituals as did Isaiah, Jeremiah, and others; his concern is that the community recognize the utter seriousness of their situation [Wolff].
2. Joel is concerned that YHWH be called upon with sincerity of heart and purpose [Crenshaw].

DISCOURSE UNIT: 1:15–20. This discourse unit comprises Stanza B of Part 1 [Wendland].

1:15

Alas[a] for[b]-the-day[c],

for[d] near[e] (is) (the-)day(-of)[f] YHWH, and-as[g]-violence[h] from[i] Shaddai[j] it-will-come.[k]

INTERTEXTUAL REFERENCE—Joel echoes in this verse several other prophetic passages, such as Ezek. 30:2–3, Zeph. 1:7, and Isa. 13:6; but the verse is perhaps best considered an allusion to a long prophetic tradition expressed in many other passages [Wendland].

LEXICON—a. **alas for-the-day** אֲהָהּ *ʾăhāh* [BDB p. 13], [Hol p. 5], [TWOT 30], 'alas' [BDB; Keil, Allen, Dillard, Wolff; KJV, NASB, NIV, NRSV], 'cry of alarm, ah!' [Hol]. TEV translates the phrase אֲהָהּ לַיּוֹם *ʾăhāh layyôm* as "what a terror that day will bring"; Crenshaw, "that day! horrors!" This phrase is not explicitly translated by REB. As Amos had done (Amos 5:18–20), Joel breaks all hope that on the much-touted day of YHWH, God will be so little discriminating as to bring defeat only to Israel's enemies and nothing but triumph to all Israel [Crenshaw].

b. **alas for-the-day** -לְ *lə-* [BDB p. 510], [Hol p. 167], [TWOT 1063]: 'for' [Keil, Wolff; KJV, NASB, NIV], not explicit [Dillard]. Allen begins a new clause here: 'alas, it is the Day'.

c. **alas for-the-<u>day</u>** יוֹם *yôm* [BDB p. 398], [Hol p. 130], [TWOT 852]: 'day' [BDB, Hol; Crenshaw, Keil, Allen, Dillard, Wolff; KJV, NASB, NIV, NRSV, TEV]. NIV translates the phrase אֲהָהּ לַיּוֹם *ʾăhāh layyôm* as "alas for that day."

d. **<u>for</u> near (is) (the-)day(-of) YHWH** כִּי *kî* particle [BDB p. 471], [Hol p. 155], [TWOT 976]: 'for' [Crenshaw, Keil, Wolff; KJV, NASB, NIV, NRSV], not explicit [Allen, Dillard; TEV].

e. **for <u>near</u> (is) (the-)day(-of) YHWH** קָרוֹב *qārôḇ* [BDB p. 898], [Hol p. 325], [TWOT 2065d]: 'near' (temporal) [BDB, Hol; Keil, Dillard, Wolff; NASB, NIV, NRSV, REB, TEV], 'imminent' [Hol; Crenshaw], 'at hand' [KJV]. Allen translates this adjective by a verb phrase: "will soon be here."

f. **for near (is) (the-)<u>day(-of)</u> YHWH** constr. of יוֹם *yôm* (see *c* above): 'day' [Keil, Dillard, Wolff; KJV, NASB, NIV, TEV].

g. **and-<u>as</u>-violence from Shaddai it-will-come** -כְּ *kə-* [BDB p. 453], [Hol p. 149], [TWOT 937]: 'like' [Crenshaw, Keil, Dillard, Wolff; NIV], 'as' [KJV, NASB, NRSV, REB]. *Kə-* functions here not as stating a resemblance between two things, but rather as giving an example of something: YHWH's judgment will bring devastation of a general type [Keil]. The sense of this occurrence of *kə-* is explained by Driver in this way: "The coming visitation will be what a devastation proceeding from the Almighty might be expected to be" [S. R. Driver, *The Minor Prophets: Nahum, Habakkuk, Zephaniah, Haggai, Zechariah, Malachi*; cited by Bewer]. In this vein, TEV translates "the day when the Almighty brings destruction", and Allen, "it is coming with mighty ruin from the Almighty." An idiomatic translation might be, 'and as theviolence that it is from Shaddai it will come'.

h. **and-as-<u>violence</u> from Shaddai it-will-come** שֹׁד *šōḏ* [BDB p. 994], [Hol p. 361], [TWOT 2331a]: 'violence' [BDB, Hol; Keil], 'destruction' [Hol; Crenshaw; KJV, NASB, NIV, NRSV, TEV], 'devastation' [BDB; Dillard], 'mighty destruction' [REB], 'might' [Wolff], 'mighty ruin' [Allen].

i. **and-as-violence <u>from</u> Shaddai it-will-come** מִן *min* [BDB p. 577], [Hol p. 200], [TWOT 1212]: 'from' [Crenshaw, Keil, Allen, Dillard, Wolff; KJV, NASB, NIV, NRSV,REB]. Here *min* introduces the agent of an action [BDB, Hol]; TEV makes the agent (שַׁדַּי *šadday*) the subject of the clause.

j. **and-as-(the)violence (that it is) from <u>Shaddai</u> it-will-come** שַׁדַּי *šadday* [BDB p. 994], [Hol p. 361], [TWOT 2333]: 'the Almighty' [Keil, Allen; KJV, NASB, NIV, NRSV, REB, TEV], 'the Devastator' [Dillard], 'Destroyer' [Crenshaw], 'Mighty One' [Wolff]. *Šadday* is a divine name, identified with YHWH [Hol].

k. **and-as-violence from Shaddai <u>it-will-come</u>** 3rd masc. sing. Qal imperf. of בּוֹא *bôʾ* [BDB p. 97], [Hol p. 34], [TWOT 212]: 'to come' [BDB, Hol; Allen, Dillard, Wolff; KJV, NASB, NIV, NRSV, REB], 'to dawn' [Crenshaw], not explicit [TEV]. Most translate with the English future tense. Wolff and REB use the present tense: 'it comes'.

QUESTION—What view was held of this verse by early historical critics?

Duhm held that this verse was inserted by a redactor in an effort to reconcile the locust plague and drought material of Joel 1–2 with the obvious apocalypse-like material of Joel 3 (3–4) [Dillard]. Bewer adopted this position, remarking that whereas the "original" Joel regarded the locust plague as judgment from YHWH (like Amos 5:18–20), the editor viewed it, as bad as it was, only as warning of the far more catastrophic day of YHWH.

QUESTION—What relation does 1:15–20 have to the preceding verses?

1. The 1:15–20 passage constitutes a personal outcry of the prophet [Keil, Wolff]. With v. 15 is imparted the recognition that the locust invasion described in the previous verses presages the coming day of YHWH, which is the theme proper of the entire book [Wolff].
2. The 1:15–20 passage constitutes a summary of the lament liturgy, an outcry to YHWH [Dillard]. (Bewer also holds this view, but only concerning 1:16–20; he considers 1:15 to be a later insertion.) This view is supported by the Syriac Peshitta, which reads in such a way as to understand a Hebrew reading of לֵאמֹר *lēʾmōr* 'saying' at the end of 1:14, thus introducing 1:15 as reported speech [Wolff].

QUESTION—How does the invasion of locusts, described in the previous verses, relate to the day of YHWH theme in Joel?

The locust invasion is described in militaristic terms, bringing to mind the many past invasions of pagan nations, some of which did far more damage than any plague of locusts. These military invasions were seen in Israel's collective consciousness as evidence of YHWH's judgment upon the nation, leading inexorably up to the great, final day of YHWH. Israel indeed ran the risk of destruction at the hands of YHWH, but if she repented and returned to the covenant, she would see instead the defeat of her enemies [Dillard]. Thus Joel sees the locust plague as a harbinger of a far more definitive judgment brought by YHWH against Israel [Crenshaw, Wolff]. Joel is able to see the locust invasion in this light because the invasion was so severe that it jeopardized the ceremonial sacrificial practices, which in turn put into question Israel's continuing covenant with YHWH. Joel's description of the locust plague in military terms therefore befits a description of the day of YHWH as well. Ultimately, then, the locust invasion is seen as playing an apocalyptic role, which explains why the prophet was so insistent in 1:3 that everyone in the covenant community pay attention to its significance [Wolff].

QUESTION—What is the nature of the exclamation אֲהָהּ *ʾăhāh̲*, which begins this verse?

Here, as elsewhere in the OT, *ʾăhāh̲* introduces a lament. However, *ʾăhāh̲* generally begins the phrase אֲהָהּ אֲדֹנָי יְהוִה *ʾăhāh ʾăd̲ōnāy yhwh* 'Ah, my Lord YHWH', but in 1:15, it appears that Joel is not interested in presenting a full liturgy of lamentation; rather, he wishes to highlight the magnitude of the coming day of YHWH [Wolff]. The short colon אֲהָהּ לַיּוֹם *ʾăhāh layyôm* 'alas for the day' is an exclamation and should be translated very forcefully [Wendland].

QUESTION—What is the literary dynamic of the phrase וּכְשֹׁד מִשַּׁדַּי *ûkəšōd miššadday* 'and-as-violence from Shaddai' ?

As in many other passages, Joel employs alliteration in this phrase, and he might be reiterating a common opinion as to the etymology of the divine name Shaddai (*šadday)*, although today one often sees given as a probable source of Shaddai the Akkadian *šadû* 'God of the mountains, mountain dweller'. The Jewish commentator Eliezer of Beaugency noted that Shaddai occurred only rarely in prophetic literature and inferred that Joel uses it only for the sake of the resulting alliteration [cited by Cohen]. The LXX translates *šadday* as Παντοκράτωρ, whence the traditional English translation 'Almighty' [Dillard].

QUESTION—To what do the two occurrences of יוֹם *yôm* 'day' refer?

They refer to the day of YHWH, when he will judge all the nations who have rebelled against him and when he will bring everything into his divine order, avenging and righting all wrongs committed throughout history. A second aspect of this judgment will be the punishment of evil in Israel [Keil, Dillard]. *Yôm* here does not refer to a period of time, but rather to an event associated with the person indicated, in this case YHWH [Wolff].

QUESTION—Where in the OT is the expression יוֹם יְהוָה *yôm yhwh* 'the day of YHWH' found?

It is found five times in Joel and eleven times outside of it, often in the context of prophecies directed against Israel (Amos 5:18, 20; Zech. 1:7, 14; Mal. 4:5 (3:23); Ezek. 13:5), but also in contexts of prophecies directed against other nations (Isa. 13:6, 9; Obad. 15). In Joel it is found in both kinds of contexts. There are, however, many expressions similar to *yôm yhwh* which should be taken into account, such as "a day for YHWH" (Ezek. 30:3), "a day of tumult for the Lord YHWH of hosts" (Isa. 22:5), and "a day of YHWH's vengeance" (Isa. 34:8) [Wolff].

QUESTION—What was the origin of the concept of "the day of YHWH"?

1. This concept had its origin mainly in the institution of the holy war [Wolff, who follows Gerhard von Rad and others on this point].
2. This concept grew out of the annual Enthronement Festival of the Hebrews, perhaps an expectation to see YHWH reveal himself at the festival [Sigmund Mowinckel, *He that Cometh* (Nashville: Abingdon Press, 1954), cited by Crenshaw].
3. This concept grew out of Israel's ancient history of theophanies—YHWH's self-revelation to his people [M. Weiss, "The Origin of the Day of the Lord Reconsidered," *Hebrew Union College Annual* 37 (1966), cited by Prinsloo].
4. This concept grew out of a common Near Eastern tradition begun by the Assyrians and Hittites of the sovereign visiting his people and inflicting

punishment upon covenant breakers in accordance with the curses pronounced at the establishment of the covenant [F. C. Fensham, "A possible origin of the concept of the Day of the Lord," *Biblical Essays*, Proceedings of the Ninth Meeting of Die Ou-Testamentiese Werkgemeeskap in Suid-Afrika (1996), cited by Prinsloo].

QUESTION—What were the characteristics of the concept of "the day of YHWH"?

Many scholars agree that this concept developed over time. One has therefore to pay attention to the specific way in which it appears in any one place in the OT. It is certain that "the day of YHWH" came to include the idea of God's revealing himself in anger. At first, this anger was directed against Israel's enemies in Israel's salvation history. Later, this anger was found to threaten also the faithless covenant community of Israel, as can be seen in Isa. 28:21. With this latter development came a shift from regarding "the day of YHWH" as a historical event to regarding it as an eschatological event yet to occur; the first oracles in this regard are found in Amos 5:18–20 and Isa. 2:6–22. Once Jerusalem had fallen to the Babylonians, "the day of YHWH" began increasingly to be applied to future eschatological judgment of the other nations. Finally, the fully developed apocalyptic "day of YHWH" came to threaten the future of both Israel and of the other nations, a fate from which there would be no escape. Thus the salvation history of Israel has not yet been fully written or realized; rather, it awaits the fulfillment of all that YHWH has decreed in his word [Wolff].

QUESTION—What relationship does this verse have to Isa. 13:6?

1. Isaiah borrows this verse almost verbatim from Joel [Keil].
2. It is difficult to say whether Joel borrowed from Isaiah and Ezekiel (Ezek. 30:2b–3a) (or from Zeph. 1:7, 14 [Wolff]), or whether he made use of a common stock of prophetic tradition [Crenshaw]. In any case, the imminence of "the day of YHWH," which is applied to other nations in Isa. 13:6 and Ezek. 30:2–3, is spoken of by Joel in relation to Judah [Wolff].

1:16

Has-not[a] before[b] our-eyes[c] food[d] been-removed,[e]
from-(the-)house(-of) our-God[f] joy[g] and-rejoicing[h]?

LEXICON—a. **has-not ... food been-removed** הֲלוֹא *hălôʾ* [BDB p. 518], [Hol p. 170]: 'is/has not' [Crenshaw, Keil, Allen, Dillard, Wolff; KJV, NASB, NRSV]. REB and TEV translate the rhetorical question introduced by *hălôʾ* as a declarative sentence.

b. **has-not before our-eyes food been-removed** נֶגֶד *neḡeḏ* [BDB p. 617], [Hol p. 226], [TWOT 1289a]: 'before' [Hol; Crenshaw, Keil, Allen, Dillard, Wolff; KJV, NASB, NIV, NRSV, REB]. Properly a noun, 'that which is in front, conspicuous', *neḡeḏ* always functions as a preposition or an adverb [BDB]. TEV translates the expression עֵינֵינוּ נֶגֶד *neḡeḏ ʿênênû* 'before our eyes' as "we look on helpless."

c. **has-not before our-<u>eyes</u> food been-removed** constr. pl. of עַיִן *ʿayin* [BDB p. 744], [Hol p. 271], [TWOT 1612a]: 'eye' [BDB, Hol; Crenshaw, Keil, Allen, Dillard, Wolff; KJV, NASB, NIV, NRSV, REB].

d. **has-not before our-eyes <u>food</u> been-removed** אֹכֶל *ʾōḵel* [BDB p. 38], [Hol p. 15], [TWOT 85a]: 'food' [BDB, Hol; Crenshaw, Keil, Allen, Dillard, Wolff; NASB, NIV, NRSV, REB], 'meat' [KJV], 'crops' [TEV]. This is the usual term for food in general; here, however, the focus is upon foodstuffs destined for the Temple sacrifices [Bewer, Crenshaw].

e. **has-not before our-eyes food <u>been-removed</u>** 3rd masc. sing. Niphal perf. of כרת *krṯ* [BDB p. 503], [Hol p. 165], [TWOT 1048]: 'to be removed' [Hol], 'to be cut off' [BDB; Crenshaw, Dillard, Wolff; KJV, NASB, NIV, NRSV, REB], 'to be destroyed' [Keil; TEV], 'to disappear' [Allen]. This verb has as a second object שִׂמְחָה וָגִיל *śimḥâ wāḡîl* 'joy and rejoicing', and with this second object TEV translates it as 'there is no....' Note that the same verb is used in 1:5.

f. **from (the-)house(-of) our-<u>God</u>** constr. of אֱלֹהִים *ʾĕlōhîm* [BDB p. 43], [Hol p. 17], [TWOT 93c]: 'God' [BDB, Hol; Crenshaw, Keil, Allen, Dillard, Wolff; KJV, NASB, NIV, NRSV, REB, TEV].

g. **<u>joy</u> and-rejoicing** שִׂמְחָה *śimḥâ* [BDB p. 970], [Hol p. 353], [TWOT 2268b]: 'joy' [BDB, Hol; Crenshaw, Keil, Allen, Dillard, Wolff; KJV, NIV, NRSV, REB, TEV], 'gladness' [BDB; NASB]. The Israelites were promised joy in their faithful obedience to the covenantal stipulations (Deut. 12:7) [Crenshaw].

h. **joy and-<u>rejoicing</u>** גִּיל *gîl* [BDB p. 162], [Hol p. 59], [TWOT 346a]: 'rejoicing' [BDB, Hol; Wolff], 'gladness' [Crenshaw, Allen, Dillard; KJV, NIV, NRSV, REB], 'exulting' [Keil], 'joy' [NASB], not explicit [TEV].

QUESTION—How is joy taken away from the house of God?

This verse, in which even the Temple routine is said to be menaced, thereby represents a reversal of the normal prophetic theme of "the day of YHWH." In earlier Israel this "day" traditionally represented judgment for the hostile nations; later it came to signal judgment also upon faithless Israel [Wendland]. Since the people lack food, the offerings presented at the Temple have also greatly diminished or have completely ceased, as have the celebratory fellowship meals, which were traditional at the time of sacrifice [Keil], and which were a sign of fellowship between the worshiper and YHWH [Dillard]. As the priests and Levites were to benefit from the grain offerings (Lev. 6:14–18), they would be particularly affected by the famine [Dillard]. Cohen specifically refers to the traditional joy reigning at the Festival of Harvest.

QUESTION—Who are the speakers in this verse?

1. They may be either the people at large or the priests, who would be very concerned over the cessation of Temple sacrifices [Bewer, Crenshaw].
2. The speaker is Joel; he asks this rhetorical question in order to stress the magnitude of the disaster which has come upon Judah [Wolff].

QUESTION—Of what is the expression נֶגֶד עֵינֵינוּ *neg̱eḏ ʿênênû* 'before our very eyes' reminiscent?

It might well be evocative of similar expressions in the old curses which were threatened upon Israel's disobedience to her covenant with YHWH. Deut. 28:31 is an example: "Your ox shall be slain before your eyes (לְעֵינֶיךָ *ləʿênêḵā*), and you shall not eat of it; your ass shall be violently taken away before your face (מִלְּפָנֶיךָ *milləp̄ānêḵā*) and shall not be restored to you."

1:17

(The-)seeds[a] have-withered[b] under[c] their-clods [d-1] / shovels,[d-2]
(the-)storehouses[e] have-been-deserted,[f] (the-)granaries[g] have-been-laid-in-ruins,[h] for[i] (the-)grain[j] has-dried-up.[k]

TEXT—Various ancient versions reflect longstanding uncertainty about the sense of the initial bicolon.

Translation	Version	Remarks
		This bicolon contains three hapax legomena, words which occur nowhere else in the OT and which, for this reason, are susceptible to various interpretations. Either the original text was already corrupt by the time that Jewish translators began treating it or the meaning of the words had already been lost. This is indicated by the disagreement among the ancient versions [Dillard].
ἐσκίρτησαν δαμάλεις ἐπὶ ταῖς φάτναις αὐτῶν 'heifers danced at their mangers'	LXX	
conputreuerunt iumenta in stercore suo 'beasts rot in their dung'	Vulgate	
ηὐρωτίασαν σιτοδοξεῖα ἀπὸ τοῦ χρισμάτων 'the granaries have rotted from their plaster'	Symmachus	

Bewer regarded this bicolon as corrupt, but as followed by the correct reading noted down by a scribe, as in Hos. 9:13. The difference between the two cases is that in Hos. 9:13, the scribe wrote כַּאֲשֶׁר־רָאִיתִי *kaʾăšer-rāʾîṯî* 'as I see', whereas no such indication is given in 1:17. For this reason, Bewer translated it as follows:

17 *Waste lie the store-houses,*
ruined the barns!
Since the corn has failed,
18 *what shall we put in them?*

Bewer derived the line *what shall we put in them?* directly from LXX (τί ἀποθήσομεν ἑαυτοῖς), which he regarded as correct.

LEXICON—a. **(the-) <u>seeds</u> have-withered** assumed pl. of פְּרֻדָה *pǝrudâ* [BDB p. 825], [TWOT 1806a]: 'seed' [Crenshaw, Allen, Dillard; KJV, NASB, NIV, NRSV, REB, TEV], 'grain of seed' [BDB], 'seed grain' [Wolff], פְּרֻדֹת *pǝrudōt* [Hol p. 297]: 'dried figs' [Hol], 'grain' [Keil]. *Pǝrudōt* is one of the three hapax legomena in this passage, and so is particularly difficult to interpret. Keil and many others regard it as coming from פרד *prd* 'to divide, separate', although this derivation is highly questionable. Moreover, BH certainly has common words for "seed" other than *pǝrudâ*. Others regard *pǝrudâ* as cognate to Syriac *prdʾ* 'grain, seed, berry' and Aramaic *perîdaʾ* 'pebble, sand, berry'. LXX's δαμάλεις 'heifers' is based on reading *pǝrudōt* as the plural of *pirdâ* 'she mule' [Crenshaw].

b. **(the-) seeds <u>have-withered</u>** 3rd common pl. Qal perf. of עבשׁ *ʿbš* [BDB p. 721], [Hol p. 264], [TWOT 837]: 'to wither' [Hol], 'to dry up' [Hol], 'to be shriveled' [Allen; NIV], 'to shrivel' [BDB; Crenshaw; NASB, NRSV, REB], 'to lie shriveled' [Wolff], 'to be parched' [Dillard], 'to moulder' [Keil], 'to be rotten' [KJV], 'to die' [TEV]. This word is another hapax legomenon and is considered by many to be related to an Arabic verb *ʿabisa* 'to contract', especially to contract the face, that is, 'to frown', hence 'to shrivel' [Crenshaw, Dillard]. Some see it as derived from Aramaic עפשׁ *ʿpš* 'to rot'; the Vulgate reflects this [Crenshaw]. But plants do not tend to rot in dry heat [Bewer].

c. **<u>under</u> their-clods/shovels** תַּחַת *taḥat* [BDB p. 1065], [Hol p. 389], [TWOT 2504]: 'under' [BDB, Hol; Crenshaw, Keil, Allen, Wolff; KJV, NASB, NRSV, REB], 'beneath' [BDB, Hol; Dillard; NIV], 'in' [TEV].

d-1. **under their-<u>clods</u>** constr. pl. of מֶגְרָפָה *meḡrāp̄â* [BDB p. 175], [TWOT 385b], or of מַגְרָף *maḡrāp̄* [Hol p. 182]: 'clod' [Keil, Dillard, Wolff; KJV, NASB, NIV, NRSV, REB], 'dry earth' [TEV], perhaps 'clod' [BDB], 'spade' [Hol], 'hoe' [Hol; Cohen], 'shovel' [Allen, Cohen, Crenshaw], 'water channel' [REB]. *Meḡrap̄ôt* is yet another hapax legomenon. Keil considers that it comes from גרף *grp̄* 'to wash away a detached piece of earth'.

d-2. **under their-<u>shovels</u>** Some consider *meḡrap̄ôt* to be related to Arabic and Aramaic words meaning "shovel" [Allen, Dillard]; there is indeed a postbiblical Hebrew word *meḡrāp̄â* 'shovel' [Crenshaw]. If 'shovel' is intended in the text, then the implication may be that the farmers, despairing over the implied drought, have uncovered the sown seed with their shovels only to find it shriveled [Allen]. Jewish commentators have usually understood *meḡrap̄ôt* in the sense of 'clods' [Dillard], derived from *grp̄* 'to sweep away' [Crenshaw]. However, Bewer regarded the derivation of 'clods' from *grp̄* as impossible and the translation as 'shovels' to be nonsensical in the context. Some have held that *meḡrāp̄* or *maḡrāp̄* is related to Arabic *gurf* 'a stream bank worn down by water' [Bewer]. This could have been the source of REB's translation "the water-channels are dry" except that REB has "clods" as well. There is also the problem that the third plural possessive pronoun "their" attached to *meḡrap̄ôṯ* has no antecedent; Crenshaw says the pronoun could possibly imply indefinite possession, i.e., the shovels of anyone. It could be tempting to omit translating the first four words of this verse were it not for a fair possibility of reconstructing their meaning based on their parallelism with the rest of the verse—it is probable that these words have something to do with grain [Crenshaw].

e. **(the-)storehouses have-been-deserted** pl. of אוֹצָר *ʾôṣār* [BDB p. 69], [Hol p. 7], [TWOT 154a]: 'storehouse' [BDB, Hol; Keil, Dillard, Wolff; NASB, NIV, NRSV], 'garner' [KJV], 'storage bin' [Crenshaw], 'granary' [Allen]. In OT times there were many different varieties of storage facilities, constructed and managed in different manners; the exact denotations of *ʾôṣār* and of מַמְּגוּרָה *mammǝgûrâ* (see *g* below) are unknown [Dillard]. The terms אֹצָרוֹת *ʾōṣārôṯ* 'storehouses' and מַמְּגֻרוֹת *mammǝgurôṯ* 'granaries' have been conflated to 'granaries' by TEV and to 'barns' by REB. The disrepair of the granaries argues that the supervisors of these important structures had become negligent in their duties [Crenshaw], or it may simply have been that the buildings had fallen into disuse [Kimchi, cited by Cohen].

f. **(the-)storehouses have-been-deserted** 3rd common pl. Niphal perf. of שׁמם *šmm* [BDB p. 1030], [Hol p. 376], [TWOT 2409]: 'to be made deserted' [Hol], 'to be in ruins' [Dillard; NIV], 'to be desolated' [BDB], 'to be desolate' [Crenshaw, Keil; NASB, NRSV], 'to be laid desolate' [KJV], 'to lie in ruins' [REB], 'to be ruined' [Allen, Wolff].

g. **(the-)granaries have-been-laid-in-ruins** pl. of מַמְּגוּרָה *mammǝgûrâ* [BDB p. 158], [Hol p. 199], [TWOT 330e]: 'granary' [BDB; Crenshaw, Dillard, Wolff; NIV, NRSV], 'storehouse' [BDB], 'barn' [Keil, Allen; KJV, NASB], 'grain pit' [Hol].

h. **(the-)granaries have-been-laid-in-ruins** 3rd common pl. Niphal perf. of הרס *hrs* [BDB p. 248], [Hol p. 84], [TWOT 516]: 'to be laid in ruins' [Hol], 'to be broken down' [KJV, NIV], 'to be torn down' [BDB; Wolff; NASB], 'to be in disrepair' [Dillard], 'to be ruined' [Crenshaw; NRSV], 'to fall down' [Keil], 'to be dilapidated' [Allen]. Since the granaries are no longer in use, they are not maintained [Keil, Wolff].

i. **for (the-)grain has-dried-up** כִּי *kî* particle [BDB p. 471], [Hol p. 155], [TWOT 976]: 'for' [Crenshaw, Wolff; KJV, NASB, NIV, REB], 'because' [Keil, Allen, Dillard; NRSV]. TEV turns the relation signaled by *kî* around: 'there is no grain to be stored, and so the empty granaries are in ruins'. The *kî* particle implies a demoralization on the part of the farmers; given the lack of harvest, they are no longer motivated to maintain the granaries [Keil, Wolff].

j. **for (the-)<u>grain</u> has-dried-up** דָּגָן *dāgān* [BDB p. 186], [Hol p. 68], [TWOT 403a]: 'grain' [BDB, Hol; Crenshaw, Allen, Dillard, Wolff; NASB, NIV, NRSV, TEV], 'corn' [BDB; Keil; KJV] (but this might be British English usage for "wheat"), 'harvest' [REB].

k. **for (the-)grain <u>has-dried-up</u>** 3rd masc. sing. Hiphil perf. of יבשׁ *yḇš* [BDB p. 386], [Hol p. 127], [TWOT 837]: 'to dry up' [BDB, Hol; NIV], 'to be dried up' [NASB], 'to dry out' [Crenshaw], 'to make dry' [BDB], 'to wither away' [Dillard], 'to wither' [Wolff], 'to fail' [NRSV], 'to be destroyed' [Keil], 'to be withered' [KJV], 'to come to naught' [REB], 'to be in a sorry state' [Allen]. TEV translates the phrase הֹבִישׁ דָּגָן *hōḇîš dāgān* 'the grain has dried up' as 'there is no grain to be stored'.

QUESTION—What conditions are implied by 1:17–20?

A drought is implied, in addition to the locust invasion, and made explicit in 1:20 [Cohen, Keil, Wolff]. The defoliation for which the locusts were responsible would have resulted in a lowered water table and would have introduced conditions of drought [Dillard]. Either the sown seed was plowed under the ground before the start of the summer rains, or it was sown at the start of the cultivating season in the vain hope of rain [Wolff].

1:18

How[a] (the-)cattle[b] groan;[c] (the-)herds(-of)[d] cattle[e] wander-in-agitation[f-1] / weep, [f-2]
for[g] there-is-no pasturage[h] for-them; indeed,[i] (the-)flocks(-of)[d] the-sheep-and-goats[j] have-suffered-punishment[k-1] / have-been-deserted.[k-2]

TEXT—A textual emendation has been proposed as follows:

Reading	Remarks
MT: נֶאְשָׁמוּ *neʾəšāmû* 'have suffered punishment' (for their guilt)	**From:** אשׁם *ʾšm* 'to suffer punishment'. **Followed by:** Jewish commentator Rashi [Cohen]. **Argument against:** The Niphal of *ʾšm* is nowhere clearly attested [Wolff].
Emendation: נָשַׁמּוּ *nāšammû* 'have been deserted'	**From:** שׁמם *šmm* 'to be desolate'. **Followed by:** Allen, Stuart, Wolff; REB. **Argument for:** If *šmm* is read here, it then forms a small inclusio with the same verb in 1:17, demarcating Strophe 2 of Stanza B [Wendland]. **Argument for:** LXX's ἠφανίσθησαν 'they have been obliterated' is regarded by Wolff as supporting the proposed emendation *nāšammû*.

NASB, NIV, and TEV simply have 'suffer', without specifying whether the suffering is moral (*ʾšm)* or physical (*ššm).*

LEXICON—a. **how (the-)cattle groan** מָה *mâ* [BDB p. 552], [Hol p. 183], [TWOT 1149]: the exclamation 'how' [Hol; Crenshaw, Keil, Wolff; KJV, NASB, NIV, NRSV, REB], 'even' [Dillard]. Allen preserves the exclamatory quality with "what groans the animals raise"; TEV turns the exclamation into a declarative statement, "the cattle bellow."

b. **how (the-)cattle groan** בְּהֵמָה *bəhēmâ* [BDB p. 96], [Hol p. 34], [TWOT 208a]: 'cattle' [BDB, Hol; Keil, Dillard; NIV, REB, TEV], 'beast' [BDB; Crenshaw, Wolff; KJV, NASB], 'animal' (in general) [Hol; Allen; NRSV]. Opinions differ as to what *bəhēmôṯ* denotes in this context. Crenshaw holds it to be domesticated cattle as distinguished from בַּהֲמוֹת שָׂדֶה *bahămôṯ śāḏệ* 'wild animals' (lit., 'beasts of the field') in 1:20. Wolff supposes that it denotes the domesticated small animals as distinct from the cattle herds in the second bicolon of this verse (עֶדְרֵי בָקָר *ʿeḏrê ḇâqâr*); the distress reaches even the small domesticated animals, revealing that the drought is indeed severe and prolonged, perhaps exacerbated by the locust invasion [Wolff].

c. **how (the-)cattle groan** 3rd fem. sing. Niphal perf. of אנח *ʾnḥ* [BDB p. 58], [Hol p. 22], [TWOT 127]: 'to groan' [Hol; Keil, Wolff; KJV, NASB, NRSV], 'to sigh' [BDB, Hol], 'to moan' [Crenshaw, Dillard; NIV, REB], 'to bellow in distress' [TEV], 'to raise groans' [Allen]. The phrases מַה־נֶּאֶנְחָה בְהֵמָה *mâ-neʾenḥâ ḇəhēmâ* 'how the cattle groan' and נָבֹכוּ עֶדְרֵי בָקָר *nâḇḵû ʿeḏrê ḇâqâr* 'the herds of cattle wander in agitation' have been conflated by TEV: "the cattle are bellowing in distress." Crenshaw interprets the verb as "to sigh inwardly."

d. **(the-)herds(-of) cattle wander-in-agitation** constr. pl. of עֵדֶר *ʿēḏer* [BDB p. 727], [Hol p. 266], [TWOT 1572a]: 'herd' [BDB, Hol; Crenshaw, Keil, Allen, Dillard, Wolff; KJV, NASB, NIV, NRSV, REB].

e. **(the-)herds(-of) cattle wander-in-agitation** בָּקָר *bāqār* [BDB p. 133], [Hol p. 46], [TWOT 274a]: 'cattle' [BDB, Hol; Allen, Wolff; NASB, NRSV, KJV], 'oxen' [Keil; REB], not explicit [Dillard, Crenshaw; NIV].

f-1. **(the-)herds(-of) cattle wander-in-agitation** 3rd pl. Niphal perf. of בוך *bûq* [BDB p. 100], [Hol p. 35], [TWOT 214]: 'to wander in agitation' [Hol], 'to mill about' [NIV], 'to be confused' [BDB], 'to be perplexed' [Dillard; KJV], 'to wander about' [NRSV], 'to wander aimlessly' [NASB], 'to wander in distress' [Allen], 'to stray about' [Wolff], 'to be bewildered' [Keil], 'to be distraught' [REB].

f-2. **(the-)herds(-of) cattle weep** 3rd pl. Niphal perf. of בכה *bḵh* [BDB p. 113], [Hol p. 39], [TWOT 243]: 'to weep' [BDB, Hol; Crenshaw]. The picture is one of cattle and herds wandering aimlessly about; the cattle sigh inwardly and the herds weep from hunger [Crenshaw], perplexed from the lack of food [Bewer, Cohen].

g. **<u>for</u> there-is-no pasturage for-them** כִּי *kî* particle [BDB p. 471], [Hol p. 155], [TWOT 976]: 'for' [Keil, Wolff], 'because' [Allen, Dillard; KJV, NASB, NIV, NRSV, REB, TEV].

h. **for there-is-no <u>pasturage</u> for-them** מִרְעֶה *mirᶜê* [BDB p. 945], [Hol p. 216], [TWOT 2185a]: 'pasturage' [BDB], 'pasture' [Hol; Keil, Allen, Dillard, Wolff; KJV, NASB, NIV, NRSV, REB, TEV], 'fodder' [Crenshaw].

i. **<u>indeed</u>, (the-)flocks(-of) the-sheep-and-goats have-suffered-punishment have-been-deserted** גַּם *gam* [BDB p. 168], [Hol p. 61], [TWOT 361a]: 'even' [Bewer, Crenshaw, Keil, Wolff; NASB, NIV, NRSV, REB], 'too' [Dillard], 'yea' [KJV], 'also' [TEV], 'and' [Allen]. Bewer explains the concessive rendition 'even' with the remark that sheep incline naturally to drier pastures and would therefore feel the drought later than cattle, which require lusher pasturage.

j. **(the-)flocks(-of) the-<u>sheep-and-goats</u>** צֹאן *ṣōʾn* [BDB p. 838], [Hol p. 302], [TWOT 1864a]: 'sheep and goats' [BDB, Hol], 'sheep' [NASB, NIV, TEV], 'small cattle' [BDB], 'flocks' [Dillard, Wolff], 'flocks of sheep' [Crenshaw, Keil, Allen; KJV, NRSV, REB].

k-1. **<u>have-suffered-punishment</u>** 3rd common pl. Niphal perf. of אשׁם *ʾšm* [BDB p. 79], [Hol p. 29], [TWOT 180]: 'to suffer punishment' [BDB, Hol], 'to suffer' [Keil, Dillard; NASB, NIV, TEV], 'to hurt' [Crenshaw], 'to succumb' [Wolff]. This verb form is viewed as signifying to suffer for the expiation of another's offense; the herds suffer the consequences of man's sin [Crenshaw, Keil]; thus the idea of animal sacrifice for human sin is evoked [Crenshaw]. Wolff regards *ʾšm* as meaning 'to become subject to punishment', but notes that this verb occurs only here in the Niphal form.

k-2. **(the-)flocks(-of) the-sheep-and-goats <u>have-been-deserted</u>** 3rd common pl. Niphal perf. of שׁמם *šmm* [BDB p. 1030], [Hol p. 375], [TWOT 2409]: 'to be made deserted' [Hol], 'to be desolated' [BDB], 'to be appalled' [BDB], 'to be made desolate' [KJV], 'to be dazed' [NRSV], 'to waste away' [Allen; REB], 'to be desolate' [Stuart].

QUESTION—What sentiment is associated with the animals described in this verse?

1. They are pictured as feeling more distress at the lamentable conditions than does the population [Dillard].
2. They are pictured as sharing the distress of the people. Joel here depicts to a degree the human-animal sharing of suffering which is so prominent at the very end of Jonah 3 [Crenshaw].

1:19

To-you(s), YHWH, I-call,[a]
for[b] **fire**[c] **has-burned**[d] **(the-)pastures(-of)**[e] **(the-)wilderness,**[f]
and-flames[g] **have-scorched**[h] **all (the-)trees(-of)**[i] **(the-)field(s).**[j]

TEXT—Bewer emends 'I call' to 'they call'. He regards the context supplied by both 1:18 and 1:20 as demanding that in 1:19 the animals cry out to YHWH, but there is no textual suppport for this emendation.

LEXICON—a. **to-you, YHWH, I-call** קרא *qrʾ* [BDB p. 894], [Hol p. 323], [TWOT 2063]: 'to call' [Hol; Allen; NIV], 'to call out' [Dillard, Wolff], 'to call unto someone' [BDB], 'to cry' [Keil; KJV, NASB, NRSV, TEV], 'to cry out' [Crenshaw; REB].

b. **for fire has-consumed** כִּי *kî* particle [BDB p. 471], [Hol p. 155], [TWOT 976]: 'for' [Crenshaw, Keil, Wolff; KJV, NASB, NIV, NRSV, REB], 'because' [Allen; TEV], not explicit [Dillard].

c. **fire has-consumed (the-)pastures(-of)** אֵשׁ *ʾēš* [BDB p. 77], [Hol p. 29], [TWOT 172]: 'fire' [BDB, Hol; Crenshaw, Keil, Allen, Dillard, Wolff; KJV, NASB, NIV, NRSV, REB, TEV]. The expressions concerning fire burning the pastures and forests in this verse are translated as figures of speech for drought by TEV, using a simile: "the pastures and trees are dried up, as though a fire had burned them."

d. **fire has-burned (the-)pastures(-of)** 3rd fem. sing. Qal perf. of אכל *ʾḵl* [BDB p. 37], [Hol p. 14], [TWOT 85]: 'to burn' [TEV], 'to consume' [BDB, Hol; Crenshaw, Allen, Dillard; REB], 'to devour' [BDB; Keil, Wolff; KJV, NASB, NIV, NRSV].

e. **(the-)pastures(-of) (the-)wilderness** pl. constr. of נָוָה *nāwâ* [BDB p. 627], [Hol p. 231], [TWOT 1322c]: 'pasture' [BDB; Keil, Wolff; KJV, NASB, NIV, NRSV, TEV], 'pasturage' [Hol], 'meadow' [BDB], 'grazing lands' [Dillard].

f. **(the-)pastures(-of) (the-)wilderness** מִדְבָּר *miḏbār* [BDB p. 184], [Hol p. 182], [TWOT 399l): 'wilderness' [BDB, Hol; Keil, Dillard; KJV, NASB, NRSV], 'range' [Wolff], 'steppe' [Bewer]. *Miḏbār* refers in general to noncultivated areas [Hol], suitable for cattle to graze [Cohen]. For the phrase נְאוֹת מִדְבָּר *nəʾôṯ hammiḏbār* NIV and REB have "the open pastures"; Crenshaw has "the pasture land"; Allen has "the prairie pastures." It is not the wild desert area of Israel [Crenshaw]. BDB's gloss of 'uninhabited land' is not helpful here.

g. **and-flames have-scorched** לֶהָבָה *lehāḇâ* [BDB p. 529], [Hol p. 173], [TWOT 1077b]: 'flame' [BDB, Hol; Crenshaw, Keil, Allen, Dillard, Wolff; KJV, NASB, NIV, NRSV, REB]. Here *lehāḇâ* is used figuratively of drought [BDB; Bewer], which view accords with TEV's rendering (see *c* above). Crenshaw, however, takes this as a metaphor for the locusts. The singular "flame" is understood as a generic reference, which allows for a plural translation.

h. **and-flames have-scorched** להט *lhṭ* [BDB p. 529], [Hol p. 173], [TWOT 1081]: 'to scorch' [Hol], 'to blaze up' [BDB], 'to burn up'

[NASB, NIV, REB], ‘to burn’ [Allen, Dillard; KJV, NRSV], ‘to consume’ [Keil], ‘to lick’ [Crenshaw], ‘to set ablaze’ [Wolff]. The phrase וְלֶהָבָה לִהֲטָה *wəlehāḇâ lihăṭâ* ‘and flames have scorched’ gives the image of flames licking the vegetation [Crenshaw].

i. **all (the-)<u>trees(-of)</u> (the-)field(s)** pl. constr. of עֵץ *ʾēṣ* [BDB p.), [Hol p. 279], [TWOT 1670a]: ‘tree’ [BDB, Hol; Crenshaw, Keil, Allen, Dillard, Wolff; KJV, NASB, NIV, NRSV, REB, TEV].

j. **all (the-)trees(-of) (the-)<u>field(s)</u>** שָׂדֶה *śāḏeh* [BDB p. 961], [Hol p. 349], [TWOT 2236b]: ‘field’ [BDB, Hol; Crenshaw, Keil, Dillard, Wolff; KJV, NASB, NIV, NRSV], ‘countryside’ [Allen]. The singular ‘field’ is here understood as a generic reference, which allows for a plural translation. *Śāḏeh* can denote either a cultivated field or uncultivated, uninhabited space [BDB]. REB translates it with a phrase: “in the open countryside.” The expression כָּל־עֲצֵי הַשָּׂדֶה *kol-ʿăṣê haśśāḏeh* denotes the trees in the countryside as distinguished from the cultivated trees [Crenshaw].

QUESTION—What is the structure of this verse?

The prayer to God is only the first three words: אֵלֶיךָ יְהוָה אֶקְרָא *ʾēleḵā yhwh ʾeqrāʾ* ‘to you, YHWH, I call’. The rest of the verse provides the motivation for the prayer. The phrase following the first three words amounts to a refrain (כִּי אֵשׁ אָכְלָה נְאוֹת מִדְבָּר *kî ʾēš ʾoḵlâ nəʾôṯ miḏbār* ‘for fire has consumed the pastures of the wilderness’) as becomes clear when the following verse, 1:20, is examined—in it the wild animals are also said to cry out to God. In this latter verse, the “refrain” also appears, but in last place [Crenshaw]; it functions to emphasize the magnitude of the disaster [Wolff].

QUESTION—Who is the referent of the first person singular pronoun in אֶקְרָא *ʾeqrāʾ* ‘I call’?

The referent is probably the prophet, who gives an example of prayer for the priests to imitate [Crenshaw], but it could be the priest leading the liturgy [Dillard]. Mowinckel maintains that psalms in the first person singular are meant for the worship leader—a priest or the king in earlier Israelite times, while Psalms in the first person plural are meant for a congregation as a whole [Sigmund Mowinckel, Review of *Tempora und Satzstellung in den Psalmen* by Diethelm Michel, *Theologische Literaturzeitung* 87: 36 (1962), cited by Wolff]. Like Crenshaw, Wolff supposes that the referent is Joel, who sets the example for the rest of the community in taking up a lament to YHWH.

QUESTION—How are אֵשׁ *ʾēš* ‘fire’ and לֶהָבָה *lehāḇâ* ‘flame’ used in this verse?

1. They are metaphors for the destruction perpetrated by the locusts: the locusts’ ravages leave the landscape blackened as if the countryside had been burned [Kimchi, cited by Cohen; Crenshaw].
2. They are metaphors for drought, as is shown by the drying up of the water courses in 1:20, a phenomenon that could not be caused by locusts

[Bewer, Keil, Wolff]. But the language of fire and flame, while serving as a metaphor, does double duty by calling to mind the theme of the day of YHWH, since such language is characteristic of descriptions elsewhere of theophanies associated with the day of YHWH, as in Zeph. 1:18 and Joel 2:3 [Wolff].

1:20

Indeed,[a] (the-)beasts(-of)[b] (the-)field(s)[c] pant[d] for-you(s),
for[e] they-have-dried-up,[f] (the-)streams(-of)[g] water,[h]
and-fire[i] has-burned[j] (the-)pastures(-of)[k] the-wilderness.[l]

LEXICON—a. **indeed** גַּם *gam* [BDB p. 168], [Hol p. 61], [TWOT 361a]: 'indeed' [Hol], 'even' [Crenshaw, Keil, Allen, Wolff; NASB, NIV, NRSV, REB, TEV], 'too' [Dillard], 'also' [KJV]. *Gam* may be used to signal added information; it may also introduce a rhetorical climax [BDB].

b. **(the-)beasts(-of) (the-)fields** constr. pl. of בְּהֵמָה *bəhēmâ* [BDB p. 96], [Hol p. 34], [TWOT 208a]: 'beast' [BDB; Crenshaw, Keil; KJV, NASB, REB], 'animal' (in general) [Hol], 'wild animal' [Hol; Dillard; NRSV]. Dillard, NIV, NRSV, and TEV translate the phrase בַּהֲמוֹת שָׂדֶה *bāhămôṯ śāḏeh* as "wild animal"; Allen has "wild beast" (also Wolff); Cohen is similar with "wild animal."

c. **(the-)beasts(-of) (the-)fields** שָׂדֶה *śāḏeh* [BDB p. 961], [Hol p. 349], [TWOT 2236b]: 'field' [BDB, Hol; Crenshaw, Keil; KJV, NASB, REB]. *Śāḏeh* can denote either a cultivated field or uncultivated, uninhabited space [BDB]. The construct relationship between בַּהֲמוֹת *bahămôṯ* 'beasts' and שָׂדֶה *śāḏeh* 'field' is generally translated as "beasts of the field." Crenshaw and REB have "beasts in the field."

d. **pant for-you** 3rd fem. sing. Qal imperf. of ערג *ʿrg* [BDB p. 788], [Hol p. 282], [TWOT 2236b]: 'to pant for' [Hol; NASB, NIV], 'to long for' [BDB; Hol], 'to pant after' [Wolff], 'to look to' [Dillard; REB], 'to cry to/unto' [Bewer, Keil; KJV, NRSV], 'to cry out' [TEV], 'to complain' [Crenshaw], 'to cry' [Allen]. The wild animals cry out to God, as in Ps. 104:21 and Job 38:41 [Crenshaw]. It is possible to use a singular verb with a plural subject, especially in the case of animals [Crenshaw].

e. **for they-have-dried-up, (the-)streams(-of) water** כִּי *kî* particle [BDB p. 471], [Hol p. 155], [TWOT 976]: 'for' [Crenshaw, Keil, Dillard, Wolff; KJV, NASB, REB], 'because' [Allen; NRSV, TEV], not explicit [NIV]. The thought introduced by this conjunction, that of the streams and rivers drying up, implies a further thought—that the animals can find no drinking water [Bewer].

f. **they-have-dried-up** 3rd common pl. Qal perf. of יבשׁ *yḇš* [BDB p. 386], [Hol p. 127], [TWOT 837]: 'to dry up' [Hol; Crenshaw, Dillard; NIV], 'to be dried up' [BDB; Keil, Wolff; KJV, NASB, NRSV, REB]. A phrase is also used, 'to be dry of water' [Allen].

g. **(the-)<u>streams(-of)</u> water** pl. constr. of אָפִיק *ʾāpîq* [BDB p. 67], [Hol p. 25], [TWOT 149a]: 'channel (of water)', that is, 'stream bed' [BDB], 'stream channel' [Hol], 'stream' [NIV, REB], 'water source' [Crenshaw, Dillard], 'water course' [NRSV], 'water brook' [Keil; NASB], 'river' [KJV]. The word *ʾāpîq* denotes the main water course of a valley [Hol]. For the phrase אֲפִיקֵי מָיִם *ʾăpîqê mâyim* 'channels of water' REB and TEV have "streams," Allen has "riverbeds," Wolff has "torrents of water." Wolff's translation is probably inspired by Ugaritic, in which a cognate expression signifies gushing fountains or springs [Crenshaw]. This expression denotes streams capable of drying up during periods of heat rather than streams coming from artesian sources (see Isa. 8:7 for the two expressions in parallel) [Crenshaw].

h. **(the-)streams(-of) <u>water</u>** מָיִם *mayim* [BDB p. 565], [Hol p. 193], [TWOT 1188]: 'water' [BDB, Hol; Crenshaw, Dillard, Wolff; KJV, NIV].

i. **and-<u>fire</u> has-burned** אֵשׁ *ʾēš* [BDB p. 77], [Hol p. 29], [TWOT 172]: 'fire' [BDB, Hol; Crenshaw, Keil, Allen, Dillard, Wolff; KJV, NASB, NRSV, REB]. Again, the phrase וְאֵשׁ אָכְלָה נְאוֹת הַמִּדְבָּר *wəʾēš ʾāk̲əlâ nəʾôt̲ hammid̲bâr* is treated as a figure of speech and is translated concretely by TEV, "the streams have become dry," based perhaps on the feeling that "pastures" is implicit in this translation.

j. **and-fire <u>has-burned</u>** 3rd fem. sing. Qal perf. of אכל *ʾk̲l* [BDB p. 37], [Hol p. 14], [TWOT 85]: 'to consume' [BDB, Hol; Allen, Dillard; REB], 'to devour' [BDB; Crenshaw, Keil, Wolff; KJV, NASB, NIV, NRSV].

k. **(the-)<u>pastures(-of)</u> the-wilderness** pl. constr. of נָוָה *nāwâ* [BDB p. 627], [Hol p. 231], [TWOT 1322c]: 'pasture' [BDB; Keil, Wolff; KJV, NASB, NIV, NRSV], 'pasturage' [Hol], 'meadow' [BDB], 'grazing land' [Dillard], not explicit [TEV].

l. **(the-)pastures(-of) the-<u>wilderness</u>** מִדְבָּר *mid̲bār* [BDB p. 184], [Hol p. 182], [TWOT 399l): 'wilderness' [BDB, Hol; Keil, Dillard; KJV, NASB, NRSV], 'range' [Wolff], 'steppe' [Bewer]. *Mid̲bār* refers in general to noncultivated areas [Hol], uninhabited lands [BDB]. The phrase נְאוֹת הַמִּדְבָּר *nəʾôt̲ hammid̲bār* is translated as "the open pastures" [NIV, REB], "the prairie pastures" [Allen], "the pasture land" [Crenshaw]. This phrase does not denote the wild desert areas of Israel, but instead the open grazing land [Crenshaw].

QUESTION—What is the significance of the streams drying up?

1. Joel may be introducing another disaster, that of drought, which he will develop more fully in the next chapter [Crenshaw].
2. This verse perpetuates the image of drought, which is a metaphor for the locusts' destruction [Simkins].

DISCOURSE UNIT: 2:1–17[16] [Keil, Dillard, Wolff; NIV]. The topic is variously given as a "Summons to penitential prayer for the removal of the judgment" [Keil], "The Day of the Lord: The Impending Disaster" [Dillard], "Call to return before the day of Yahweh" [Wolff], and "An army of locusts" [NIV]. This discourse unit comprises Part 1, Oracle 2, in Wendland's analysis.

Comments on this discourse unit: This discourse unit is the second part of the prophet's announcement of coming judgment and of his call to repentance [Keil]. Much of Joel's language depicting the coming judgment and YHWH's might occurs elsewhere in the OT, but 2:1–13 seems to be especially drawn from Isa. 13:1–13 (compare 2:2, 5 with Isa. 13:4, and 2:2 with Isa. 13:4). This discourse unit is divided into a number of subsections: 2:1–2 constitutes "A Cry of Alarm, Warning of Attack"; 2:3–11 constitutes "The Divine Army as Locusts;" 2:12–14 constitutes an "Offer of Repentance;" and 2:15–17 constitutes a "Summons to Fasting and Prayer at the Temple" [Dillard]. Early historical critics wanted to excise from the putative original Joel the passages that concern the day of YHWH, considering that such passages were added later by another hand. Such passages include 2:1b–2a: *for (the-)day(-of) YHWH is-coming, for (it is) near. (A-)day(-of) darkness and-gloom, (a-)day(-of) cloud-masses and-gloom.* However, one notes that if 2:1b–2a were not present, the reader would have to wait until 2:11 to discover that the enemy approaching Jerusalem is, in fact, the army of YHWH. Moreover, this discourse unit is full of motifs characteristic of the day of YHWH theme in several other prophets. There is, for example, the military motif, which, on the basis of Isa. 13:2, Ezek. 30:3, and Zeph. 1:16, leads one to conclude that Joel is drawing heavily from a well-established prophetic tradition. Another motif is the darkness on the day of YHWH, as in Deut. 4, 5:22–2, Amos 5:18–203, and Zeph. 1:15, part of which is quoted in Joel 2:2. There is thus no need to remove from a putative original Joel the day of YHWH passages [Wolff, also Crenshaw, Keil]. Generally, the language in this discourse unit is more intense than in Joel 1, as befits the thematic heightening: From the locust plague of Joel 1, admittedly extremely severe, the reader is transported to the coming day of YHWH, which infinitely outweighs in magnitude the theme of Joel 1. Thus, for example, the picture of the buzzing of locusts in Joel 1 is replaced by the sound of chariots rumbling over the mountains in 2:5. Finally, Joel's heavy drawing upon earlier prophetic themes and language drives home the insistent message that the day of YHWH, foretold for so long, will soon come [Wolff].

QUESTION—What literary forms are exhibited in this discourse unit?

1. In 2:4–7 there is a series of similes in which comparisons are brought to the characteristics of an invading enemy. Already in Isa. 5:28–30 there is such a series; a similar series is found in Hab. 1:8–9 and in Jer. 4:13.

---

[16] The Masoretes marked this section (with פ) as ending at the close of 2:14.

However, Joel's series is the longest and reveals that he was influenced by Ezekiel in his use of the simile marker כְּמַרְאֵה *kəmarʾēh* 'like the appearance of'. Thus we find that Joel is working toward an apocalyptic style [Wolff].

2. In 2:12–14 there is a summons to repentance, which is different from a summons to communal lamentation in that the latter focuses on a calamity, while the former focuses upon YHWH's will and threat of punishment of disobedience [Wolff].
3. In 2:15–17 there is a series of commands accompanying the summons to repentance; these correspond to the series of commands in 1:14, which conclude a summons to lamentation [Wolff].

DISCOURSE UNIT: 2:1–11 [Cohen, Crenshaw]. Cohen gives the topic as "The invasion of the locusts"; Crenshaw, as "YHWH's efficient army." This discourse unit comprises Stanza C in Wendland's analysis.

Comments on this discourse unit: That these eleven verses constitute a distinct discourse unit is evident by (1) the thematic unity; (2) the transition expression וְגַם־עַתָּה *wəgam ʿattâ* 'but even now' in 2:12, which introduces the topic of repentance; and (3) the introduction of a new theme, that of Zion in 2:1, and the heavy use of לְפָנָיו *ləpānâw* 'before it' and its variant מִפָּנָיו *mippānâw* [Crenshaw].

QUESTION—What is the relationship between the locust plague described in Joel 1 and the disaster described in this discourse unit?

1. They are the same plague or successive plagues [Bewer, Simkins]. This view interprets Joel 1–2 concretely, regarding the plague or plagues as historical, for 2:25 speaks of the years the locusts have eaten. Against this view, it is argued that the same locust attack cannot be depicted in both Joel 1 and 2:1–11 because the verbs in the former are mainly in the perfect tense (depicting an accomplished event), and in the latter, mainly in the imperfect (depicting an event in the course of occurring, or an event yet to occur). Moreoever, the account in 2:1–11, unlike the one in Joel 1, is qualified (in 2:12ff.) as being perhaps contingent upon lack of repentance in the people. In addition, the account in Joel 1, although it describes a very severe locust attack, does not match the uniqueness claimed for the invasion in Joel 2 [Crenshaw].
2. The locust plague of Joel 1 is a metaphor for a foreign invasion, while that of 2:1–11 also represents the coming of an enemy, in this case the Assyrians or Babylonians [Stuart]. The invaders, coming generally from the north (2:20), rule in Jerusalem (2:17), and the Gentile nations are therefore judged by God (4:4–14, 19 (3:4–14, 19)). Inspiration is drawn from Exodus 10, in which a plague of locusts defeated powerful Egypt.
3. The locust plague of Joel 1 is historical. It was meant as a warning against the foreign military invasion depicted in 2:1–11 as another locust plague, or perhaps it was meant as a warning to Israel against all of her enemies. This view occurs in the Targum. Garrett has a similar view,

offering at the same time a number of reasons, in addition those offered by Wolff (whose view is stated in 4 below), for understanding Joel 2 as describing an armed invasion:

a. The plea in 2:17 that YHWH would rescue Judah from disgrace among the nations fits a time of threatened foreign invasion much more than does a threatened locust plague.
b. If 2:8 is understood as depicting the Judeans' attempt to defend themselves with arms, then only a foreign invasion can be implied; 2:1–11 shows the invaders aiming at capturing the city, which as a military goal could not be the intention of locusts.
c. If one accepts the MT in 2:17, then the political goal of the invaders must be to rule over Judah, also something impossible for locusts.
d. The arrogance charged to the invaders in 2:20 would be inconceivable if imputed to locusts.
e. The term "northerner" (2:20), if applied to locusts, would conflict with its identification with the Assyrians (Isa. 14:31; Zeph. 2:13) and the Babylonians (Jer. 6:1, 22).

4. The locust plague of Joel 1 is historical and was meant as a prophetic precursor to the event depicted figuratively as another locust plague in 2:1–11: the coming of YHWH with his army to overcome evil and usher in his rule. In Joel 2 are many expressions featured in descriptions of theophanies elsewhere in the OT.[17] The descriptive power of the Joel 2 passage is drawn, not from nature, but from apocalyptic language [Wolff]. It recapitulates the locust plague of Joel 1 (without ever overtly mentioning locusts) [Wolff], but this time the meaning of the plague is far greater than a simple agricultural disaster. This presumed greater meaning matches the spiritual and eschatological thrust of Joel 4 (3), which promises deliverance from the threats represented figuratively in 2:1–11 [Allen, Dillard]. (Keil also appears to have this same essential viewpoint).

QUESTION—How is the admitted ambiguity of the relationship between Joel 1 and 2:1–11 to be evaluated?

On the one hand, Joel's original hearers may have felt no ambiguity; our uncertainty may stem from our ignorance of their current events. On the other hand, it is possible that the original reference to a historical plague of locusts, transmuted into a text fit for liturgical use in a variety of contexts, acquired an ambiguity which necessarily sprang from the new liturgical function of the book. Another aspect of the book's ambiguity lies in the fact that Joel does not specify the sins the people are being asked to repent of. This ambiguity may be another reflection of the liturgical use to which this book seems to have been put [Dillard].

---

[17] Wolff thinks that this invasion is identical to what was threatened in Jer. 1:14–15, 4:6, 6:1, 22, and Ezek. 38:6, 15, and 39:2.

2:1

Blow[a] **(a-)ram's-horn**[b] **on**[c]**-Zion,**[d] **and-sound-an-alarm**[e] **on**[f]**-(the-)mountain(-of)**[g] **my-holiness.**[h]

Let- all (the-)inhabitants(-of)[i] **the-land**[j] **-tremble**[k] **/ All (the-)inhabitants (-of)**[i] **the-land**[j] **will-tremble,**[k] **for**[l] **(the-)day(-of)**[m] **YHWH is-coming,**[n] **for**[o] **(it is) near.**[p]

LEXICON—a. **<u>blow</u> (a-)ram's-horn** masc. pl. Qal imper. of תקע *tq*ᶜ [BDB p. 1075], [Hol p. 394], [TWOT 2541]: 'to blow' (a wind instrument) [BDB, Hol; Keil, Allen, Dillard, Wolff; KJV, NASB, NIV, NRSV, REB, TEV]. Crenshaw translates the phrase תִּקְעוּ שׁוֹפָר *tiqᶜû šôp̄ār* 'blow a trumpet' as "sound the alarm."

b. **blow <u>(a-)ram's-horn</u>** שׁוֹפָר *šôp̄ār* [BDB p. 1051], [Hol p. 364], [TWOT 2449c]: 'ram's horn' [Hol], 'trumpet' [Keil, Dillard; KJV, NASB, NIV, NRSV, REB, TEV], 'horn' (for blowing) [BDB; Allen, Wolff]. The *šôp̄ār* was a ram's horn adapted as a wind instrument, quite different from a metal trumpet [Wolff].

c. **<u>on</u>-Zion** -בְּ *bə-* [BDB p. 88], [Hol p. 32], [TWOT 193]: 'on' [Wolff ; TEV], 'in' [Crenshaw, Allen, Dillard; KJV, NASB, NIV, NRSV, REB], 'upon' [Keil].

d. **on-<u>Zion</u>** צִיּוֹן *ṣiyyôn* [BDB p. 851], [Hol p. 306], [TWOT 1910]: 'Zion' [BDB; Crenshaw, Keil, Allen, Dillard, Wolff; KJV, NASB, NIV, NRSV, REB, TEV]. This is the first direct reference to the city of Jerusalem, although Jerusalem can be inferred as early as 1:8–9 [Crenshaw].

e. **and-<u>sound-an-alarm</u>** masc. pl. Hiphil imper. of רוע *rû*ᶜ [BDB p. 929], [Hol p. 336], [TWOT 2135]: 'to sound the/an alarm' [Allen, Dillard, Wolff; NASB, NIV, NRSV, REB, TEV], 'to shout in alarm' [Hol], 'to shout an alarm' [KJV], 'to raise a shout' [BDB], 'to cause to sound (a trumpet)' [Keil], 'to shout the warning' [Crenshaw]. *Rû*ᶜ can mean to shout either in triumph or in distress [BDB].

f. **<u>on</u>-(the-)mountain(-of) my-holiness** -בְּ *bə-* [BDB p. 88], [Hol p. 32], [TWOT 193]: 'on/upon' [Crenshaw, Keil, Dillard, Wolff; NASB, NIV, NRSV, REB], 'in' [Allen; KJV].

g. **on-(the-)<u>mountain(-of)</u> my-holiness** הַר *har* [BDB p. 249], [Hol p. 83], [TWOT 517a]: 'mountain' [BDB, Hol; Crenshaw, Keil, Allen, Dillard, Wolff; KJV, NASB, NRSV, REB], 'hill' [BDB; NIV, TEV].

h. **on-(the-)mountain(-of) my-<u>holiness</u>** constr. of קֹדֶשׁ *qōḏeš* [BDB p. 871], [Hol p. 314], [TWOT 1990a]: 'holiness' [BDB, Hol]. The noun *qōḏeš* here denotes God's quality of holiness [Hol]. It is translated by some as an adjective: "holy" [Keil, Dillard, Wolff; KJV, NASB, NIV, NRSV, REB], "sacred" [Crenshaw, Allen; TEV].

i. **(the-)<u>inhabitants(-of)</u> the-land** constr. pl. masc. part. of ישׁב *yšḇ* [BDB p. 442], [Hol p. 146], [TWOT 922]: 'to inhabit' [Keil, Wolff; KJV, NASB, NRSV, REB], 'to dwell' [BDB, Hol], 'to live' [Hol; Dillard; NIV]. The phrase כֹּל יֹשְׁבֵי הָאָרֶץ *kol yōšəḇê hāʾāreṣ* 'all who inhabit the land' is translated as "every citizen" [Crenshaw], "people of Judah" [TEV], and "the country's population" [Allen]. Most translate it in local terms, denoting all Israelites. Wolff is more universal. Crenshaw understands אֶרֶץ *ʾereṣ* (see *j* below) as "the world," but evidently, judging by his translation "every citizen," regards it as a figure of speech signifying the land of Israel.

j. **(the-)inhabitants(-of) the-land** אֶרֶץ *ʾereṣ* [BDB p. 76], [Hol p. 28], [TWOT 167]: 'land' [BDB, Hol; Keil, Dillard; KJV, NASB, NIV, NRSV, REB], 'territory' [BDB], 'Judah' [TEV], 'world' [Wolff], 'country' [Allen].

k. **let- all (the-)inhabitants(-of) the-land –tremble** 3rd masc. pl. Qal jussive of רגז *rḡz* [BDB p. 919], [Hol p. 332], [TWOT 2112]: 'to tremble' [Hol; Crenshaw, Keil, Dillard, Wolff; KJV, NASB, NIV, NRSV, REB, TEV], 'to be agitated' [BDB], 'to quake' [BDB; Allen]. Here the word has the force of being shaken from one's spiritual deadness or apathy [Keil]. Keil regards it as third person masculine plural Qal imperfect, translating it as a future: 'all will tremble' (also Wolff). All translate יִרְגְּזוּ *yirgəzû* as an exhortation, 'let all tremble', except Crenshaw.

l. **for (the-)day(-of) YHWH is-coming** כִּי *kî* particle [BDB p. 471], [Hol p. 155], [TWOT 976]: 'for' [Keil, Dillard, Wolff; KJV, NASB, NIV, NRSV, REB], 'because' [Crenshaw, Allen], not explicit [TEV].

m. **(the-)day(-of) YHWH** constr. of יוֹם *yôm* [BDB p. 398], [Hol p. 130], [TWOT 852]: 'day' [BDB, Hol; Crenshaw, Keil, Allen, Dillard, Wolff; KJV, NASB, NIV, NRSV, REB, TEV].

n. **for (the-)day(-of) YHWH is-coming** 3rd masc. sing. Qal perf. [Keil] or 3rd masc. sing. Qal part. of בוא *bôʾ* [BDB p. 97], [Hol p. 34], [TWOT 212]: 'to come' [BDB, Hol; Crenshaw, Keil, Allen, Dillard, Wolff; KJV, NASB, NIV, NRSV, REB, TEV]. According to Keil, juxtaposition of the Qal perfect with the following statement that the day of YHWH is near implies that the day of YHWH is happening continuously throughout history, until its final fulfillment at the end of the ages. Others translate it with a more or less imminent future (e.g., 'is coming'). On the other hand, Wolff takes the adjective *qārôḇ* 'near' in the following clause as justifying the interpretation of *bāʾ* as a Qal participle, 'coming', as in Ezek. 7:7.

o. **for (it is) near** כִּי *kî* particle [BDB p. 471], [Hol p. 155], [TWOT 976]: 'for' [Keil; KJV], 'indeed' [Crenshaw, Dillard, Wolff], 'surely' [NASB], not explicit [Allen; NIV, NRSV, REB, TEV].

p. **for (it is) near** קָרוֹב *qārôḇ* [BDB p. 898], [Hol p. 325], [TWOT 2065d]: 'near (temporal)' [BDB, Hol; Crenshaw, Keil, Dillard, Wolff; NASB, NRSV], 'close at hand' [NIV], 'imminent' [Hol], 'nigh at hand' [KJV], 'at hand' [REB]. TEV translates this adjective by an adverb, "soon"; Allen, by a verb phrase, "will soon be here." At first glance, it would seem that with *qārôḇ* here בָּא *bāʾ* 'has come' could not be understood as a perfect verb form [Crenshaw], but see Keil's explanation in *n* above. Both Joel and Ezekiel associate the ideas of nearness and coming (Ezek. 7:7) [Crenshaw].

QUESTION—Who is the speaker in this verse?

The speaker must be YHWH; this is inferred from the word קָדְשִׁי *qoḏšî* 'my holiness'. YHWH is actually warning his own people of the impending attack. It is possible that YHWH's words extend through 2:10 [Crenshaw].

QUESTION—What is the meaning of וְהָרִיעוּ *wəhārîᶜû*, and how does this verb stand in relation to the earlier expression תִּקְעוּ שׁוֹפָר *tiqᶜû šôpār* 'blow a ram's horn'?

1. *Wəhārîᶜû* is a form of the verb רוע *rûaᶜ* 'to shout (either in triumph or in distress)' [BDB]. Thus *wəhārîᶜû* stands in complementary parallelism to the previous expression in this verse.
2. *Wəhārîᶜû* probably denotes here the manner of sounding the ram's horn, not in a festive way as normal, but rather to warn of approaching danger. Thus *wəhārîᶜû* stands in synonymous parallelism with the first verb in this verse. Moreover, this alarm is not sounded in order that the people might assemble for fasting or for repentance, but instead that the people might flee for their lives [Wolff].

QUESTION—To whom are the commands תִּקְעוּ *tiqᶜû* 'blow' and וְהָרִיעוּ *wəhārîᶜû* 'raise a shout' addressed?

1. Literally, they seem to be addressed to the city's sentinels, who stand high in the guard towers on the wall watching for any approaching enemy. In this case, the prophet Joel is functioning as a prophetic sentinel [Crenshaw].
2. They are addressed to the priests, as is evident from a comparison of this verse to 2:15–16 [Keil].

QUESTION—What was the use of the שׁוֹפָר *šôpār* 'ram's horn' in ancient Israel?

The *šôpār* was blown to give a summons for a variety of military purposes: to give the army a command to attack, to warn of an enemy's approach, and to muster an army. It was also blown in worship, both at the crowning of monarchs and during worship processions. In 2:1 the warning is of imminent judgment by YHWH. In 2:15 the *šôpār* is to be heard as a summons to national repentance before YHWH [Dillard], or to a collective lamentation before him. The sounding of horns is associated with the day of YHWH in Zeph. 1:14–16, with YHWH's judging the world in Ps. 98:6–9, and with theophanies in general in the spirit of the Mount Sinai theophany. Both Hosea and Jeremiah feature the sounding of the ram's horn to announce the military-like approach of YHWH in judgment and punishment. Joel sounds this same theme [Wolff].

QUESTION—What is meant by בְּצִיּוֹן *bəṣîyôn* 'at Zion' and הַר קָדְשִׁי *har qoḏšî* 'the mountain of my holiness'?

The reference to Zion signifies the summit of Mount Moriah, the Temple mount in Jerusalem, where the throne of YHWH was, as in Ps. 2:6 [Keil]; by extension the expression came to mean Jerusalem. There was a very long tradition of deities dwelling on high mountaintops in the ancient world [Crenshaw, Wolff]. Presumably *qoḏšî* 'my holiness' in this phrase concerns not so much YHWH's moral perfection as his exclusive "otherness"—he is incomparable to any human quality: In other words, his ownership of the mountain in question is exclusive .

QUESTION—What were the Israelites' feelings regarding Zion (i.e., Jerusalem)?

Zion was felt to be unconquerable because YHWH watched over it unceasingly. The unsuccessful Assyrian attempt against the city reinforced this belief. The Babylonian conquest of Jerusalem was attributed to YHWH, for the Babylonians were his instrument for chastising Israel. But if now YHWH himself comes against the city, there is no help to be found [Crenshaw].

QUESTION—What is the significance of the trumpet blast and the shout?

They are signals of alarm, as in time of war at an enemy's approach; in this case, however, they are a prophetic alarm calling for repentance, similar to that sounded by other men of God at approaching judgment [Keil, Dillard]. Another way of expressing this view is to think of the trumpet blast as a warning to the people to flee from the enemy; here, the enemy turns out to be YHWH himself and the sole way to flee from him is to run toward him, that is, to repent [Wolff].

2:2

(A-)day(-of)[a] darkness[b] and-gloom,[c] **(a-)day(-of) cloud-masses[d] and-gloom;[e]**

(MT) like[f]-dawn[g-] being-spread[h] over[i]-the-mountains,[j]

(ET) like[f] blackness[g-2] being-spread[h] over[i]-the-mountains,[j]

(is/comes[k])(a-)people[l] numerous[m] and-vast,[n]

such-as[o] has- not[p] -happened[q] **from-the-far-past,[r]**

and-after[s]-it not continuing[t] **to (the-)years(-of)[u] generations[v] and-generations.**

INTERTEXTUAL REFERENCE—Bicolon α–β evokes a long tradition of prophetic language describing the self-revelation of YHWH, as in Deut. 4, 5:22–23; Zeph. 1:15; and Amos 5:18–20 [Crenshaw, Keil, Dillard, Wendland, Wolff]. Bicolon γ–δ evokes the Exod. 10:14–15 description of Egypt under the locust plague sent by YHWH. Once more Joel redirects an earlier description of judgment of YHWH's enemies against YHWH's own covenant people [Wendland, Wolff].

SYNTAX—Wolff views colon α as belonging with the last part of 2:1—'for near is the time of darkness and gloom, a day of cloud masses and gloom.'

TEXT—The MT text is not followed here by all versions:

Reading	Remarks
MT: שַׁחַר *šaḥar* 'dawn'	**Followed by:** Cohen, Crenshaw, Keil, Wolff. **Argument against:** The comparison of cloud masses and gloom to the spread of dawn over the mountains is difficult; one would instead expect a swarm of locusts, which can block out sunlight, to spread "like darkness."
Emendation: שָׁחֹר *šāḥōr* 'blackness'	**Followed by:** NRSV, REB, TEV. **Achieved by:** Alteration of the Hebrew vowel points.

LEXICON—a. **(a-)day(-of) darkness and-gloom** constr. of יוֹם *yôm* [BDB p. 398], [Hol p. 130], [TWOT 852]: 'day' [BDB, Hol; Keil, Allen, Dillard, Wolff; KJV, NASB, NIV, NRSV, REB, TEV], 'time' [Crenshaw].

b. **(a-)day(-of) darkness and-gloom** חֹשֶׁךְ *ḥōšek* [BDB p. 365], [Hol p. 119], [TWOT 769a]: 'darkness' [BDB, Hol; Crenshaw, Keil, Dillard; KJV, NASB, NIV, NRSV, REB]. Allen, Wolff, and TEV translate this noun by an adjective: "dark."

c. **(a-)day(-of) darkness and-gloom** אֲפֵלָה *ʾăpēlâ* [BDB p. 66], [Hol p. 25], [TWOT 145c]: 'gloom' [Dillard; NASB, NIV, NRSV, REB], 'gloominess' [BDB; KJV], 'calamity' [BDB], 'obscurity' [Keil], 'murkiness' [Crenshaw], 'darkness' [BDB, Hol]. Allen, Wolff, and TEV translate this noun by an adjective: "gloomy."

d. **(a-)day(-of) cloud-masses and-gloom** עָנָן *ʿānān* [BDB p. 777], [Hol p. 278], [TWOT 1655a]: 'cloud-mass' [BDB], 'mass of clouds' [Hol], 'cloud' [BDB; Keil, Crenshaw, Dillard, Wolff; KJV, NASB, NIV, NRSV, REB]. Allen translates this noun by an adjective: "cloudy" (also TEV). Both this word and the following one, עֲרָפֶל *ʿărāpel*, are collective nouns, denoting great masses of clouds that obscure YHWH from view [Crenshaw].

e. **(a-)day(-of) cloud-masses and-gloom** עֲרָפֶל *ʿărāpel* [BDB p. 791], [Hol p. 284], [TWOT 1701b]: 'gloom' [Hol], 'darkness' [Hol], 'thick darkness' [KJV, NASB, NRSV], 'heavy cloud' [BDB], 'blackness' [NIV], 'cloudy night' [Keil], 'obscurity' [Dillard], 'haze' [Crenshaw], 'dense fog' [REB]. Some translate this noun by an adjective: Allen has "lowering"; Wolff, "dense"; TEV, "black."

f. **like dawn/blackness being-spread over-the-mountains** -כְּ *kə-* [BDB p. 453], [Hol p. 149], [TWOT 937]: 'like' [Hol; Crenshaw, Keil, Allen, Dillard, Wolff; NIV, NRSV, REB, TEV], 'as' [KJV, NASB].

g-1. **like dawn being-spread over-the-mountains** שַׁחַר *šaḥar* [BDB p. 1007], [Hol p. 366], [TWOT 2369a]: 'light before dawn' [Hol], 'light of dawn' [Wolff], 'dawn' [BDB; Crenshaw, Dillard; NASB, NIV], 'morning dawn' [Keil], 'morning' [KJV].

g-2. **like <u>blackness</u> being-spread over-the-mountains** שָׁחֹר *šāḥōr* [BDB p. 1007], [Hol p. 366], [TWOT 2368b]: 'blackness' [Allen; NRSV, REB], 'black' [BDB, Hol]; 'darkness' [TEV].

h. **<u>being-spread</u> over-the-mountains** masc. sing. Qal pass. part. of פרשׂ *prś* [BDB p. 831], [Hol p. 299], [TWOT 1832]: 'to spread' [Dillard; KJV, NIV, TEV], 'to spread out' [BDB; Hol], 'to be spread' [Keil, Wolff; NASB, NRSV, REB], 'to engulf' [Crenshaw], 'to cover' [Allen]. The subject of פָּרֻשׂ *pāruś* 'spreading' could, syntactically, be either שַׁחַר *šaḥar* 'dawn' or עָם *ᶜām* 'people', but the athnach under הֶהָרִים *hehārîm* 'the mountains' shows that the Masoretes took 'dawn' as the subject [Crenshaw]. Nevertheless, Bewer understood the subject of *pāruś* 'spreading' to be *ᶜām* 'people'. He regarded the locusts as covering the mountains on the ground, rather than in the air, and so their wings would have been unable to reflect the sun's rays (see the second question below).

i. **being-spread <u>over</u>-the-mountains** עַל *ᶜal* [BDB p. 757], [Hol, p. 273], [TWOT 1624p): 'over' [Hol; Keil, Dillard; NASB, REB, TEV], 'across' [Wolff; NIV], 'upon' [KJV, NRSV].

j. **being-spread over-the-<u>mountains</u>** pl. of הַר *har* [BDB p.), [Hol p. 83], [TWOT 517a]: 'mountain' [BDB, Hol; Crenshaw, Keil, Allen, Dillard, Wolff; KJV, NASB, NIV, NRSV, REB, TEV].

k. **<u>(is/comes)</u> (a-)people numerous and-vast** Most commentators and versions supply a verb here: 'to come' [Dillard; NIV, NRSV], 'to be' [NASB], 'to appear' [Allen, REB], 'to advance' [TEV], 'to approach' [Wolff]. Neither Keil nor KJV, however, supplies a verb.

l. **(is/comes) (a-)<u>people</u> numerous and-vast** עָם *ᶜām* [BDB p. 766], [Hol, p. 275], [TWOT 1640a]: 'a people' [BDB, Hol; Crenshaw, Keil, Wolff; KJV, NASB], 'army' [Dillard; NIV, NRSV, TEV], 'host' [REB], 'horde' [Allen].

m. **<u>numerous</u> and-vast** רַב *rab̲* [BDB p. 912], [Hol p. 330], [TWOT 2099a]: 'numerous' [Hol; Crenshaw, Wolff], 'large' [NIV], 'many' [BDB], 'great' [BDB; Keil, Dillard; KJV, NASB, NRSV], 'vast' [Allen; REB]. TEV translates the phrase רַב וְעָצוּם *rab̲ wəᶜāṣûm* 'numerous and vast' as "great."

n. **numerous and-<u>vast</u>** עָצוּם *ᶜāṣûm* [BDB p. 783], [Hol p. 280], [TWOT 1673d]: 'vast' [Hol], 'mighty' [BDB, Hol; Crenshaw, Wolff; NASB, NIV], 'strong' [Keil; KJV], 'powerful' [Dillard; NRSV], 'countless' [REB], 'massive' [Allen]. This word connotes strength in numbers [BDB, Hol].

o. **<u>such-as</u> has- not -happened from-the-far-past** כְּמוֹ *kəmô* [BDB p. 455], [Hol p. 159], [BDB 938]: 'such as' [NIV], 'like' [BDB; Crenshaw, Keil, Allen, Wolff; KJV, NASB, NRSV, REB, TEV), 'just like' [Hol], 'the likes' [Dillard].

p. **such-as has- <u>not</u> -happened from-the-far-past** לֹא *lō*ʾ [BDB p. 518], [Hol p. 170], [TWOT 1064]: 'not' [Hol; Keil; KJV], 'never' [Crenshaw, Allen, Dillard, Wolff; NASB, NIV, NRSV, REB, TEV].

q. **such-as <u>has</u>- not -<u>happened</u> from-the-far-past** 3rd masc. sing. Niphal perf. of היה *hyh* [BDB p. 224], [Hol p. 78], [TWOT 491]: 'to happen' [Hol], 'to occur' [Hol], 'to be' [Keil, Dillard, Wolff; KJV, NASB, NIV, NRSV, TEV], 'to appear' [Crenshaw], 'to be known' [REB].

r. **such-as has- not -happened from-the-<u>far-past</u>** עוֹלָם *ʿôlām* [BDB p. 761], [Hol p. 267], [TWOT 1631a]: 'long time ago' [Hol], 'the dim past' [Hol], 'of old' [Dillard, Wolff; NIV, NRSV], 'from all eternity' [Keil], 'ever' [KJV], 'before' [Allen], not explicit [Crenshaw; NASB, TEV]. This word denotes a point in time as far in the past as imaginable [Wolff].

s. **and-<u>after</u>-it not continuing** constr. of אַחַר *ʾaḥar* [BDB p. 29], [Hol p. 10], [TWOT 68b]: 'after' [BDB, Hol; Keil; KJV, NASB, NRSV], 'ever' [Dillard; NIV], 'again' [Crenshaw, Allen; TEV], 'afterwards' [Wolff]. Properly a noun, *ʾaḥar* functions here as an adverb.

t. **and-after-it not <u>continuing</u>** 3rd masc. sing. Qal part. of יסף *ysp̄* [BDB p. 414], [Hol p. 137], [TWOT 876]: 'to continue' [Hol], 'to be' [Keil, Dillard; KJV, NASB, NIV, NRSV, REB], 'to come again' [Wolff], not explicit [Allen].

u. **continuing to (the-)<u>years(-of)</u> generations and-generations** pl. constr. of שָׁנָה *šānâ* [BDB p. 1040], [Hol p. 378], [TWOT 2419a]: 'year' [Hol; Keil, Allen, Dillard; NASB].

v. **(the-)years(-of) <u>generations</u> and-<u>generations</u>** דּוֹר *dôr* [BDB p. 189], [Hol p. 69], [TWOT 418b]: 'generation' [BDB, Hol; Keil, Dillard, Wolff; NASB]. The singular is here understood as a generic reference, which allows for a plural translation. For the phrase עַד־שְׁנֵי דּוֹר וָדוֹר *ʿad̲ šənê dôr wād̲ôr* NIV and NRSV have "in ages to come"; REB has "in all the ages to come"; KJV and NASB have "to the years of many generations"; Crenshaw, "in the remote future"; Wolff , "to most distant generations"; Allen, "for years and years to come." In TEV it is not translated explicitly. According to Wolff, this phrase denotes all time to come.

QUESTION—What is the function of the line יוֹם חֹשֶׁךְ וַאֲפֵלָה יוֹם עָנָן וַעֲרָפֶל *yôm ḥōšek̲ waʾăpēlâ yôm ʿānān waʿărāpel (a-)day(-of) darkness and-gloom, (a-)day(-of) cloud-masses and-gloom*?

It is a metaphor. The darkness is that brought by the swarms of locusts that blot out the sunlight [Keil]. It may also be a metaphor for grief and sadness [Cohen]. At the same time, it is traditional OT theophanic language, describing God's revelation of himself at Mount Sinai (Deut. 4, 5:22–23). It is very reminiscent of Zeph. 1:15 [Crenshaw, Keil, Dillard, Wolff], in which appears exactly the first line of 2:2. Moreover, the description of the day of YHWH as dark and menacing is reminiscent of Amos 5:18–0

[Crenshaw]. Worthy of note also is the description of the locust plague in Exod. 10:22 as חֹשֶׁךְ־אֲפֵלָה *ḥōšek̲-ăpēlâ* 'darkness of gloom'. YHWH, who often revealed himself in awe-inspiring ways to rescue Israel, now is about to reveal himself in the same terms, but this time in order to wage war against Israel. Only he who has saved Israel so many times in the past is able to overthrow her [Wolff].

QUESTION—What is the point of the simile כְּשַׁחַר פָּרֻשׂ עַל־הֶהָרִים *kəšaḥar pāruś ʿal-hehārîm* 'like the dawn being spread over the mountains'?

1. The simile means to say that the locust invasion, seen coming from far off, casts a faint glow as the sunlight reflects off the locust wings, and that this glow spreads as the invasion approaches. The locusts' arrival, of course, turns the land dark since they blot out the sunlight [Crenshaw, Keil].[18]
2. The simile probably means to say that the locust invasion appears as suddenly as the sun appears over the mountains [Wolff].

QUESTION—To what does the expression עַם רַב וְעָצוּם *ʿam rab̲ wəʿāṣûm* 'a vast and mighty people' refer?

1. It refers to the vast swarm of locusts [Cohen, Keil]. This expression, which resembles גוֹי ... עָצוּם וְאֵין מִסְפָּר *gôy ... ʿāṣûm wəʾên mispār* 'a people mighty and without number' in 1:6, is the first hint that the invasion described in this part of Joel 2 is actually a locust attack, as in Joel 1 [Crenshaw].
2. It refers to the army of YHWH. Although this expression is similar to the one in 1:6, which admittedly refers to a vast locust invasion, it resembles even more an expression, from which it certainly receives inspiration, in Isa. 13:4, דְּמוּת עַם־רָב (*dəmût̲ ʿam rāb̲* 'like a great people'), which clearly stands in the context of the day of YHWH, in which he will come to judge all nations [Wolff].

QUESTION—What is the point of וְאַחֲרָיו לֹא יוֹסֵף עַד־שְׁנֵי דּוֹר וָדוֹר *wəʾaḥărāyw lōʾ yôsēp̄ ʿad̲-šənê dôd̲ wād̲ôd̲* 'and after it not continuing to the years of generation to generation'?

It is that this locust invasion is unique in Israel's history [Dillard].

QUESTION—What rhetorical device does Joel employ in this strophe?

He employs here the technique of thematic reversal. Unlike in Isa. 13:1–13, as well as in other passages, the day of YHWH results in the overthrow of Babylon, Joel applies this concept against Jerusalem herself [Wendland]. This thematic reversal is also signaled by the locust invasion, which is the inverse of the plague YHWH had sent against Egypt before

---

[18] Keil cites *Journey through Abyssinia* by Francis Alvarez, a Portuguese monk: "The day before the arrival of the locusts we could infer that they were coming, from a yellow reflection in the sky, proceeding from their yellow wings. As soon as this light appeared, no one had the slightest doubt that an enormous swarm of locusts was approaching."

freeing Israel from slavery: now he has sent it against Israel herself [Dillard].

2:3

Before[a]-it fire[b] burns,[c] and-after[d]-it flames[e] scorch.[f]
Like[g]-(the-)Garden(-of)[h] Eden (is) the-land[i] before-it, and-after-it (a-)wilderness(-of)[j] desolation[k]
and- there-is[l] -absolutely[m] nothing/no one spared[n] from-it [o-1]/of-it.[o-2]

INTERTEXTUAL REFERENCE—Bicolon α–β is reminiscent of Ps. 97:3: "fire goes before him, and scorches his enemies all about." Joel here redirects the Psalm reference; instead of its being applied to YHWH's (and Israel's) enemies, Joel applies it to Israel herself.

LEXICON—a. before-it לִפְנֵי *lip̄nê* [BDB p. 815], [Hol p. 293], [TWOT 1782b]: 'before (spatial)' [BDB, Hol; Crenshaw, Keil, Dillard, Wolff; KJV, NASB, NIV, NRSV], 'ahead' [Allen]. REB translates the phrase לְפָנָיו *ləp̄ānāyw* 'before it' as "their vanguard." *Lip̄nê*, which functions as a compound preposition, is formally composed of the proclitic -לְ *lə*- and the construct of פָּנִים *pānîm* 'face'. TEV conflates the larger expression 'before it a fire has burned, and after it flames have scorched' (לְפָנָיו אָכְלָה אֵשׁ וְאַחֲרָיו תְּלַהֵט לֶהָבָה *ləp̄ānāyw ʾāḵəlâ ʾēš wəʾaḥărāyw təlahēṭ lehâḇâ*) and translates it with a simile: "like fire they eat up the plants." *Ləp̄ānāyw* 'before it' is prominent due to its sentence-initial position, as is *wəʾaḥărāyw* 'and after it', due to its clause-initial position.

b. **before-it fire burns** אֵשׁ *ʾēš* [BDB p. 77], [Hol p. 29], [TWOT 172]: 'fire' [BDB, Hol; Crenshaw, Keil, Dillard, Allen, Wolff; KJV, NASB, NIV, NRSV, REB].

c. **before-it fire burns** 3rd fem. sing. Qal perf. of אכל *ʾḵl* [BDB p. 37], [Hol p. 14], [TWOT 85]: 'to burn' [Keil, Dillard], 'to consume' [Crenshaw, Allen; NASB], 'to devour' [Hol; Wolff; KJV, NIV, NRSV, REB]. The commentators and versions use the English present tense here.[19]

---

[19] The verb אָכְלָה *ʾāḵəlâ* 'has consumed' presumably exhibits the so-called prophetic perfect tense here, a little-understood use of the perfect tense which projects an event into the future. Waltke, calling it an "accidental perfective," regards it as the use of the perfect tense to present a future event as vivid and completed. Gesenius (§106n) attributes the implied completed aspect of the prophetic perfect to the supreme confidence of the prophet in foretelling an imminent event (hence also the label "perfective of confidence"). He comments that this usage of the perfect tense frequently appears in close association with verbs in the imperfect tense. In Keil's view, the imminence of the events so marked often justifies a translation using the English present tense. In Joel, the prophetic perfect characterizes certain discrete portions of the text: 2:3–6 and 2:10–11 (within the section 2:1–11); 2:21–23 (within the section 2:18–27); and 4:15–16 (within the section 4:12–21).

d. **and-<u>after</u>-it flames scorch** constr. of אַחַר *ʾaḥar* [BDB p. 29], [Hol p. 10], [TWOT 68b]: 'after' [BDB, Hol], 'behind' [BDB; Crenshaw, Keil, Allen, Dillard, Wolff; KJV, NASB, NIV, NRSV]. The REB translates the phrase אַחֲרָיו *ʾaḥărâw* 'after it' as "their rearguard."

e. **<u>flames</u> scorch** לֶהָבָה *lehāḇâ* [BDB p. 529], [Hol p. 173], [TWOT 1077b]: 'flame' [BDB, Hol; Crenshaw, Keil, Allen, Dillard, Wolff; KJV, NASB, NIV, NRSV, REB]. The singular is here understood as a generic reference, which allows for a plural translation.

f. **flames <u>scorch</u>** 3rd fem. sing. Piel imperf. of להט *lhṭ* [BDB p. 529], [Hol p. 173], [TWOT 1081]: 'to scorch' [Hol], 'to blaze' [Dillard, Wolff; NIV], 'to set ablaze' [BDB], 'to flame' [Keil], 'to burn' [Allen; KJV, NASB, NRSV], 'to lick' [Crenshaw], not explicit [REB].

g. **<u>like-</u>(the-)Garden(-of) Eden (is) the-land before-it** -כְּ *kə-* [BDB p. 453], [Hol p. 149], [TWOT 937]: 'like' [BDB, Hol; Crenshaw, Allen, Dillard, Wolff; NASB, NIV, NRSV], 'as' [Keil; KJV]. The REB turns the simile introduced by *kə-* into a metaphor: "before them the land is a garden of Eden."

h. **like-(the-)<u>Garden(-of)</u> Eden (is) the-land before-it** constr. of גַּן *gan* [BDB p. 171], [Hol p. 63], [TWOT 367a]: 'garden' [BDB, Hol; Crenshaw, Keil, Allen, Dillard; KJV, NASB, NIV, NRSV, REB, TEV]. Wolff translates גַּן־עֵדֶן *gan-ʿēḏen* 'the Garden of Eden' as "like the Delightful Garden."

i. **like-(the-)Garden(-of) Eden (is) the-<u>land</u> before-it** אֶרֶץ *ʾereṣ* [BDB p. 76], [Hol p. 28], [TWOT 167]: 'land' [BDB, Hol; Crenshaw, Keil, Allen, Dillard, Wolff; KJV, NASB, NIV, NRSV, REB, TEV].

j. **(a-)<u>wilderness(-of)</u> desolation** constr. of מִדְבָּר *midbār* [BDB p. 184], [Hol p. 182], [TWOT 399l): 'wilderness' [BDB, Hol; Crenshaw, Keil, Dillard, Wolff; KJV, NASB, NRSV], 'desert' [TEV], 'waste' [REB], 'heath' [Allen]. The NIV translates this noun as an adjective in the phrase "desert waste."

k. **(a-)wilderness(-of) <u>desolation</u>** שְׁמָמָה *šəmāmâ* [BDB p. 1031], [Hol p. 376], [TWOT 2409b]: 'desolation' [Hol; Wolff], 'waste' [BDB; NIV], 'devastation' [BDB]. The noun *šəmāmâ* connotes terror or sinister feelings because of ruin or abandonment [Hol]. It is translated as an adjective by some: Crenshaw, Keil, Allen, KJV, NASB, NRSV, and REB have "desolate"; Dillard has "devastated"; TEV has "barren."

l. **and- <u>there-is</u> -absolutely nothing/no one spared from/of-it** 3rd fem. sing. Qal perf. of היה *hyh* [BDB p. 224], [Hol p. 78], [TWOT 491], 'to be' [BDB, Hol; Wolff], 'to remain' [Keil]. This verb appears to be an example of the so-called prophetic perfect.

m. **and- there-is -<u>absolutely</u> nothing/no one spared from/of-it** גַּם *gam* [BDB p. 168], [Hol p. 61], [TWOT 361a]: 'even' [Keil], 'yea' [KJV], 'in fact' [Allen], not explicit [Crenshaw; NASB, NIV, REB, TEV]. The particle *gam* serves to signal emphasis or intensity [Hol].

n. **and- there-is -absolutely nothing/no one spared from-it/of-it** פְּלֵיטָה *pəlêṭâ* [BDB p. 812], [Hol p. 292], [TWOT 1774d]: 'what is spared' [Hol], 'escaped remnant' [BDB], 'escape' [Allen, Dillard, Wolff]. Crenshaw, Keil, KJV, NASB, NIV, NRSV, and TEV translate this noun as a verb, "escapes"; REB has "survives." *Pəlêṭâ* is taken here to refer to any portion of the land which has not suffered YHWH's judgment [Bewer, Keil], but some [BDB, Hol; Crenshaw) understand it as referring to human survivors. Crenshaw sees *pəlêṭâ* as a military term for 'survivor', by analogy with Gen. 45:7 and 2 Sam. 15:14.

o-1. **and- there-is -absolutely nothing/no one spared from-it** לוֹ *lô* (consisting of the proclitic -לְ *lə-* and the 3rd masc. sing. pronoun): most versions and commentators take this pronoun to refer to the invading army, that is, 'nothing escapes from the army' [Allen, Dillard, Wolff; KJV, NASB, NIV, NRSV, REB, TEV].

o-2. **and- there-is -absolutely nothing/no one spared of-it** לוֹ *lô* (consisting of the proclitic -לְ *lə-* and the 3rd masc. sing. pronoun): Keil takes this pronoun to refer to the land itself; that is, none of the land escapes destruction. Allen remarks that such would indeed be the normal interpretation of *lô* after פְּלֵיטָה *pəlêṭâ* 'escape, escaped remnant'; but by analogy with the other occurrences of pronominal suffixes in this passage, Allen favors the majority view.

QUESTION—What is the referent of the 3rd masc. sing. pron. "it" in the expressions לְפָנָיו *ləpānāyw* 'before it' and וְאַחֲרָיו *wəʾaḥărāyw* 'and after it'?

It is probably the same as the referent to *wəʾaḥărāyw* in the preceding verse: the invading army [Dillard, Wolff]. YHWH's army comes with fire, YHWH himself being so viewed elsewhere [Wolff]. NRSV follows this interpretation.

QUESTION—What is the significance of the expression כְּגַן־עֵדֶן *kəgan ʿēḏen* 'like the Garden of Eden'?

God's treatment of Israel as his choice possession continues the paradise theme that has its origin in Genesis. But the theme is here reversed as Joel describes the garden's transformation from paradise to devastation [Dillard]. Of course, here the image of the Garden of Eden means to denote concretely the well-kept, fertile land of Israel. Joel draws upon the language of Ezek. 36:35, but note that the Garden of Eden motif in Joel describes what is *lost* due to the invading army of YHWH, whereas both in Ezekiel and in Isa. 51:3 the motif functions as the *hope* for the future of Jerusalem [Cohen, Wolff].

QUESTION—What is the implied agency in the following expression: לְפָנָיו אָכְלָה אֵשׁ וְאַחֲרָיו תְּלַהֵט לֶהָבָה *ləpānāyw ʾāḵəlâ ʾēš wəʾaḥărāyw təlahēṭ lehāḇâ* 'before it fire has consumed and after it flames scorch'?

1. The implied agency is the fire of YHWH's judgment. It is reminiscent of the fire—the lightning—attending the plague of hail in Egypt (Exod. 9:23–24) as well as of the theophanic fire that marked some of YHWH's

self-revelations, for example, to Moses at Sinai (Exod. 19:16–18; see also Ps. 97:3) [Keil, Wolff].

2. The implied agency is perhaps the poetic flames of YHWH's judgment, or it might be comparing the sound and destructive effect of the locust invasion to that of a raging fire [Dillard]. Cohen cites the Jewish commentator Metsudath David as regarding the fire as a metaphor for the locusts.
3. The implied agency is the drought implied in 1:19. This view must be held by those who consider that the calamity depicted in this passage is a locust invasion, whether the same as in Joel 1 or a second one. However, against this view it is argued, that if a drought occurs before the locusts, then there will be nothing left for them to destroy [Wolff].
4. The implied agency is the locust invasion of Joel 2, which preceded that of Joel 1 [Bewer].

QUESTION—What is the referent of the pronoun in the expression וְגַם־פְּלֵיטָה לֹא־הָיְתָה לּוֹ *wəgam pəlêṭâ lōʾ hāyəṯâ lô and there was absolutely nothing spared from-it/of-it*?

1. The referent is הָאָרֶץ *hāʾāreṣ* 'the land', *pəlêṭâ lô* being a partitive expression, "of it." The whole thought is that none of the land escapes the devastation. It is strongly suggested by 2 Sam. 15:4, Judg. 21:17, and Ezra 9:13 that the preposition -לְ *lə-* can introduce only the escaped person or thing [Keil]. In this view, the expression in question reads "and there was nothing spared of the land."
2. The referent is עַם רַב וְעָצוּם *ʿam raḇ wəṣûm (a)-people numerous and-vast* (2:2) [Allen, Bewer, Cohen, Stuart, Wolff; KJV, NASB, NIV, NRSV, REB, TEV]. In this view, the expression in question effectively reads "and nothing was spared from the enemy."

2:4

As[a]-(the-)appearance(-of)[b] horses[c] (is) their-appearance, and-as-horsemen[d] so[e] they-run.[f]

LEXICON—a. **as-(the-)appearance(-of) horses** -כְּ *kə-* [BDB p. 453], [Hol p. 149], [TWOT 937]: 'like' [Hol; Keil, Dillard, Allen, Wolff; NASB, REB], 'as' [KJV]. Crenshaw translates כְּמַרְאֵה סוּסִים *kəmarʾēh sûsîm* 'as the appearance of horses' as "resembles horses." Allen translates כְּמַרְאֵה סוּסִים מַרְאֵהוּ *kəmarʾēh sûsîm marʾēhû* as "they look like horses" [so also TEV].

b. **as-(the-)appearance(-of) horses** constr. of מַרְאֶה *marʾeh* [BDB p. 909], [Hol p. 213], [TWOT 2095i]: 'appearance' [BDB, Hol; Crenshaw, Keil, Dillard, Wolff; KJV, NASB, NIV, NRSV, REB], 'sight' [BDB].

c. **horses** pl. of סוּס *sûs* [BDB p. 692], [Hol p. 254], [TWOT 1477]: 'horse' [BDB, Hol; Crenshaw, Keil, Allen, Dillard, Wolff; KJV, NASB, NIV, NRSV, REB, TEV]. In this passage סוּסִים *sûsîm* 'horses' probably denotes a chariot corps [Wolff, following Kurt Galling, "Der

Ehrenname Elisas und die Entrückung Elias," *Zeitschrift für Theologie und Kirche* 53: 134–35 (1956)].

d. **and-as-<u>horsemen</u> so they-run** pl. of פָּרָשׁ *pārāš* [BDB p. 832], [Hol p. 299], [TWOT 1836a]: 'horseman' [BDB, Hol; KJV], 'rider' [Hol], 'cavalry' [Allen, Dillard; NIV, REB], 'riding horse' [Keil], 'war horse' [Wolff; NASB, NRSV, TEV], 'steed' [Crenshaw]. While *pārāš* is the term for war horse [Crenshaw], here פָּרָשִׁים *pārāšîm* very likely denotes horses pulling war chariots, following the probable sense of סוּסִים *sûsîm* [Wolff].

e. **and-as-horsemen <u>so</u> they-run** כֵּן *kēn* [BDB p. 485], [Hol p. 159], [TWOT 964b]: 'so' [BDB, Hol; Keil; KJV, NASB], 'thus' [BDB, Hol], 'like' [Crenshaw, Dillard, Wolff; NRSV, REB], 'just like' [Allen], not explicit [NIV].

f. **<u>they-run</u>** 3rd masc. pl. Qal imperf. of רוּץ *rûṣ* [BDB p. 930], [Hol p. 336], [TWOT 2137]: 'to run' [BDB, Hol; Keil, Dillard, Wolff; KJV, NASB, TEV], 'to gallop' [Crenshaw], 'to gallop along' [NIV], 'to charge' [Allen; NRSV, REB]. The verb ending ן- *-n* is archaic and is probably used to stress the force of the sentence [Wolff].

QUESTION—What is the point of similarity between locusts and horses?

1. It is the cumulative effect of an overwhelming horde, locusts being similar in this respect to the power of a cavalry charge. The Israelites associated horses mainly with armies; it was for his army that Solomon imported horses [Cohen, Crenshaw, Dillard, Wolff].
2. It lies in a certain resemblance of a locust's head to a horse's head and in the swiftness of their running [Keil]. The resemblance between locusts and the heads of horses has been recognized in various cultures (cf. the German *Heupferd* 'hayhead' and also Rev. 9:7) [Crenshaw, Wolff].

2:5

Like[a]-(the-)sound(-of)[b] chariots,[c] over[d] (the-)summits(-of)[e] the-mountains[f] they-leap[g];
like-(the-)sound(-of) (a-)flame(-of)[h] fire[i] devouring[j] stubble,[k]
like-(a-) mighty[l] -people[m] prepared-for[n] battle.[o]

LEXICON—a. **<u>like</u>-(the-)sound(-of) chariots** -כְּ *kə-* [BDB p. 453], [Hol p. 149], [TWOT 937]: 'like' [Hol; Crenshaw, Keil, Allen, Dillard, Wolff; KJV, REB, TEV], 'as' [NASB, NRSV].

b. **like-(the-)<u>sound(-of)</u> chariots** constr. of קוֹל *qôl* [BDB p. 876], [Hol p. 315], [TWOT 1998a]: 'sound' [BDB, Hol], 'noise' [Allen; NASB, KJV, NIV], 'rumbling' [Keil; NRSV], 'rumbling sound' [Wolff], 'rumble' [Crenshaw], 'din' [REB], 'rattling' [Bewer]. Dillard translates this noun as a verb, "sound"; likewise, TEV has "rattle."

c. **<u>chariots</u>** pl. of מֶרְכָּבָה *merkāḇâ* [BDB p. 939], [Hol p. 215], [TWOT 2163f]: 'war chariot' [BDB, Hol], 'chariot' [Bewer, Crenshaw, Keil, Allen, Dillard, Wolff; KJV, NASB, NIV, NRSV, REB, TEV].

d. <u>over</u> (the-)summits(-of) the-mountains they-leap עַל *ʿal* [BDB p. 757], [Hol p. 273], [TWOT 1624p): 'over' [Hol; Allen, Dillard; NIV, REB], 'on' [Crenshaw, Keil; KJV, NASB, NRSV, TEV], 'across' [Wolff].

e. **over (the-)<u>summits(-of)</u> the-mountains they-leap** constr. pl. of רֹאשׁ *rōʾš* [BDB p. 910], [Hol p. 329], [TWOT 2097]: 'top (of mountain)' [BDB, Hol; Crenshaw, Keil, Allen, Dillard, Wolff; KJV, NASB, NIV, NRSV, TEV], 'peak' [REB].

f. **(the-)summits(-of) the-<u>mountains</u>** pl. of הַר *har* [BDB p. 249], [Hol p. 83], [TWOT 517a]: 'mountain' [BDB, Hol; Crenshaw, Keil, Allen, Dillard, Wolff; KJV, NASB, NIV, NRSV, TEV], not explicit [REB].

g. **<u>they-leap</u>** 3rd masc. pl. Piel imperf. of רקד *rqd* [BDB p. 955], [Hol p. 346], [TWOT 2214]: 'to leap' [BDB; Keil, Allen; KJV, NASB, NIV, NRSV, TEV], 'to dance' [BDB, Hol],'to skip' [Dillard], 'to pop' [Crenshaw], 'to bound' [REB], 'to crackle' [Wolff].

h. **(a-)<u>flame(-of)</u> fire** constr. of לַהַב *lahab̲* [BDB p. 529], [Hol p. 173], [TWOT 1077a]: 'flame' [BDB, Hol; Keil, Allen, Dillard; KJV, NRSV, REB]. The phrase כְּקוֹל לַהַב אֵשׁ *kəqôl lahab̲ ʾēš* is translated as "like a crackling fire" [NIV], "like the crackling of flame" [Keil; NASB, NRSV, and REB are similar], "like lapping flames" [Dillard], "like the popping of fire" [Crenshaw], "like the crackling sound of a flaming fire" [Wolff]. For כְּקוֹל לַהַב אֵשׁ אֹכְלָה קָשׁ *kəqôl lahab̲ ʾēš ʾōk̲əlâ qâš* 'as the sound of a flame of fire devouring stubble' TEV has "they crackle like dry grass on fire."

i. **(a-)flame(-of) <u>fire</u>** אֵשׁ *ʾēš* [BDB p. 77], [Hol p. 29], [TWOT 172]: 'fire' [BDB, Hol; Wolff; KJV, NASB], not explicit [REB]. Allen translates this noun as an adjective, "fiery."

j. **<u>devouring</u> stubble** fem. sing. Qal part. of אכל *ʾk̲l* [BDB p. 37], [Hol p. 14], [TWOT 85]: 'to devour' [Hol; Crenshaw, Keil, Dillard, Wolff; KJV, NRSV], 'to consume' [Allen; NASB, NIV], 'to burn up' [REB].

k. **devouring <u>stubble</u>** קַשׁ *qaš* [BDB p. 905], [Hol p. 326], [TWOT 2091a]: 'stubble' [Hol; Crenshaw, Keil, Allen, Wolff; KJV, NASB, NIV, NRSV, REB], 'chaff' [Dillard], 'dry grass' [TEV].

l. **like-(a-) <u>mighty</u> –people** עָצוּם *ʿāṣûm* [BDB p. 783], [Hol p. 280], [TWOT 1673d]: 'mighty' [BDB, Hol; Dillard, Wolff; NASB, NIV], 'strong' [Keil; KJV], 'vast' [Hol; REB], 'powerful' [NRSV], 'formidable' [Crenshaw], 'great' [TEV], 'massive' [Allen]. The word *ʿāṣûm* connotes great numbers or quantity [Hol] and therefore great strength [BDB], often in a military sense [Dillard].

m. **(a-)mighty –<u>people</u>** עָם *ʿām* [BDB p. 766], [Hol p. 275], [TWOT 1640a]: 'a people' [Hol; Keil, Wolff; KJV, NASB], 'army' [Crenshaw, Dillard; NIV, NRSV, TEV], 'host' [REB], 'horde' [Allen].

n. **prepared-for battle** masc. sing. Qal pass. part. of ערך *ʿrk* [BDB p. 789], [Hol p. 283], [TWOT 1694]: 'to be prepared' [Hol], 'to be put in order' [Hol], 'to be set in order' [BDB], 'to be equipped' [Keil], 'to be set in array' [KJV], 'to be organized for' [Crenshaw], 'to be arranged' [NASB], 'marshalled' [Allen]. The phrase עֱרוּךְ מִלְחָמָה *ʿĕrûk milḥāmâ* denotes 'drawn up for battle' [Hol; Dillard; NRSV, NIV], 'lined up ready for battle' [TEV], 'in battle array' [REB], 'arrayed for battle' [Wolff], 'marshaled for battle' [Allen].

o. **prepared-for battle** מִלְחָמָה *milḥāmâ* [BDB p. 536], [Hol p. 197], [TWOT 1104c]: 'battle' [BDB; Crenshaw, Allen, Dillard, Wolff; KJV, NASB, NIV, REB, TEV], 'combat' [Hol], 'war' [BDB, Hol], 'conflict' [Keil].

QUESTION—How is the language of this verse intensified over the language of Joel 1?

The picture of the buzzing of locusts in Joel 1 is replaced by the sound of war chariots rumbling over the mountains toward Jerusalem [Wolff].

QUESTION—What is the point of similarity in the simile of burning stubble?

It is that burning stubble makes a crackling sound, similar to the sound of a swarm of locusts [Cohen].

QUESTION—What are the elements of OT theophany in this verse?

The militaristic language in general, as well as fire and chaff [Dillard].

QUESTION—What does the extended metaphor in this verse depict?

1. The locusts are depicted in military terms [Crenshaw].
2. YHWH's apocalyptic army is depicted [Wolff].

2:6

Before[a]-it (the-)peoples[b] tremble[c]; all faces[d] gather[e] heat.[f]

TEXT—The meaning of קִבְּצוּ פָארוּר *qibbəṣû pāʾrûr* 'they gather heat' is uncertain: The LXX's reading πᾶν πρόσωπον ὡς πρόσκαυμα χύτρας 'every face is like a scorched pot', seems to have come from reading the Hebrew פָּרוּר *pārûr* 'pot' for *pāʾrûr* 'heat' [Dillard]. Perhaps the point of similarity is heat, based on the fact that the pot was fired as it was made or that the pot might glow when in use over a fire. In any case, the comparison probably has to do with the gathering of heat. Hence, the best guess at the meaning here is 'they gather heat' [Wolff].

LEXICON—a. **before-it** מִפְּנֵי *mippənê* [BDB p. 815], [Hol p. 293]: 'before' [Keil, Dillard, Wolff; NASB, NRSV], 'on account of' [Hol], 'at the sight of' [NIV], 'in its path' [Crenshaw], 'at their advance' [Allen]. KJV translates מִפָּנָיו *mippānāyw* 'before it' semiliterally, "before their face"; TEV's translation is free, "as they approach," as is REB's, "at their onset." The complex preposition *mippənê* consists of *min* 'from' and the construct of פָּנִים *pānîm* 'face'.

b. **(the-)peoples tremble** pl. of עָם *ʿām* [BDB p. 766], [Hol p. 275], [TWOT 1640a]: 'a people' [Hol; KJV, NRSV], 'people' [Crenshaw,

Allen, Wolff; NASB], 'nation' [Keil, Dillard; NIV, REB], 'everyone' [TEV].

c. **(the-)peoples <u>tremble</u>** 3rd masc. pl. Qal imperf. of חול *hûl* [BDB p. 296], חיל *hîl* [Hol p. 102], [TWOT 623]: 'to tremble' [Hol; Keil; REB], 'to be in anguish' [NASB, NIV, NRSV], 'to be terrified' [Dillard; TEV], 'to be much pained' [KJV], 'to writhe' [BDB; Crenshaw, Wolff], 'to writhe in terror' [Allen].

d. **all <u>faces</u> gather heat** פָּנִים *pānîm* [BDB p. 815], [Hol p. 293], [TWOT 1782a]: 'face' [Hol; Keil, Allen, Dillard, Wolff; KJV, NASB, NIV, NRSV, REB, TEV], 'visage' [Crenshaw].

e. **<u>gather</u> heat** 3rd pl. Piel perf. of קבץ *qbṣ* [BDB p. 867], [Hol p. 312], [TWOT 1983]: 'to gather' [Crenshaw; KJV], 'to withdraw' [Keil], 'to be drained of' [REB]. For the phrase קִבְּצוּ פָארוּר *qibbəṣû pā'rûr* Holladay has "glows (of face in excitement)"; NASB, NIV, and TEV have "turn/turns pale"; NRSV, "grow pale"; Keil, "withdraws their redness [i.e., turns pale]"; Dillard, "to contort in dread"; REB, "to be drained of colour." BDB assumes that the sense is to glow with dread (of faces); Wolff translates it "all faces are aglow," and Allen "every face is flushed." The primary sense of *qbṣ* is 'to gather, collect' [BDB], 'to gather together' [Hol]. Most translate it using the English present tense. KJV uses the future tense: "they shall gather blackness."

f. **gather <u>heat</u>** פָּארוּר *pā'rûr* [BDB p. 802], [Hol p. 288], [TWOT 1727b]: 'heat' [Hol], 'redness' [Keil], 'blackness' [Cohen, KJV], 'sorrow' [Crenshaw], 'colour' [REB]. Some, assuming a root of פור *pûr* 'to boil, to heat', translate it similarly to Dillard: "every face gathers heat, becomes flushed." The idea of faces glowing from excitement seems drawn from a presumed link between *pā'rûr* and פאר *p'r* 'to beautify, glorify', or to another unknown root פאר *p'r*, as in BDB. The Jewish commentator Ibn Ezra posited an idea of faces withdrawing their beauty. Cohen objects that the verb קבץ *qbṣ* 'to gather' is not used in this sense. Another Jewish commentator, Eliezer of Beaugency, suggests "all faces have gathered wrinkles," indicating anxiety, as a piece of meat wrinkles when it is boiling in water [Cohen]. Some extract from "glow" the further idea of "to become pale" [Dillard]. Keil reaches this latter interpretation by viewing *pā'rûr* as the healthy glow of cheeks, which is withdrawn (קבץ *qbṣ* 'to withdraw') at the terrible sight, leaving the face pale. Whatever the literal reading, the context may be assumed to suggest a terrified population [Crenshaw].

QUESTION—What kind of language is Joel using in this verse?

Here Joel is using the language of OT theophany and of the day of YHWH; the peoples are said to tremble before YHWH's self-revelation. Psalms 96 and 97, Isa. 13:8–9, Jer. 5:22, and Ezek. 30:16 use such language to describe the day of YHWH [Crenshaw, Wolff].

QUESTION—To what does the pronoun in מִפָּנָיו *mippānāyw* 'before it' refer?

The pronoun refers to the invading army [Crenshaw, Keil, Wolff].

QUESTION—Who are meant by the term עַמִּים *ʿammîm* 'the peoples'?

1. This term most likely refers literally to the various ethnic groups surrounding Israel, as well as Israel herself [Allen, Stuart].
2. Beyond the literal reference, the prophet probably uses *ʿammîm* in an exaggerated manner to denote the Israelites [Crenshaw].

2:7

Like-valiant-men[a] they-run,[b] like-men(-of)[c] war[d] they-scale[e] (the-) wall,[f]

(each) man goes[g] in-his-paths,[h] (MT) and- they-do- -not -abandon[i] their-path.[j] (ET$_1$) and- they-do- -not bend-aside[i] their-path.[j] (ET$_2$) and- they-do- -not -turn-aside[i] their-path.[j]

TEXT—Some commentators and versions follow the MT, while others follow various proposed emendations:

Reading	Coming from	Remarks
יְעַבְּטוּן *yəʿabbəṭûn* **(MT)**	עבט *ʿbṭ* 'to receive or give security for a debt' (from an otherwise unused Piel stem)	**Sense:** 'They do not exchange their own paths with another' [the Jewish commentator Kimchi, who derives an idea of exchange from this verb—cited by Cohen]. **Followed by:** Keil, Wolff; KJV, TEV.
	—or from—	
	a different verb, עבט *ʿbṭ*, supposed by some to be a variant of עבת *ʿbṯ* 'to weave'	**Sense:** 'They do not entangle their paths' [cited by Cohen].
	—or from—	
	a different verb, עבט *ʿbṭ*, cognate to an Arabic verb, 'to spoil something'	**Sense:** 'They do not spoil their paths'. **Proposed by:** S. R. Driver [Allen].
יְעַוְּתוּן *yəʿawwəṯûn* **(emendation)**	עות *ʿwṯ* 'to be crooked'	**Sense:** 'They do not bend aside'. **Followed by:** Dillard; NASB, NIV, NRSV.
יִטּוּן *yiṭṭûn* **(emendation)**	נטה *nṭh* 'to turn aside'	**Sense:** 'They do not turn aside'.

The LXX's οὐ μὴ ἐκκλίνωσιν τὰς τρίβους αὐτῶν 'they do not make fall their steps' is inconclusive, as it does not appear to support any suggested reading.

LEXICON—a. **like-<u>valiant-men</u> they-run** pl. of גִּבּוֹר *gibbôr* [BDB p. 150], [Hol p. 53], [TWOT 310b]: 'valiant man' [BDB], 'hero' [Hol; Keil], 'champion' [Hol], 'warrior' [Dillard, Wolff; NIV, NRSV, REB,

TEV], 'mighty man' [KJV, NASB], 'soldier' [Crenshaw, Allen]. The picture is of an irresistible military attack [Cohen].

b. **they-run** 3rd masc. pl. Qal imperf. of רוץ *rûṣ* [BDB p. 930], [Hol p. 336], [TWOT 2137]: 'to run' [BDB, Hol; Keil, Dillard, Wolff; KJV, NASB], meaning they run to attack [Keil], 'to charge' [Allen; NIV, NRSV, REB], 'to attack' [Crenshaw; TEV]. Most translate using the English present tense. KJV employs the future tense: "they shall run." This word ends the short first colon; the parallel second colon, much expanded, gives the impression of a burgeoning attack [Crenshaw].

c. **men(-of) war** constr. pl. of אִישׁ *ʾîš* [BDB p. 35], [Hol p. 13], [TWOT 83a]: 'man' [BDB, Hol; Allen, Dillard, Wolff; KJV]. The singular *ʾîš* functions distributively when acting as the subject of a plural verb in Hebrew [Dillard].

d. **war** מִלְחָמָה *milḥāmâ* [BDB p. 536], [Hol p. 197], [TWOT 1104c]: 'combat' [Hol], 'war' [BDB, Hol; Allen, Wolff; KJV], [NIV], 'battle' [BDB]. Crenshaw translates the phrase כְּאַנְשֵׁי מִלְחָמָה *kəʾanšê milḥāmâ* 'like men of war' as "like warriors" (also Keil). NASB, NIV, NRSV, REB, and TEV have "like soldiers." Dillard has "like men of war" and Allen "like men at war."

e. **they-scale (the-) wall** 3rd masc. pl. Qal imperf. of עלה *ʿlh* [BDB p. 748], [Hol p. 273], [TWOT 1624]: 'to scale' [Crenshaw, Allen, Dillard, Wolff; NIV, NRSV, REB], 'to ascend' [BDB; Hol], 'to climb' [Keil; KJV, NASB, TEV]. KJV employs the English future tense; most translate with the present tense.

f. **wall** חוֹמָה *ḥômâ* [BDB p. 327], [Hol p. 97], [TWOT 674c]: 'wall (i.e., city wall)' [BDB, Hol; Crenshaw, Keil, Allen, Dillard, Wolff; KJV, NASB, NIV, NRSV, REB, TEV]. References to the city wall place Joel's prophetic ministry after the rebuilding of Jerusalem's wall, for Neh. 2:13 and 4:1 suggest that the wall, although extensively damaged by the Babylonians, had not been completely destroyed [Dillard].

g. **(each) man goes in-his-paths** 3rd masc. pl. Qal imperf. of הלך *hlḵ* [BDB p. 229], [Hol p. 79], [TWOT 498]: 'to go' [BDB, Hol; Crenshaw, Keil], 'to keep' [NRSV, REB], 'to march' [Dillard; KJV, NASB, NIV, TEV], 'to move ahead' [Allen, Wolff].

h. **in-his-paths** constr. pl. of דֶּרֶךְ *dereḵ* [BDB p. 202], [Hol p. 74], [TWOT 453a]: 'path' [Hol], 'way' [BDB; Keil, Wolff; KJV], 'course' [NRSV], 'line' [NASB, NIV, REB], 'trail' [Crenshaw]. For the expression בִּדְרָכָיו *biḏrāḵâw* Allen, Dillard, and TEV have 'straight ahead."

i. **and- they-do- -not -abandon their-path** 3rd masc. pl. Piel imperf. עבט *ʿḇṭ* [BDB p. 716], [Hol p. 262], [TWOT 1555]: 'to abandon' [Hol], 'to lend' [Kimchi, cited by Cohen], 'to change' [Hol; Keil, Wolff; TEV], 'to swerve' [NIV, NRSV], 'to deviate' [Dillard; NASB], 'to break' [KJV], 'to encroach' [Crenshaw]. Crenshaw translates the phrase וְלֹא יְעַבְּטוּן אָרְחוֹתָם *wəlōᵓ yəᶜabbəṭûn ᵓōrḥôṯām* 'they do not abandon their path' as "it [each locust] does not encroach on others' paths"; REB has "with no confusion in the ranks"; and Allen has "without overlapping their tracks."

j. **their-path** constr. pl. of אֹרַח *ᵓōraḥ* [BDB p. 73], [Hol p. 27], [TWOT 161a]: 'path' [Crenshaw; Keil; NASB, NRSV], 'stretch of path' [Hol], 'way' [BDB], 'course' [Dillard, Wolff; NIV], 'rank' [KJV], 'direction' [TEV], 'track' [Allen]. This term refers to a designated route of march [Wolff].

QUESTION—What is the theme of this verse?

1. It is that YHWH's coming judgment is as overwhelming and irresistible as the assault of the locusts [Keil]. The OT often compares military invasions to those of locusts (Judg. 6:5; Prov. 30:27; Isa. 33:4; Jer. 46:23; 51:14, 27). Joel, however, reverses the image, comparing the locust invasion to a military invasion [Dillard].
2. It is that the assault of YHWH's apocalyptic army is irresistible. It does not wreak devastation in the fields as do locusts, but instead invades Jerusalem. However severe a locust invasion might be, this attack is even more so; military weapons, which are powerless against locusts, have even less power against this assault; every house in the city, however susceptible to the entry of locusts, is even more so in this case [Wolff].

2:8

And-one[a] does- not -crowd[b] another[c]; everyone[d] goes[e] in-his-(own-) way[f];
(MT1) and-through[g] the-weapons[h-1] they-burst[i]; (MTT1) they-do- not -stop[j] (MTT2) they-are- not -hurt.[j]
(MT2) and-through[g] the-water-channel[h-2] they-descend[i]; they-do- not -stop.[j]

TEXT—The MT is capable of various interpretations, as summarized below:

and-through the-weapons they-burst	שֶׁלַח *šelaḥ* 'weapon' נפל *npl* 'to fall'	Cohen, Dillard, Keil, Wolff; KJV, NASB, NIV, NRSV, REB, TEV
they-do- not -stop	בצע *bṣᶜ* 'to stop'	Dillard, Wolff; NASB, NIV, NRSV, TEV
they-are- not -hurt	בצע *bṣᶜ* 'to stop'	Cohen, Keil; KJV
and-through the-water-channel they-descend	שֶׁלַח *šelaḥ* 'water channel' נפל *npl* 'to fall'	Allen, Crenshaw

LEXICON—a. **and-one does- not -crowd another** אִישׁ *ᵓîš* [BDB p. 35], [Hol p. 13], [TWOT 83a]: 'one' [Crenshaw, Dillard; KJV], 'each one' [Hol]. The primary sense of *ᵓîš* is 'man' [Hol]. The same thought is conveyed by the plural pronoun 'they' later in this verse [Keil; NIV, NRSV].

b. **and-one <u>does-</u> not <u>-crowd</u> another** 3rd masc. pl. Qal imperf. of דחק *dḥq* [BDB p. 191], [Hol p. 70], [TWOT 424]: 'to crowd' [BDB; Dillard; NASB], 'to press' [Keil], 'to afflict' [Hol], 'to jostle' [Allen; NIV, NRSV, REB], 'to thrust' [BDB; KJV], 'to shove' [Crenshaw] 'to push aside' [Wolff]. TEV conflates וְאִישׁ אָחִיו לֹא יִדְחָקוּן גֶּבֶר בִּמְסִלָּתוֹ יֵלֵכוּן *wə'îš 'āḥîw lō' yidḥāqûn geḇer bimsillāṯû yēlēḵûn* 'and one does not crowd another; everyone goes in his own way' and translates it as "[they do not] get in each other's way."

c. **and-one does- not -crowd <u>another</u>** constr. of אָח *'āḥ* [BDB p. 26], [Hol p. 8], [TWOT 62a]: 'another' [Crenshaw; KJV], 'one another' [Keil; NRSV], 'other' [Hol; Dillard, Wolff], 'each other' [Allen; NIV, TEV], 'neighbour' [REB]. The primary sense of *'āḥ* is 'brother' [Hol], and the Hebrew text reads אָחִיו *'āḥîw*, literally 'his brother'.

d. **<u>everyone</u> goes in-his-(own-) way** גֶּבֶר *geḇer* [BDB p. 149], [Hol p. 55], [TWOT 310a]: 'everyone' [Hol; Keil; KJV], 'each' [BDB; Crenshaw, Allen, Dillard, Wolff; NIV, NRSV, REB], 'each other' [NASB]. The primary sense of *geḇer* is 'young, strong man' [BDB, Hol].

e. **everyone <u>goes</u> in-his-(own-) way** 3rd masc. pl. Qal imperf. of הלך *hlḵ* [BDB p. 229], [Hol p. 79], [TWOT 498]: 'to go' [BDB, Hol; Keil], 'to march' [Dillard, Wolff; NASB, NIV], 'to keep to' [NRSV, REB], 'to walk' [KJV], 'to tread' [Crenshaw], 'to follow' [Allen].

f. **in-his-(own-) <u>way</u>** constr. of מְסִלָּה *məsillâ* [BDB p. 700], [Hol p. 203], [TWOT 1506d]: 'way' [Crenshaw, Dillard], 'path' [Keil, Wolff; KJV, NASB], 'track' [NRSV], 'course' [REB], 'set path' [Allen]. NIV translates this noun as an adverb: "straight ahead." The primary sense of *məsillâ* is 'highway' [BDB, Hol], meaning 'built-up road' [Hol], but the word is used in various figurative senses, as in this passage where it means the march of the locusts [BDB]. As 'set path' implies, *məsillâ* apparently denotes here the path that each locust should take. NIV's "straight ahead" is a reasonable rendering.

g. **and-<u>through</u>** בַּעַד *ba'aḏ* [BDB p. 126], [Hol p. 43], [TWOT 258]: 'through' [Keil, Allen; NASB, NIV, NRSV, TEV], 'among' [BDB], 'upon' [KJV], 'into' [Crenshaw], 'through the midst of' [Wolff], 'against' [Dillard]. The primary sense of the preposition *ba'aḏ* is 'away from' [BDB]. REB translates the phrase וּבְעַד הַשֶּׁלַח יִפֹּלוּ לֹא יִבְצָעוּ *ûḇ'aḏ haššelaḥ yippōlû lō' yiḇṣā'û* as "weapons cannot halt their attack."

h-1. **and-through the-<u>weapons</u> they-burst** שֶׁלַח *šelaḥ* [BDB p. 1019], [Hol p. 372], [TWOT 2394a]: 'weapon' [BDB; Cohen, Keil; NRSV, REB], 'sword' [KJV], 'javelin' [Hol], 'dart' [Hol], 'missile' [BDB; Wolff], 'defense' [Dillard, NASB, NIV, TEV]. The singular is here understood as a generic reference, which allows for a plural translation. A *šelaḥ* is not a throwing weapon but rather one held in the hand, such as a sword, or even a shield, as in 2 Chron. 32:5 [Keil]. The LXX has ἐν τοῖς βέλεσιν αὐτῶν πεσοῦνται 'among their spears they fall', seeming to regard *šelaḥ* as a spear for throwing. However, as no weapon of war would be useful against locusts, some have suggested that *šelaḥ* here denotes 'frontwall', as it is cognate to the Akkadian *šalḫu*, which bears that sense; this word would then refer ahead to the city wall mentioned in the next verse [Dillard].

h-2. **and-through the-water-channel they-descend** שֶׁלַח *šelaḥ* [Hol p. 372]: 'water channel' [Hol], 'tunnel' [Crenshaw], 'aqueduct' [Allen]. Some see in *šelaḥ* a reference to the waters of Shiloah (Isa. 8:6), supposing that the locusts came through that water system, which brought the water of the Gihon Spring to the reach of the inhabitants of Jerusalem [Gösta W. Ahlström, *Joel and the Temple Cult of Jerusalem*, Supplement to *Vetus Testamentum* 21 (Leiden: Brill, 1971), cited by Dillard]. It is in this vein that Crenshaw translates the word as "tunnel."

i. **they-burst/ they-descend** 3rd masc. pl. Qal imperf. of נפל *npl* [BDB p. 656], [Hol p. 241], [TWOT 1392]: 'to burst' [NASB, NRSV], 'to break through' [Cohen], 'to attack' [Wolff], 'to fall' [Hol; KJV], 'to fall headlong' [Keil], 'to plunge' [NIV], 'to descend' [Crenshaw], 'to swarm' [TEV], 'to press headlong' [Allen], 'to hurtle' [Dillard]. The primary sense of *npl* is 'to fall by accident'. Although the sense of 'to fall upon' as in an attack seems to generally occur with the preposition עַל *ᶜal* [BDB], that sense seems fairly appropriate for this verse even without the preposition. *Npl* certainly denotes intentional descent in Gen. 24:64 [Crenshaw].

j. **they-do- not -stop** 3rd masc. pl. Qal imperf. of בצע *bṣᶜ* [BDB p. 130], [Hol p. 45], [TWOT 267]: 'to stop' [Hol; Wolff], 'to break off' [BDB; Dillard], 'to break ranks' [NASB, NIV], 'to be halted' [NRSV], 'to halt one's course' [Allen], 'to break away' [Crenshaw]. TEV translates the phrase לֹא יִבְצָעוּ *lōᵓ yibṣāᶜû* as "and nothing can stop them." The primary concrete sense of *bṣᶜ* is 'to cut off, break off', here applied to the locusts' course [BDB]. It was, however, traditional to consider that *bṣᶜ* was used here intransitively and in effect passively: 'to cut oneself (to be cut) to pieces': the locusts are not hurt by the defenders' weapons [Cohen, Keil], 'to be wounded' [KJV]. Keil used this understanding to argue that 2:1–11 actually concerned not locusts (for locusts would not be hurt by military weapons), but in fact YHWH's heavenly army. Similarly, Crenshaw, in viewing the attacking enemy as a portent of the day of YHWH, concludes that the imagery becomes strained, based as it is upon the figure of a locust attack.

2:9

Against[a]-the-city[b] they-rush,[c] upon[d]-the-wall[e] they-run[f]; into[g]-the-houses[h] they-go-up,[i]
through[j]-the-windows[k] they-go[l] as[m]-the-thief.[n]

LEXICON—a. **against-the-city they-rush** -בְּ *bə-* [BDB p. 88], [Hol p. 32], [TWOT 193]: 'against' [TEV], 'upon' [NIV, NRSV], 'through' [Dillard], 'in' [Crenshaw, Keil; KJV], 'on' [NASB], 'into' [Allen; REB].

b. **against-the-city they-rush** עִיר *ʿîr* [BDB p. 746], [Hol p. 272], [TWOT 1615]: 'city' [BDB, Hol; Crenshaw, Keil, Allen, Dillard, Wolff; KJV, NASB, NIV, NRSV, REB, TEV]. The noun *ʿîr* denotes a walled settlement of houses and other buildings, as opposed to an unwalled village.

c. **against-the-city they-rush** 3rd masc. pl. Qal imperf. of שׁקק *šqq* [BDB p. 1055], [Hol p. 383], [TWOT 2640]: 'to rush' [BDB, Hol; Allen; NASB, NIV, TEV], 'to leap on' [Hol; Cohen; NRSV], 'to range' [Dillard], 'to run about' [BDB; Keil], 'to run' [BDB], 'to run to and fro' [KJV], 'to rush about' [Crenshaw], 'to burst' [REB], 'to assault' [Wolff]. *Šqq* always implies menacing movement [Crenshaw].

d. **upon-the-wall they-run** -בְּ *bə-* (see *a* above): 'upon' [Keil; KJV, NRSV], 'along' [NIV, REB], 'on' [Crenshaw, Dillard; NASB], 'over' [TEV], 'up' [Allen].

e. **upon-the-wall they-run** חוֹמָה *ḥômâ* [BDB p. 327], [Hol p. 97], [TWOT 674c]: 'wall' [BDB; Crenshaw, Keil, Allen, Dillard, Wolff; KJV, NASB, NIV, NRSV, REB, TEV], 'city wall' [Hol]. *Ḥômâ* denotes a defensive wall around a settlement.

f. **upon-the-wall they-run** 3rd masc. pl. Qal imperf. of רוץ *rûṣ* [BDB p. 930], [Hol p. 336], [TWOT 2137]: 'to run' [BDB, Hol; Keil, Allen, Dillard; KJV, NASB, NIV, NRSV, TEV], 'to race' [REB], 'to storm' [Wolff].

g. **into-the-houses they-go-up** -בְּ *bə-* (see *a* above): 'into' [Keil, Allen, Dillard; NASB, NIV, NRSV, REB], 'upon' [KJV].

h. **into-the-houses they-go-up** pl. of בַּיִת *bayiṯ* [BDB p. 108], [Hol p. 38], [TWOT 241]: 'house' [BDB, Hol; Crenshaw, Keil, Allen, Dillard, Wolff; KJV, NASB, NIV, NRSV, REB, TEV].

i. **into-the-houses they-go-up** 3rd masc. pl. Qal imperf. of עלה *ʿlh* [BDB p. 748], [Hol p. 273], [TWOT 1624]: 'to go up' [BDB, Hol], 'to ascend' [BDB, Hol], 'to climb' [BDB; Keil, Allen, Dillard; NASB, NIV], 'to climb up' [KJV, NRSV, TEV], 'to enter' [Crenshaw], 'to scale' [Wolff]. The primary sense of *ʿlh* is 'to ascend'; in this case, the invaders' entry into the city's houses is seen as part of their ascent starting from outside the city walls [Crenshaw].

j. **through-the-windows they-go** constr. of בַּעַד *baʿaḏ* [BDB p. 126], [Hol p. 43], [TWOT 258a]: 'through' [BDB, Hol; Crenshaw, Keil,

Dillard, Wolff; NASB, NIV, NRSV, REB, TEV], 'in through' [Allen], 'at' [KJV].

k. **through-the-windows they-go** pl. of חַלּוֹן *ḥallôn* [BDB p. 319], [Hol p. 105], [TWOT 660c]: 'window' [BDB; Crenshaw, Keil, Allen, Dillard, Wolff; KJV, NASB, NIV, NRSV, REB, TEV], 'window opening' [Hol]. *Ḥallôn* denotes a hole in a wall to admit light and air [Hol]; the windows were filled with latticework [Cohen].

l. **through-the-windows they-go** 3rd masc. pl. Qal imperf. of בּוֹא *bôʾ* [BDB p. 97], [Hol p. 34], [TWOT 212]: 'to go' [Hol; Crenshaw, Dillard], 'to enter' [Wolff; NASB, NIV, NRSV, REB], 'to come' [Keil; Allen], 'to enter in' [KJV], 'to go in' [TEV].

m. **they-go as-the-thief** -כְּ *kə-* [BDB p. 453], [Hol p. 149], [TWOT 937]: 'like' [Hol; Crenshaw, Keil, Allen, Dillard, Wolff; KJV, NASB, NIV, NRSV, REB, TEV].

n. **they-go as-the-thief** גַּנָּב *gannāḇ* [BDB p. 170], [Hol p. 63], [TWOT 364b]: 'thief' [BDB, Hol; Crenshaw, Keil, Dillard, Wolff; KJV, NASB, NIV, NRSV, REB, TEV], 'burglar' [Allen]. This noun has the Hebrew definite article prefixed, but the singular noun form with the definite article stands for a plural collective or a generic idea.

2:10

Before[a]-it (the-)earth[b] quakes,[c] (the-)heavens[d] tremble;[e]
(the-)sun[f] and-(the-)moon[g] grow-dark,[h] and-(the-)stars[i] draw-back[j] their-light.[k]

INTERTEXTUAL REFERENCE—Joel has already alluded to Isa. 13:6 (in 1:15). Here he alludes to Isa. 13:10, 13, presenting the same heavenly vocabulary in inverted order (treating "sun" and "moon" together):

Isa. 13:10, 13					**Joel 2:10**		
כּוֹכָבִים	*ḵôḵāḇîm*	'stars'	a	d´	אֶרֶץ	*ʾereṣ*	'earth'
שֶׁמֶשׁ, יָרֵחַ	*šemeš, yārēaḥ*	'sun, moon'	b	c´	שָׁמַיִם	*šāmāyim*	'heavens'
שָׁמַיִם	*šāmāyim*	'heavens'	c	b´	שֶׁמֶשׁ, יָרֵחַ	*šemeš, yārēaḥ*	'sun, moon'
אֶרֶץ	*ʾereṣ*	'earth'	d	a´	כּוֹכָבִים	*ḵôḵāḇîm*	'stars'

This lexical reversal reflects Joel's reversal of Isaiah's theme: Isaiah marshals the heavenly phenomena as accompaniment to the attack of YHWH's army against Babylon, while Joel applies them to the army's attack against Judah [Wendland].

LEXICON—a. **before-it (the-)earth quakes** לִפְנֵי *lip̄nê* [BDB p. 815], [Hol p. 293], [TWOT 1782b]: 'before' (in a spatial sense) [Hol; Keil, Dillard, Wolff; KJV, NASB, NIV, NRSV], 'ahead' [Allen]. Crenshaw translates לְפָנָיו *ləpānâw* 'before it' as "in its vanguard"; TEV has "as they advance"; REB has "at their onset."

b. **before-it (the-)<u>earth</u> quakes** אֶרֶץ *ʾereṣ* [BDB p. 76], [Hol p. 28], [TWOT 167]: 'earth' [Hol; Crenshaw, Keil, Allen, Wolff; KJV, NASB, NIV, NRSV, REB, TEV], 'land' [Dillard].

c. **before-it (the-)earth <u>quakes</u>** 3rd fem. sing. Qal perf. of רגז *rgz* [BDB p. 919], [Hol p. 332], [TWOT 2112]: 'to quake' [Hol; Keil, Allen, Wolff; KJV, NASB, NRSV], 'to shake' [Hol; NIV, REB, TEV], 'to tremble' [Crenshaw, Dillard]. KJV employs the English future tense in translation, but most commentators and translators use the English present tense.

d. **(the-)<u>heavens</u> tremble** שָׁמַיִם *šāmayim* [BDB p. 1029], [Hol p. 375], [TWOT 2407a]: 'heavens' [Hol; Keil, Dillard, Wolff; KJV, NASB, NRSV, REB], 'sky' [Hol; Crenshaw, Allen; NIV, TEV].

e. **(the-)heavens <u>tremble</u>** 3rd pl. Qal perf. of רעשׁ *rʿš* [BDB p. 950], [Hol p. 344], [TWOT 2195]: 'to tremble' [Keil, Wolff; KJV, NASB, NIV, NRSV, TEV], 'to quake' [BDB, Hol; Crenshaw], 'to shake' [BDB, Hol; Dillard], 'to shudder' [REB], 'to vibrate' [Allen]. KJV employs the English future tense in translation, but most commentators and translators use the English present tense.

f. **(the-)<u>sun</u> and-(the-)moon** שֶׁמֶשׁ *šemeš* [BDB p. 1039], [Hol p. 378], [TWOT 2417a]: 'sun' [Hol; Crenshaw, Keil, Allen, Dillard, Wolff; KJV, NASB, NIV, NRSV, REB, TEV].

g. **(the-)sun and-(the-)<u>moon</u>** יָרֵחַ *yārēaḥ* [BDB p. 437], [Hol p. 144], [TWOT 913a]: 'moon' [BDB, Hol; Crenshaw, Keil, Allen, Dillard, Wolff; KJV, NASB, NIV, NRSV, REB, TEV].

h. **(the-)sun and-(the-)moon <u>grow-dark</u>** 3rd pl. Qal perf. of קדר *qḏr* [BDB p. 871], [Hol p. 313], [TWOT 1989]: 'to grow dark' (as in an eclipse) [Hol; Allen, Dillard; NASB, TEV], 'to be dark' [BDB; KJV], 'to be darkened' [Crenshaw, Wolff; NIV, NRSV, REB], 'to turn black' [Keil]. *Qḏr* often appears in texts prophesying divine judgment and punishment, as also in Jer. 4:28; words derived from this verb root often carry a strong nuance of sorrow [TWOT]. KJV employs the English future tense in translation, but most commentators and translators use the English present tense. The Hebrew verb appears to be an example of the so-called prophetic perfect.

i. **and-(the-)<u>stars</u>** pl. of כּוֹכָב *kôḵāḇ* [BDB p. 456], [Hol p. 152], [TWOT 942a]: 'star' [Hol; Crenshaw, Keil, Allen, Dillard, Wolff; KJV, NASB, NIV, NRSV, REB, TEV].

j. **and-(the-)stars <u>draw-back</u> their-light** 3rd pl. Qal perf. of אסף *ʾsp̄* [BDB p. 62], [Hol p. 23], [TWOT 140]: 'to draw back' (transitive) [Hol], 'to withdraw' [Keil; KJV, NRSV], 'to recall' [Dillard], 'to gather' [Crenshaw], 'to withhold' [REB]. The expression אָסְפוּ נָגְהָם *ʾāsəpû noḡhām* is translated "no longer shine" [NIV, TEV], "lose their brightness" [NASB], "stars stop shining" [Allen], and "the brightness is extinguished" [Wolff]. KJV employs the English future tense in translation, but most commentators and translators use the English present tense. The Hebrew verb appears to be an example of the so-called prophetic perfect.

k. **draw-back their-<u>light</u>** constr. of נֹגַהּ *nōḡah̠* [BDB p. 618], [Hol p. 226], [TWOT 1290a]: 'light' [Dillard; REB], 'gleam' [Hol], 'brightness' [BDB; Wolff; NASB], 'shining' [Hol; Keil; KJV, NRSV], 'splendor' [Crenshaw].

QUESTION—What is the syntactic organization of 2:10–11?

The uniqueness of the circumstantial clauses in 2:10b–11a is shown by their word order, which is unusual: subject–verb–optional object. (Normal BH word order, as is illustrated in 2:10a, is verb–subject–optional object.) These circumstantial clauses appear following the cosmic description of the day of YHWH and before the explanation (the circumstantial portion is in bold type here):

The earth quakes before it
the heavens tremble—
while sun and moon are darkened,
the brighteness of the stars is extinguished
and Yahweh lifts up his voice before his army—
for exceedingly great is his encampment;
indeed, mighty is he who carries out his word.
Indeed, the Day of Yahweh is great and very terrible.
[Wolff]

QUESTION—To what does the pronoun in לְפָנָיו *ləp̄ānâw* 'before it/him' refer?

1. The pronoun refers to the army of locusts. The earth trembles, not so much because of the locusts, but because the Lord is coming in judgment [Keil]. The identification of the pronoun with the locust army gains force with the recognition that Joel has used expressions for 'before' also in 2:3 and 6 with apparent reference to the locust army [Crenshaw].
2. Instead of referring to the locusts, which would require a plural pronoun, the singular pronoun probably refers ahead to "YHWH," explicit in the following verse. This view recognizes an abrupt change of subject in 2:10, accompanied by a change from imperfect to perfect tenses in the verbs (the perfect tense verbs here carrying accompanying material). The 2:10–11 passage depicts a cosmic shaking of the sort that not even the most massive locust invasion could produce, but only the day of YHWH (see the description of this day in Isa. 13:10 and Ezek. 32:7–8) [Crenshaw, Wolff].

QUESTION—What are the exegetical considerations of the term רעשׁ *r*ʿ*š* ‘to shake’ in the phrase רָעֲשׁוּ שָׁמָיִם *rā*ʿ*ăšû šāmāyim* ‘the heavens tremble’?

By postexilic times, *r*ʿ*š* ‘to tremble’ was part of the vocabulary associated with the end of the age, which would be marked by an undoing of creation and a return to a chaos reminiscent of that described in of Genesis 1. The heavenly bodies would be shaken; then YHWH would execute his final judgment [Brevard S. Childs, “Enemy from the North and the Chaos Tradition,” *Journal of Biblical Literature* 78:188–90 (1959), cited by Dillard]. Such a return to chaos, betokened by the shaking of the heavenly bodies, represents an undoing of creation. This shaking accompanied the theme of theophany, which in turn, had been incorporated by before Joel’s time into the day of YHWH scenario [Wolff].

2:11

And[a]-YHWH utters[b] his-voice[c] before[d] his-army,[e]
surely/for[f] great[g] (is) (the-)power(-of)[h] his-army,[i] indeed/for[j] mighty[k] (is) (the-) one-carrying-out[l] his-word,[m]
indeed/for[n] great[o] (is) (the-)day(-of) YHWH and fearful[p] (its-)power,[q] and-who (can-)endure-it[r]?

LEXICON—a. **and-YHWH utters** -וְ *wə- waw* connective [BDB p. 251], [Hol p. 84], [TWOT 519]: ‘and’ [Keil, Wolff; NASB], ‘then’ [Crenshaw]; not explicit [Dillard; NRSV, REB, TEV]. Allen takes -וְ *wə-* as introducing a circumstantial construction: “as YHWH thunders.”

b. **utters his-voice** 3rd masc. sing. Qal perf. of נתן *ntn* [BDB p. 678], [Hol p. 249], [TWOT 1443]: ‘to utter’ [KJV, NASB, NRSV], ‘to give’ [Hol; Dillard], ‘to lift up’ [Wolff]. The expression נָתַן קוֹלוֹ *nāṯan qôlô* is translated “thunders” [Keil, Allen; NIV, REB, TEV], “thunders commands” [TEV], “spoke” [Crenshaw]. KJV employs the English future tense, but most commentators and translators use the English present tense. The Hebrew verb appears to be an example of the so-called prophetic perfect.

c. **utters his-voice** constr. of קוֹל *qôl* [BDB p. 876], [Hol p. 315], [TWOT 1998a]: ‘voice’ [Hol; Wolff; KJV, NASB, NRSV], ‘orders’ [Dillard], ‘commands’ [TEV].

d. **and-YHWH utters his-voice before his-army** לִפְנֵי *lip̄nê* [BDB p. 815], [Hol p. 293], [TWOT 1782b]: ‘before’ [Keil, Wolff; KJV, NASB], ‘at the head of’ [Allen; NIV, NRSV], ‘to’ [Dillard; TEV]. The phrase לִפְנֵי חֵילוֹ *lip̄nê ḥêlô* ‘before his army’ is translated as “in his army’s presence” by Crenshaw and, more freely, “as he leads his host” by REB.

e. **his-army** constr. of חַיִל *ḥayil* [BDB p. 298], [Hol p. 102], [TWOT 624a]: ‘army’ [BDB, Hol; Crenshaw, Keil, Allen, Dillard, Wolff; KJV, NASB, NIV, NRSV, TEV], ‘host’ [REB].

f. <u>**surely/for**</u> **great (is) (the-)power(-of) his-army** כִּי *kî* particle [BDB p. 471], [Hol p. 155], [TWOT 976]: 'for' [Crenshaw, Keil, Allen, Dillard, Wolff; KJV], 'surely' [NASB], not explicit [NIV, NRSV, REB, TEV].

g. <u>**great**</u> **(is) (the-)power(-of) his-army** רַב *rab* [BDB p. 912], [Hol p. 330], [TWOT 2099a]: 'great' [Hol]. The expression רַב מְאֹד *rab məʾōd* is translated as "vast" [Allen; NRSV], "beyond number" [NIV], "most numerous" [Dillard], "very great" [Keil; KJV, NASB], "exceedingly great" [Wolff], "particularly numerous" [Crenshaw], "mighty" [REB]. TEV conflates the clauses כִּי רַב מְאֹד מַחֲנֵהוּ כִּי עָצוּם עֹשֵׂה דְבָרוֹ *kî rab məʾōd maḥănēhû kî ʿāṣûm ʿōśēh dəbārô* 'for great is the power of his army, for mighty is the one carrying out his word' and translates it as "the troops that obey him are many and mighty."

h. **great (is) (the-)**<u>**power**</u>**(-of) his-army** מְאֹד *məʾōd* [BDB p. 547], [Hol p. 180], [TWOT 1134a]: 'power' [Hol], 'might' [BDB, Hol]. This word functions here as an intensifier and is so recognized by all commentators and versions.

i. **his-**<u>**army**</u> constr. of מַחֲנֶה *maḥăneh* [BDB p. 334], [Hol p. 190], [TWOT 690c]: 'army' [BDB, Hol; REB], 'host' [BDB; NRSV], 'forces' [NIV], 'soldiers' [Dillard], 'camp' [Keil; KJV, NASB], 'encampment' [Crenshaw, Wolff], 'troops' [TEV], 'battalion' [Allen].

j. <u>**indeed/for**</u> **mighty (is) (the-) one-carrying-out his-word** כִּי *kî* particle (see *f* above): 'for' [Keil; KJV, NASB], 'and' [Allen; NIV], 'indeed' [Wolff], not explicit [REB, Dillard; NRSV].

k. <u>**mighty**</u> **(is) (the-) one-carrying-out his-word** עָצוּם *ʿāṣûm* [BDB p. 783], [Hol p. 280], [TWOT 1673d]: 'mighty' [Hol; Crenshaw, Wolff; NIV], 'vast' [Hol], 'numberless' [NRSV], 'powerful' [Dillard], 'strong' [Keil; KJV, NASB], 'countless' [REB], 'massive' [Allen].

l. <u>**one-carrying-out**</u> **his-word** sing. masc. Qal part. constr. of עשׂה *ʿśh* [BDB p. 793], [Hol p. 284], [TWOT 1708]: 'to carry out' [Hol; Crenshaw, Wolff; NASB], 'to obey' [NIV, NRSV, TEV], 'to do' [Dillard; REB], 'to execute' [Allen; KJV]. Keil translates this participle as a single noun, "executor." TEV translates עֹשֵׂה דְבָרוֹ *ʿōśēh dəbārô* 'one carrying out his word' as "that obey him."

m. **one-carrying-out his-**<u>**word**</u> constr. of דָּבָר *dābār* [BDB p. 182], [Hol p. 67], [TWOT 399a]: 'word' [Hol; Keil, Wolff; KJV, NASB], 'command' [NIV, NRSV], 'will' [Dillard], 'decree' [Crenshaw], 'bidding' [REB], 'order' [Allen].

n. <u>**indeed/for**</u> **great (is) (the-)day(-of) YHWH** כִּי *kî* particle (see *f* above): 'for' [Crenshaw, Keil, Dillard; KJV], 'truly' [NRSV], 'indeed' [Wolff], not explicit [Allen; NASB, NIV, REB]. TEV makes *kî* signal an exclamation here: "how terrible."

o. <u>**great**</u> **(is) (the-)day(-of) YHWH** גָּדוֹל *gādôl* [BDB p. 152], [Hol p. 55], [TWOT 315d]: 'great' [Hol; Crenshaw, Keil, Dillard, Wolff;

KJV, NASB, NIV, NRSV, REB], 'momentous' [Allen]. TEV conflates the expression כִּי־גָדוֹל יוֹם־יְהוָה וְנוֹרָא מְאֹד *kî-gāḏôl yôm-yhwh wənôrāʾ məʾōḏ* 'for great is the day of YHWH and fearful its power' and translates it as "how terrible is the day of the Lord!"

p. **and <u>fearful</u> (its-)power** Niphal part. of ירא *yrʾ* [BDB p. 431], [Hol p. 142], [TWOT 907]: 'fearful' [Crenshaw], 'to be feared' [Hol], 'terrible' [Allen, Keil, Wolff; KJV, NRSV, REB], 'dreadful' [Dillard; NIV], 'awesome' [NASB].

q. **and fearful (its-)<u>power</u>** מְאֹד *məʾōḏ* (see *h* above). In the expression וְנוֹרָא מְאֹד *wənôrāʾ məʾōḏ*, this word functions as an intensifier and is so recognized by all commentators and versions. It is generally rendered "very" or "exceedingly," as in "very fearful."

r. **and-who (can-)<u>endure</u>-it** 3rd masc. sing. Hiphil imperf. of כול *kûl* [BDB p. 465], [Hol p. 152], [TWOT 962]: 'to endure' [Hol; Keil, Dillard, Wolff; NASB, NIV, NRSV, REB], 'to abide' [KJV], 'to stand' [Crenshaw], 'to survive' [TEV], 'to withstand' [Allen].

QUESTION—How does this verse function in this discourse unit?

It defines an inclusio, for it provides a second explicit reference to the day of YHWH, as 2:1 does [Crenshaw].

QUESTION—To what does וַיהוָה נָתַן קוֹלוֹ *wayhwh nāṯan qôlô* 'and YHWH utters his voice' refer?

1. The expression's immediate literal reference is to the thunder of a storm; in its more extended meaning, it signals the final judgment brought by YHWH. This is similar to Isa. 13:10 and Ezek. 32:7, which employ the ideas of a storm together with the darkening of the sun, moon, and stars as accompaniments to the judgment day; in Matt. 24:29 and Mark 13:24–25 Christ also links these ideas [Keil]. YHWH's final judgment necessarily implies that he will reveal himself, and OT theophanies were indeed generally accompanied by thunder and storm [Dillard].
2. It refers to an implicit proclamation by which the people were warned to repent in order to avoid the coming judgment of the day of YHWH [Cohen].
3. It refers to the orders given by YHWH to his advancing army [TEV]. Thunder is said to accompany YHWH's commands to his armies in Ps. 18:14, 46:7, and Amos 1:2 [Crenshaw].

QUESTION—What is the referent of the phrase עֹשֵׂה דְבָרוֹ *ʿōśēh dəḇārô* 'the one carrying out his word'?

The referent is YHWH's army [Crenshaw, Wolff], which the Jewish commentators Rashi and Kara understood to be the locusts [Cohen]. It is worth noting, however, that ancient versions diverge in their understanding of this passage. The Targum Jonathan and the Greek version of Symmachus understand YHWH's army (the 'encampment') in their respective readings, עַבְדֵי *ʿaḇdê* 'servants of' and οἱ ποιοῦντες 'those who do'. The LXX makes YHWH's work of 2:10 the referent (ὅτι ἰσχυρὰ ἔργα λόγων αὐτοῦ 'for great are the deeds of his words') [Wolff].

QUESTION—What is the referent of דְּבָרוֹ *dəḇārô* 'his word'?

1. It is probably YHWH's word which earlier prophets had received (see Jer. 1:12) [Wolff].
2. It is the commands YHWH gives to his army [Dillard; TEV].
3. It is the sentence of judgment YHWH passes upon the nations [Keil].

QUESTION—What kind of question is וּמִי יְכִילֶנּוּ *ûmî yəḵîlenû* 'and who can endure it?

It is a rhetorical question and is to be understood as implying that no one can endure it [Cohen, Dillard]. This question marks the emotional low point of the entire book [Wendland].

QUESTION—What is the nature of the three occurrences of the particle כִּי *kî* and the clauses that they introduce in this verse?

1. In these occurrences, *kî* functions to affirm the statements it introduces: 'indeed', 'surely'. Joel is here expressing awe [Dillard, Wendland].
2. In these occurrences, *kî* functions to set forth the three reasons for which YHWH utters his voice [Keil].
3. These occurrences of *kî* look back to the first part of 2:10, giving the reasons for the earth to quake and the heavens to shake; the intervening material is composed of circumstantial clauses (see 2:10) [Wolff; Crenshaw also leans to this opinion].

DISCOURSE UNIT: 2:12–17 [Cohen, Crenshaw, Wendland; NIV, TEV]. Crenshaw calls the topic "a call to return to YHWH and to lament"; NIV has "rend your heart"; TEV has "call to repentance" (also Cohen). The unit comprises Stanza D [Wendland].

Comments on this discourse unit: Lexical cohesion in this unit is promoted by a series of terms relating to the religious life of the Jews—"fasting," "weeping," "blessing," "offering," "libation," "ram's horn," "to sanctify a fast," "to announce a religious gathering," "to sanctify an assembly," "porch" (of the Temple), "altar," "priests," and "ministers of YHWH." In addition, this unit features many commands addressed to the priests and people [Crenshaw] as well as two notable contrasts: (1) The ram's horn call in 2:15 summons the people *toward* YHWH in contrast to their flight *away from* judgment on the day of YHWH in 2:1. (2) The referent of אַחַר *ʾaḥar* 'after' in 2:3 is the devastation left behind by the invading locusts, which is in contrast to the referent of *ʾaḥar* in 2:14, namely the blessing it is hoped that YHWH will leave behind after coming to his people [Crenshaw].

2:12

Yet-even[a] now,[b] (the-)declaration(-of)[c] YHWH:
return(p)/turn(p)[d] to-me with[e]-all your(p)-heart[f] and-with[g]-fasting[h]
and-with-weeping[i] and-with-rites-of-mourning.[j]

SYNTAX—The syntax of the phrase וְגַם־עַתָּה נְאֻם־יְהוָה *wəḡam-ʿattâ nəʾum-yhwh and-indeed now (the-)declaration(-of) YHWH* is disputed:

<table>
<tr><th>Expression</th><th>Viewed as</th><th>Sense of cola α—γ</th><th></th></tr>
<tr><td>wəḡam-ʿattâ 'but-even now'</td><td>start of reported speech</td><td rowspan="2">' "Yet even now," declares YHWH, "return to me with all your heart...." '</td><td rowspan="2">Followed by: Most commentators and versions.</td></tr>
<tr><td>nəʾum-yhwh 'oracle-of YHWH'</td><td>speech margin</td></tr>
<tr><td>wəḡam-ʿattâ nəʾum -yhwh 'but-even now (the-)oracle(-of) YHWH'</td><td>a single independent phrase</td><td>'But even now the oracle of YHWH is valid: "Return to me with all your heart...." '</td><td>Proposed by: Wolff.</td></tr>
<tr><td></td><td colspan="3">Argument for: Wolff's view entails taking cola γ–δ as a citation from the prophetic tradition (cf. Amos 4:6–11; Hos. 3:5; 14:2; Jer. 3:10; 24:7) and treating these two cola as the content of YHWH's declaration. The prophet is then seen as resuming his own speech in 2:13. In this way, Wolff accounts for the first person reference to YHWH in 2:12 and the resumption of third person reference to YHWH in 2:13.
Argument against: Crenshaw argues against Wolff's view. He points out that alternation between first and third person in prophetic oracles is common and may be ascribed to the prophet's intimate role as spokesman for YHWH.</td></tr>
</table>

SYNTAX—The MT has an athnach—a kind of interpretative punctuation mark—at the end of בְּכָל־לְבַבְכֶם *bəḵol-ləḇaḇḵem* 'with all your heart', indicating that the Masoretes considered the first half of the verse to end at this point. Thus the call to turn to YHWH is explicitly set off from the outward manner in which the people are to return [Crenshaw].

LEXICON—a. **yet-even now** וְגַם *wəḡam* [BDB p. 168], [Hol p. 61], [TWOT 361a]. The expression וְגַם־עַתָּה *wəḡam ʿattâ* is translated "yet even now" [Hol; Keil; NASB, NIV, NRSV, REB], "but even now" [Crenshaw, Wolff; TEV], "even now" [Dillard], "therefore also now" [KJV]. *Gam* is an emphasizing and associating particle [Hol] and is certainly one of the devices used by Joel to begin this discourse unit emphatically. It also begins a new topic; an adversative force (e.g., "but even now") is required by the theme of the imminence of the day of YHWH [Wolff]. Most other commentators and versions appear to agree with Wolff's position. Allen, however, translates it as simply "now is the time."

b. **yet-even now** עַתָּה *ʿattâ* [BDB p. 774], [Hol p. 287], [TWOT 1650c]: 'now' [all commentators and versions]. This word indicates that the time for repentance, the theme of this verse, is short [Wolff].

c. **(the-)declaration(-of) YHWH** constr. of נְאֻם *nəʾum* [BDB p. 610], [Hol p. 223], [TWOT 1272a]: 'declaration' [BDB, Hol], 'saying' [Keil], 'oracle' [Crenshaw, Wolff]. This noun is also translated as a verb: 'to declare' [NASB, NIV], 'to say' [Dillard; KJV, NRSV, REB, TEV]. Crenshaw translates the phrase נְאֻם־יְהוָה *nəʾum-yhwh* 'the declaration of YHWH' as "a divine oracle."

d. **return(p)/turn(p) to-me** masc. pl. Qal imper. of שׁוּב *šûḇ* [BDB p. 996], [Hol p. 362], [TWOT 2340]: 'to return' [BDB, Hol; Crenshaw, Allen, Wolff; NASB, NIV, NRSV], 'to come back' [Hol], 'to turn' [Keil, Dillard; KJV], 'to turn back' [REB]. The phrase שֻׁבוּ עָדַי בְּכָל־לְבַבְכֶם *šuḇû ʿāḏay bəḵol-ləḇaḇḵem* 'return/turn to me with all your heart' is interpreted, amplified, and translated concretely by TEV: "repent sincerely and return to me." But see the questions below for another opinion regarding the use of *šûḇ* here.

e. **with-all your(p)-heart** -בְּ *bə-* [BDB p. 88], [Hol p. 32], [TWOT 193]: 'with' [Crenshaw, Keil, Dillard, Wolff; KJV, NASB, NIV, NRSV]. The proclitic *bə-* here expresses superficial instrument [Hol]. Allen and also REB translate בְּכָל־לְבַבְכֶם *bəḵol-ləḇaḇḵem* 'with all your heart' as "wholeheartedly."

f. **with-all your(p)-heart** constr. of לֵבָב *lēḇāḇ* [BDB p. 523], [Hol p. 172], [TWOT 1071a]: 'heart' [BDB, Hol; Keil, Dillard, Wolff; KJV, NASB, NIV, NRSV], 'will' [BDB], 'mind' [Crenshaw]. *Lēḇāḇ* is normally glossed 'heart', but it is doubtful that it ever means the physical organ. What *lēḇāḇ* undoubtedly denotes is the seat of intelligence, reason, and the will [Wolff (b)].

g. **and-with-fasting** -בְּ *bə-* (see *e* above): 'with' [all commentators and versions]. It is clear that this second occurrence of *bə-* introduces expressions of exterior manner, whereas the first occurrence (see *e* above) introduces an expression of interior attitude.

h. **and-with-fasting** צוֹם *ṣôm* [BDB p. 847], [Hol p. 304], [TWOT 1890a]: 'fasting' [BDB, Hol; Crenshaw, Keil, Allen, Dillard, Wolff; KJV, NASB, NIV, NRSV, REB, TEV].

i. **and-with-weeping** בְּכִי *bəḵî* [BDB p. 113], [Hol p. 40], [TWOT 243b]: 'weeping' [Hol; Crenshaw, Keil, Allen, Dillard, Wolff; KJV, NASB, NIV, NRSV, REB, TEV].

j. **and-with-rites-of-mourning** מִסְפֵּד *mispēḏ* [BDB p. 704], [Hol p. 204], [TWOT 1530a]: 'rites of mourning' [Hol], 'mourning' [Crenshaw, Keil, Dillard, Wolff; KJV, NASB, NIV, NRSV, REB, TEV], 'wailing' [BDB], 'lamenting' [Allen].

QUESTION—What is the significance of 2:12–14?

1. Verses 2:12–14 constitute a summons to national repentance. This summons is signaled by the phrase נְאֻם־יְהוָה *nəʾum-yhwh* 'oracle of

YHWH', which normally introduces a prophecy [Dillard], but which appears in Joel only in this passage, where it introduces a very prominent expression of hope: if the people truly turn to YHWH, he may still relent from judging his people [Crenshaw, Keil]. Verse 2:12 is reminiscent of 2 Chron. 6:28 and 7:14 [Dillard]. The expression וְגַם־עַתָּה *wəḡam ʿattâ* 'yet even now' evidently does not relate to the invasion described in 2:1–9, for that has already occurred, but rather to the day of YHWH, described in 2:10–11 [Crenshaw, Wolff].

2. Within an honor-shame model, these verses are regarded as a summons to the people to mourn before YHWH. Such mourning would be the appropriate way to publicly honor him in time of suffering. This summons stands in stark contrast to the people's present posture, in which, ashamed at no longer being able to perform the Temple sacrifices, they have silently withdrawn from public worship [Simkins].

QUESTION—What is the significance of the speech margin נְאֻם־יְהוָה *nəʾum-yhwh* 'oracle of YHWH'?

This is the only occurrence of this formulaic expression in Joel, and so it carries heavy prominence. It marks a crisis, a turning point: in addition to the prospect of facing the apocalyptic army of YHWH, the people are also issued an ultimatum, cast in terms of an invitation, to turn to him [Wolff]. This verse is the first in Joel to present direct reported speech of YHWH, and it can be seen as foreshadowing Part 2 of the book, which is composed mostly of reported speech of YHWH [Wendland].

QUESTION—What is the significance of the command וְשֻׁבוּ *wəšûḇû* 'return/turn'?

1. This command means to completely reorient oneself to YHWH, both in thought and in behavior. The word שׁוּב *šûḇ* 'to return' was part of the vocabulary of repentance and prophecy long before Joel's time; from the times of Amos, Hosea, and Jeremiah, it was associated with vocabulary relating to the day of YHWH [Wolff].
2. In the OT *šûḇ* sometimes refers, not to repentance, but to the people's response to YHWH's salvation, as in Isa. 44:21–23: "turn to me, for I have redeemed you." Here the sense is not 'repent', but 'acknowledge', YHWH's salvation. Within an honor-shame model, Joel is then seen as summoning the people to continue to demonstrate their loyalty to YHWH by honoring him in public worship, even in the midst of suffering [Simkins].

QUESTION—Of what is the phrase וְשׁוּבוּ אֶל־יְהוָה אֱלֹהֵיכֶם *wəšûḇû ʾel-yhwh ʾĕlōhêḵem* 'return to YHWH your God' reminiscent?

It is reminiscent of Deut. 4:30, 30:2, and Mal. 3:1–3, although this last passage includes an expression of reciprocity on the part of YHWH [Crenshaw].

QUESTION—What significance is attached to Joel's admonition to engage in rites of mourning before YHWH?

1. Although some OT prophets are considered by many commentators to be against the use of religious ceremonies (since they sometimes anathematize them as dead rituals), this passage shows that Joel is not against the use of ritual when it comes from sincere intention [Wolff].
2. In a society characterized by a strong honor-shame dynamic, Joel's summons to engage in rites of mourning before YHWH evokes perfectly what should be the community's appropriate and loyal response to YHWH in times of suffering [Simkins].

2:13

And[a]-tear(p)[b] your(p)-heart(s)[c] and[d]-not (only) your(p)-garment(s),[e]
and[f]-turn(p)/return(p)[g] to[h]-YHWH your(p)-God,[i] for[j] gracious[k] and-compassionate[l] (is) he,
slowness(-of)[m] anger[n] and-great[o] (in) faithfulness[p] and[q]-relenting[t] from[s] the-intended-evil.[t]

INTERTEXTUAL REFERENCE—One part of this verse is very close to Exod. 34:6 [Crenshaw, Wendland].

SYNTAX—An athnach stands in the MT at the end of אֶל־יְהוָה אֱלֹהֵיכֶם *ʾel-yhwh ʾĕlōhêḵem* 'to YHWH your God', thus setting off the exhorted human activity from YHWH and his nature [Crenshaw].

LEXICON—a. **and-tear(p) your(p)-heart(s)** -וְ *wə- waw* connective [BDB p. 251], [Hol p. 84], [TWOT 519]: 'and' [Keil; KJV, NASB]. This word signals an additive relation, which Crenshaw, Allen, Dillard, Wolff, REB, NRSV, and TEV express with a new clause or sentence.

b. **and-tear(p) your(p)-heart(s)** masc. pl. Qal imper. of קרע *qrʿ* [BDB p. 902], [Hol p. 326], [TWOT 2074]: 'to tear' [BDB; Allen; TEV], 'to tear up' [Hol], 'to rend' [Crenshaw, Keil, Dillard, Wolff; KJV, NASB, NIV, NRSV, REB]. TEV translates וְקִרְעוּ לְבַבְכֶם וְאַל־בִּגְדֵיכֶם *wəqirʿû ləḇaḇḵem wəʾal-biḡdêḵem* 'and tear your hearts and not your garments' less figuratively: "let your broken heart show your sorrow; tearing your clothes is not enough."

c. **and-tear(p) your(p)-heart(s)** constr. of לֵבָב *lēḇāḇ* [BDB p. 523], [Hol p. 172], [TWOT 1071a]: 'heart' [BDB, Hol; Keil, Allen, Dillard, Wolff; KJV, NASB, NIV, NRSV, REB, TEV], 'inner disposition' [Crenshaw]. *Lēḇāḇ* refers to the seat of human reason and will. The singular is here understood as a generic reference, which allows for a plural translation.

d. **and-not your(p)-garments** -וְ *wə- waw* connective [BDB p. 251], [Hol p. 84], [TWOT 519]: 'and' [Crenshaw, Keil, Dillard, Wolff; KJV, NASB, NRSV, REB]. This word signals an additive relation, which the TEV expresses with a new clause.

e. **and-not (only) your(p)-garment(s)** constr. of בֶּגֶד *beḡeḏ* [BDB p. 93], [Hol p. 33], [TWOT 198d]: 'garment' [BDB, Hol; Keil, Dillard, Wolff; KJV, NASB, NIV, REB], 'clothes' [Hol; Crenshaw, Allen; TEV], 'clothing' [BDB; NRSV]. The singular 'garment' is here understood as a generic reference, which allows for a plural translation.

f. **and-turn(p)/return(p) to-YHWH** -וְ *wə-* *waw* connective [BDB p. 251], [Hol p. 84], [TWOT 519]: 'and' [Keil, Allen, Dillard; KJV, REB], 'now' [NASB], 'then' [Crenshaw]. This word signals an additive relation, which Wolff, NRSV, and TEV express with a new clause or sentence.

g. **and-turn(p)/return(p) to-YHWH** masc. pl. Qal imper. of שׁוּב *šûḇ* [BDB p. 996], [Hol p. 362], [TWOT 2340]: 'to turn' [Dillard; KJV], 'to return' [BDB, Hol; Crenshaw, Allen, Wolff; NASB, NRSV], 'to turn back' [BDB; REB], 'to come back' [Hol; TEV].

h. **to-YHWH** אֶל *ʾel* [BDB p. 39], [Hol p. 16], [TWOT 91]: 'unto/to' [all lexica, commentators, and versions].

i. **to-YHWH your(p)-God** constr. of אֱלֹהִים *ʾĕlōhîm* [BDB p. 43], [Hol p. 16], [TWOT 93c]: 'God' [all lexica, commentators, and versions].

j. **for gracious and-compassionate (is) he** כִּי *kî* particle [BDB p. 471], [Hol p. 155], [TWOT 976]: 'for' [Crenshaw, Keil, Dillard, Wolff; KJV, NIV, NASB, NRSV, REB], 'because' [Allen], not explicit [TEV].

k. **gracious and-compassionate (is) he** חַנּוּן *ḥannûn* [BDB p. 337], [Hol p. 110], [TWOT 694d]: 'gracious' [BDB, Hol; Keil, Dillard, Wolff; KJV, NASB, NIV, NRSV, REB], 'merciful' [Crenshaw], 'kind' [TEV], 'kindly' [Allen]. In the OT *ḥannûn* qualifies only "God" [BDB] and signifies the good will which a superior party shows an inferior party [Wolff].

l. **compassionate** רַחוּם *raḥûm* [BDB p. 933], [Hol p. 337], [TWOT 2146c]: 'compassionate' [BDB, Hol; Crenshaw, Allen, Dillard; NASB, NIV, REB], 'merciful' [Keil, Wolff; KJV, NRSV], 'full of mercy' [TEV]. *Raḥûm* denotes the tenderness a parent might show his children [Wolff].

m. **slowness(-of) anger and-great (in) faithfulness** constr. of assumed אֶרֶךְ *ʾārēḵ* [BDB p. 74], [Hol p. 28], [TWOT 162b]: in combination with אַף *ʾap̄* (see *n* below), 'slow' [Hol; Dillard; NIV, NRSV], 'long-suffering' [Keil; REB], 'slow to anger' [BDB; Dillard; KJV, NASB], 'patient' [Crenshaw, Wolff; TEV], 'so patient' [Allen].

n. **slowness(-of) anger** dual of אַף *ʾap̄* [BDB p. 60], [Hol p. 24], [TWOT 133a]: 'anger' [BDB, Hol; Dillard; KJV, NIV, NRSV]. Literally, אַפַּיִם *ʾappayim* (the plural of *ʾap̄*) means 'nostrils' [Hol].

o. **and-great (in) faithfulness** רַב *raḇ* [BDB p. 912], [Hol p. 330], [TWOT 2099a]: 'great' in quantity [BDB, Hol; Keil; KJV], 'abounding' [Wolff; NASB, NIV, NRSV], 'lavish' [Allen].

p. **<u>faithfulness</u>** חֶסֶד *ḥesed* [BDB p. 338], [Hol p. 111], [TWOT 698a]: 'faithfulness' [Hol], 'steadfast love' [Wolff; NRSV], 'love' [NIV], 'kindness' [BDB; Keil; KJV], 'goodness' [BDB], 'lovingkindness' [NASB], 'loyal love' [Allen]. The expression וְרַב־חֶסֶד *wərab̲-ḥesed̲* is translated as "unfailingly faithful" [Dillard], "ever constant" [REB], "abundantly loyal" [Crenshaw], and "he keeps his promise" [TEV].

q. **<u>and</u>-relenting from the-intended-evil** -וְ *wə-* *waw* connective [BDB p. 251], [Hol p. 84], [TWOT 519]: 'and' [Keil, Dillard, Wolff; KJV, NASB]. Crenshaw, REB, and TEV express the additive relation with a new clause, Allen with a new phrase.

r. **<u>relenting</u>** 3rd masc. sing. Niphal part. of נחם *nḥm* [BDB p. 636], [Hol p. 234], [TWOT 1344]: 'to relent' [Dillard; NASB, NIV, NRSV], 'to regret' [Hol], 'to have a change of heart' [Hol], 'to suffer oneself to repent' [Keil], 'to repent (of ill done to others)' [BDB; Crenshaw, Wolff; KJV]. Several amplify the phrase וְנִחָם עַל־הָרָעָה *wəniḥām ᶜal-hārāᶜâ* 'and relenting from the evil', translating it "ready always to relent when he threatens disaster" [REB], "he is always ready to forgive and not punish" [TEV], and "ready to relent" [Allen]. Since YHWH commits no wrong, the focus of this word, when it is applied to him, is upon his change of mind: he relents from inflicting punishment—rather than upon sorrow for wrong committed by him [Dillard].

s. **relenting <u>from</u> the-intended-evil** עַל *ᶜal* [BDB p. 752], [Hol p. 272], [TWOT 1624p): 'from' [Dillard; NIV, NRSV], 'of' [Keil, Wolff; KJV, NASB], 'about' [Crenshaw], 'over' [Allen].

t. **<u>intended-evil</u>** רָעָה *rāᶜâ* [BDB p. 949], [Hol p. 342], [TWOT 2191c]: 'intended evil' [Hol], 'evil' [BDB; Keil, Wolff; KJV, NASB], 'intended harm' [Hol], 'punishing' [NRSV], 'doing harm' [Dillard], 'harm' [Crenshaw], 'disaster' [REB], 'punishment' [Allen]. TEV translates this noun as a verb, "punish"; NIV, as a verb phrase, "sending calamity." Here *rāᶜâ* connotes ruin or disaster [Wolff]. This "evil," of course, is the punishment intended by God. It is evil from a human point of view only and certainly not from God's point of view, since divine punishment cannot be considered a moral wrong.

QUESTION—What are the general features of this verse?

This verse reverts from divine speech to speech about God in the third person. It also uses the weaker preposition אֶל *ᵓel* 'to' instead of the stronger עַד *ᶜad̲* 'to' found in Hos. 14:2 and Amos 4:6 [Crenshaw].

QUESTION—What considerations affect the interpretation of the expression וְשׁוּבוּ *wəšûb̲û* 'and return/turn'?

The rendering 'return' would probably imply that the people were guilty of some sin left unstated by Joel. The rendering 'turn' would not necessarily imply that the people were guilty of specific sin against YHWH, but that they should rather turn to him in trust. Joel does not use the verb שׁוּב *šûb̲* in the sense in which Hosea and Jeremiah used it: they used it to denote the abandoning of the worship of idols. Nor does he use it in the sense of

Amos, Isaiah, and Ezekiel: they used it to denote the abandoning of wrong behavior. Rather, Joel employs *šûḇ* in the Deuteronomistic sense of hearing and obeying the word of YHWH [Wolff].

QUESTION—What is the significance of וְקִרְעוּ לְבַבְכֶם וְאַל־בִּגְדֵיכֶם *wəqirᶜû ləḇaḇḵem wəʾal-biḡḏêḵem* 'and tear up your hearts and not your garments'?

It is that God desires repentance from the heart, not merely outward signs of it. Tearing one's clothes apart to put on sackcloth is an outward act of remorse, insufficient in the face of the need to "tear up one's heart" [Dillard], which is to have true contrition for sin, as in Ps. 51:19 [Keil]. Thus Joel echoes the same opposition to empty rituals as do other prophets before him—Isaiah, Jeremiah, Amos, and Micah. Joel is not, however, against ritual as such—he specifically admonishes the people to fast, weep, and mourn. Therefore a translation should read, in effect, 'and not *only* your garments'. *Lēḇaḇ*, normally mistranslated as 'heart', was in BH the seat of the will and thought, while the feelings were situated in the kidneys [Crenshaw]. The emphasis is upon sincere singleness of purpose necessary for repentance or upon the ritual expression of repentance, and not upon emotionalism (which would be presumed from the usual misunderstanding of the meaning of *lēḇaḇ*).

QUESTION—What is the import of the *kî* particle in this verse?

Here *kî* introduces the grounds for Joel's exhortation to turn to YHWH: Joel does not look to past instances of YHWH's deliverance, but rather to his inherent qualities of patience and faithfulness [Crenshaw].

QUESTION—What is the source elsewhere in the Old Testament of the phrase כִּי־חַנּוּן וְרַחוּם הוּא אֶרֶךְ אַפַּיִם וְרַב־חֶסֶד וְנִחָם עַל־הָרָעָה *kî-ḥannûn wəraḥûm hûʾ ʾereḵ ʾappayim wəraḇ-ḥeseḏ wəniḥām ᶜal-hārāᶜâ* 'for he is gracious and compassionate, slow to anger and great in faithfulness, and relents from the evil?'

1. It apparently comes from Jon. 4:2. Some scholars view this and similar lists of YHWH's saving attributes as a kind of liturgical confession. This "creed," reluctantly enunciated by Jonah concerning the pagan Ninevites, is here applied by Joel to YHWH's own people [Dillard, Wolff]. The view that Jonah is the source of this quotation by Joel is strengthened by the fact that 2:14a also appears to come from Jonah (Jon. 3:9a). Even the contexts are similar. In both Jonah and Joel, YHWH's repenting of intended evil is hoped for on the basis of the people's first returning to him [Wolff].
2. The earliest source is Exod. 34:6–7: "YHWH is God compassionate and gracious (רַחוּם וְחַנּוּן *raḥûm wəhannûn*), slow to anger (אֶרֶךְ אַפַּיִם *ʾereḵ ʾappayim*) and great in faithfulness and truth (וְרַב־חֶסֶד וֶאֱמֶת *wəraḇ-ḥeseḏ weʾĕmeṯ*)." This statement, which is of a creedal nature, occurs in various forms elsewhere in the OT: Num. 14:18; Pss. 86:15; 103:8; 145:8; Nah, 1:3; Jon. 4:2; and Neh. 9:17, 31. Although Joel

2:13 is very similar to Jon. 4:2, it is unclear who borrowed it from whom [Crenshaw].

QUESTION—What is the significance of the phrase וְנִחָם עַל־הָרָעָה *wəniḥām ᶜal-hārāᶜâ* 'and relenting from the evil' for this "creedal statement"?

This phrase represents a kind of expansion of the "creed." It served to apply the "creed" to the coming judgment announced by the prophets in an effort to motivate the people's repentance [Wolff].

QUESTION—What is the relation signaled by the *waw* connective attached to וְנִחָם עַל־הָרָעָה *wəniḥām ᶜal-hārāᶜâ* 'and relenting from the evil'?

It is tantamount to a result relation: as a result of his compassion and forbearance, God relents from inflicting harm [Dillard]. (But note that the mood of "to relent" here must be one of possibility, ability or desire: he might relent, he can relent, or he desires to relent. This mode does not appear to be one which signals habitual action, that he always relents, for the prophet explicitly indicates only possibility, not certainty, in the next verse— מִי יוֹדֵעַ *mî yôḏēaᶜ* 'who knows?').

2:14

Who (is) (the-)one-knowing[a] (whether) he-will-turn[b] and-relent[c] and-leave[d] behind[e]-him blessing,[f]
sacrifice[g] and-drink-offering[h] for-YHWH our-God?[i]

LEXICON—a. **who (is) (the-)one-knowing** masc. sing. Qal part. of ידע *yḏᶜ* [BDB p. 393], [Hol p. 128], [TWOT 848]: 'to know' [BDB, Hol; Keil, Allen, Dillard; KJV, NASB, NIV, NRSV]. The phrase מִי יוֹדֵעַ *mî yôḏēaᶜ* 'who knows' is translated with the adverb "perhaps" by Crenshaw, Wolff, and TEV. The REB translates it as "it may be."

b. **(whether) he-will-turn and-relent** 3rd masc. sing. Qal imperf. of שׁוּב *šûḇ* [BDB p. 996], [Hol p. 362], [TWOT 2340]: 'to turn' [Crenshaw, Keil, Allen, Dillard, Wolff; KJV, NASB, NIV, NRSV], 'to return' [BDB, Hol], 'to turn back' [REB]. TEV translates the phrase יָשׁוּב וְנִחָם *yāšûḇ wəniḥām* 'will turn and relent' as "will change his mind."

c. **(whether) he-will-turn and-relent** 3rd masc. sing. Piel perf. of נחם *nḥm* [BDB p. 636], [Hol p. 234], [TWOT 1344]: 'to relent' [Crenshaw, Allen, Dillard; NASB, NRSV, REB], 'to comfort' [Hol], 'to have pity' [NIV], 'to repent' [Keil, Wolff], 'to repent (of ill done to others)' [BDB; KJV].

d. **and-leave behind-him blessing** 3rd masc. sing. Hiphil perf. of שׁאר *šʾr* [BDB p. 983], [Hol p. 357], [TWOT 2307]: 'to leave something or someone remaining' [Hol], 'to leave' [BDB; Crenshaw, Keil, Allen, Dillard, Wolff; KJV, NASB, NIV, NRSV, REB]. TEV translates the phrase וְהִשְׁאִיר אַחֲרָיו בְּרָכָה *wəhišʾîr ʾaḥărâw bərāḵâ* 'and leave after him blessing' concretely as "and bless you with abundant crops."

e. **and-leave <u>behind</u>-him blessing** constr. of אַחַר *ʾaḥar* [BDB p. 29], [Hol p. 10], [TWOT 68b]: 'behind' [BDB, Hol; Keil, Allen, Dillard, Wolff; KJV, NASB, NIV, NRSV, REB]. Crenshaw translates the expression אַחֲרָיו *ʾaḥărāyw* 'behind him' as "in his wake."

f. **<u>blessing</u>** בְּרָכָה *bərāḵâ* [BDB p. 139], [Hol p. 50], [TWOT 285b]: 'blessing' [BDB, Hol; Crenshaw, Keil, Allen, Dillard, Wolff; KJV, NASB, NIV, NRSV, REB]. TEV interprets *bərāḵâ* 'blessing' concretely and translates it "abundant crops."

g. **<u>sacrifice</u> and-drink-offering** מִנְחָה *minḥâ* [BDB p. 585], [Hol p. 202], [TWOT 1214a]: 'sacrifice' [Hol], 'tribute' [BDB], 'offering' [BDB; Allen], 'grain offering' [Dillard; NASB, NIV, NRSV, REB], 'meat offering' [Keil; KJV, NIV], 'meal offering' [Wolff], 'cereal offering' [Crenshaw]. The REB and TEV translate מִנְחָה וָנֶסֶךְ לַיהוָה אֱלֹהֵיכֶם *minḥâ wānesek laywhw ʾĕlōhêḵem* 'sacrifice and drink offering for YHWH your God' as a result concept: REB has "blessing enough for grain-offerings and drink-offerings to be presented to the Lord your God"; TEV has "then you can offer him grain and wine."

h. **and-<u>drink-offering</u>** נֶסֶךְ *neseḵ* [BDB p. 651], [Hol p. 239], [TWOT 1375a]: 'drink offering' [BDB, Hol; Keil; KJV, NIV, NRSV, REB], 'libation' [Crenshaw, Allen, Dillard, Wolff; NASB].

i. **for-YHWH our-<u>God</u>** constr. of אֱלֹהִים *ʾĕlōhîm* [BDB p. 43], [Hol p. 16], [TWOT 93c]: 'God' [all lexica, commentators, and versions].

QUESTION—What is the significance of מִי יוֹדֵעַ *mî yôḏēaᶜ* 'who knows'?

1. With this phrase, Joel continues to cite the account of Jonah, specifically Jon. 3:9; or at least the two texts continue to resemble each other [Crenshaw]. The phrase means 'perhaps', but in a particular sense: It casts doubt not on God's readiness to forgive and restore, but rather upon the readiness of the population to seize upon that forgiveness, for the people might be too complacent in the face of the teaching of YHWH's forgiving nature or they might be too despairing of his forgiveness [Crenshaw, Keil].
2. Paradoxically, although God is only too ready to forgive, his forgiveness is never engineered by man's repentance and so must never be presumed upon. In this sense also, the phrase *mî yôḏēaᶜ* is very appropriate [Edmond Jacob, Carl-A. Keller, and Samuel Amsler, *Osée, Joel, Abdias, Jonas, Amos*, Commentaire de l'Ancien Testament 11a (Neuchâtel: Delachaux & Niestlé, 1965), cited by Dillard; Wolff]. *Mî yôḏēaᶜ* must therefore spring from the humble attitude of one who is caught in judgment [Wolff].
3. God is forgiving, but Israel's sins are perhaps too great for God to forgive [twelfth-century Jewish commentator Kimchi, cited by Cohen].
4. The phrase means "whoever knows he has sinned should repent" [Targum and Rashi, cited by Cohen].

QUESTION—What is the meaning of יָשׁוּב *yāšûḇ* in the phrase יָשׁוּב וְנִחָם *yāšûḇ wəniḥām* 'he will turn/return and relent'?

Yāšûḇ may mean to turn away from anger. In a longer expression in Exod. 32:12, in which the two verbs *šûḇ* and נחם *nḥm* appear, Joel's exhortation to the people to turn is balanced by his speaking of YHWH as perhaps turning away from his anger [Crenshaw, Wolff]. The notions that YHWH is slow to anger and that he might turn from his anger, the basis for the idea of 'perhaps', underscore the knowledge that YHWH is not a slave to his emotions [Wolff].

QUESTION—What is the meaning of וְהִשְׁאִיר אַחֲרָיו *wəhiš'îr 'aḥărāyw* 'and he may leave behind him'?

It is that YHWH, having come to render judgment, may instead leave a blessing upon his people before he returns to where he came from [Keil], blessing being the opposite of judgment [Crenshaw]. Leaving a blessing would then be seen as the evidence that YHWH had turned away from his anger [Wolff].

QUESTION—What is the relation of מִנְחָה וָנֶסֶךְ *minḥâ wānesek* 'sacrifice and drink offering' to the preceding בְּרָכָה *bərāḵâ* 'blessing'?

It is one of explanatory apposition: YHWH may prosper the agriculture so as to allow the people to bring him offerings from their produce [Keil]. This phrase employs synecdoche, a figure of speech in which a part stands for a whole: the offerings stand for something much larger in quantity than themselves, a successful harvest [Cohen, Crenshaw], and, in fact, the renewal of life itself [Wolff]. At the same time the expression לַיהוָה אֱלֹהֵיכֶם *layhwh 'ĕlōhêḵem* 'for YHWH your God' stresses that this life is not to be lived for itself, but rather in a covenantal relationship with YHWH [Crenshaw], a life possible only through his compassion [Wolff].

QUESTION—What are the intertextual dynamics of אַחֲרָיו *'aḥărāyw* 'after him' in the phrase וְהִשְׁאִיר אַחֲרָיו בְּרָכָה *wəhiš'îr 'aḥărāyw bərāḵâ* 'and leave a blessing after him'?

The use of the word *'aḥărāyw* here recalls the use of the same word in 2:3: 'and after it (*wə'aḥărāyw*) flames have scorched'. But whereas 2:3 describes destruction wrought by the divine army, 2:14 refers to the divine mercy which repentance may elicit [Crenshaw, Wolff].

2:15

Blow(p)[a] (a-)ram's-horn[b] on[c]-Zion,[d]
announce-a-holy(p)[e] fast,[f] call(p)[g] (a-)solemn-assembly.[h]

LEXICON—a. **blow(p)** **(a-)ram's-horn** masc. pl. Qal imper. of תקע *tq'* [BDB p. 1075], [Hol p. 394], [TWOT 2541]: 'to blow' a wind instrument [BDB, Hol; Crenshaw, Keil, Allen, Dillard, Wolff; KJV, NASB, NIV, NRSV, REB, TEV].

b. **blow(p) (a-)ram's-horn** שׁוֹפָר *šôpār* [BDB p. 1051], [Hol p. 364], [TWOT 2449c]: 'ram's horn' [Hol; Crenshaw], 'trumpet [Keil, Dillard; KJV, NASB, NIV, NRSV, REB, TEV], 'horn' (for blowing) [BDB;

Allen, Wolff]. The trumpet blast is not to signal the approach of danger as in 2:1, but a religious assembly [Cohen].

c. **on-Zion** -בְּ *bə-* [BDB p. 88], [Hol p. 32], [TWOT 193]: 'on' [Dillard, Wolff; TEV], 'in' [Crenshaw, Keil, Allen, Dillard; KJV, NASB, NIV, NRSV, REB].

d. **Zion** צִיּוֹן *ṣiyyôn* [BDB p. 851], [Hol p. 306], [TWOT 1910]: 'Zion' [BDB; Crenshaw, Keil, Allen, Dillard, Wolff; KJV, NASB, NIV, NRSV, REB], 'Mount Zion' [TEV].

e. **announce-a-holy(p) fast** masc. pl. Piel imper. of קדשׁ *qdš* [BDB p. 873], [Hol p. 313], [TWOT 1990]: 'to announce' [Wolff], 'to order' [Allen], 'to appoint a holy day' [Hol], 'to observe as holy' [BDB], 'to declare' [NIV], 'to proclaim' [Dillard], 'to sanctify' [Keil; KJV, NRSV], 'to inaugurate' [Crenshaw], 'to consecrate' [NASB], 'to give orders for' [TEV], 'to appoint' [REB].

f. **(a-)fast** צוֹם *ṣôm* [BDB p. 847], [Hol p. 304], [TWOT 1890a]: 'fast' [BDB, Hol; Keil, Dillard; KJV, NASB, NRSV, TEV], 'holy fast' [Crenshaw, Wolff; NIV], 'solemn fast' [REB], 'sacred fast' [Allen].

g. **call(p) (a-)solemn-assembly** masc. pl. Qal imper. of קרא *qrʾ* [BDB p. 894], [Hol p. 323], [TWOT 2063]: 'to call' [Hol; KJV, NIV, NRSV, TEV], 'to proclaim' [Keil, Allen, Dillard, Wolff; NASB, REB], 'to summon' [BDB; Hol], 'to announce' [Crenshaw]. This word implies the proclamation of a solemn assembly and a banning of work on that day [Gösta W. Ahlström, *Joel and the Temple Cult of Jerusalem*, Supplement to *Vetus Testamentum* 21 (Leiden: Brill, 1971), cited by Dillard].

h. **(a-)solemn-assembly** עֲצָרָה *ʿăṣārâ* [BDB p. 783], [Hol p. 281], [TWOT 1675c]: 'solemn assembly' [KJV, NASB, NRSV], 'festive assembly' [Hol], 'sacred assembly' [BDB; NIV], 'assembly' [TEV], 'meeting' [Keil], 'convocation' [Dillard], 'solemn holiday' [Wolff], 'religious gathering' [Crenshaw], 'day of abstinence' [REB], 'special service' [Allen]. Keil says that *ʿăṣārâ* denotes a meeting for the purposes of worship.

QUESTION—To whom is the command תִּקְעוּ שׁוֹפָר בְּצִיּוֹן *tiqʿû šôpār bəṣiyyôn* 'blow a trumpet on Zion' addressed?

1. It is probably addressed to the Temple officials [Dillard].
2. The addressees are ambiguous: if the priests are addressed, then one would expect for them to be addressed directly in the second person in 2:17 as well [Crenshaw].

QUESTION—What role is played by 2:15–17?

1. These verses consitute a summons to national repentance in the Temple [Keil, Dillard]. Not only does Joel take pains to ensure that everyone in the community participate, but he also provides in 2:17 the very prayer that should be used [Keil]. Crenshaw assumes that Joel's exhortation in 2:12–14 is true, that the command to inner repentance has been heeded by the priests and people, and that, thus encouraged, Joel now calls them to external rites of sorrow.

2. These verses comprise a set of instructions for the fresh turning to YHWH to which the prophet has summoned the people. These instructions are parallel to the instructions given in 1:13–14 for the lamentation announced in 1:5–12 [Wolff].
3. Bewer proposes that the imperatives of 2:15–17 be rendered so as to indicate narration: the ram horn was blown, a fast was announced, a religious gathering was scheduled, etc. Narration is presumed to be necessary in order to pave the way for the narration of YHWH's merciful response beginning in 2:18. But no version lends any support for such a reading [Crenshaw].

2:16

Gather(p)[a] (the-)people,[b] announce-(a)-sacred(p)[c] assembly,[d]
gather(p)[e] (the-) elders,[f]
gather(p)[g] (the-)children[h] and[i]-those-who-suck[j] (the-)breasts,[k]
let- (the-)bridegroom[l] come-out[m] from-his-chamber[n] and-(the-)bride[o] from-her-bridal-chamber.[p]

LEXICON—a. **gather(p) (the-)people** 3rd masc. pl. Qal imper. of אסף *ʾsp̄* [BDB p. 62], [Hol p. 23], [TWOT 140]: 'to gather' [BDB, Hol; Dillard, Wolff; KJV, NASB, NIV, NRSV], 'to gather together' [Keil; REB, TEV], 'to collect' [BDB], 'to assemble' [Crenshaw, Allen].

b. **gather(p) (the-)people** עָם *ᶜām* [BDB p. 766], [Hol p. 275], [TWOT 1640a]: 'people' [BDB, Hol; Crenshaw, Keil, Allen, Dillard, Wolff; KJV, NASB, NIV, NRSV, REB, TEV]. Here *ᶜām* denotes the population of the covenantal community.

c. **announce-a-sacred(p) assembly** masc. pl. Piel imper. of קדשׁ *qḏš* [BDB p. 873], [Hol p. 313], [TWOT 1990]: 'to arrange' [Allen], 'to sanctify' [Crenshaw, Keil, Wolff; KJV, NASB, NRSV], 'to appoint a holy day' [Hol], 'to consecrate' [NIV], 'to proclaim' [Dillard], 'to observe as holy' [BDB], 'to appoint' [REB]. TEV translates the phrase קַדְּשׁוּ קָהָל *qaddəšû qāhāl* 'sanctify the assembly' as "prepare them for a sacred meeting." This preparation prohibited work, food, and marital relations [Crenshaw, Wolff]. On this basis, the phrase *qaddəšû qāhāl* should be understood as calling upon the religious leaders to get the population ready to assemble in order to call upon YHWH.

d. **announce-a-sacred(p) assembly** קָהָל *qāhāl* [BDB p. 874], [Hol p. 314], [TWOT 1991a]: 'assembly' [BDB, Hol; Keil; NIV], 'convocation' [BDB, Hol; Dillard], 'congregation' [BDB; Crenshaw, Wolff; KJV, NASB, NRSV], 'sacred meeting' [TEV], 'religious meeting' [Allen], 'solemn assembly' [REB].

e. **gather(p) (the-) elders** 3rd masc. pl. Qal imper. of קבץ *qḇṣ* [BDB p. 867], [Hol p. 312], [TWOT 1983]: 'to gather' [BDB, Hol; Allen], 'to collect' [BDB], 'to assemble' [Hol; Wolff; KJV, NASB, NRSV], 'to bring together' [Crenshaw, Keil; NIV], 'to summon' [Dillard; REB], 'to bring' [TEV].

f. **(the-) elders** pl. of זָקֵן *zāqēn* [BDB p. 278], [Hol p. 91], [TWOT 574b]: 'elders' [BDB, Hol; Dillard; KJV, NASB, NIV, REB], 'old men' [Keil; Allen], 'the aged' [NRSV], 'the elderly people' [Crenshaw], 'the old people' [Wolff; TEV]. Here the term probably denotes the aged people, not the class of local leaders [Wolff].

g. **gather(p) (the-)children** 3rd masc. pl. Qal imper. of אסף *ʾsp̄* (see *e* above): 'to gather' [Wolff; REB, TEV], 'to assemble' [Allen].

h. **(the-)children** pl. of עוֹלָל *ʿôlāl* [BDB p. 760], [Hol p. 267], [TWOT 1579d]: 'child' [BDB, Hol; Keil, Allen, Dillard, Wolff; KJV, NASB, NIV, NRSV, REB, TEV], 'infant' [Crenshaw]. In the OT *ʿôlāl* covers a range of meaning. Here where it is followed by an expression denoting small babies, it probably designates small children as opposed to babies [Dillard].

i. **and-those-who-suck (the-)breasts** -וְ *wə- waw* connective [BDB p. 251], [Hol p. 84], [TWOT 519]: 'even' [Allen, Dillard, Wolff; NRSV, REB, TEV], 'and' [all other versions].

j. **those-who-suck (the-)breasts** pl. constr. Qal part. of ינק *ynq* [BDB p. 413], [Hol p. 136], [TWOT 874]: 'to suck' [BDB, Hol; Wolff; KJV], 'to nurse' [Dillard; NIV], 'to feed' [Crenshaw]. Keil translates this participle as "suckling"; NASB and NRSV have "infant"; REB, "babe."

k. **(the-)breasts** dual. of שַׁד *šaḏ* [BDB p. 994], [Hol p. 361], [TWOT 2332a]: 'breast' [Hol; Crenshaw; KJV, NIV]. The construct relationship between יֹנְקֵי *yōnəqê* 'those who suck' and שָׁדָיִם *šāḏāyim* 'breasts' is translated locatively by Crenshaw: "on breasts." Keil, Dillard, Wolff, NIV, NRSV, and REB have "at the breast." NASB has a noun phrase, "nursing infant"; Allen has "breastfed babies." TEV translates וְיֹנְקֵי שָׁדָיִם *wəyōnəqê šāḏāyim* 'the sucklings of breasts' as "babies."

l. **let- (the-)bridegroom come-out from-his-chamber** חָתָן *ḥāṯān* [BDB p. 368], [Hol p. 120], [TWOT 781c]: 'bridegroom' [BDB, Hol; Crenshaw, Keil, Dillard, Wolff; KJV, NASB, NIV, NRSV, REB], 'newlywed' [Allen]. The two clauses יֵצֵא חָתָן מֵחֶדְרוֹ וְכַלָּה מֵחֻפָּתָהּ *yēṣēʾ ḥāṯān mēḥeḏrô wəḵallâ mēḥuppāṯāh̠* 'let the bridegroom come out from his chamber and the bride from her bridal chamber' are conflated by TEV: "even newly married couples must leave their homes and come."

m. **come-out from-his-chamber** 3rd masc. sing. jussive of יצא *yṣʾ* [BDB p. 422], [Hol p. 139], [TWOT 893]: 'to come out' [BDB, Hol; NASB], 'to come forth' [Hol], 'to go out' [BDB; Keil], 'to leave' [Crenshaw, Allen, Dillard, Wolff; NIV, NRSV, REB], 'to go forth' [KJV]. The REB expresses the jussive by an extra verb in English: "bid the bridegroom leave." The jussive is not as strong as the imperative form and probably reflects the prophet's awareness of the grave situation facing the nation, one which would compel even bridegrooms, normally exempt from military service for a year, to participate in the national mourning [Crenshaw].

n. **<u>chamber</u>** constr. of חֶדֶר *ḥeḏer* [BDB p. 293], [Hol p. 96], [TWOT 612a]: 'chamber' [BDB; Keil, Dillard; KJV], 'dark room' [Hol], 'room' [BDB; Crenshaw, Wolff; NASB, NIV, NRSV], 'wedding chamber' [REB], 'bedroom' [Allen]. *Ḥeḏer* refers to the most secluded rooms of a house, to which newly married couples would naturally repair [Crenshaw, Wolff].

o. **and-(the-)<u>bride</u> from-her-bridal-chamber** כַּלָּה *kallâ* [BDB p. 483], [Hol p. 158], [TWOT 986a]: 'bride' [BDB, Hol; Crenshaw, Keil, Allen, Dillard, Wolff; KJV, NASB, NIV, NRSV, REB].

p. **<u>bridal-chamber</u>** constr. of חֻפָּה *ḥuppâ* [BDB p. 342], [Hol p. 112], [TWOT 710b]: 'bridal chamber' [Hol; NASB], 'chamber' [BDB; Crenshaw, Wolff; NIV], 'room' [Keil], 'canopy' [Dillard; NRSV], 'closet' [KJV], 'bower' [REB], 'place of honeymoon' [Allen].

QUESTION—Why does Joel take pains to include all the Jewish population, even infants, in his summons to repentance?

1. Joel does so, because all the population are deeply implicated in guilt before YHWH [Keil]. Although nursing mothers seem to have been exempt from worship obligations (see 1 Sam. 1:21–24), both they and their infants were to be present for this extraordinary convocation, such was the dire necessity of the entire people in this instance [Dillard, Wolff]. Joel is aware from the Isaiah (Isa. 13:16) and Ezekiel (Ezek. 30:17–18) passages concerning the day of YHWH that disaster will come to whole populations, not just to the fighting men. Similar references to brides and bridegrooms are also in Jer. 7:34 and 16:9 [Wolff].
2. The presence of even little infants is probably intended to arouse YHWH's pity [Kimchi, cited by Cohen; Crenshaw] and to move the adults to repentance [Cohen]. In this and the following verses, Joel is very specific about who should participate in the national mourning (everyone) and the manner in which the priests should lead the people, even down to the precise place in which the priests should stand [Crenshaw].

QUESTION—What is meant by חֻפָּה *ḥuppâ* 'bridal chamber'?

Ḥuppâ seems to have originally denoted the tent or room in which a marriage was consummated. In postbiblical times it came to signify the canopy under which the wedding was performed [Dillard], but it is referred to in Jewish law as the normal place of spousal cohabitation [Wolff]. The summons of even bride and groom suggests that even important human activities must be postponed in order that everyone may participate in the mass repentance before YHWH [Cohen, Dillard].

QUESTION—What is the rhetorical style of this verse?

The series of imperatives has a short, abrupt air, not dissimilar to military commands. The effect is one of urgency [Crenshaw].

2:17

Between[a] the-porch[b] and-the-altar[c] let- the-priests[d] -weep,[e]
(the-)ministers(-of)[f] YHWH, and[g]-let-them-say,[h] YHWH, look-compassionately(s)[i] upon your(s)-people,[j]
and[k]-do- not -hand-over(s)[l] your(s)-possession[m] to-mockery,[n] (MT) that (the-) nations[p] should-rule[o-1] over-them; (ET) to-scoffing[o-2] among-them (the-)nations;[p]
why[q] should-they-say among[r]-the-peoples,[s] where[t] (is) their-God[u]?

TEXT—The MT reading is לִמְשָׁל־בָּם גּוֹיִם *limšāl bām gôyim* 'that the nations should rule over them'. This view is summarized as follows (taken from Wolff):

MT consisting of		Remarks
לִמְשָׁל *limšāl*	proclitic -לְ *lə-* 'to' + Qal infin. of משׁל *mšl* 'to gain dominion over'	**Followed by:** Luther, Wolff, KJV.
בָּם *bām*	proclitic -בְּ *bə-* + the 3rd masc. pl. pron. 'them'; complement of 'over them'	**Supported by LXX:** μὴ δῷς τὴν κληρονομίαν σου εἰς ὄνειδος τοῦ κατάρξαι αὐτῶν ἔθνη 'do not give over your inheritance to the nations to rule over them in shame'.
גּוֹיִם *gôyim*	'nations', subject of verb	**Supported by Vulgate:** *ut dominentur eis Nationes* 'that the nations may rule over them'.

The ET reading is לִמְשַׁל בָּם גּוֹיִם *limšal bām gôyim* 'to scoffing among them, the nations' (see the semiliteral rendering of 2:17 in bold). This reading is summarized as follows:

Emendation consisting of		Remarks
לִמְשַׁל *li mšal*	the proclitic -לְ *lə-* 'to' + the construct of מָשָׁל *māšāl* 'scoffing' (the final vowel in *limšāl* is repointed to *limšal* to achieve the constr. form of the noun *māšāl* 'scoffing')	**Followed by:** Most commentators and versions. **Argument for:** The prophet perhaps intended that both 'to rule' and 'to taunt' be recognized here [Crenshaw].
בָּם *bām*	the proclitic -בְּ *bə-* + the 3rd masc. pl. pron. 'them'; complement of 'among them'	**Argument against:** The notion of taunting or mocking became necessary when interpreters assumed that the invaders were locusts, whether of the same plague or a different one from that described in Joel 1 [Wolff].
גּוֹיִם *gôyim*	'nations', in apposition with 'them'	**Argument against:** Apposition between the object of a preposition (as in *bām* 'among them') and the following noun is rare in BH [Dillard].

LEXICON—a. **<u>between</u> the-porch and-to-the-altar** בַּיִן *bayin* [BDB p. 107], [Hol p. 38], [TWOT 239a]: 'between' [BDB, Hol; Crenshaw, Keil, Allen, Dillard, Wolff; KJV, NASB, NIV, NRSV, REB, TEV]. *Bayin* is properly a noun signifying 'interval, space between' [BDB].

b. **the-<u>porch</u>** אוּלָם *ʾûlām* [BDB p. 17], [Hol p. 12], [TWOT 45c]: 'porch' [BDB; Crenshaw, Keil, Allen, Dillard; KJV, NASB, REB], 'vestibule' [Hol; Wolff; NRSV], 'entrance of the Temple' [TEV], 'temple porch' [NIV].

c. **and-to-the-<u>altar</u>** מִזְבֵּחַ *mizbēaḥ* [BDB p. 258], [Hol p. 188], [TWOT 525b]: 'altar' [BDB; Crenshaw, Keil, Allen, Dillard, Wolff; KJV, NASB, NIV, NRSV, REB, TEV].

d. **let- the-<u>priests</u> -weep** pl. of כֹּהֵן *kōhēn* [BDB p. 463], [Hol p. 152], [TWOT 959]: 'priest' [all lexica, commentators, and versions].

e. **let- the-priests -<u>weep</u>** 3rd masc. pl. jussive of בכה *bkh* [BDB p. 113], [Hol p. 39], [TWOT 243]: 'to weep' [BDB, Hol; Crenshaw, Keil, Allen, Dillard, Wolff; KJV, NASB, NIV, NRSV, REB, TEV], 'bewail' [BDB]. The REB also supplies 'stand': "let the ... ministers of the Lord stand weeping."

f. **(the-)<u>ministers(-of)</u> YHWH** masc. pl. constr. Piel part. of שׁרת *šrṯ* [BDB p. 1058], [Hol p. 384], [TWOT 2472]: 'to minister' [BDB; Crenshaw, Allen, Dillard, Wolff; KJV, NASB, NIV, NRSV, REB], 'to serve' [BDB; TEV], 'servant' [Keil]. The construct relationship between מְשָׁרְתֵי *məšārəṯê* 'ministers' and יְהוָה *yhwh* 'YHWH' is expressed by the preposition 'before' in the NIV: "who minister before the Lord." Keil expresses it with the preposition 'of': "servants of."

g. **<u>and</u>-let-them-say** -וְ *wə- waw* connective [BDB p. 251], [Hol p. 84], [TWOT 519]: 'and' [Keil; KJV, NASB, REB,TEV]. Crenshaw, Dillard, Wolff, NIV, and NRSV express the additive relation with a new clause or sentence.

h. **and-<u>let-them-say</u>** 3rd masc. pl. jussive of אמר *ʾmr* [BDB p. 55], [Hol p. 21], [TWOT 118]: 'to say' [BDB, Hol; Crenshaw, Keil, Allen, Dillard, Wolff; KJV, NASB, NIV, NRSV, REB], 'to pray' [TEV].

i. **YHWH, <u>look-compassionately(s)</u> upon your(s)-people** masc. sing. Qal imper. of חוּס *ḥûs* [BDB p. 299], [Hol p. 98], [TWOT 626]: 'to look compassionately' [Hol], 'to spare' [Keil; KJV, NASB, NIV, NRSV, REB], 'to have pity' [Crenshaw; TEV], 'to take pity' [Allen], 'to pity' [BDB; Wolff]. *Ḥûs* normally connotes the flowing of tears at the sight of suffering [Wolff].

j. **upon your(s)-<u>people</u>** constr. of עָם *ʿām* [BDB p. 766], [Hol p. 275], [TWOT 1640a]: 'people' [BDB, Hol; Crenshaw, Keil, Allen, Wolff; KJV, NASB, NIV, NRSV, REB, TEV]. The word *ʿām* denotes a people, emphasizing its ethnic unity [Hol].

k. **<u>and</u>-do- not -hand-over(s) your(s)-possession to-mockery** -וְ *wə- waw* connective [BDB p. 251], [Hol p. 84], [TWOT 519]: 'and' [Crenshaw, Keil; KJV, NASB, NRSV], not explicit [Allen, Wolff; NIV, REB, TEV].

l. **<u>do</u>- not -<u>hand-over(s)</u> your(s)-possession to-mockery** 2nd masc. sing. Qal imperf. of נתן *nṯn* [BDB p. 678], [Hol p. 249], [TWOT 1443]: 'to hand over' [Wolff], 'to give' [BDB, Hol; Keil; KJV], 'to make' [NASB,

NIV, NRSV], 'to expose' [REB], 'to surrender' [Crenshaw], 'to permit' [Allen].

m. **your(s)-<u>possession</u>** constr. of נַחֲלָה *naḥălâ* [BDB p. 635], [Hol p. 234], [TWOT 1342a]: 'possession' [Allen, Wolff], 'heritage' [Hol; NRSV, KJV], 'inheritance' [Keil, Dillard; NASB, NIV], 'people' [REB], 'property' [Crenshaw]. TEV employs the pronoun 'us' instead of the second person pronoun in *naḥălâṯəkâ* 'your possession'. *Naḥălâ* is used here in a sense rather similar to the OT use of סְגֻלָּה *səḡullâ* 'treasured possession' [Crenshaw, Wolff]. The traditional translations, 'inheritance' or 'heritage', although these are the root meaning of the noun, miss the sense of the word here [Wolff].

n. **to-<u>mockery</u>** חֶרְפָּה *ḥerpâ* [BDB p. 357], [Hol p. 117], [TWOT 749a]: 'mockery' [NRSV], 'abuse' [Hol], 'scorn' [Hol], 'disgrace' [Hol], 'reproach' [Crenshaw, Dillard; KJV, NASB], 'insult' [REB], 'object of scorn' [NIV], 'object of reproach' [BDB], 'shame' [Keil, Wolff]. TEV renders the noun *ḥerpâ* by a verb: "Do not let other nations despise us." Allen translates, "do not permit your possession to be ridiculed."

o-1. **that (the-)nations <u>should-rule</u> over-them** Qal infin. of מֹשׁל *mšl* [BDB p. 605, [Hol p. 219], [TWOT 1259]: 'to rule' [BDB, Hol; KJV], 'to gain dominion over' [BDB, Hol].

o-2. **to-<u>scoffing</u> among-them (the-)nations** constr. of מָשָׁל *māšāl* [BDB p. 605], [Hol p. 219], [TWOT 1258a]: 'saying' [Hol]. *Māšāl* here denotes a scoffing remark habitually aimed at a particular object of scorn [Keil], 'taunt' [Dillard], 'byword' [BDB; NASB, NIV, NRSV, REB]. This noun is rendered as a verb by some: 'to mock' [Crenshaw; TEV], 'to scoff' [Keil]. Allen has a noun phrase: "a swear word to be bandied about." The true construct of *māšāl* features a *paṯaḥ* in the second syllable; to understand a construct here requires a repointing of the MT.

p. **(the-)<u>nations</u>** pl. of גּוֹי *gôy* [BDB p. 156], [Hol p. 57], [TWOT 326e]: 'nation' [all commentators and versions except Keil, Wolff, KJV], 'heathen' [Keil; KJV], 'foreign nation' [Wolff].

q. **<u>why</u> should-they-say among-the-peoples** לָמָּה *lāmmâ* [BDB p. 552], [Hol p. 184]: 'why' [BDB, Hol; Crenshaw, Allen, Wolff; NASB, NIV, REB], 'wherefore' [Keil; KJV]. TEV translates the rhetorical question introduced by this interrogative particle as a prayer: "Do not let other nations despise us and mock us by saying...."

r. **<u>among</u>-the-peoples** -בְּ *bə-* [BDB p. 88], [Hol p. 32], [TWOT 193]: 'among' [Hol; Crenshaw, Keil, Allen, Dillard, Wolff; KJV, NASB, NIV, NRSV].

s. **the-<u>peoples</u>** pl. of עַם *ʿām* (see *j* above): 'people' [BDB, Hol; Crenshaw, Allen, Wolff; KJV, NASB, NIV, NRSV], 'nation' [Keil, Dillard; REB, TEV].

t. **<u>where</u> (is) their-God** אַיֵּה *ʾayyēh* [BDB p. 32], [Hol p. 12], [TWOT 75a]: 'where' [Hol; Crenshaw, Keil, Allen, Dillard, Wolff; KJV, NASB, NIV, NRSV, REB, TEV]. This is an interrogative particle.

u. **their-<u>God</u>** pl. constr. of אֱלֹהִים *ʾĕlōhîm* [BDB p. 43], [Hol p. 16], [TWOT 93c]: 'God' [BDB, Hol; Crenshaw, Keil, Allen, Dillard, Wolff; KJV, NASB, NIV, NRSV, REB, TEV].

QUESTION—What function of the priests is alluded to in this verse?

Here the priests are depicted in their liturgical role, that of leading the assembled people in repentance [Keil].

QUESTION—What place is indicated by the phrase בֵּין הָאוּלָם וְלַמִּזְבֵּחַ *bên hāʾûlām wəlammizbēaḥ* 'between the porch and the altar'?

It is just before the door of the holy place [Keil], near where stood the altar for burning offerings [Crenshaw]. It was while standing in this spot that the priests habitually interceded for the people through the sacrifices and their prayers [Dillard], for this spot served to separate the people from the holy place [Crenshaw]. It was also in this spot where a group of men turned their backs upon YHWH to worship the sun, as recounted in Ezek. 8:16. It is also the area of murder to which Christ referred in Matt. 23:35 [Wolff].

QUESTION—What is the significance of יִבְכּוּ *yiḇkû* 'let them weep'?

If this is read as a jussive form, which is normally weaker than an imperative, it may imply that the priests were already mourning. On the other hand, *yiḇkû* can also be read as an imperfect, 'they will weep' [Crenshaw].

QUESTION—What is the nature of the question 'Where is their God'?

This is a rhetorical question, mocking the covenant that existed between YHWH and Israel. It was by thus appealing to YHWH's honor that the priests might induce him to avert his punishment [Keil]. The question would most naturally have been sounded by the ethnic groups surrounding the Jews [Cohen], but might well have been in the minds of more than a few of Joel's countrymen [Crenshaw]. Wolff points out that such a question is much more powerful when it is assumed that Judah is faced, not with another agricultural crisis of invading locusts, but rather with the threat of extermination.

QUESTION—What is the discourse role of this strophe?

This strophe forms the peak of Part 1. In it, the prophet gives the substance of the prayer with which the priests are to intercede for the nation. Note that Stanza D implies two grounds for the prayer, that YHWH is merciful (2:13–14) and that YHWH's honor is in question (2:17) [Wendland].

Part 2 of Joel

All commentators recognize that Part 2 consists of 2:18–4:21 (3:21). For Bewer, Crenshaw, Keil, Allen, Dillard, and Wolff, 2:18, which begins the second half, or which perhaps functions as a transition between the halves, implies that Judah responds positively to the prophet's appeal to turn to YHWH.

Dillard characterizes Part 2 as "the Lord's answer." Keil entitles it "the promise of God to avert the judgment, and bestow an abundant blessing." Whereas Part 1 presents the reality of present judgment and the threat of coming judgment, Part 2 presents YHWH's answer to the cries for help which his people have sounded [Dillard].

DISCOURSE UNIT: 2:18–3:5 (2:18–32) [Allen, Wolff]. Wolff calls the topic "new life for all who call upon Yahweh"; Allen calls it "material and spiritual promises"; and Stuart, "restoration and the outpouring of the Spirit."

Comments on this discourse unit: In this discourse unit, one is led to the culminating declaration (2:27) of YHWH's sovereignty among his covenant people. The maintenance of 2:27's integrity in this passage by VanGemeren is in contrast to the view of Prinsloo that 2:27 was added by a redactor.

This discourse unit begins the book's second half and is introduced by 2:18 (but see the discussion under "SYNTAX" in 2:18 below), which gives the turning point in the book, and which introduces YHWH's plan for answering his people in their repentance: he will rescue them from their distress and defeat their enemies. Moreover, this section has the form of an assurance oracle in response to a cry for help. (This is discussed under 2:19 in connection with the use of הִנֵּה *hinnēh* 'behold' followed by a participle as a principal mark of such oracles. Another formal element of this kind of oracle is direct speech attributed to YHWH, which is presumably seen as more comforting than indirect speech.)

Unlike the many commentators and versions that take 3:1 (2:28) as beginning a major discourse unit, Wolff sees 3:1 (2:28) as signaling an explanation of the preceding verse, therefore as starting only the second half of a two-part oracle.

The intricate relationships of the various elements of this discourse unit lead one to view this text as a highly structured literary piece drawing on a variety of genre traditions [Wolff].

DISCOURSE UNIT: 2:18–27 [Cohen, Crenshaw, Keil, Dillard]. Cohen calls the topic "God's response"; Crenshaw, "replacing what the locusts consumed"; Keil, "destruction of the army of locusts, and renewal of the spiritual and earthly blessings"; Dillard, "the Lord's answer to the immediate disaster: locusts." This discourse unit comprises Stanza A′ [Wendland].

2:18

Then[a]- YHWH -was-zealous[b] for-his-land,[c] **and[d]-he-took-pity[e] on his-people.** [f]

SYNTAX—The sudden shift in this verse from exhortation to narration is signaled by the wayyiqtol verb form וַיְקַנֵּא *wayəqannēʾ* 'YHWH was zealous'. Commentators have asked, "Is this shift too abrupt?"

"No, not too abrupt."	**Recommended action**	**Remarks**
Most commentators and versions.	Do nothing.	**Argument for:** An abrupt transition from a lamentation to a narration of rescue characterizes other psalms of lament [Dillard].

"Yes, too abrupt."	**Recommended action**	**Remarks**
Bewer	Begin the narration at 2:15 by repointing the imperative verb forms of the exhortation and prayer of 2:15–17 as wayyiqtol forms.	**Argument against:** The main verbs in 2:15–16 are clearly imperatives, as is shown by their thematic parallelism with the verbs in 1:14 [Wolff].
Budde[20]	Continue the priests' prayer in 2:17 to 2:18; do this by repointing the vowel of the relevant verbs to make them jussives, expressing a wish.	**Argument for:** The name 'YHWH' is repeated in 2:19. **Argument against:** The repetition of 'YHWH' in 2:19 suggests that 2:18 functions as an independent paragraph and that 2:19 accounts for the assessment in 2:18 that YHWH was indeed zealous for his people [Wolff].

LEXICON—a. **then- YHWH -was-zealous** -וְ *wə- waw* of the attached wayyiqtol verb form [BDB p. 251], [Hol p. 84], [TWOT 519]: 'then' [Crenshaw, Keil, Allen, Wolff; KJV, NASB, NIV, NRSV, REB, TEV]. Dillard expresses the additive relation with a new clause.

b. **YHWH -was-zealous** 3rd masc. sing. Piel wayyiqtol verb form of קנא *qnʾ* [BDB p. 888], [Hol p. 320], [TWOT 2038]: 'to be zealous' [BDB, Hol; Cohen; NASB], 'to be jealous' [BDB; Keil, Dillard; KJV, NIV], 'to become jealous' [Crenshaw, Wolff; NRSV], 'to show ardent

---

[20] Karl Budde, "Der Umschwung in Joel 2," *Orientalistische Literaturzeitung* 22 (1919); cited by Wolff.

love' [REB], 'to show concern' [TEV], 'to show passionate concern' [Allen]. All commentators and versions employ the English past tense except KJV, NASB, and NIV, which employ the future tense. *Qnʾ* means here to express a very strong attachment to a person or object. Such emotion may result in violence against those who would reject YHWH, as when YHWH punishes Israel's enemies (Ezek. 36:5–6) or even the faithless in Israel (Ezek. 5:13) [TWOT 2038]. Such zealousness resulting in saving action for someone else represents a development of the sense of *qnʾ*; earlier in time, as in Exod. 20:5, the word denoted exclusive attachment in the semantic domain of worship [Wolff].

c. **then- YHWH -was-zealous for-his-land** constr. of אֶרֶץ *ʾereṣ* [BDB p. 76], [Hol p. 28], [TWOT 167]: 'land' [Hol; Crenshaw, Keil, Dillard, Wolff; KJV, NASB, NIV, NRSV, REB, TEV], 'territory' [Hol], 'country' [Allen].

d. **and-he-took-pity on his-people** -וְ *wə- waw* of the attached wayyiqtol verb form [BDB p. 251], [Hol p. 84], [TWOT 519]: 'and' [Crenshaw, Keil, Allen, Wolff; KJV, NASB, NIV, NRSV, REB]. Dillard and TEV express the additive relation with a new clause or sentence.

e. **he-took-pity** 3rd masc. sing. wayyiqtol verb form of חמל *ḥml* [BDB p. 328], [Hol p. 108], [TWOT 676]: 'to take pity' [NIV], 'to take compassion' [Hol], 'to look with compassion' [Dillard], 'to have pity' [NASB, NRSV], 'to be moved with compassion' [REB], 'to pity' [KJV], 'to feel pity' [Wolff], 'to have mercy' [TEV], 'to have compassion' [Crenshaw, Keil], 'to spare' [Allen]. All commentators and versions employ the English past tense except KJV, NASB and NIV, which employ the future tense.

f. **on his-people** constr. of עָם *ʿām* [BDB p. 766], [Hol p. 275], [TWOT 1640a]: 'people' [BDB, Hol; Crenshaw, Keil, Allen, Dillard, Wolff; KJV, NASB, NIV, NRSV, REB, TEV].

QUESTION—What is the literary function of 2:18?

Together with the narration in 1:4, it gives the whole book a narrative cast. It is this narrative which Joel is concerned that the present generation pass on to the younger.

QUESTION—What are the implications of 2:18?

1. This verse begins in effect YHWH's answer to his people's present distress. The prophet uses a completed verbal aspect (*was-zealous, and-he-took-pity*) as he looked with assurance into the distant future [Stuart].
2. Wolff says that this verse immediately implies that Israel did indeed return to YHWH. Similarly, the Jewish commentator Kimchi saw implicit in this verse the information that in taking pity on his people, YHWH had driven away the locusts [Cohen]. In the long run, this verse begins the prophet's recital of the future deliverance promised by YHWH. YHWH's promise of help in the present economic collapse

points ahead to his promise of salvation in the great day which is still coming [Wolff].

2:19

And[a]- YHWH -answered[b] and-said[c] to-his-people,[d] behold[e]-me about-to-send[f] to-you(p)
the-grain[g] and-the-wine[h] and-the-oil,[i] and[j]-you(p)-will-be-satisfied[k] with-it,
and[l]- I-will- -not -make[m] you(p) any-longer[n] (a-)disgrace[o] among-the-nations.[p]

LEXICON—a. **and- YHWH –answered** -וְ *wə- waw* of the attached wayyiqtol verb form [BDB p. 251], [Hol p. 84], [TWOT 519]: 'and' [Keil; NASB]. Crenshaw, Allen, Dillard, Wolff; NIV, NRSV, REB, and TEV express the additive relation with a new clause or sentence.

b. **and- YHWH -answered and-said** 3rd masc. sing. Qal wayyiqtol verb form of ענה *ʿnh* [BDB p. 772], [Hol p. 277], [TWOT 1650]: 'to answer' [Hol; Crenshaw, Keil, Dillard, Wolff; KJV, NASB, REB, TEV], 'to reply' [NIV]. Allen expresses this verb with the phrase "in reply"; NRSV has "in response." Most commentators and versions translate it with the past tense, but the KJV, NASB, and NIV have the future tense. The verb *ʿnh* 'to answer' signals the beginning of a prophecy in response to a cry for help [Wolff].

c. **and- YHWH -answered and-said** 3rd masc. sing. Qal wayyiqtol verb form of אמר *ʾmr* [BDB p. 55], [Hol p. 21], [TWOT 118]: 'to say' [Hol; Keil, Allen, Dillard, Wolff; KJV, NASB, NRSV, REB], not explicit [Crenshaw; NIV, TEV].

d. **to-his-people** constr. of עָם *ʿām* [BDB p. 766], [Hol p. 275], [TWOT 1640a]: 'people' [BDB, Hol; Allen, Dillard, Wolff; KJV, NASB, NRSV], not explicit [Crenshaw, Keil; NIV, REB].

e. **behold-me about-to-send to-you(p)** הִנֵּה *hinnēh* [BDB p. 243], [Hol p. 82], [TWOT 510a]: 'behold' [Hol; Keil, Dillard; KJV, NASB], 'look' [Crenshaw], not explicit [Allen; NIV, REB, TEV]. The exclamation הִנְנִי *hinnî* 'behold me' followed by a participle is the device which most often marks assurance oracles answering a cry for help, especially in the postexilic period [Wolff].

f. **behold-me about-to-send to-you(p)** masc. sing. Qal part. of שׁלח *šlḥ* [BDB p. 1018], [Hol p. 371], [TWOT 2394]: 'to send' [BDB, Hol; Crenshaw, Keil, Dillard, Wolff; KJV, NASB, NIV, NRSV, REB], 'to give' [TEV], 'to supply with' [Allen]. Dillard uses the English present progressive tense as do NIV, NRSV, and TEV (e.g., "I am sending you"). A kind of imminent future, reflecting the sense of הִנֵּה *hinnēh* followed by a participle, is used by Wolff: "I am now about to send...."

g. **the-grain and-the-wine and-the-oil** דָּגָן *dāḡān* [BDB 186], [Hol p. 68], [TWOT 403a]: 'grain' [Hol; Crenshaw, Allen, Dillard, Wolff; NASB, NIV, NRSV, TEV], 'corn' [Keil; KJV, REB]. *Dāḡān* is the generic term for grains and cereals, which in Israel essentially comprise wheat and barley [Dillard]. The translation "corn" probably reflects standard British English for "wheat."

h. **and-the-wine** תִּירוֹשׁ *tîrôš* [BDB p. 440], [Hol p. 389], [TWOT 2505]: 'wine' [Hol; Allen; KJV, NRSV, TEV], 'new wine' [Crenshaw, Keil, Dillard, Wolff; NASB, NIV, REB]. *Tîrôš* is an archaic word found in ritual and poetic texts [Hol].

i. **and-the-oil** יִצְהָר *yiṣhār* [BDB p. 844], [Hol p. 140], [TWOT 1883c]: 'oil' [Crenshaw, Keil, Allen; KJV, NASB, NIV, NRSV, REB], 'olive oil' [Hol; Wolff; TEV], 'fresh oil' [Dillard].

j. **and-you(p)-will-be-satisfied with-it** -וְ *wə-* *waw* connective [BDB p. 251], [Hol p. 84], [TWOT 519]: 'and' [Dillard; KJV, NASB, NRSV, REB, TEV]. Crenshaw expresses the additive relation with a new clause. Keil considers it a relation of purpose as does Wolff (e.g., "that ye may be satisfied"). Allen renders it as a descriptive clause: "as much as you want."

k. **you(p)-will-be-satisfied with-it** 2nd masc. pl. Qal perf. of שׂבע *śḇᶜ* [BDB p. 959], [Hol p. 348], [TWOT 2231]: 'to be satisfied' [BDB; Crenshaw, Keil; KJV, NASB, NRSV, TEV], 'to be satiated' [Hol], 'to have enough' [Dillard], 'to have one's fill' [Wolff] 'to satisfy fully' [NIV], 'to have in plenty' [REB]. *Śḇᶜ* most often occurs in a context about having enough to eat [TWOT].

l. **and- I-will- -not -make you(p) any-longer (a-)disgrace** -וְ *wə-* *waw* connective (see *j* above): 'and' [Keil, Dillard, Wolff; NASB, NRSV, KJV]. Crenshaw, Allen, NIV, and REB express the additive relation with a new clause or sentence.

m. **and- I-will- -not -make you(p) any-longer** 1st sing. Qal imperf. of נתן *nṯn* [BDB p. 678], [Hol p. 249], [TWOT 1443]: 'to make someone to be something' [Hol; Crenshaw, Keil, Dillard; KJV, NASB, NIV, NRSV], 'to give over' [Wolff]. The root meaning of *nṯn* is 'to give'. For the clause וְלֹא־אֶתֵּן אֶתְכֶם עוֹד חֶרְפָּה בַּגּוֹיִם *wəlōʾ-ʾettēn ʾeṯkem ᶜôḏ ḥerpâ baggôyim* 'and I will no longer make you a disgrace among the nations' REB has "I will expose you no longer to the reproach of other nations"; TEV has "other nations will no longer despise you"; Allen has "I shall no longer allow you to be ridiculed by the nations."

n. **and-I-will- not -make you(p) any-longer** עוֹד *ᶜôḏ* [BDB p. 728], [Hol p. 267], [TWOT 1576]: 'again' [Hol; Dillard], 'no longer' [Allen; REB, TEV], 'no more' [Keil, Wolff; KJV, NRSV], 'never again' [Crenshaw; NASB, NIV].

o. **(a-)disgrace** חֶרְפָּה *ḥerpâ* [BDB p. 357], [Hol p. 117], [TWOT 749a]: 'disgrace' [Hol], 'reproach' [Crenshaw, Keil, Dillard; KJV, NASB, REB], 'mockery' [NRSV], 'object of reproach' [BDB], 'object of scorn' [NIV], 'shame' [Wolff]. Allen expresses this noun by a verb, "to be ridiculed."

p. **among-the-nations** pl. of גּוֹי *gôy* [BDB p. 156], [Hol p. 57], [TWOT 326e]: 'nation' [all commentators and versions except KJV], 'heathen' [KJV].

QUESTION—What is the implication of the phrase וַיַּעַן יְהוָה וַיֹּאמֶר לְעַמּוֹ *wayyaᶜan yhwh wayyōʾmer ləᶜammô* 'then YHWH answered and said to his people'?

1. It is the assurance that YHWH will restore his people in the future, after they will have undergone defeat and deportation at the hands of the invaders [Stuart].
2. It is that the priests and people did actually follow the prophet's exhortation to humble themselves before YHWH and cry out to him for pardon and help [Cohen, Keil, Wolff].

QUESTION—What is the significance of the various elements in this verse?

The reference to grain, wine, and oil is a clear reminder of the Israelites' need that was mentioned in Joel 1 [Cohen; cf. Deut. 7:13 and 11:14]—but only of their need for sustenance, for there is no reference to any resumption of Temple sacrifices. The promise to end the people's disgrace relates to 2:1–17 and especially to 2:17 itself [Wolff].

2:20

And[a]-the-northerner[b] I-will-remove[c] from-you(p),
and[d]-I-will-drive[e]-it to (a-)land[f] (a-)dry-country[g] and-(a-)sinister-desolation,[h]
its-front-end[i] into[j] the- eastern[k] -sea[l] and-its-rear[m] into the-western[n] -sea.
And[o]- its-stench[p] -will-go-up[q] and[r]- its-foul-odor[s] -will-go-up,[t]
(MT) because/indeed[u] he/it-has-done[v] great-things[w]
(ET) for[u] I-have-done[v] great-things.[w]

TEXT—The MT הִגְדִּיל *higdîl* 'he/it has done' is emended by Bewer to אַגְדִּיל *ʾagdîl* 'I have done great things', in which "I" refers to YHWH. Bewer calls the MT "improbable." Stuart concurs. The MT is accepted by the other commentators and all the English versions consulted. The LXX and the Targum also support the MT [Stuart].

LEXICON—a. **and-the-northerner** -וְ *wə- waw* connective [BDB p. 251], [Hol p. 84], [TWOT 519]: 'and' [Keil], 'but' [Wolff; KJV, NASB]. Crenshaw, Allen, Dillard, NIV, NRSV, REB, and TEV express the additive relation with a new clause or sentence.

b. **and-the-northerner** צְפוֹנִי *ṣəpônî* [BDB p. 861], [Hol p. 309], [TWOT 1953c]: 'northerner' [BDB, Hol; Crenshaw, Allen, Wolff], 'northern one' [Keil], 'northern peril' [REB], 'northern army' [Dillard; KJV, NASB, NIV, NRSV]. TEV interprets and expands the word *ṣəpônî*: "the locust army that came from the north."

c. **I-will-remove from-you(p)** 1st Hiphil imperf. of רחק *rḥq* [BDB p. 934], [Hol p. 338], [TWOT 2151]: 'to remove' [BDB, Hol; Keil, Dillard; KJV, NASB, NRSV, REB, TEV], 'to move someone far away'

[Hol], 'to put far away' [BDB], 'to drive' [NIV], 'to drive away' [Wolff], 'to thrust from' [Crenshaw], 'to relieve ... send far away' ("of the northerners I shall relieve you, sending them far away") [Allen].

d. **and-I-will-drive-it to (a-)land** -וְ *wə- waw* of the attached weqatal verb form [BDB p. 251], [Hol p. 84], [TWOT 519]: 'and' [Keil, Wolff; KJV, NASB, NRSV, REB, TEV]. Crenshaw, Allen, Dillard, and NIV express the additive relation with a new clause or sentence.

e. **and-I-will-drive-it to (a-)land** 1st sing. Hiphil weqatal verb form of נדח *nḏḥ* [BDB p. 623], [Hol p. 229], [TWOT 1304]: 'to drive' [Crenshaw, Keil, Allen, Dillard; KJV, NASB, NRSV, TEV], 'to thrust out' [BDB], 'to banish' [BDB; REB], 'to scatter' [Hol], 'to disperse' [Hol], 'to push' [NIV], 'to expel' [Wolff]. *Nḏḥ* means to cause to scatter and flee, as a defeated army does [Crenshaw]. The object pronoun attached to this verb is translated "it" by most commentators and versions and refers to "the northerner." TEV has "[I will] drive some of them into the desert."

f. **(a-)land** אֶרֶץ *ʾereṣ* [BDB p. 76], [Hol p. 28], [TWOT 167]: 'land' [Hol; Crenshaw, Keil, Dillard, Wolff; KJV, NASB, NIV, NRSV REB], 'territory' [Hol], 'country' [Allen]. TEV translates the phrase אֶרֶץ צִיָּה וּשְׁמָמָה *ʾereṣ ṣîyâ ûšəmāmâ* 'a dry and desolate land' as "the desert."

g. **(a-)land (a-)dry-country and-(a-)sinister-desolation** צִיָּה *ṣîyâ* [BDB p. 851], [Hol p. 305], [TWOT 1909a]: 'dry country' [Hol], 'waterless region' [Hol], 'dryness' [BDB], 'drought' [Keil]. Some render this noun with an adjective: 'barren' [KJV], 'parched' [Allen, Wolff; NASB, NIV, NRSV], 'arid' [REB], 'dry [Dillard], 'thirsty' [Crenshaw].

h. **and-(a-)sinister-desolation** שְׁמָמָה *šəmāmâ* [BDB p. 1031], [Hol p. 376], [TWOT 2409b]: 'sinister desolation' [Hol], 'desert' [Keil]. Some render this noun with an adjective: 'desolate' [Crenshaw, Dillard, Wolff; KJV, NASB, NRSV], 'waste' [Allen; REB], 'barren' [NIV].

i. **its-front-end into the- eastern -sea** constr. of פָּנִים *pānîm* [BDB p. 815], [Hol p. 293], [TWOT 1782a]: 'front end' [NRSV], 'front side' [Hol], 'front columns' [NIV], 'vanguard' [Crenshaw, Wolff; NASB, REB], 'face' [KJV], 'advance force' [Dillard], 'van' [Keil], 'front ranks' [Allen; TEV]. The words פָּנִים *pānîm* 'front end' and סוֹף *sôp̄* 'end' seem to imply a large invading force, whether of soldiers or locusts.

j. **into the- eastern –sea** אֶל *ʾel* [BDB p. 39], [Hol p. 16], [TWOT 91]: 'into' [Hol; Keil, Dillard, Wolff; NASB, NIV, NRSV, REB, TEV], 'toward' [KJV], 'to' [Crenshaw, Allen]. The root meaning of the preposition *ʾel* is 'toward' [Hol], of either motion or direction [BDB].

k. **the- eastern –sea** קַדְמֹנִי *qaḏmōnî* [BDB p. 870], [Hol p. 313], [TWOT 1988f]: 'eastern' [Hol; Dillard, Wolff; NASB, NIV, NRSV, REB], 'east' [KJV], 'in the east' [Allen], 'eastward' [Crenshaw], 'front' [Keil]. TEV renders the expression הַיָּם הַקַּדְמֹנִי *hayyām haqqaḏmōnî* as "the Dead Sea," which the twelfth-century Jewish commentator Kimchi regarded it to be [cited by Cohen]. In OT times, the Israelites indicated compass directions as if one stood facing east [Crenshaw].

l. **the- eastern –sea** יָם *yām* [BDB p. 410], [Hol p. 135], [TWOT 871a]: 'sea' [BDB, Hol; Crenshaw, Keil, Allen, Dillard, Wolff; KJV, NASB, NIV, REB].

m. **and-its-rear into the- western -sea** constr. of סוֹף *sôp̄* [BDB p. 693], [Hol p. 254], [TWOT 1478a]: 'rear' [Keil; NRSV], 'rearguard' [Hol; Crenshaw, Dillard, Wolff; NASB, REB], 'end' [BDB], 'hinder part' [KJV], 'those in the rear' [NIV], 'rear ranks' [Allen; TEV]. Wolff says that this Aramaized word indicates a late date for the Book of Joel.

n. **the- western –sea** אַחֲרוֹן *ʾaḥărôn* [BDB p. 30], [Hol p. 11], [TWOT 68f]: 'western' [BDB, Hol; Dillard, Wolff; NASB, NIV, NRSV, REB], 'westward' [Crenshaw], 'in the west' [Allen], 'utmost' [KJV], 'hinder' [Keil]. TEV translates the expression הַיָּם הָאַחֲרוֹן *hayyām hāʾaḥărôn* as "the Mediterranean."

o. **and- its-stench -will-go-up** -וְ *wə- waw* of the attached weqatal verb form [BDB p. 251], [Hol p. 84], [TWOT 519]: 'and' [Keil; KJV, NASB, NIV]. Crenshaw, Allen, Dillard, Wolff, NRSV, REB, and TEV express the additive relation with a new clause or sentence.

p. **its-stench -will-go-up** constr. of בְּאֹשׁ *bəʾōš* [BDB p. 93], [Hol p. 33], [TWOT 195a]: 'stench' [BDB, Hol; Crenshaw, Allen, Dillard, Wolff; NASB, NIV, NRSV, REB], 'stink' [Keil; KJV]. In TEV the phrase וְעָלָה בָאְשׁוֹ וְתַעַל צַחֲנָתוֹ *wəʿālâ ḇāʾəšû wəṯaʿal ṣaḥănāṯô* 'and its stench will go up and its odor will go up' is conflated and restructured: "their dead bodies will stink."

p. **its-stench -will-go-up** 3rd masc. sing. Qal perf. weqatal verb form of עלה *ʿlh* [BDB p. 748], [Hol p. 272], [TWOT 1624]: 'to go up' [BDB, Hol; NIV, REB], 'ascend' [BDB; Keil, Dillard], 'to come up' [KJV], 'to arise' [NASB], 'to rise up' [NRSV], 'to rise' [Crenshaw, Allen, Wolff].

r. **and- its-foul-odor -will-go-up** -וְ *wə- waw* connective [BDB p. 251], [Hol p. 84], [TWOT 519]: 'and' [Keil; KJV, NASB, NRSV, REB]. Crenshaw, Allen, Dillard, Wolff, and NIV express this as an appositive relation with a new clause or sentence.

s. **its-foul-odor -will-go-up** constr. of צַחֲנָה *ṣaḥănâ* [BDB p. 850], [Hol p. 305], [TWOT 1904a]: 'foul odor' [Crenshaw], 'stench (of putrefaction)' [BDB, Hol], 'foul smell' [Allen, Wolff; NASB, NRSV, REB], 'ill savour' [KJV], 'smell' [Dillard; NIV], 'corruption' [Keil]. This noun occurs only here in the OT, but its parallelism with בְּאֹשׁ *bəʾōš* 'stench' makes it easy to understand [Crenshaw]. The stench of decaying corpses can characterize the aftermath of a locust invasion as well as that of a battle [Crenshaw, Dillard].

t. **its-foul-odor -will-go-up** 3rd fem. sing. Qal imperf. of עלה *ʿlh* (see *p* above).

u. <u>**because/indeed**</u> **he/it-has-done great-things** כִּי *kî* particle [BDB p. 471], [Hol p. 155], [TWOT 976]: 'because' [KJV], 'because of' [Allen], 'for' [Crenshaw, Keil, Dillard, Wolff; NASB]. NIV and REB express the additive relation with a new sentence. TEV employs what seems to an explanatory relation: "I will destroy them...." NIV and NRSV understand *kî* as an intensive, "surely."

v. **he/it-<u>has-done great-things</u>** 3rd masc. sing. Hiphil perf. of גדל *gdl* [BDB p. 152], [Hol p. 56], [TWOT 315]: 'to make something great' [Hol]. The expression הִגְדִּיל לַעֲשׂוֹת *hiḡdîl laᶜăśôṯ* means 'to accomplish great things' [Hol]. It is normally a positive statement—in the next verse it is said of YHWH himself [Crenshaw] and many translate it accordingly: "he/it/they has/have done great things" [Keil, Dillard; KJV, NASB, NIV, NRSV, REB], "he has acted great" [Wolff]. However, in the context of 2:20, relating to Israel's defeated foe, this phrase is pejorative and is better translated "he has acted reprehensibly," "he has acted in a proud and grandiose manner, going beyond his divinely-given task of correction" (cf. Isa. 10:5–19; Hab. 2:6–19) [Crenshaw], or at least "he has acted arrogantly and boastfully in his own might" [Keil]. Allen has "because of their high and mighty deeds." The implied singular subject of this clause is understood to be "the northerner" [Allen, Cohen, Crenshaw, Dillard, Keil, Wolff; KJV, NASB, NIV, NRSV, REB, TEV], a view supported by the LXX and the Targum [Stuart]. On the other hand, Bewer emends the text to אַגְדִּיל *ᵓaḡdîl* 'I have acted great', referring to YHWH; he calls the MT "improbable." Stuart concurs in this view. This understanding would of course put a different complexion on Wendland's recursive structure of anadiplosis between 2:20 and 2:21, although such a structure would still exist. TEV expands כִּי הִגְדִּיל לַעֲשׂוֹת *kî hiḡdîl laᶜăśôṯ* based on implicit information: "I will destroy them because of all they have done to you."

w. **he/it-<u>has-done</u> great-things** Qal infin. of עשׂה *ᶜśh* [BDB p. 793], [Hol p. 56], [TWOT 1708]: 'to do' [Hol], 'to act' [Crenshaw].

QUESTION—What is the relationship of this verse to the preceding verse?

This verse expands upon the promise given in 2:19b: God will ensure that his people will never suffer disgrace again by driving away their attackers [Wolff].

QUESTION—To what does הַצְּפוֹנִי *haṣṣəp̄ônî* 'the northerner' refer?

1. An expanded translation would be 'the northern army'. This might refer to locusts, which tend to come from the north, or to the traditional enemies of Israel, or to an archetypical apolocalyptic foe [Dillard].
2. Although the language combines allusions to both locusts and the divine army of YHWH, *haṣṣəp̄ônî* probably should be taken as referring to a locust attack [Crenshaw]. This is the view of the Jewish commentator Ibn Ezra [cited by Cohen], as well as of Cohen himself. Cohen explains that locusts usually attack Israel from the southeast, but that the expression "the north" probably had become stylized as the direction of

danger, regardless of any actual points of the compass (cf. Jer. 1:14; 10:22; Ezek. 38:6, 15). Cohen notes that some regard *haṣṣəp̄ônî* as indicating here the direction of the locusts' travel (coming from the southeast), instead of the direction of their origin.

3. *Haṣṣəp̄ônî* probably refers initially to a locust plague and, in a fashion more removed, to an invading army [Keil]. The Jewish commentator Jepheth regarded it as referring to an invading army [cited by Cohen].
4. *Haṣṣəp̄ônî* refers, in terms of invading locusts (although locusts are never overtly named), to an invading final enemy of Israel, the same one spoken of by Jeremiah and Ezekiel. This attack, although described in mythological terms, will indeed occur in historical time and will mark the end times as well, although Joel makes no attempt to identify this final enemy with any known people [Wolff].

QUESTION—What are the literary and cultural allusions of the term הַצְּפוֹנִי *haṣṣəp̄ônî* 'the northerner'?

The gods of the Canaanites lived in the north, and there are scriptural allusions to the north as the divine home (Job 37:22; Ps. 48:3; Ezek. 1:4). In addition, many OT passages refer to the north as the direction from which Israel's enemies came and would come (e.g., Isa. 41:25; Jer. 1:13–15). It is certainly possible that for the Israelites the second concept was reinforced by the first [Crenshaw, Dillard, Wolff]. In postexilic literature there is certainly increasing emphasis laid upon an archetypical, apocalyptic foe also to come from the north [Dillard, Wolff], a foe whose coming would signal the day of YHWH [Crenshaw].

QUESTION—What is the logical relationship between bicolon γ–δ, *and-I-will-drive-it to (a-)land (a-)dry-country and-(a-)sinister-desolation*, and bicolon ε–ζ, *its-front-end into the- eastern -sea and-its-rear into the- western –sea* ?

1. The relationship is one of temporal simultaneity: the middle of the invading force (viewed by Allen as locusts) is driven into the desert and the two ends into the two seas. Implied is a strong wind rising in the northwest (as in Exod. 10:19), which blows the front end of the invading locusts into the Dead Sea; then the wind shifts to blowing from the northeast and thus blows the rear end into the Mediterranean Sea [Allen]. Thus TEV has "[I will] drive some of them into the desert. Their front ranks will be driven into the Dead Sea, their rear ranks into the Mediterranean." Stuart's view of the relationship between these bicola is similar, but he applies it to an invading army. The three fates of the invading army—to be driven far away, to be divided, and to be drowned—correspond to three curses with which Israel is threatened in the case that she is unfaithful to YHWH (see Deut 30:4; 28:25; and 28:20).
2. The relationship is one of temporal succession: the invaders are driven first into the desert, and then into the seas [Wolff].

QUESTION—What is the significance of the four directions, north ("the northerner"), east ("the eastern sea"), south ("a dry and desolate land"), and west ("the western sea")?

As in Zech. 2:6, the four directions connote a universality; the judgment upon the "northerner" is complete and final [Dillard].

QUESTION—What area is signified by אֶרֶץ צִיָּה וּשְׁמָמָה *ʾereṣ ṣîyâ ûšəmāmâ (a-)dry-country and-(a-)sinister-desolation*?

It signifies the desert lands to the east and south of Israel [Crenshaw].

QUESTION—What is the symbolic import of הַיָּם הָאַחֲרוֹן *hayyām hāʾaḥărôn* 'the western sea (the Mediterranean)'?

The sea in Jewish lore represented chaos, opposed to YHWH and his order. It is into the sea that his enemies are consigned [Dillard].

QUESTION—Whose are the בְּאשׁ *bəʾōš* 'stench' and צַחֲנָה *ṣaḥănâ* 'odor'?

They belong to the army of locusts and, by extension, to whatever further foe may be intended [Dillard]. There are numerous ancient accounts of the stench raised by millions of dead locusts [Cohen, Crenshaw, Keil, Dillard].

2:21

Do- not -be-afraid(s),[a] field[b]; shout-with-joy(s)[c] and[d]-rejoice(s),[e]
for[f] YHWH has-done[g] great-things.[h]

The beginning of this strophe is marked by a change of speaker, from YHWH back to Joel.

INTERTEXTUAL REFERENCE—Joel here evokes Ps. 126:3: 'YHWH has done great things (הִגְדִּיל יְהוָה לַעֲשׂוֹת *higdîl yhwh laʿăśôṯ*) for us; we are filled with joy'. Joel, however, reverses the terms: his command to the fields to be joyful precedes his reason, while the psalmist follows his reason with a statement of joy [Wendland].

LEXICON—a. **do- not -be-afraid(s), field** 2nd fem. sing. Qal imperf. of ירא *yrʾ* [BDB p. 431], [Hol p. 142], [TWOT 907]: 'to be afraid' [Hol; NIV, TEV], 'to fear' [Hol; Crenshaw, Keil, Allen, Dillard, Wolff; KJV, NASB, NRSV, REB]. The words אַל־תִּירְאִי *ʾal-tîrəʾî* 'do not be afraid' are Joel's second device marking an assurance oracle that answers a cry for help [Wolff]. (The first is הִנֵּה *hinnēh* 'behold'—see *e* under 2:19.)

b. **field** אֲדָמָה *ʾădāmâ* [BDB p. 9], [Hol p. 4], [TWOT 25b]: 'field' [TEV], 'ground' [Hol; Allen, Cohen], 'land' [Crenshaw, Dillard, Wolff; KJV, NASB, NIV], 'earth' [Keil; REB], 'soil' [NRSV]. The singular "field" is here understood as a generic reference, which allows for a plural translation. A more literal rendering is "ground" [Cohen].

c. **shout-with-joy(s) and-rejoice(s)** fem sing. Qal imper. of גיל *gîl* [BDB p. 162), [Hol p. 59], [TWOT 346]: 'to shout with joy' [Hol], 'to rejoice' [Allen, Dillard; NASB, REB], 'to be joyful' [TEV], 'to be glad' [Wolff; KVJ, NIV, NRSV], 'to exult' [Keil], 'to be happy' [Crenshaw]. When they are paired, as they are here, *gîl* and *śmḥ* (see *e* below), both of which mean 'to rejoice', are most often found in connection with the joy of harvest. In this case, *gîl* and *śmḥ* reflect the reversal of the disaster chronicled in Joel 1, in which שִׂמְחָה וָגִיל *śimḥâ wāḡîl* 'joy and rejoicing' have been removed from the Temple [Wolff].

d. **and-rejoice(s)** -וְ *wə- waw* connective [BDB p. 251], [Hol p. 84], [TWOT 519]: 'and' [Crenshaw, Keil, Allen, Dillard, Wolff; KJV, NASB, NIV, NRSV, REB, TEV].

e. **and-rejoice(s)** fem. sing. Qal imper. of שׂמח *śmḥ* [BDB p. 970], [Hol p. 352], [TWOT 2268]: 'to rejoice' [BDB, Hol; Crenshaw, Keil, Wolff; KJV, NIV, NRSV], 'to be glad' [BDB, Hol; Allen, Dillard; NASB, REB, TEV].

f. **for YHWH has-done great-things** כִּי *kî* particle [BDB p. 471], [Hol p. 155], [TWOT 976]: 'for' [Crenshaw, Keil, Dillard, Wolff; KJV, NASB, NRSV, REB], 'surely' [REB], Allen and TEV translate this conjunction as a preposition: "because of."

g. **YHWH has-done great-things** 3rd masc. sing. Hiphil perf. of גדל *gḏl* [BDB p. 152], [Hol p. 56], [TWOT 315]: 'to make something great' [Hol]. See 2:20 for a discussion of the phrase הִגְדִּיל לַעֲשׂוֹת *hiḡdîl laʿăśôṯ*. This phrase is variously translated: "to do great things" [Keil, Dillard; KJV, NASB, NIV, NRSV, REB], "to act mightily" [Crenshaw], "to act great" [Wolff]. Allen translates כִּי־הִגְדִּיל יְהוָה לַעֲשׂוֹת *kî-hiḡdîl yhwh laʿăśôṯ* as a complex noun phrase: "because of Yahweh's great and mighty deeds"; TEV translates it "because of all the Lord has done for you." Most translations and commentators employ the English present perfect tense; the future tense is employed by KJV. This verb appears to be an example of the so-called prophetic perfect. The repetition of this expression in two succeeding verses is a word play, since the first occurrence has a negative meaning and the second a positive [Wolff].

h. **YHWH has-done great-things** Qal infin. of עשׂה *ʿśh* [BDB p. 793], [Hol p. 56], [TWOT 1708]: 'to do' [Hol].

QUESTION—What is the nature of the change of person in 2:21–24?

1. The change to the third person in reference to YHWH is characteristic of hymns of thanksgiving (see Ps. 85:9–14, for example) [Wolff].
2. The change to the third person in reference to YHWH indicates that the speaker in this strophe is the prophet. This is unusual for Part 2 of Joel, which consists mainly of reported speech of YHWH in the first person—just the opposite of the situation in Part 1, where most of the speech is attributed to the prophet in the first person. In this strophe, the prophet's exclamation has the form of a response of praise to the promises of YHWH and is certainly a deliberate rhetorical device [Wendland].

QUESTION—What progression is indicated in 2:21–2:23?

In 2:21, Joel addresses the fields; in 2:22, he addresses the wild animals, and in 2:23, he addresses the inhabitants. The progression is therefore from the least important to the most important, from inanimate to animate to human [Dillard]. However, not too much should be made of such progression, for the emphasis is upon the combined effect of well-being for the land and its people. As the terms *gîl* and *śmḥ* 'to rejoice' (see *c* above) refer to the reversal of the disaster portrayed in Joel 1, so also are the references to the fields, wild animals, and inhabitants reminiscent of the suffering fields (1:10), animals (1:18, 20), and inhabitants (1:5, 11, 13–14), with this difference, that the prophet announces here the reversal of Israel's economic woes [Wolff].

2:22

Do- not -be-afraid(p),[a] beasts(-of)[b] (the-)field(s)[c]; for[d] (the-)pastures(-of)[e] (the)wilderness[f] have-become-green,[g]
for[h] (the-)tree(s)[i] have-yielded[j] their[k]-fruit;[l] (the-)fig-tree(s)[m] and-the-vine(s)[n] have-given[o] their-strength.[p]

LEXICON—a. **do- not -be-afraid(p)** 2nd masc. pl. imperf. Qal of ירא *yr*ʾ [BDB p. 431], [Hol p. 142], [TWOT 907]: 'to be afraid' [Hol; KJV, NIV, TEV], 'to fear' [Hol; Crenshaw, Keil, Allen, Dillard, Wolff; NASB, REB, NRSV]. Imperative forms sometimes occur in the second person masculine plural even when the addressee is feminine, as is the case here: בַּהֲמוֹת *bahămôṯ* 'animals' [Dillard, Wolff].

b. **beasts(-of)** **(the-)field(s)** pl. constr. of בְּהֵמָה *bəhēmâ* [BDB p. 96], [Hol p. 34], [TWOT 208a]: 'beast' [Crenshaw, Keil, Wolff; KJV, NASB, REB], 'animal' [Hol].

c. **beasts(-of)** **(the-)field(s)** This is an older form (also singular) of שָׂדֶה *śāḏeh* [BDB p. 961], [Hol p. 349], [TWOT 2236b]: for בַּהֲמוֹת שָׂדַי *bahămōṯ śāḏay*, 'beasts of the field' [Crenshaw, Keil, Wolff; KJV, NASB], 'beasts in the field' [REB], 'wild animals' [Hol; Dillard; NIV], 'animals' [TEV], 'animals of the field' [NRSV], 'wild beasts' [Allen]. The root meaning of *śāḏeh* is 'open country, open field' [Hol].

d. **for** **(the-)pastures(-of)** **(the-)wilderness** **have-become-green** כִּי *kî* particle [BDB p. 471], [Hol p. 155], [TWOT 976]: 'for' [Crenshaw, Keil, Dillard, Wolff; KJV, NASB, NIV, NRSV, REB], not explicit [TEV].

e. **(the-)pastures(-of)** **(the-)wilderness** constr. pl. of נָוָה *nāwâ* [BDB p. 627], [Hol p. 231], [TWOT 1322c]: 'pasture' [Keil, Allen, Dillard, Wolff; KJV, NASB, NRSV, TEV], 'open pasture' [NIV, REB], 'pasture land' [Crenshaw], 'pasturage' [Hol].

f. **(the-)wilderness** מִדְבָּר *miḏbār* [BDB p. 184], [Hol p. 182], [TWOT 399l): 'wilderness' [Hol; KJV, NASB, NRSV], 'desert' [Hol; Keil], 'range' [Wolff], 'prairie' [Allen], not explicit [Crenshaw, Dillard; NIV, REV, TEV]. *Miḏbār* denotes uncultivated land [Hol].

g. **have-become-green** 3rd pl. Qal perf. of דשׁא *dš*ʾ [BDB p. 205], [Hol p. 75], [TWOT 456]: 'to become green' [Crenshaw, Keil, Dillard; NIV], 'to be green' [Hol; Wolff; NRSV, REB, TEV], 'to turn green'

[Allen; NASB], 'to grow green' [BDB], 'to spring' [KJV], 'to sprout' [BDB], 'to put forth lush growth' [Crenshaw]. Crenshaw gives the meaning of this word as a present state of verdure (e.g., "are green" or "have turned green"), as do KJV, NASB, and TEV. Keil and NIV express it as a state of becoming green; Crenshaw, Dillard, and REB, as a future state of verdure. This verb appears to be an example of the so-called prophetic perfect.

h. **<u>for</u> (the-)tree(s) have-yielded their-fruit** כִּי *kî* particle [BDB p. 471], [Hol p. 155], [TWOT 976]: 'for' [Keil; KJV, NASB], 'indeed' [Wolff], not explicit [Crenshaw, Allen, Dillard; NIV, NRSV, REB, TEV].

i. **(the-)<u>tree(s)</u>** עֵץ *ʿēṣ* [BDB p. 781], [Hol p. 279], [TWOT 1670a]: 'tree' [Hol; Crenshaw, Keil, Allen, Dillard, Wolff; KJV, NASB, NIV, NRSV, REB, TEV]. In BH the singular is often used colloquially for the plural [Hol]. KJV, NASB, and NRSV, however, all have "tree."

j. **<u>have-yielded</u> their-fruit** 3rd masc. sing. Qal perf. of נשׂא *nśʾ* [BDB p. 669], [Hol p. 246], [TWOT 1421]: 'to yield' (fruit) [Hol], 'to bear' [Keil, Allen, Dillard, Wolff; KJV, NASB, NIV, NRSV, REB, TEV], 'to produce' [Crenshaw]. The root meaning of *nśʾ* is 'to lift, raise high' [Hol]. The English past tense is employed by Crenshaw and NASB; the present tense or present progressive tense by Keil, Wolff, KJV, NIV, and TEV; the future tense by Dillard and REB. This verb appears to be an example of the so-called prophetic perfect.

k. **<u>their</u>-fruit** 3rd masc. sing. poss. pron. in Hebrew, which agrees in number with עֵץ *ʿēṣ* 'tree'.

l. **their-<u>fruit</u>** constr. of פְּרִי *pərî* [BDB p. 826], [Hol p. 297], [TWOT 1809a]: 'fruit' [Hol; Crenshaw, Keil, Allen, Dillard, Wolff; KJV, NASB, NIV, NRSV, REB, TEV].

m. **<u>fig-tree</u> and-the-vine have-given their-strength** תְּאֵנָה *təʾēnâ* [BDB p. 1061], [Hol p. 386], [TWOT 2490]: 'fig tree' [Hol; Keil, Allen, Wolff; KJV, NASB, NIV, NRSV], 'fig' [Crenshaw, Dillard; REB, TEV]. The singular can be taken for generic reference [Hol].

n. **fig-tree and-the-<u>vine</u>** גֶּפֶן *gep̄en* [BDB p. 172], [Hol p. 63], [TWOT 372a]: 'vine' [Crenshaw, Keil, Allen, Dillard, Wolff; KJV, NASB, NIV, NRSV, REB], 'grape vine' [Hol], 'grapes' [TEV]. The singular can be taken for generic reference [Hol].

o. **<u>have-given</u> their-strength** 3rd masc. pl. of נתן *ntn* [BDB p. 678], [Hol p. 249], [TWOT 1443]: 'to give' [Hol; Wolff; NRSV], 'to yield' [Crenshaw, Keil, Allen, Dillard; KJV, NASB, NIV, REB]. Crenshaw and NASB use the English past tense; Wolff, KJV, NIV, REB, and TEV the present or present progressive tense; Dillard the future tense. This verb appears to be an example of the so-called prophetic perfect.

p. **their-<u>strength</u>** חַיִל *ḥayil* [BDB p. 298], [Hol p. 102], [TWOT 624a]: 'strength' [Keil; KJV], 'wealth' [Hol; Dillard], 'harvest' [REB], 'riches' [NIV], 'full yield' [NRSV], 'produce' [Crenshaw, Wolff], 'maximum crop' [Allen]. NASB translates this noun by an adverbial phrase, "in full." The root sense of *ḥayil* is 'strength, ability' [Wolff]; *ḥayil* 'strength' stands in synonymous parallelism with פְּרִי *pərî* 'fruit' [Wolff]. The LXX translates it literally: καὶ συκῆ ἔδωκαν τὴν ἰσχὺν αὐτῶν 'and the fig has given its strength'. TEV translates the phrase תְּאֵנָה וָגֶפֶן נָתְנוּ חֵילָם *tə'ēnâ wāgep̄en nātənû ḥêlām* as "there are plenty of figs and grapes."

2:23

And[a]-sons(-of)[b] Zion,[c] rejoice(p)[d] and-be-glad(p)[e] in[f]-YHWH your(p)-God,[g]
(MT1) for[h] he-has-given[i] to-you(p) the-early-rain[j-1] for[k]-righteousness[l] / in-due-measure,[l]
(MT2) for[h] he-has-given[i] to-you(p) the-teacher[j-2] for[k]-righteousness,[l]
(ET) for[h] he-has-given[i] to-you(p) food [j-3] according-to[k] righteousness[l] / in-due-measure,[l]
and[m]-he-has-brought-down[n] to-you(p) showers,[o]
(the-)early-rain[p] and-(the-)late-rain,[q] (as) in-the-former-times.[r]

TEXT—The different understandings of הַמּוֹרֶה *hammôreh* are summarized in the following diagram:

Reading	Remarks
MT's *hammôreh* should be read literally as 'the rain'.	**Followed by:** Most commentators and versions. **Supported by:** Talmud. **For a similar ambiguity:** See Hos. 10:12, 'he will teach justice' or 'let it rain' [Hol].
MT's *hammôreh* should be read literally as 'the teacher'. **Followed by:** Keil; Rashi, Ibn Ezra.	**Identity of Teacher:** This reading was seen as referring to Messiah. **Riddle of Qumran Community:** This reading may identify the central figure of the Qumran community, "the teacher of righteousness." Many suspect that it was at Qumran that "rain" was misread as "teacher."
Supported by:	Targum.
Hammôreh should be emended to מַאֲכָל *ma'ăk̄āl* 'food' or בִּרְיָה *biryâ* 'food'.	**Followed by:** Wolff; REB. **Supported by:** LXX (τὰ βρώματα), Old Latin (*escas*) [Dillard]. **Argument for:** The sense 'food' matches the theme of the previous verses [Wolff].

TEXT—The MT reading בָּרִאשׁוֹן *bāri'šôn* is unambiguous. Wolff, however, posits an original reading of כָּרִאשׁוֹן *kāri'šôn* (see *r* below), saying that such is necessary if one finds that the context better supports a sense of "as formerly" than "in the first month."

LEXICON—a. **and-sons(-of) Zion** -וְ *wə- waw* connective [BDB p. 251], [Hol p. 84], [TWOT 519]: 'and' [Keil, Allen, Wolff], 'then' [KJV]. Crenshaw, Dillard, NIV, NRSV, REB, and TEV express the additive relation with a new clause or sentence.

b. **sons(-of) Zion** pl. constr. of בֵּן *bēn* [BDB p. 119], [Hol p. 42], [TWOT 254]: 'sons' [Keil, Allen, Wolff], 'children' [Hol; Crenshaw, Dillard; KJV, NRSV], 'people' [NIV, REB, TEV], 'citizens' [Crenshaw].

c. **Zion** צִיּוֹן *ṣiyyôn* [BDB p. 851], [Hol p. 306], [TWOT 1910]: 'Zion' [all lexica, commentators, and versions].

d. **rejoice(p) and-be-glad(p)** masc. pl. Qal imper. of גִּיל *gîl* [BDB p. 162), [Hol p. 59], [TWOT 346]: 'to shout with joy' [Hol], 'to rejoice' [Crenshaw, Allen, Dillard; REB], 'to be glad' [Wolff; KJV, NRSV, TEV], 'to exult' [Keil]. The NIV conflates the phrase גִּילוּ וְשִׂמְחוּ *gîlû wəśimḥû* 'rejoice and be glad' and translates it as "rejoice."

e. **and-be-glad(p)** masc. pl. Qal imper. of שׂמח *śmḥ* [BDB p. 970], [Hol p. 352], [TWOT 2268]: 'to rejoice' [BDB, Hol; Keil, Wolff; KJV, NRSV, TEV], 'to be glad' [BDB; Crenshaw, Allen, Dillard; REB].

f. **in-YHWH your(p)-God** -בְּ *bə-* [BDB p. 88], [Hol p. 32], [TWOT 193]: 'in' [Crenshaw, Keil, Dillard, Wolff; KJV, NIV, NRSV, REB], 'at' [TEV], 'because of' [Allen]. The Targum Jonathan to the Prophets paraphrased בַּיהוָה *bayhwh* 'in YHWH' as 'in the word of YHWH' [Wolff], consistent with a general rabbinic tendency to speak of God as more distant from his creation than portrayed by the Hebrew Scriptures.

g. **in-YHWH your(p)-God** constr. of אֱלֹהִים *ʾĕlōhîm* [BDB p. 43], [Hol p. 16], [TWOT 93c]: 'God' [all lexica, commentators, and versions].

h. **for he-has-given to-you(p)** כִּי *kî* particle [BDB p. 471], [Hol p. 155], [TWOT 976]: 'for' [Crenshaw, Keil, Allen, Wolff; KJV, NIV, NRSV], not explicit [Dillard]. The REB translates the logical relation expressed by *kî* with a relative clause, "who gives you ..."; and TEV with a substantive clause: "at what the Lord your God has done for you."

i. **he-has-given to-you(p)** 3rd masc. sing. Qal perf. of נתן *nṯn* [BDB p. 678], [Hol p. 249], [TWOT 1443]: 'to give' [Hol; Crenshaw, Allen, Keil, Dillard, Wolff; KJV, NIV, NRSV, REB, TEV]. Crenshaw, KJV, NIV, NRSV, and TEV use the English present perfect tense; Keil, Wolff, and REB, the present tense; Allen and Dillard, the future tense. Crenshaw says that since this clause stands as the reason for which the children of Zion should rejoice, the verb *nṯn* should be translated as completed action. This verb appears to be an example of the so-called prophetic perfect.

j-1. **the-early-rain** מוֹרֶה *môreh* [BDB p. 435], [Hol p. 187], [TWOT 910b]: 'early rain(s)' [Crenshaw, Dillard; NRSV], 'autumn rains' [Allen; NIV, TEV], 'former rain' [KJV], 'rain' [Hol]. The usual term for "early rain" is יוֹרֶה *yôreh*; *môreh* appears to occur with this sense only in this verse and in Ps. 84:7 [Crenshaw; TWOT]. BDB considers this and the following lexical item as homonyms derived from the same verb root, ירה *yrh* 'to throw, shoot, teach' [BDB], whereas Holladay considers this lexical item to be derived from ירה *yrh* 2, and and the following (see *j-2*) to be derived from ירה *yrh* 3.

j-2. **the-teacher** מוֹרֶה *môreh* [BDB p. 435], [Hol p. 187], [TWOT 910c]: 'teacher' [BDB, Hol; Keil].

k. **for/according-to** -לְ *lə-* [BDB p. 510], [Hol p. 167], [TWOT 1063]: 'for' [Keil, Dillard; NRSV], 'in' [Crenshaw; NIV, REB], 'according to' [Wolff], 'in token of' [Allen].

l. **righteousness/in-due-measure** צְדָקָה *ṣədāqâ* [BDB p. 842], [Hol p. 303], [TWOT 1879b]: 'righteousness' [Keil; NIV], 'covenant righteousness' [Wolff], 'covenant harmony' [Allen], 'justice' [Hol], 'vindication' [Crenshaw, Dillard; NRSV], 'due measure' [REB], 'just measure' [Cohen], 'season' [Crenshaw], 'moderately' [KJV]. *Ṣədāqâ* carries a wide range of meaning (see the second of the questions below).

m. **and-he-has-brought-down to-you(p) showers** -וַ *wə- waw* of the attached wayyiqtol verb form [BDB p. 251], [Hol p. 84], [TWOT 519]: 'and' [Crenshaw; Keil, Allen, Wolff; KJV]. Dillard, NIV, NRSV, REB, and TEV express the additive relation with a new clause or sentence.

n. **and-he-has-brought-down to-you(p) showers** 3rd masc. sing. Hiphil wayyiqtol verb form of ירד *yrd* [BDB p. 432], [Hol p. 143], [TWOT 909]: 'to bring down' [Hol], 'to cause to fall' [Dillard], 'to pour down' [NRSV, TEV], 'to send' [NIV, REB], 'to send down' [BDB; Crenshaw, Allen], 'to cause to come down' [Keil; KJV], 'to make fall' [Wolff]. Crenshaw, NASB, and TEV use the English present perfect or past tense; Keil, NIV, and REB, the present tense; Dillard and KJV, the future tense. This wayyiqtol verb form is used in parallel with the prophetic perfect of נָתַן *nātan* 'he has given'.

o. **showers** גֶּשֶׁם *gešem* [BDB p. 177], [Hol p. 65], [TWOT 389a]: 'shower' [BDB; Crenshaw], 'rain shower' [Hol], 'rain' [BDB; Allen, Dillard, Wolff; KJV, REB], 'abundant rain' [NRSV], 'abundant showers' [NIV], 'rainfall' [Keil], not explicit [TEV]. *Gešem* is BH's general term for "rain" [Dillard].

p. **(the-)early-rain and-(the-)late-rain** מוֹרֶה *môreh* (see *j-1* above): 'early rain' [Keil, Wolff; NRSV], 'autumn rains' [Allen; NIV, REB], 'early showers' [Crenshaw], 'former rain' [Dillard; KJV], 'winter rain' [TEV]. The phrase מוֹרֶה וּמַלְקוֹשׁ *môreh ûmalqôš* 'the early and later rains' simply signifies the normal rainy season [Dillard] and stands in apposition to גֶּשֶׁם *gešem* 'showers' [Crenshaw], as in Jer. 5:24 [Wolff]. The early rains come in October [Cohen].

q. **(the-)early-rain and-(the-)late-rain** מַלְקוֹשׁ *malqôš* [BDB p. 545], [Hol p. 199], [TWOT 1127b]: 'late rain' (March-April) [Hol], 'late showers' [Crenshaw], 'latter rain' [BDB; Keil, Dillard, Wolff; KJV], 'later rain' [NRSV], 'spring rain' [BDB; Allen; NIV, REB, TEV]. Rain is hoped for as late as in April, so that the dryness of the coming summer might not be too severe [Wolff].

r. **(as) in-the-former-times** רִאשׁוֹן *riʾšôn* [BDB p. 911], [Hol p. 329], [TWOT 2097c]: 'former' [BDB, Hol], 'as before' [Allen, Dillard; NIV, NRSV, TEV], 'as previously' [Crenshaw], 'as formerly' [Wolff], 'as of old' [REB], 'first of all' [Keil], 'in the first month' [KJV].

QUESTION—What is the correct understanding of הַמּוֹרֶה *hammôreh*, 'the rain' or 'the teacher'?

1. It is 'the teacher' [Keil]. A number of ancient versions as well as most early commentators adopted the interpretation of 'teacher'. The Vulgate, for example, reads *doctorem iustitiae* 'the teacher of righteousness', and Symmachus reads τὸν ὑποδεικνύοντα. Doubtlessly, *môreh* later in this verse signifies 'early rain'; there is, however, no other unamibiguous attestation of *môreh* signifying 'early rain' in the OT. (The meaning of *môreh* in Ps. 84:7 cannot be considered clear.) Elsewhere it is *yôreh* which means 'early rain'. One may therefore conclude that Joel indulged in word play on *hammôreh* by writing *môreh* instead of *yôreh* for 'early rain'. The occurrence of *hammôreh* is unique by virtue of the definite article, for all references to 'rain' in this passage (*môreh* and מַלְקוֹשׁ *malqôš* 'late rain') appear without the article [Keil].
2. As the MT stands, it is 'the teacher'. However, evidence points to an original reading signifying 'food', either מַאֲכָל *maʾăkāl* 'food' or בִּרְיָה *biryâ* 'food', or perhaps מָזוֹן *māzôn* 'food' [Wolff].[21]
3. It is 'the rain' [the other commentators and all versions]. The context of 2:23 makes it probable that the correct understanding of *hammôreh* [Crenshaw, Dillard] is 'the rain'. This position was also held by Kimchi, as well as Calvin [Keil]. Although admittedly rare, the use of *môreh* to mean 'rain' in Ps. 84:7 allows one to understand *môreh* here in the same way. In fact, rabbinic tradition considered the rain as a teacher, for from it the people learned when to harvest crops and when to strengthen their houses against it [Wolff].

---

21 Although he offers no explanation of how an original reading signifying 'food' became transformed to 'the teacher', Wolff points out that the MT's 'teacher' does indeed fit the well-known expectation in Rabbinic Judaism of a great teacher who would come in the end times and provide the answers to everyone's questions [Wolff, citing Gert Jeremias, *Der Lehrer der Gerechtigkeit*, Studien zur Umwelt des Neuen Testaments 2 (Göttingen: Vandenhoeck & Ruprecht, 1963)].

QUESTION—What is meant by the expression לִצְדָקָה *liṣdāqâ*?

1. It means 'for righteousness'. *Ṣədāqâ* always refers to an ethical quality, never to a physical one, and so it could never mean 'in due measure, at the normal time and in normal amounts'. In conjunction with the noun הַמּוֹרֶה *hammôreh* 'the teacher' some understand solely the Messiah who is to come, and others solely the ensemble of prophets and true teachers yet to come. The problem is that the context necessitates that the Jews of Joel's time, those who have suffered the locusts' attacks, be also the recipients of this 'teacher'. Keil concludes, then, that by this phrase Joel means himself along with Moses and all the true teachers who came to the Israelites; he also looks ahead as well to those who are yet to come, including the Messiah, who will be the ultimate realization of this prophecy.
2. It perhaps refers to being rescued by YHWH from hardship. This view accompanies an understanding of *môreh* as 'rain' [Dillard].
3. It refers to how *môreh* 'rain' is given: "in due measure." This view is derived from an understanding that the root sense of *ṣədāqâ* and its cognates in ancient Near Eastern texts concerns the order stemming from the nature of creation itself. So a rendering such as 'early rain in an orderly fashion (i.e., in due season)' is indicated [Crenshaw]. KJV's "moderately," REB's "in due measure," and TEV's "the right amount" are along this line. Cohen understands *liṣdāqâ* in the same way.
4. If a textual reading of בִּרְיָה *biryâ* 'food' instead of *môreh* 'rain' is adopted, *ṣədāqâ* can then be understood as referring to motivation for the gift: "food as YHWH has promised in his covenant" [Crenshaw, Wolff]. Even so, REB, which adopts a reading of 'food', interprets *ṣədāqâ* as 'in due measure'.

QUESTION—What relationship to the preceding phrase is signaled by the *waw* in the phrase וַיּוֹרֶד לָכֶם גֶּשֶׁם *wayyôred lākem gešem* 'and I brought (or, will bring) down to you rain'?

1. Consequence is signaled: the blessings of rain come as a result of righteous teaching. (Understood here is the reading of הַמּוֹרֶה לִצְדָקָה *hammôreh liṣdāqâ* as 'the teacher for righteousness'.) All the other benefits referred to in the rest of this chapter, both physical and spiritual, and even all of YHWH's actions detailed in Joel 3, stand as consequence signaled by this *waw* [Keil].
2. A more or less equivalent relation is signaled: *gešem* 'rain, showers' is equivalent to *hammôreh* 'the rain' [Crenshaw, who understands *hammôreh* as 'the rain'].

QUESTION—What relation does the phrase וַיּוֹרֶד לָכֶם גֶּשֶׁם *wayyôred lākem gešem* 'and I brought down to you rain' have to מוֹרֶה וּמַלְקוֹשׁ *môreh ûmalqôš* 'early and late rain'?

The second phrase gives precision to the first, which concerns only rain in general [Crenshaw, Keil].

QUESTION—Who are meant in the expression וּבְנֵי צִיּוֹן *ûḇənê ṣîyôn* 'and the sons of Zion'?

Literally this phrase denotes the inhabitants of Jerusalem, but here it is used figuratively to mean all Israelites, for YHWH is about to rescue all the land from the suffering it has experienced [Keil].

QUESTION—What is the sense of the expression בָּרִאשׁוֹן *bāriʾšôn*?

1. This expression denotes, as in other OT passages, the month of Nisan, the first month of the Jewish year (March–April) [Targum Jonathan to the Prophets, Talmud, Jewish commentators Rashi, Ibn Ezra, Kimchi—cited by Cohen]. KJV has "the first *month.*" But this understanding accords badly with "early rains," since the early rains are expected to fall in October–November [Crenshaw, Dillard, Wolff]. On the other hand, Nisan accords well with the coming of the later rains [Crenshaw].
2. This expression could be taken to refer to the restoration of the very first blessed conditions of Israel, hence "as at first" [Crenshaw].
3. This expression, translated by Keil as "first of all," indicates that YHWH will pour out upon Israel physical blessings first—here symbolized by rainfall; this implies that at a later time he will pour out the spiritual blessings referred to later in this chapter and in Joel 3 [Keil].
4. According to Wolff, this expression probably denotes 'as in the former [times]', as in the LXX, which reads καθὼς ἔμπροσθεν. However, one must then presume that καθὼς ἔμπροσθεν reflects an original BH reading of כָּרִאשׁוֹן *kāriʾšôn*, which is properly "formerly." This fits better than *bāriʾšôn* in parallel with לִצְדָקָה *liṣḏāqâ* 'according to righteousness', since *bāriʾšôn* always denotes the first month of the Jewish year [Wolff].

2:24

And[a]- the-threshing-floors(-of)[b] grain[c] -will-be-full,[d] and[e]- the-wine-vats[f] -will-overflow[g] (with) new-wine[h] and-olive-oil.[i]

LEXICON—a. **and- the-threshing-floors(-of) grain -will-be-full** -וְ *wə-waw* of the attached weqatal verb form [BDB p. 251], [Hol p. 84], [TWOT 519]: 'and' [Keil; KJV, NASB]. Crenshaw, Allen, Dillard, Wolff, NIV, NRSV, REB, and TEV express the additive relation with a new clause or sentence.

b. **the-threshing-floors(-of) grain** pl. constr. of גֹּרֶן *gōren* [BDB p. 175], [Hol p. 64], [TWOT 383a]: 'threshing floor' [BDB, Hol; Allen, Dillard, Wolff; NASB, NIV, NRSV, REB], 'granary' [Crenshaw], 'barn' [Keil], 'threshing place' [TEV], 'floor' [KJV]. The threshing floor consisted of a circle of ground, trampled hard by feet, usually located on a hilltop, so the wind could easily carry away the chaff once the sheaves were beaten [Bewer].

c. **grain** בָּר *bar* [BDB p. 135], [Hol p. 47], [TWOT 288b]: 'grain' [Hol; Crenshaw, Dillard, Wolff; NASB, NIV, NRSV, REB, TEV], 'corn' [BDB; Keil], 'wheat' [Allen; KJV]. *Bār* denotes grain which has been cleaned and threshed [Hol; Crenshaw]; the word seems to be used by Joel interchangeably with דָּגָן *dāḡān* 'grain' (see 1:10, 17; 2:19) [Crenshaw].

d. **will-be-full** 3rd pl. Qal weqatal verb form of מלא *mlʾ* [BDB p. 569], [Hol p. 195], [TWOT 1195]: 'to be full' [BDB, Hol; Crenshaw, Dillard, Wolff; KJV, NASB, NRSV, TEV], 'to become full of' [Keil], 'to be heaped with' [NIV, REB], 'to be crammed' [Allen]. Most commentators and versions employ the English future tense; the present tense is employed by Crenshaw, also Keil.

e. **and- the-wine-vats -will-overflow** -וְ *wə- waw* of the attached weqatal verb form [BDB p. 251], [Hol p. 84], [TWOT 519]: 'and' [Keil, Allen; KJV, NASB, REB]. Crenshaw, Dillard, Wolff, NIV, NRSV, and TEV express the additive relation with a new clause or sentence.

f. **the-wine-vats -will-overflow** pl. of יֶקֶב *yeqeḇ* [BDB p. 428], [Hol p. 141], [TWOT 900a]: 'wine vat' [BDB, Hol], 'vat' [Crenshaw, Keil, Allen, Dillard, Wolff; KJV, NASB, NIV, NRSV, REB]. TEV has a phrase giving the vats' location: "the pits beside the presses." Here *yeqeḇ* denotes a hole excavated in rock which received the juice from grapes trodden out in the winepress, which was situated to one side and higher [BDB, Hol]. Occasionally several such excavations were employed in a descending row, in order to produce a clearer juice [Bewer]. The term is applied also to the vats dug for the production of olive oil [Keil].

g. **the-wine-vats -will-overflow** 3rd pl. Hiphil weqatal verb form of שׁוּק *šûq* [BDB p. 1003], [Hol p. 365], [TWOT 2351]: 'to overflow' [BDB, Hol; Allen, Dillard, Wolff; KJV, NASB, NIV, NRSV, REB, TEV], 'to flow over' [Keil], 'to spill over' [Crenshaw]. Most commentators and versions employ the English future tense; the present tense is employed by Crenshaw, also Keil. There is in *šûq* a sense of the container or storage space being too constricted to hold all that must be held [Crenshaw]. The Hebrew word וְהֵשִׁיקוּ *wəhēšîqû* 'will overflow' is onomatopoeic, suggesting the sound of wine being poured out [Cohen].

h. **will-overflow (with) new-wine and-olive-oil** תִּירוֹשׁ *tîrôš* [BDB p. 440], [Hol p. 389], [TWOT 2505]: 'new wine' [BDB; Crenshaw, Wolff; NASB, NIV, REB], 'wine' [Hol; Keil, Allen, Dillard; KJV, NRSV, TEV]. *Tîrôš* is an archaic word found in ritual and poetic texts [Hol].

i. **and-olive-oil** יִצְהָר *yiṣhār* [BDB p. 844], [Hol p. 140], [TWOT 1883c]: 'olive oil' [Hol; Wolff; TEV], 'fresh oil' [BDB], 'oil' [Crenshaw, Keil, Allen, Dillard; KJV, NASB, NIV, NRSV, REB].

QUESTION—What is the theme of this verse?

This verse presents some of the results of a bountiful harvest, which is in turn the consequence of normal rainfall [Cohen]. The words "grain, new wine, and oil" have in this verse the same significance that they have in 1:10, but here the context is positive [Wendland].

2:25

And[a]-I-will-repay[b] to-you(p) the-years/two-fold[c] which/that-which the-locusts[d] have-eaten,[e]
the-creeping-locusts[f] and-the-young-locusts[g] and-the-flying-locusts,[h]
my- great[i] -army[j] which I-sent[k] against[l]-you(p).

The speaker shifts again from the prophet to YHWH at the beginning of this verse. In addition, this verse presents a reversal of the destruction portrayed in 1:4.

TEXT—Some have disputed the reading of הַשָּׁנִים *haššānîm* 'the years'. Bewer regards the LXX's τῶν ἐτῶν 'the years' as reflecting a corrupted text, and he emends *haššānîm* to הַשְּׁמָנִים *hašmānîm* 'the rich fruits'. Stuart reads so as to understand 'twofold'.

LEXICON—a. **and-I-will-repay to-you(p)** -וְ *wə- waw* of the attached weqatal verb form [BDB p. 251], [Hol p. 84], [TWOT 519]: 'and' [Keil, Wolff; KJV]. Crenshaw, Dillard, NIV, NRSV, REB, and TEV express the additive relation with a new clause or sentence. Allen specifies a result relation, "and so"; NASB specifies a temporal relation, "then."

b. **I-will-repay to-you(p)** 1st sing. Piel weqatal verb form of שׁלם *šlm* [BDB p. 1022], [Hol p. 373], [TWOT 2401]: 'to repay' [Hol; Keil, Dillard; NIV, NRSV], 'to make amends' [Hol], 'to recompense' [BDB; REB], 'to restore' [Wolff; KJV], 'to give back' [Allen], 'to give back what has been lost' [TEV], 'to make up' [Crenshaw; NASB].

c. **And-I-will-repay to-you(p) the-years** pl. of שָׁנָה *šānâ* [BDB p. 1040], [Hol p. 378], [TWOT 2419a]: 'year' [BDB, Hol; Crenshaw, Keil, Allen, Dillard, Wolff; KJV, NASB, NIV, NRSV, REB, TEV]. Implicit in the construction וְשִׁלַּמְתִּי...אֶת־הַשָּׁנִים *wəšillamtî ... ʾet-haššānîm* 'and I will repay ... the years' is the content of the repayment: 'and I will repay ... the produce of the years' [Keil]. In other words, *haššānîm* 'the years' is a metaphor for the lost harvests of those years [Crenshaw].

d. **which/that-which the-locusts have-eaten** אַרְבֶּה *ʾarbeh* [BDB p. 916], [Hol p. 26], [TWOT 2103a]: 'locust' [Hol; Keil, Dillard, Wolff; KJV, NIV], 'swarming locust' [Crenshaw, Allen; NASB, NRSV], 'swarmer' [REB]. The singular is here understood as a generic reference, which allows for a plural translation. (The same is true for the other singular references in this verse to varieties of locust.)

e. **which/that-which the-locusts have-eaten** 3rd masc. sing. Qal perf. of אכל *ʾkl* [BDB p. 37], [Hol p. 14], [TWOT 85]: 'to eat' [Hol; Keil, Allen, Wolff; KJV, NASB, NIV, NRSV, REB, TEV], 'to devour' [Dillard], 'to consume' [Crenshaw]. TEV translates this phrase, which extends through three designations of locusts, "in the years when swarms of locusts ate your crops" (...אֶת־הַשָּׁנִים אֲשֶׁר אָכַל הָאַרְבֶּה *ʾet-haššānîm ʾăšer ʾākal hāʾarbeh...* 'the years which the locusts have eaten').

f. **the-<u>creeping-locusts</u>** יֶלֶק *yeleq* [BDB p. 410], [Hol p. 135], [TWOT 870a]: 'creeping locust' [NASB], 'locust' [Hol], 'hopper' [Allen, Dillard, Wolff; NRSV, REB], 'great locust' [NIV], 'cankerworm' [KJV], 'jumper' [Crenshaw], 'licker' [Keil].

g. **and-the-<u>young-locusts</u>** חָסִיל *ḥāsîl* [BDB p. 340], [Hol p. 111], [TWOT 701a]: 'young locust' [NIV], 'leaping locust' [Dillard], 'grub' [REB], 'caterpiller' [KJV], 'stripping locust' [NASB], 'finisher' [Crenshaw], 'devourer' [Keil], 'jumper' [Wolff], 'destroyer' [Allen; NRSV]. Holladay identifies *ḥāsîl* as a specific but indeterminate stage of the locust's development, while BDB views *ḥāsîl* as a kind of locust.

h. **and-the-<u>flying-locusts</u>** גָּזָם *gāzām* [BDB p. 160], [Hol. 58], [TWOT 338a]: 'flying locust' [Dillard], 'locust' [BDB; REB], 'the other locusts' [NIV], 'palmerworm' [KJV], 'cutter' [NRSV], 'chewer' [Crenshaw]. Holladay vacillates between regarding *gāzām* as a locust just turned mature and about to fly, and a locust in its caterpillar stage.

i. **my- <u>great</u> -army** גָּדוֹל *gāḏôl* [BDB p. 152], [Hol p. 55], [TWOT 315d]: 'great' [BDB, Hol; Keil, Allen, Dillard, Wolff; KJV, NASB, NIV, NRSV, REB], 'mighty' [Crenshaw], not explicit [TEV].

j. **my- great -<u>army</u>** constr. of חַיִל *ḥayil* [BDB p. 298], [Hol p. 102], [TWOT 624a]: 'army' [Allen, Keil, Wolff; KJV, NASB, NIV, NRSV, REB, TEV]. *Ḥayil* has here a military sense, in contrast to its use in 2:22, in which it stands for the yield of fruit trees [Wolff].

k. **which <u>I-sent</u> against-you(p)** 1st sing. Piel perf. of שׁלח *šlḥ* [BDB p. 1018], [Hol p. 371], [TWOT 2394]: 'to send' [Hol; Crenshaw, Keil, Dillard, Wolff; KJV, NASB, NIV, NRSV, REB, TEV], 'to launch' [Allen]. Here Joel states unambiguously, and in military terms, that the locusts were sent by YHWH. This passage is similar to Amos 4:10 in ascribing divine origin to various calamities [Crenshaw].

l. **which I-sent <u>against</u>-you(p)** -בְּ *bə-* [BDB p. 88], [Hol p. 32], [TWOT 193]: 'against' [Crenshaw, Allen, Dillard; NRSV, REB, TEV], 'among' [Keil, Wolff; KJV, NASB, NIV].

QUESTION—What is the discourse function of this verse?

This verse begins the third utterance (2:25–2:27) of this discourse unit, in which reference to YHWH shifts back to first person. This verse provides a second expansion of YHWH's promise of help in 2:19, parallel to that contained in 2:21–24, for in it he promises to make up for the damage done by the locusts [Wolff].

QUESTION—What is the sense of the expression וְשִׁלַּמְתִּי לָכֶם אֶת־הַשָּׁנִים *wəšillamtî lākem ʾet-haššānîm* 'and I will restore to you the years'?

This clause implies that the harvests of a number of years have been lost to the locusts. It employs the verb שׁלם *šlm*, which concerns legal restitution for damages suffered. The expression is a metonymy, in which "years" stands for the lost harvests [Ibn Rashi, cited by Cohen; Wolff].

QUESTION—How is the list of locust terms organized in אֲשֶׁר אָכַל הָאַרְבֶּה הַיֶּלֶק וְהֶחָסִיל וְהַגָּזָם *ʾăšer ʾāḵal hāʾarbeh hayyeleq wəheḥāsîl wəhaggāzām*?

1. The list is organized in the order of the locust's life cycle [Dillard], with *ʾarbeh*, the generic term "locust," at the head. A *waw* connective is attached to the last two terms, indicating that the last three terms are in coordination and are together in apposition to *ʾarbeh* [Keil, Wolff]. The four locust terms in this passage are the same as in 1:4; the difference is that in the earlier passage *ʾarbeh* appears, not as the generic term for locust, but as a specific term.
2. Ibn Ezra considered the locust terms to denote four different species [cited by Cohen].
3. Jewish tradition identifies the locust terms in this list with political forces. The Targum Jonathan to the Prophets glosses the four terms as 'peoples, tongues, governments, and kingdoms'; and a sixth-century A.D. LXX manuscript gives a fivefold gloss: 'Egyptians, Babylonians, Assyrians, Greeks, Romans' [Dillard, Wolff].

QUESTION—What is the significance of the plural form of הַשָּׁנִים *haššānîm* 'years'?

1. It indicates that the locusts ruined the harvest for more than one year [Crenshaw].
2. It does not prove that the locust plague lasted over more than one year; the plural form is either used indefinitely, as in Gen. 21:7, or used to indicate the locusts' vast destructive force [Keil]. Indeed, harvests in the years immediately following a locust attack can be significantly impaired [Dillard].

2:26

And[a]-you(p)-will-eat[b] in-plenty[c] and[d]-be-satisfied,[e] and-you(p)-will-praise[f] (the-)name(-of)[g] YHWH your(p)-God,[h]
who has-worked[i] wonderfully[j] for[k]-you(p), and[l]- my-people[m] will- not -be-ashamed[n] (again) for-all-time.[o]

LEXICON—a. <u>and</u>-you(p)-will-eat in-plenty -וְ *wə- waw* of the attached weqatal verb form [BDB p. 251], [Hol p. 84], [TWOT 519]: 'and' [Keil; KJV, NASB], 'now' [TEV], 'then' [Wolff]. Crenshaw, Allen, Dillard, NIV, NRSV, and REB express the additive relation with a new clause or sentence.

b. <u>you(p)-will-eat</u> in-plenty 2nd masc. pl. Qal weqatal verb form of אכל *ʾkl* (see *e* under 2:25): 'to eat' [Keil, Allen, Wolff; KJV, NASB, NIV, NRSV, REB, TEV], 'to have food' [Dillard], 'to consume food' [Crenshaw].

c. you(p)-will-eat <u>in-plenty</u> Qal infin. of אכל *ʾkl* [BDB p. 37], [Hol p. 14], [TWOT 85]: 'to eat' [BDB, Hol], 'in plenty' [KJV, NRSV], 'continually' [Crenshaw], 'plenty to eat' [NASB, NIV, TEV], 'really'

[Wolff], not explicit [Allen, Dillard; REB]. This infinitive functions as an intensifier.

d. **and-be-satisfied** -וְ wə- *waw* connective [BDB p. 251], [Hol p. 84], [TWOT 519]: 'and' [Crenshaw, Keil, Allen, Dillard, Wolff; KJV, NASB, NRSV, TEV], 'until' [NIV, REB].

e. **be-satisfied** Qal infin. of שׂבע *śbᶜ* [BDB p. 959], [Hol p. 348], [TWOT 2231]: 'to be satisfied' [Crenshaw, Keil; KJV, NASB, NRSV, REB, TEV], 'to be satiated' [Hol], 'to be sated' [Wolff], 'to have one's fill' [Dillard], 'to be full' [NIV]. Allen translates this verb as a noun phrase, "your fill."

f. **and-you(p)-will-praise (the-)name(-of) YHWH** 2nd masc. pl. Piel weqatal verb form of הלל *hll* [BDB p. 237], [Hol p. 80], [TWOT 500]: 'to praise' [Hol; Crenshaw, Keil, Allen, Dillard, Wolff; KJV, NASB, NIV, NRSV, REB, TEV]. This verb is often found in the context of adoration of God [Crenshaw].

g. **you(p)-will-praise (the-)name(-of) YHWH** constr. of שֵׁם *šēm* [BDB p. 1027], [Hol p. 374], [TWOT 2405]: 'name' [BDB, Hol; Crenshaw, Keil, Allen, Dillard, Wolff; KJV, NASB, NIV, NRSV, REB]. TEV recognizes this as a metonymy and translates it nonfiguratively: "you will praise the Lord your God."

h. **YHWH your(p)-God** constr. of אֱלֹהִים *ʾĕlōhîm* [BDB p. 43], [Hol p. 16], [TWOT 93c]: 'God' [all lexica, commentators, and versions].

i. **who has-worked wonderfully for-you(p)** 3rd masc. sing. Qal perf. of עשׂה *ᶜśh* [BDB p. 793], [Hol p. 284], [TWOT 1708]: 'to work' [Crenshaw, Allen; NIV], 'to do' [BDB, Hol; Keil, Dillard; REB, TEV], 'to deal' [Wolff; KJV, NASB, NRSV].

j. **who has-worked wonderfully for-you(p)** -לְ *lə-* a proclitic and Hiphil infin. of פלא *plʾ* [BDB p. 810], [Hol p. 291], [TWOT 1768]: 'wonderfully' [Crenshaw], 'to do wonderful things' [Hol; REB, TEV], 'wondrously' [Keil, Wolff; KJV, NASB, NRSV], 'wondrous things' [Dillard], 'wonders' [Allen; NIV]. The word לְהַפְלִיא *ləhap̄lîʾ* is used adverbially here [Wolff].

k. **who has-worked wonderfully for-you(p)** עִם *ᶜim* [BDB p. 767], [Hol p. 275], [TWOT): 'for' [Allen, Dillard; NIV, REB, TEV], 'with' [Hol; Keil, Wolff; KJV, NASB, NRSV], 'in common with' [Hol], 'among' [Crenshaw]. In spite of the various renderings, *ᶜim* would appear to have a benefactive force here.

l. **and- my-people will- not -be-ashamed** -וְ *wə- waw* connective [BDB p. 251], [Hol p. 84], [TWOT 519]: 'and' [Crenshaw, Keil, Allen, Dillard, Wolff; KJV, NRSV, REB], 'then' [NASB]. NIV expresses the additive relation with a new clause, TEV with a new sentence.

m. **my-people** constr. of עָם *ᶜām* [BDB p. 766], [Hol p. 275], [TWOT 1640a]: 'people' [all lexica, commentators, and versions].

n. **will- not -be-ashamed** 3rd masc. pl. Qal imperf. of בושׁ *bûš* [BDB p. 101], [Hol p. 36], [TWOT 222]: 'to be ashamed' [Hol; KJV], 'to be shamed' [Crenshaw; NIV], 'to be put to shame' [Keil, Dillard, Wolff; NASB, NRSV, REB], 'to be despised' [TEV], 'to be humiliated' [Allen].

o. **for-all-time** -לְ *lə-* a proclitic and עוֹלָם *ᶜôlām* [BDB p. 761], [Hol p. 267], [TWOT 1631a]: 'for all time' [Hol], 'for ever' [Hol], 'to all eternity' [Keil], 'again' [Dillard]; (with the negation לֹא *loᵓ* 'not') 'never again' [Crenshaw, Allen; NIV, NRSV, REB, TEV], 'never' [KJV, NASB], 'never more' [Wolff].

QUESTION—What is the relationship of the first part of this verse with the preceding verse?

YHWH's promise that Israel will have abundant food (2:26) amplifies the statement that he will make up the lost harvests to the Israelites (2:25) [Wolff].

QUESTION—What is the force of the verb and two infinitives in the passage וַאֲכַלְתֶּם אָכוֹל וְשָׂבוֹעַ *waᵓăkaltem ᵓākôl wəśābôaᶜ* 'and you will eat in plenty and be satisfied'?

The two infinitives lend a great deal of emphasis to the verb; it is as if the appetites of the famished Israelites were contrasted with that of the locusts described earlier in the book. Even this enormous appetite will be forever satisfied by God [Crenshaw].

QUESTION—What is the textual status of the phrase וְלֹא־יֵבֹשׁוּ עַמִּי לְעוֹלָם *wəlōᵓ-yēbōšû ᶜammî ləᶜôlām* 'and my people shall never again be put to shame' in this verse?

This phrase is considered by many to have been erroneously copied from the end of the next verse: The pronominal reference in the expression 'my people' is a first person reference to YHWH, whereas the previous phrases imply third person reference to him. This phrase functions much better as the conclusion of the recognition formula of the next verse [Wolff].

QUESTION—How does Joel develop the concept of shame to this point?

The concept of shame is first introduced in 1:11–12, where it is to be an attribute of the farmers: הֹבִישׁוּ אִכָּרִים *hōbîšû ᵓikkārîm* 'be ashamed, you farmers' (1:11). This shame then becomes a property of all the nation before the day of YHWH: וְאַל־תִּתֵּן נַחֲלָתְךָ לְחֶרְפָּה *wəᵓal-titten naḥălātəkā ləḥerpâ* 'and do not give your inheritance to disgrace' (2:17). In the present passage, Joel describes the removal of this shame [Dillard]. The verb יֵבֹשׁוּ *yēbōšû* 'will be ashamed' in this passage continues the word play that Joel has pursued between בּוֹשׁ *bûš* 'to be ashamed' and יבשׁ *ybš* 'to be dry': 1:11 and 2:26 have *bûš*, and 1:12, 17 have *ybš* [Crenshaw].

2:27

And[a]-you(p)-will-know[b] that[c] I (am) in-(the-)midst(-of)[d] Israel;
I (am) YHWH your(p)-God,[e] and[f]-there-is-no[g] other,[h] and[i]- my-people[j] will- -not -be-ashamed[k] (again) for-all-time.[l]

LEXICON—a. **and-you(p)-will-know** -וְ *wə- waw* of the attached weqatal verb form [BDB p. 251], [Hol p. 84], [TWOT 519]: 'and' [Keil, Wolff;

KJV]. Dillard, NRSV, and REB express the additive relation with a new clause or sentence. Crenshaw, Allen, NIV, and TEV signal a chronological relation: 'then'. NASB signals a result relation: 'thus'.

b. **and-you(p)-will-know** 2nd masc. pl. Qal weqatal verb form of ידע *yḏʿ* [BDB p. 393], [Hol p. 128], [TWOT 848]: 'to notice' [Hol], 'to know' [Crenshaw, Keil, Allen, Dillard, Wolff; KJV NASB, NIV, NRSV, REB, TEV].

c. **that I (am) in-(the-)midst(-of) Israel** כִּי *kî* particle [BDB p. 471], [Hol p. 155], [TWOT 976]: 'that' [Crenshaw, Keil, Allen, Dillard, Wolff; KJV NASB, NIV, NRSV, REB, TEV].

d. **I (am) in-(the-)midst(-of) Israel** constr. of קֶרֶב *qereḇ* [BDB p. 899], [Hol p. 324], [TWOT 2066a]: 'midst' [Hol; Crenshaw, Keil, Dillard, Wolff; KJV NASB, NRSV]. TEV translates this noun as a preposition, "among"; Allen and NIV have "in." REB translates it as an adjective, "present."

e. **I (am) YHWH your(p)-God** constr. of אֱלֹהִים *ʾělōhîm* [BDB p. 43], [Hol p. 16], [TWOT 93c]: 'God' [all lexica, commentaries, and versions].

f. **and-there-is-no other** -וְ *wə-* *waw* connective [BDB p. 251], [Hol p. 84], [TWOT 519]: 'and' [Keil, Allen, Dillard, Wolff; KJV NASB, NIV, NRSV, REB, TEV]. Crenshaw expresses the additive relation with a new clause.

g. **and-there-is-no other** constr. of אַיִן *ʾayin* [BDB p. 34], [Hol p. 13], [TWOT 81]: 'not' [Hol]. The root meaning of *ʾayin* is 'absence' [Hol].

h. **and-there-is-no other** עוֹד *ʿôḏ* [BDB p. 728], [Hol p. 267], [TWOT 1576]: 'other' [Crenshaw], '(no) one besides' [Hol]; for the expression וְאֵין עוֹד *wəʾên ʿôḏ* 'and none else' [Keil; KJV], 'and no one else' [Wolff]; 'and there is no other' [Allen, Dillard; NASB, NIV, NRSV, TEV].

i. **and- my-people will- -not -be-ashamed** -וְ *wə-* *waw* connective [BDB p. 251], [Hol p. 84], [TWOT 519]: 'and' [Crenshaw, Keil, Allen, Dillard, Wolff; KJV NASB, NRSV, REB]. NIV expresses the additive relation with a new clause, TEV with a new sentence.

j. **my-people** constr. of עַם *ʿām* [BDB p. 766], [Hol p. 275], [TWOT 1640a]: 'people' [Hol; Crenshaw, Keil, Allen, Dillard, Wolff; NASB, KJV, NIV, NRSV, REB, TEV].

k. **will- -not -be-ashamed** 3rd masc. pl. Qal imperf. of בּוֹשׁ *bûš* [BDB p. 101], [Hol p. 36], [TWOT 222]: 'to be ashamed' [Hol; KJV], 'to be shamed' [Crenshaw; NIV], 'to be put to shame' [Keil, Dillard, Wolff; NASB, NRSV, REB], 'to be despised' [TEV], 'to be humiliated' [Allen].

l. **for-all-time** -לְ *lə-* a proclitic and עוֹלָם *ʿôlām* [BDB p. 761], [Hol p. 267], [TWOT 1631a]: 'for all time' [Hol], 'for ever' [Hol], 'to all eternity' [Keil], 'again' [Dillard]; (with the negation לֹא *lōʾ*) 'never again' [Crenshaw, Allen; NIV, NRSV, REB, TEV], 'never' [KJV, NASB], 'never more' [Wolff].

QUESTION—What is the form and rhetorical function of this verse?

This verse comprises a "recognition formula," which Joel expands much more than is customary [Crenshaw, Wolff]. It serves to authenticate the oracle to which it is attached. The formula occurs more generally as "you will know that I am the Lord"; it is usually cast, as here, as the result of some marvelous action of God [Dillard]. (Other instances of the formula are found in Exod. 20:2; Deut. 5:6; Isa. 45:5; 45:6; Ezek. 2:5; 5:13; 6:7, 10, 13–14; 7:4, 9, 27 [Crenshaw].) Here the recognition formula has even more weight than usual, being expanded by a concluding promise that YHWH's people will never again experience shame. Besides functioning as authentication of the oracle it accompanies, the recognition formula also means to direct attention beyond the marvelous work in question—in this case the reversal of Israel's poor fortunes—to YHWH, the author of that reversal. Ultimately, this recognition formula draws all the rest of the discourse unit to itself: the gift of YHWH's Spirit, the coming day of judgment upon all the earth, and his deliverance of the Israelites who have responded to his call with love and loyalty—all of these will demonstrate that it is YHWH and none other who has been active in the midst of Israel [Wolff].

QUESTION—What is the sense of the expression וִידַעְתֶּם כִּי בְקֶרֶב יִשְׂרָאֵל אָנִי *wiyḏaʾtem kî ḇəqereḇ yiśrāʾēl ʾānî* 'and you will know that I am in the midst of Israel'?

This expression, which occurs only a few times elsewhere in the OT, functions as part of the recognition formula in this passage. It appears to signify that YHWH is the God who will keep on acting for Israel, since the final clause of this verse points to the future [Wolff].

QUESTION—What is the function of the repetition of וְלֹא־יֵבֹשׁוּ עַמִּי לְעוֹלָם *wəlōʾ-yēḇōšû ʿammî ləʿôlām* 'and my people shall never again be put to shame'?

1. The repetition of this phrase, which first occurs in the preceding verse, serves to conclude this section [Keil].
2. The repetition of this phrase, coupled with the preceding recognition formula, does not signal closure, but instead looks forward to the promise of the outpouring of God's Spirit in 3:1–5 (2:28–32) [Wolff].
3. Beginning with Wellhausen, this phrase has not been viewed as a repetition at all; rather, the corresponding phrase in 2:26 is considered to have been placed there by scribal error [Wolff].
4. The repetition of this phrase pinpoints the ultimate reason for which Israel will have no more shame, namely, that YHWH is within her [Ibn Ezra, cited by Cohen].

DISCOURSE UNIT: 3:1–4:21 (2:28–3:21) [Keil, Dillard]. Keil gives the topic as "judgment upon the world of nations, and glorification of Zion"; Dillard, "the Lord's answer to the impending disaster: the day of the Lord."

DISCOURSE UNIT: 3:1–5 (2:28–32) [Crenshaw; NIV, TEV]. The topic is variously given as "the Day of the Lord" [NIV, TEV], "signs and portents" [Crenshaw], "Yahweh's promise to renew his people" [Wendland].
Comments on this discourse unit: (1) A formulaic expression for an event in the future opens this unit: וְהָיָה *wəhāyâ* 'and it will be'. (2) The first part of this unit may be said to constitute an oracle of YHWH, while the second part constitutes instruction from the prophet [Crenshaw]. (3) A possible translation problem in 3:4 (2:31) is that YHWH is the one who speaks of "the day of YHWH."

DISCOURSE UNIT: 3:1–2 (2:28–29) [NASB]. The topic is "the Promise of the Spirit" [NASB].

3:1 (2:28)
And[a]-it-will-happen[b] after[c]-this,[d]
I-will-pour-out[e] my-spirit[f] upon[g] all[h] flesh,[i] and[j]- your(p)-sons[k] and-your(p)-daughters[l] -will-prophesy[m];
your(p)-old-people/old-men[n] will-dream[o] dreams[p]; your(p)-young-men[q] will-see[r] visions.[s]

INTERTEXTUAL REFERENCE—(1) This verse is similar to Ezek. 39:29 (see *e* below) [Wendland, Wolff]. (2) This verse appears to evoke the incident recorded in Num. 11:1–12:8 [Allen, Stuart, Wendland].

TEXT—The text of this verse is not in doubt. However, the LXX's translation contains a partitive idea: ἐκχεῶ ἀπὸ τοῦ πνεύματός μου 'I will pour out some of my spirit'. Wolff thinks this comes from the influence of Num. 11:17, 25. In contrast, the Greek translations of Aquila and Symmachus both read simply τὸ πνεῦμά μου 'my spirit'. The Targum Jonathan to the Prophets interprets the sense of רוּחִי *rûḥî* 'my spirit' as רוּחַ קָדְשִׁי *rûaḥ qoḏšî* 'my holy spirit' [Wolff].

LEXICON—a. **and-it-will-happen after-this** -וְ *wə- waw* of the attached weqatal verb form [BDB p. 251], [Hol p. 84], [TWOT 519]: 'and' [Keil, Dillard; KJV, NASB, NIV]; 'then' [NRSV]. Crenshaw, Allen, Wolff, REB, and TEV express the additive relation with a new clause or sentence.

b. **it-will-happen** 3rd masc. sing. Qal weqatal verb form of היה *hyh* [BDB p. 224], [Hol p. 78], [TWOT 491]: 'to happen' [BDB, Hol], 'to come to pass' [Keil, Dillard; KJV], 'to come about' [NASB]; not explicit [Crenshaw, Allen, Wolff; NIV, REB, TEV].

c. **after-this** pl. constr. of אַחַר *ʾaḥar* [BDB p. 29], [Hol p. 10], [TWOT 68b]: 'after' [BDB, Hol]. Properly a noun, *ʾaḥar* functions here as a preposition. The expression אַחֲרֵי־כֵן *ʾaḥărê-ḵēn*, which is infrequent in the OT [Wolff], is variously translated: "after this"

[NASB, REB], "afterward(s)" [BDB; Crenshaw, Keil, Allen, Wolff; KJV, NIV, NRSV, TEV], "after these things" [Dillard].

d. **after-this** כֵּן *kēn* [BDB p. 485], [Hol p. 159], [TWOT 964b]: 'thus' [BDB, Hol].

e. **I-will-pour-out my-spirit upon all flesh** 1st sing. Qal imperf. of שׁפך *šp̄k* [BDB p. 1049], [Hol p. 381], [TWOT 2444]: 'to pour out' [BDB, Hol; Keil, Allen, Dillard, Wolff; KJV, NASB, NIV, NRSV, REB, TEV], 'to endow' [Crenshaw]. *Šp̄k* denotes a pouring out of a liquid. In 1 Sam. 1:15 and Ps. 62:9 it is used figuratively to express the free sharing of thoughts and emotions. Often God's Spirit is spoken of in terms of water, and so the gift of the Spirit is associated with the idea of pouring out (see Isa. 44:3; Ezek. 39:29; Zech. 12:10). Bewer sees in this verb a connotation of abundant giving, a sense found in the NT as well [Dillard, Wolff]. The use of *šp̄k* is all the more pointed here when one remembers the larger context of drought upon Israel: The land will have water, and its people the water of YHWH's Spirit [Dillard].

f. **my-spirit** constr. of רוּחַ *rûaḥ* [BDB p. 924], [Hol p. 334], [TWOT 2131a]: 'spirit' [all lexica, commentators, and versions except Crenshaw], 'vital force' [Crenshaw].

g. **upon all flesh** עַל *ʿal* [BDB p. 752], [Hol p. 272], [TWOT 1624p): 'upon' [Keil, Allen; KJV], 'onto' [BDB, Hol], 'on' [Dillard, Wolff; NASB, NIV, NRSV, REB, TEV], not explicit [Crenshaw].

h. **upon all flesh** constr. of כֹּל *kōl* [BDB p. 481], [Hol p. 156], [TWOT 985a]: 'all' [BDB, Hol; Crenshaw, Keil, Dillard, Wolff; KJV, NASB, NIV, NRSV, REB]. The noun *kōl* denotes a totality of something [BDB, Hol]. Allen translates the expression כָּל־בָּשָׂר *kol-bāśār* as "everybody."

i. **upon all flesh** בָּשָׂר *bāśār* [BDB p. 142], [Hol p. 51], [TWOT 291a]: 'flesh' [BDB, Hol; Keil, Dillard, Wolff; KJV, NRSV], 'mankind' [NASB, REB], 'people' [NIV], 'everyone' [TEV]. The primary sense of *bāśār* is 'animal musculature' [TWOT]. Crenshaw identifies *bāśār* with Joel's addressees: 'all of you'. The expression כָּל־בָּשָׂר *kol-bāśār* denotes variously 'men and beasts' (Gen. 6:12–17), 'the world of men' (Num. 16:22), 'the world of beasts' (Gen. 9:19), 'any man' (Deut. 5:23), and 'every man' (Isa. 40:6) [Hol].

j. **and- your(p)-sons and-your(p)-daughters -will-prophesy** -וְ *wə- waw* of the attached weqatal verb form [BDB p. 251], [Hol p. 84], [TWOT 519]: 'and' [Keil; KJV, NASB], 'so that' [Crenshaw]. Allen, Dillard, Wolff, NIV, NRSV, REB, and TEV express the additive relation with a new clause or sentence.

k. **your(p)-sons** pl. constr. of בֵּן *bēn* [BDB p. 119], [Hol p. 42], [TWOT 254]: 'son' [BDB, Hol; Keil, Allen, Dillard, Wolff; KJV, NASB, NIV, NRSV, REB, TEV], 'boy' [Crenshaw]. The plural can denote 'children' in general [BDB, Hol]. The phrase 'sons and daughters' probably denotes the young generation [Crenshaw].

l. **and-your(p)-daughters** pl. constr. of בַּת *bat* [BDB p. 123], [Hol p. 51], [TWOT 254b]: 'daughter' [all lexica, commentators, and versions except Crenshaw], 'girl' [Crenshaw].

m. **will-prophesy** 3rd pl. Niphal weqatal verb form of נבא *nbʾ* [BDB p. 612], [Hol p. 84], [TWOT 1277]: 'to prophesy' [BDB; Keil, Allen, Dillard; KJV, NASB, NIV, NRSV, REB], 'to be in prophetic ecstasy' [Hol], 'to act as a *nāḇîʾ*' [Hol], 'to speak oracles on YHWH's behalf' [Crenshaw], 'to proclaim YHWH's message' [TEV], 'to become a prophet' [Wolff]. In more ancient uses of this verb in the OT, *nḇʾ* means to be in religious ecstasy with or without song and music; in later uses, it refers to religious instruction with occasional predictions [BDB].

n. **your(p)-old-people/old-men will-dream dreams** pl. constr. of זָקֵן *zāqēn* [BDB p. 278], [Hol p. 91], [TWOT 574b]: 'old people [Crenshaw; TEV], 'old men' [Keil, Allen, Dillard, Wolff; KJV, NASB, NIV, NRSV, REB]. The plural form can denote 'old men and/or women', although it often denotes elders who exercise authority [BDB, Hol]. Here it probably does not denote 'elder' as a community functionary, but rather simply 'old man', because of the designations of other age groups in the same passage [Dillard].

o. **will-dream dreams** 3rd masc. pl. Qal imperf. of חלם *ḥlm* [BDB p. 321], [Hol p. 106], [TWOT 663]: 'to dream' [BDB, Hol; Keil, Dillard; KJV, NASB, NIV, NRSV, REB]. Crenshaw translates the expression 'to dream dreams' as "discern YHWH's will through dreams"; Allen, also TEV, as "have dreams."

p. **dreams** pl. of חֲלוֹם *ḥălôm* [BDB p. 321], [Hol p. 105], [TWOT 663a]: 'dream' [BDB, Hol; Crenshaw, Keil, Dillard, Wolff; KJV, NASB, NIV, NRSV, REB, TEV].

q. **your(p)-young-men will-see visions** pl. constr. of בָּחוּר *bāḥûr* [BDB p. 104], [Hol p. 36], [TWOT 231a]: 'young men' [BDB, Hol; Keil, Allen, Dillard, Wolff; KJV, NASB, NIV, NRSV, REB], 'young adults' [Crenshaw], 'young people' [TEV]. This term denotes young men old enough to serve in the army [Bewer].

r. **will-see visions** 3rd pl. masc. Qal imperf. of ראה *rʾh* [BDB p. 906], [Hol p. 328], [TWOT 2095]: 'to see' [all lexica, commentators, and versions except Crenshaw]. Crenshaw translates 'to see visions' as "become visionaries."

s. **visions** pl. of חִזָּיוֹן *ḥizzāyôn* [BDB p. 303), [Hol p. 99], [TWOT 633e]: 'vision' [BDB, Hol; Keil, Allen, Dillard, Wolff; KJV, NASB, NIV, NRSV, REB, TEV].

QUESTION—How should אַחֲרֵי־כֵן *ʾaḥărê-ḵēn* 'after this' be understood?

1. It should be understood as signaling temporal sequence, after the things described in the previous material [Dillard], either 2:12–17 (i.e., after the prophet has exhorted the people to turn to YHWH and after their presumable compliance) or 2:24–27 (i.e., after YHWH will have restored material prosperity) [Crenshaw, Wolff]. A temporal

understanding of ʾaḥărê-ḵēn is strengthened by Peter's reinterpretation in Acts 2 of the phrase as καὶ ἔσται ἐν ταῖς ἐσχάταις ἡμέραις 'and it will be in the last days' (based on, but going further than, the LXX's καὶ ἔσται μετὰ ταῦτα 'and after these things'), for Peter's phrase clearly refers to the *eschaton*, the end times [Dillard]. The phrase ʾaḥărê-ḵēn 'after this' introduces all the promised events in the rest of the book, even across the major discourse discontinuity after 3:5 (2:32), signaling that YHWH will indeed continue to be in the midst of his people as stated in 2:27 [Wolff].

2. It should be understood as referring back to 2:23—'after you receive the early and latter rains'—and as introducing a second result of YHWH's gift of הַמּוֹרֶה *hammôreh* 'the teacher' (2:23) [Keil]. A Jewish understanding is similar: ʾaḥărê-ḵēn is viewed as referring to the era of the Messiah (Kimchi, cited by Cohen].
3. It should be understood as signaling here an explanation of the preceding verse. In this way, 2:18–27, which promises YHWH's people freedom from hunger and enemies, is seen as promising also the outpouring of YHWH's Spirit of 3:1–5 (2:28–32) and as consequently awaiting the Pentecost of Acts 2 to be realized. The importance of this may be appreciated when one realizes that YHWH's saving presence among his people, asserted in Joel 2:27, will be permanent and not subject to their continued sinfulness; the means by which YHWH will render his people continually faithful to himself will be the outpouring of his Spirit. Closely linked to this work of the Spirit is YHWH's coming judgment on all things as symbolized by the cosmic shaking in Joel 3:1–5 (2:28–32). The salvation and judgment will both culminate when Christ returns [VanGemeren].

QUESTION—What is the function of 3:1–2 (2:28–29)?

It is to give YHWH's response to the apocalyptic threat which will come upon Israel [Dillard].

QUESTION—What is the rhetorical function of the phrase אֶשְׁפּוֹךְ אֶת־רוּחִי *ʾešpôḵ ʾeṯ-rûḥî* 'I will pour out my spirit'?

This phrase and its repetition at the end of the next verse form an inclusio (a textual unit bounded on both ends by identical or similar material) [Crenshaw].

QUESTION—In what sense should רוּחַ *rûaḥ* 'spirit' be taken in this passage?

1. Here *rûaḥ* should be taken as that divine dynamic which empowers the moral and spiritual life of mankind. (It is not identical to רוּחַ אֱלֹהִים *rûaḥ ʾĕlōhîm* of Gen. 1:2, which is concerned with the first principle of life in this world [Keil].) This force, which works only at God's command, is necessary for the accomplishing of God's will and for the obedience to his lawsas promised in Ezekiel 11 and 36), and stands in contrast to weak humanity (see Isa. 31:3; see also Ps. 51:12–13 for a reference to the stabilizing power of God's *rûaḥ*) [Wolff].

2. By *rûaḥ* Joel has nothing in mind beyond YHWH's empowering his people to experience the ecstatic states regarded by many as necessary for OT prophets to give utterance to their messages [Bewer]. In the OT, God's *rûaḥ* is represented most often as working to inspire prophecy [Dillard].
3. *Rûaḥ* should be taken here as the spirit of recognition of God, that divine power which will enable its recipients to recognize God fully (see also Isa. 1:9). According to the twelfth-century Jewish commentator Kimchi [cited by Cohen], complete freedom from sin will come with the full recognition of God.

QUESTION—What are the OT antecedents for Joel's theme of the outpouring of YHWH's spirit?

This verse belongs to the theme, starting with Moses' prayer in Num. 11:29 and continuing on to Jer. 31:33–34 and Ezek. 11:19–20 and 36:26–27, that all Israelites are, or should be, inspired at various times by YHWH's spirit [Crenshaw]. It is certainly true that the Holy Spirit was not absent from ancient Israel; he was in fact YHWH's only fully spiritual link with Israel. Even so, YHWH's presence with OT prophets and other personages cannot be characterized by any general spiritual outpouring. This was reserved for the Christian era, beginning with the Pentecost outpouring described in Acts 2 [Keil].

QUESTION—What does Joel mean by כָּל־בָּשָׂר *kol-bāśār* 'all flesh'?

1. In this passage, Joel is referring to all Israelites; the context of 2:19–3:5 (2:19–2:32) suggests as much [twelfth-century Jewish commentator Ibn Ezra, cited by Cohen; also Bewer, Crenshaw, Dillard, Wolff]. That *kol-bāśār* has this sense here is supported by the fact that YHWH's speech in this discourse unit begins (in 2:19) with distinguishing the future salvation and blessing of Israel from the doom that will come upon her attackers and from the judgment that will come upon the other nations, as is presented in 4:1–8 (3:1–8) [Wolff].[22] This does not mean to say that the ultimate fulfillment of 3:1–2 (2:28–29) need be restricted to Israelites, for this passage is applied by Paul to the church, the "new Israel," in Rom. 9:6–15. Moreover, in Gal. 3:27–28, Paul speaks of Christians clothing themselves in Christ, the same image used in reference to YHWH's Spirit in Judg. 6:34, 1 Chron. 12:19, and 2 Chron. 24:20. Paul means there would be no more class distinctions [Dillard]. This remaking of the covenant people of YHWH is taken up in 3:1–2 (2:28–29), and ultimately *kol-bāśār* here in 3:1 (2:28) must be

[22] The prophecy in Zech. 12:10 is similar: "and I will pour out on the sons of David and on the inhabitants of Jerusalem a spirit gracious and compassionate" [Crenshaw, Dillard]. Moreover, Joel is here clarifying Ezek. 39:29: "I will no longer hide my face from them, for I will pour out my Spirit on the house of Israel, declares the Sovereign LORD" (NIV).

qualified by the corresponding expression, כֹּל אֲשֶׁר־יִקְרָא בְּשֵׁם יְהוָה *kōl ʾăšer-yiqrāʾ bəšēm yhwh* ‘every one who calls on the name of YHWH’, in 3:5 (2:32) [VanGemeren]. The particular force of *kol-bāśār* in this passage is to stress the feeble humanity of the Israelites: it is their entire being and life that need the divine energizing [Wolff].

2. In this passage Joel means all mankind. *Bāśār* ‘flesh’ denotes the quality of mankind which renders mankind incapable of eternal life and of life with God. An example of the word with this meaning is in Gen. 6:3: ‘and YHWH said, my Spirit shall not strive with man (בָאָדָם *ḇāʾāḏām*) forever, for he is flesh’ (בְּשַׁגַּם הוּא בָשָׂר *bəšaggam hûʾ ḇāśār*) [Keil]. The Jewish commentator Rashi [cited by Cohen] regards Joel as meaning all those who receive from God a responsive heart (see also Ezek. 36:26).

QUESTION—What is the significance of בְּנֵיכֶם וּבְנוֹתֵיכֶם *bənêḵem ûḇənôṯêḵem* ‘your sons and your daughters’?

This could refer either to the younger generation of that day, or to a later generation; however, in view of the further reference to בַּחוּרֵיכֶם *baḥûrêḵem* ‘your young men’, it probably means the former [Crenshaw].

QUESTION—How are the groups of people mentioned in this verse and the next related to each other and to the expression כָּל־בָּשָׂר *kol-bāśār* ‘all flesh’?

1. Joel uses the expression *kol-bāśār* to refer to all the Israelites for the sake of inclusiveness and to emphasize the feeble humanity of the Israelites; he then lists various groups within this designation: sons and daughters (i.e., the young generation), young men (probably with the idea of young strong soldiers), old people, and then slaves [Crenshaw, Wolff].
2. While it is true that the various groups listed by Joel should be taken as subgroups of *kol-bāśār*, which in turn should be understood most immediately as referring to all Israelites, it does not follow that the sense of *kol-bāśār* need be ultimately restricted to only the Israelites [Keil].

QUESTION—What is the significance of the three media of inspiration mentioned in this verse—prophecy (וְנִבְּאוּ *wənibbəʾû* ‘and [your sons and daughters] will prophesy’), dreams (חֲלֹמוֹת *ḥălōmôṯ*), and visions’ (חֶזְיֹנוֹת *ḥezyōnôṯ*)?

Some commentators see them as distributed among the groups of people previously mentioned (e.g., dreams with old people), but most think that Joel actually is pointing to one reality by means of three parallel statements. For Bewer and Crenshaw, that reality is that all groups among YHWH’s people will have every sort of access to his presence and power. Similarly for Keil, who sees prophecy (נבא *nḇʾ* ‘to prophesy’) as the generic term embracing the experience of both dreams and visions, it is that the Holy Spirit and all his gifts will come to all the people. Wolff explains this outpouring of YHWH’s spirit as providing new access to

YHWH's inspiration and as signaling a new relationship between Israel and YHWH, one more free and immediate than ever before and one which will treat all Israelites alike before him. Joel expresses this goal in terms of language about prophecy, dreams, and visions, implying that Israel will become a nation of prophets. He concentrates, not upon any specific message a prophet might proclaim, but rather upon the free access to YHWH's spirit which will characterize the nation.

This view accords with current thinking reflected by TWOT (1277) that the verb *nḇʾ* 'to prophesy' was derived in BH from the noun נביא *nāḇîʾ*, which in turn signifies a spokesman. Joel's emphasis is upon the intimacy with YHWH required for the role of a prophet; the entire nation will have this intimacy with their God.

QUESTION—What is the principal association of this passage to the Pentateuch?

This verse seems to hark back to Num. 11:1–12:8, for there are numerous correspondences between the Numbers passage and 3:1–2 (2:28–29): (1) in both there is the problem of lack of food for YHWH's people;(2) the ideas of dreams and visions appear in both;(3) Joel's reference to בַּחוּרֵיכֶם *baḥûrêḵem* 'your young men' recalls Num. 11:28; and(4) Moses' prayer that all Israel would prophesy, empowered by the Spirit, is clearly germane to Joel. In 3:1–2 (2:28–29), Joel sees by faith that Moses' prayer will finally be granted [Dillard, Wolff]. Yet the content of the prophetic activity seems less the Torah than YHWH's future actions; the goal of the prophecy is something much greater than the restoration of the worship and service of YHWH as it had been known in centuries past [Wolff]. It is that the covenant community's moral life will be transformed by unfettered access of each person to YHWH [Allen, Stuart].

QUESTION—What principal association to other OT prophets does this passage have?

Joel amplifies the promise in Ezek. 39:29: "I will no longer hide my face from them, for I will pour out my Spirit (אֲשֶׁר שָׁפַכְתִּי אֶת־רוּחִי *ʾăšer šāpaḵtî ʾeṯ-rûḥî*) on the house of Israel, declares the Sovereign LORD." The Ezek. 39:29 promise is given in the context of YHWH's promise to release his covenant people from foreign enslavement. While Joel follows a tradition of Isaiah in connecting the gift of God's Spirit with a return of prosperity to the land (Isa. 44:2–5), he also connects the return of prosperity to a militaristic picture, that of YHWH driving out the great army of locusts (2:25), as in Ezek. 39:29 and Zech. 12:9–10 [Wolff].

3:2 (2:29)

And-even[a] upon the-servants[b] and-upon the-maidservants[c] in-those[d] -days,[e] I-will-pour-out my-spirit.

TEXT—In the MT there is no personal pronoun associated with הָעֲבָדִים *hāʿăḇāḏîm* 'the servants' and הַשְּׁפָחוֹת *haššəpāḥôṯ* 'the maidservants'. Different translations have viewed this fact in different ways:

Approach	Support	Reason
View the lack of pronoun as a problem and supply a 1st sing. pronoun: καὶ ἐπὶ τοὺς δούλους **μου** καὶ ἐπὶ τὰς δούλας **μου** super servos **meos** et ancillas **meas**	Later LXX tradition (followed in Acts 2:18) [Wolff] Old Latin Version [Wolff]	These translators regarded the lack of possessives qualifying “servants” and “maidservants” as strange [Crenshaw]. Not accepting the implicit 2nd pl. poss. pronoun, which suggests that YHWH’s *r̲ûaḥ* would become available even to common slaves, these translators supplied the 1st sing. poss. pronoun in order to make the passage refer instead to God’s servants [Keil].
View the lack of pronoun as a problem and regard the Hebrew definite article as filling the role of a 2nd pl. poss. pronoun.	Crenshaw; NIV	
View the lack of pronoun as not a problem and translate literally, ‘the servants’, ‘the maid servants’.	All other English versions; Vulgate	

LEXICON—a. **and-even upon the-servants** וְגַם *wəḡam* [BDB p. 168], [Hol p. 61], [TWOT 361a]: ‘even’ [BDB, Hol; Allen; NIV, NRSV, REB, TEV], ‘and even’ [Wolff; NASB], ‘too’ [Crenshaw], ‘and also’ [Keil, Dillard; KJV]. *Wəḡam* associates two elements together with an intensive nuance [Hol].

b. **the-servants** pl. of עֶבֶד *ᶜeb̲ed̲* [BDB p. 713], [Hol p. 262], [TWOT 1553a]: ‘servant’ [BDB, Hol; KJV, NIV, TEV], ‘slave’ [BDB, Hol; Allen, Dillard; REB], ‘male slave’ [Crenshaw], ‘man servant’ [Keil, Wolff], ‘male servant’ [NASB, NRSV].

c. **and-upon the-maidservants** pl. of שִׁפְחָה *šip̄ḥâ* [BDB p. 1046], [Hol p. 380], [TWOT 2442a]: ‘maidservant’ [BDB, Hol; Keil, Wolff], ‘female slave’ [Hol], ‘maid’ [BDB], ‘female slave [Crenshaw], ‘slave girl’ [Dillard; REB], ‘slave-woman’ [Allen], ‘female servant’ [Dillard; NASB], ‘handmaid’ [KJV]. Biblical Hebrew has two terms meaning ‘female slave’: אָמָה *ʾāmâ* and שִׁפְחָה *šip̄ḥâ*. The latter seems to denote a servant who is not as closely tied to the employer’s family as the former [Dillard].

d. **in- those -days I-will-pour-out my-spirit** 3rd pl. pronoun, pl. of הוּא *hûʾ* [BDB p. 214], [Hol p. 77], [TWOT 504]: ‘those’ [all lexica, commentators, and versions]. This pronoun funtions as a demonstrative qualifying יָמִים *yomîm* ‘days’ [TWOT]. The expression בַּיָּמִים הָהֵמָּה

bayyomîm hāhēmmâ is translated as “in those days” [Keil, Allen, Dillard, Wolff; KJV, NASB, NIV, NRSV, REB], “at that time” [Crenshaw; TEV].

e. **in- those -<u>days</u>** pl. of יוֹם *yôm* [BDB p. 398], [Hol p. 130], [TWOT 852]: ‘day’ [BDB, Hol].

QUESTION—To whom does עַל־הָעֲבָדִים וְעַל־הַשְּׁפָחוֹת *ʿal-hāʿăḇāḏîm wəʿal-haššəp̄āḥôṯ* ‘upon the servants and the maidservants’ refer?

1. These are the Jews’ male and female slaves who convert to following the Torah [Ibn Ezra, cited by Cohen; Allen, Dillard, Stuart, Wolff] (see Exod. 20:10; Deut. 5:14–15, 12:12).
2. These are foreigners who come to help the nation of Israel [Kimchi, cited by Cohen].

QUESTION—What is the significance of the reference to servants and slaves?

It is that they will have the same access to YHWH’s Spirit as anyone else in Israel; social status and even gender will be no barrier to inspiration from YHWH or to full participation in the community of YHWH’s people. Slaves in ancient Israel were to participate in the Sabbaths and in worship before YHWH (Exod. 20:10; Deut. 5:14; 12:12; 16:11] [Crenshaw, Wolff]. There is no record of a slave in the OT who prophesies in YHWH’s name [Keil], but some of the literary prophets took up the cause of the enslaved (see, e.g., Jer. 34:8–22, Amos 2:6–7; 5:11–12) [Wolff].

QUESTION—What is the referent of the temporal expression בַּיָּמִים הָהֵמָּה *bayyomîm hāhēmmâ* ‘in those days’?

It is the same as that of the temporal expression in the preceding verse, אַחֲרֵי־כֵן *ʾaḥărê-ḵēn* ‘after this’ [Crenshaw].

QUESTION—What is the significance of 3:1–2 (2:28–29) for the church?

It is that all Christians are to be prophets, with the Holy Spirit dwelling in them. All Christians therefore are obligated to testify of God’s truth to their generation, just as the OT prophets were obligated to testify to theirs concerning the “burden” or message with which YHWH charged them. The priesthood of all believers is accompanied by the “prophethood” of all believers [Dillard].

3:3 (2:30)

And[a]-I-will-place[b] signs[c] in-the-heavens[d] and-on-the-earth,[e] blood[f] and-fire[g] and-billows(-of)[h] smoke.[i]

TEXT—The versions of this verse in the LXX and in Acts 2:19 are displayed here, together with their differences from the MT.

Document	Translation	Remarks
LXX	καὶ δώσω τέρατα ἐν τῷ οὐρανῷ καὶ ἐπὶ τῆς γῆς αἷμα καὶ πῦρ καὶ ἀτμίδα καπνοῦ	LXX is very close to the MT.
Acts 2:19	καὶ δώσω τέρατα ἐν τῷ οὐρανῷ **ἄνω** καὶ **σημεῖα** ἐπὶ τῆς γῆς **κάτω**, αἷμα καὶ πῦρ καὶ ἀτμίδα καπνοῦ	These elements are in addition to what is found in the MT: ἄνω 'above' κάτω 'below' σημεῖα 'signs' These additions follow later LXX mss. [Dillard, Stuart, Wolff].

LEXICON—a. **and-I-will-place signs** -וְ *wə- waw* of the attached weqatal verb form [BDB p. 251], [Hol p. 84], [TWOT 519]: 'and' [Keil, Wolff; KJV, NASB]. Crenshaw, Allen, Dillard, NIV, NRSV, REB, and TEV express the additive relation with a new clause or sentence.

b. **I-will-place** 1st sing. Qal weqatal verb form of נתן *ntn* [BDB p. 678], [Hol p. 249], [TWOT 1443]: 'to place' [Dillard, Wolff], 'to give' [BDB, Hol; Keil; TEV], 'to set' [Crenshaw, Allen; REB], 'to show' [KJV, NIV, NRSV], 'to display' [NASB].

c. **signs** pl. of מוֹפֵת *môp̄ēṯ* [BDB p. 68], [Hol p. 187], [TWOT 152a]: 'sign' [BDB, Hol; Dillard], 'omen' [Hol], 'portent' [BDB; Crenshaw, Allen, Wolff; NRSV, REB], 'wonder' [BDB; Keil; KJV, NASB, NIV], 'warning' [TEV]. TEV amplifies 'warnings' by giving its object: 'warnings of that day'. *Môp̄ēṯ* denotes a phenomenon of nature [Keil], but which is extraordinary and which is taken to represent something extraordinary [Crenshaw, Wolff]. The term מוֹפְתִים *môp̄ətîm* 'wonders' was applied in Joel's day to the ten plagues of Egypt [Wolff].

d. **in-the-heavens and-on-the-earth** שָׁמַיִם *šāmayim* [BDB p. 1029], [Hol p. 375], [TWOT 2407a]: 'heavens' [BDB, Hol; Keil, Dillard; KJV, NIV, NRSV], 'sky' [BDB, Hol; Crenshaw, Allen, Wolff; NIV, REB, TEV]. The expression בַּשָּׁמַיִם וּבָאָרֶץ *baššāmayim ûḇāʾāreṣ* 'in the heavens and on the earth' means 'everywhere' [Crenshaw].

e. **in-the-heavens and-on-the-earth** אֶרֶץ *ʾereṣ* [BDB p. 76], [Hol p. 28], [TWOT 167]: 'earth (totality of land)' [Hol; Crenshaw, Keil, Allen, Dillard, Wolff; KJV, NASB, NIV, NRSV, REB, TEV].

f. **blood and-fire and-billows(-of) smoke** דָּם *dām* [BDB p. 196], [Hol p. 28], [TWOT 436]: 'blood' [all lexica, commentators, and versions except TEV], 'bloodshed' [TEV].

g. **and-fire** אֵשׁ *ʾēš* [BDB p. 77], [Hol p. 29], [TWOT 172]: 'fire' [all lexica, commentators, and versions].

h. **and-billows(-of) smoke** pl. constr. of תִּימָרָה *tîmārâ* [BDB p. 1071], [Hol p. 389], [TWOT 2523d]: 'billow' [NIV], 'column' [BDB, Hol;

Allen, Dillard; NASB, NRSV, REB], 'pillar' [Keil; KJV], 'cloud' [TEV], 'mushrooms' [Wolff]. Crenshaw translates this noun with a participle: 'mushrooming'. The word is applied only to rising smoke [Hol]. If it is from the same root as תָּמָר *tāmār* 'date-palm', then it presumably denotes the billowing of rising smoke in a shape reminiscent of the date palm [Dillard].

i. **smoke** עָשָׁן *ʿāšān* [BDB p. 798], [Hol p. 286], [TWOT 1712a]: 'smoke' [all lexica, commentators, and versions].

QUESTION—What is the significance of the three terms דָּם וָאֵשׁ וְתִימֲרוֹת עָשָׁן *dām wāʾēš wətîmărôt ʿāšān* 'blood and fire and billows of smoke'?

These terms, which are images of destruction on earth, are in a chiasm with the two expressions in the following verse, which are images of change in the heavens:

דָּם *dām* 'blood'
אֵשׁ *ʾēš* 'fire'
תִּימֲרוֹת עָשָׁן *tîmărôt ʿāšān* 'billows of smoke'

הַשֶּׁמֶשׁ יֵהָפֵךְ לְחֹשֶׁךְ *haššemeš yēhāpēk ləḥōšek* 'the sun shall be turned to darkness'
וְהַיָּרֵחַ לְדָם *wəhayyārēaḥ lədām* 'and the moon to blood'

The first three images, those of 3:3 (2:30), are images of battle and destruction of lives and of cities, although some have suggested that 'billows of smoke' represents either a storm in the desert or a volcanic eruption [Bewer, Crenshaw, Wolff]. Keil says that the expression is reminiscent of the smoke that enveloped Mount Sinai when YHWH descended upon it (Exod. 19:18). Here, according to Kimchi [cited by Cohen], the images function as the harbingers of YHWH's judgment, as the Israelites would recall the blood and fire accompanying the plagues YHWH sent upon Egypt (Exod. 7:17; 9:24). Stuart, however, regards these images, not as harbingers of YHWH's approaching judgment, but as phenomena associated directly with his judgment; he remarks that the expression לִפְנֵי בּוֹא יוֹם יְהוָה *lipnê bôʾ yôm yhwh* in the next verse can be understood as "in the presence of the coming of the day of YHWH" as easily as "before the coming of the day of YHWH."

QUESTION—What was (or will be) the fulfillment of 3:3–3:5 (2:30–2:32)?

Destruction in connection with YHWH's judgment is proposed as the fulfilment, but opinions differ as to which particular destruction is in view:

1. The destruction of Jerusalem by the Babylonians [Grotius, also Turretius, cited by Keil].
2. Assaults upon the Jews by surrounding ethnic groups in postexilic times [cited by Keil].
3. The last judgment [Tertullian, cited by Keil].
4. The totality of destruction of human power and empire, beginning with the destruction of Jerusalem by the Romans (well after the Pentecost

outpouring), continuing on with the destruction of the Roman Empire and every human empire and domination after that, until all power opposed to YHWH is destroyed, as described in 3:2 (4:2). God's continuous judgment falling upon these powers was the reason for Peter's exhortation in Acts 2:40 on the day of Pentecost, σώθητε ἀπὸ τῆς γενεᾶς τῆς σκολιᾶς ταύτης 'save yourselves from this wicked generation' [Keil].

3:4 (2:31)

The-sun[a] shall-be-turned[b] to-darkness[c] and-the-moon[d] (shall-be-turned) to-blood,[e]

before[f] (the-)day(-of)[i] YHWH comes[j] the-great[g] and-the-fearful[h] (day).

LEXICON—a. **the-sun** שֶׁמֶשׁ *šemeš* [BDB p. 1039], [Hol p. 378], [TWOT 2417a]: 'sun' [all lexica, commentators, and versions].

b. **the-sun shall-be-turned into-darkness** 3rd masc. sing. Niphal imperf. of הפך *hpk̲* [BDB p. 245], [Hol p. 82], [TWOT 512]: 'to be turned into something' [BDB, Hol; Dillard; KJV, NASB, NIV, NRSV, REB], 'to turn into something' [Keil], 'to become' [Wolff].

c. **into-darkness** חֹשֶׁךְ *ḥōšek̲* [BDB p. 365], [Hol p. 119], [TWOT 769a]: 'darkness' [most lexica, commentators, and versions]. Crenshaw and TEV translate יֵהָפֵךְ לְחֹשֶׁךְ *yēhāpēk̲ ləḥōšek̲* as "will be darkened"; Wolff, as "becomes darkened."

d. **and-the-moon (shall-be-turned) to-blood** יָרֵחַ *yārēaḥ* [BDB p. 437], [Hol p. 144], [TWOT 913a]: 'moon' [all lexica, commentators, and versions].

e. **to-blood** דָּם *dām* [BDB p. 196], [Hol p. 28], [TWOT 436]: 'blood' [most lexica, commentators, and versions]. Some use adjectival phrases: 'blood-red' [Crenshaw], 'as red as blood' [TEV], 'bloody' [Wolff].

f. **before the- day(-of) YHWH comes** לִפְנֵי *lip̄nê* [BDB p. 815], [Hol p. 293], [TWOT 1782b]: 'before' [all lexica, commentators, and versions].

g. **the-great and-the-fearful (day)** גָּדוֹל *gād̲ôl* [BDB p. 152], [Hol p. 55], [TWOT 315d]: 'great' [all lexica, commentators, and versions except Crenshaw]. Crenshaw treats this adjective as an adverb, translating הַגָּדוֹל וְהַנּוֹרָא *haggād̲ôl wəhannôrāʾ* as "greatly awesome." He also takes this expression as adverbial, modifying the transforming of the sun and moon, although most others seem to treat it as modifying "the day of YHWH."

h. **and-the-fearful (day)** masc. sing. Niphal part. of ירא *yrʾ* [BDB p. 431], [Hol p. 142], [TWOT 907]: 'to be fearful' [BDB], 'to be feared' [Hol], 'to be dreadful' [BDB; Dillard; NIV], 'terrible' [Keil, Wolff; KJV, NRSV, REB, TEV], 'awesome' [Crenshaw; NASB].

i. **before the- <u>day(-of)</u> YHWH comes** constr. of יוֹם *yôm* [BDB p. 398], [Hol p. 130], [TWOT 852]: 'day' [all lexica, commentators, and versions].

j. **before the- day(-of) YHWH <u>comes</u>** Qal infin. constr. of בּוֹא *bôʾ* [BDB p. 97], [Hol p. 34], [TWOT 212]: 'to come' [all lexica, commentators, and versions except Crenshaw], 'to dawn' [Crenshaw].

QUESTION—What is the nature of the parallelism between הַשֶּׁמֶשׁ *haššemeš* 'the sun' and הַיָּרֵחַ *hayyārēaḥ* 'the moon'?

The relation is synchronous, not diachronic; that is, the text is not saying that there shall be signs by day and signs by night, but rather that even phenomena affecting the moon shall be visible because of the darkness falling during the day [Stuart]. For this reason, although one could explain a reddish appearance to the moon as the result of sandstorms or of fire raging in the area [Crenshaw] or of natural lunar eclipses, Joel is probably referring to changes in the moon that everyone recognizes as unnatural, portending catastrophe on a cosmic scale [Wolff].

QUESTION—What relation does this verse have with the preceding verse?

The inverted Hebrew word order shows that this verse is off-line in its predictive genre. Thus this verse is an explanatory expansion of the previous verse, rather than a piece of new information [Wolff].

QUESTION—What significance lies in the image of the darkened sun?

1. Joel uses this image in 2:10 and in 4:15 (3:15) as a feature of the day of YHWH. The fright caused to ancient peoples by solar eclipses might be an element in the power of this image. The darkened sun is found elsewhere among the prophets, in Amos 8:9, Isa. 13:10, 34:4, Ezek. 32:7–8, and Jer. 4:23 [Crenshaw]; it reminds one of the plague of darkness sent by YHWH upon Egypt (Exod. 10:21), as do the signs mentioned in the previous verse. Some, like Calvin, have taken the description of these celestial phenomena as metaphors for the entire creation's being filled with terrifying premonitions of God's coming judgment upon man, but there is no reason why Joel should not be understood literally here. There is indeed a strong connection between the degree of mankind's righteousness and the well-being of creation, over which man has been placed in charge [Keil].
2. The eleventh-century Jewish commentator Rashi understood the sun's darkening as a divine device to counter those who worshiped the sun [cited by Cohen].
3. These signs were understood by the twelfth-century Jewish commentator Ibn Ezra to be harbingers of divine punishment coming upon the nations of Gog and Magog [cited by Cohen]; thirteenth-century Jewish commentator Rambam understood them as presaging divine judgment upon all the nations [cited by Cohen]; twelfth-century Jewish commentator Kimchi understood them as presaging divine judgment upon Israel herself during her involvement in the war with Gog and Magog [cited by Cohen].

QUESTION—What is the significance of יוֹם יְהוָה *yôm yhwh* 'the day of YHWH' in this passage?

It is that, for Israel, the effect of the day of YHWH has been reversed. In 2:1–10, that day was about to bring judgment and disaster to Israel, but now that YHWH has heard the cries of his people, it will free them from their hardships and enemies [Wendland, Wolff].

3:5 (2:32)

And[a]-it-will-be[b] (that) everyone[c] who calls[d] on-(the-)name(-of)[e] YHWH will-escape,[f]

for[g] on-(the-)mountain(-of)[h] Zion and-in-Jerusalem there-will-be[i] escape[j] as[k] YHWH said,[l]

and-among-the-survivors[m] whom YHWH will-call.[n]

TEXT—The MT's reading of the final phrase is not in serious doubt; the Greek versions of both Aquila and Theodotion support it. The LXX, however, reads καὶ εὐαγγελιζόμενοι 'and bearing good news', which suggests a textual reading of וּמְבַשְּׂרִים *ûməḇaśrîm* (from בשׂר *bśr* 'to bring news'), instead of the MT וּבַשְּׂרִידִים *ûḇaśrîḏîm* 'and among the survivors'. The Syriac version reads 'as the Lord has said to those who survive, whom the Lord appoints' [Wolff].

SYNTAX—The syntactic role of the phrase *and-among-the-survivors whom YHWH will-call* is disputed:

Syntactic role	Resulting sense	Followed by
A dependent clause indicating beneficiary of *will-escape*	"for on Mount Zion and in Jerusalem there will be escape, as YHWH said, **for the survivors whom YHWH will call.**"	KJV, NASB, NIV, REB. The preposition בְּ- *bə-* 'among' amounts here to indicating a beneficiary.
An independent clause, coordinate with *there-will-be escape*	"for on Mount Zion and in Jerusalem there will be escape, as YHWH said, **and among the survivors shall be those whom YHWH will call.**"	Cohen, Keil; NRSV. The preposition *bə-* is taken here in one of its normal senses, "among."

LEXICON—a. **and-it-will-be** וְ- *wə- waw* of the attached weqatal verb form [BDB p. 251], [Hol p. 84], [TWOT 519]: 'and' [Keil, Dillard, Wolff; KJV, NASB, NIV], 'then' [NRSV, REB], 'but' [Allen; TEV]. Crenshaw expresses the additive relation with a new clause.

b. **and-it-will-be** 3rd masc. sing. Qal weqatal verb form of היה *hyh* [BDB p. 224], [Hol p. 78], [TWOT 491]: 'to be' [Dillard], 'to happen' [BDB, Hol], 'to come to pass' [Keil; KJV], 'to come about' [NASB], not explicit [Allen, Wolff; NIV, NRSV, REB, TEV]. Crenshaw translates the verb וְהָיָה *wəhāyâ* as a temporal expression, "henceforth."

c. **(that) everyone who calls on-(the-)name(-of) YHWH** כֹּל *kōl* [BDB p. 481], [Hol p. 156], [TWOT 985a]: 'everyone' [Crenshaw, Keil, Allen, Wolff; NIV, NRSV, REB], 'all' [BDB, Hol; Keil, Dillard;

TEV], 'whoever' [NASB], 'whosoever' [KJV]. The noun *kōl* denotes a totality of something [BDB, Hol].

d. **who calls on-(the-)name(-of) YHWH** 3rd masc. sing. Qal imperf. of קרא *qr*ᵓ [BDB p. 894], [Hol p. 323], [TWOT 2063]: 'to call' [Hol; Keil, Allen, Dillard, Wolff; KJV, NASB, NIV, NRSV], 'to implore' [Crenshaw], 'to invoke' [REB], 'to ask for help' [TEV]. The expression קְרֹא בְּשֵׁם *qərōᵓ bəšēm* means to invoke someone's name [BDB]. Note that the two instances of *qr*ᵓ 'to call' in this verse form a kind of inclusio [Crenshaw]. The proclitic -בְּ *bə-* in *bəšēm* 'on the name of', indicates, strictly speaking, accompaniment (e.g., 'with'). The expression אֲשֶׁר־יִקְרָא בְּשֵׁם יְהוָה *ᵓăšer-yiqrāᵓ bəšēm yhwh* means, literally, one in prolonged contact with YHWH by praying to him. The contact denoted by קרא *qr*ᵓ is foremost that of worship, as in Gen. 12:8; there can also be a nuance of public witness to the truth of YHWH among the nations while surrounded by the pantheon of the nations' gods, as in Isa. 41:25; 44:5, Isa. 12:4; and Ps. 105:1 [Wolff].

e. **on-(the-)name(-of) YHWH** constr. of שֵׁם *šēm* [BDB p. 1027], [Hol p. 374], [TWOT 2405]: 'name' [all lexica, commentators, and versions except Crenshaw and TEV]. Crenshaw and TEV, understanding *šēm* to be a metonymy for YHWH himself, omit "name." TEV has "who ask the LORD"; Crenshaw has "who implores YHWH." In the OT, *šēm* came to function as a figure of speech meaning YHWH, particularly in the semantic areas of worship and fidelity (cf. Prov. 18:10) [Crenshaw].

f. **will-escape** 3rd masc. sing. Niphal imperf. of מלט *mlṭ* [BDB p. 572], [Hol p. 197], [TWOT 1198]: 'to escape' [BDB], 'to get oneself to safety' [Hol], 'to avoid harm' [Crenshaw], 'to be saved' [Keil, Dillard, Wolff; NIV, NRSV, REB, TEV], 'to be delivered' [KJV, NASB], 'to be safe' [Allen]. *Mlṭ* means to survive great danger [Crenshaw].

g. **for on-(the-)mountain(-of) Zion and-in-Jerusalem** כִּי *kî* particle [BDB p. 471], [Hol p. 155], [TWOT 976]: 'for' [Crenshaw, Keil, Dillard, Wolff; KJV, NASB, NIV, NRSV, TEV], 'because' [Allen], not explicit [REB].

h. **on-(the-)mountain(-of) Zion** constr. of הַר *har* [BDB p. 249], [Hol p. 83], [TWOT 517a]: 'mountain' [BDB, Hol], 'mount' [Crenshaw, Keil, Allen, Dillard, Wolff; KJV, NASB, NIV, NRSV, REB]. TEV conflates the phrase בְּהַר־צִיּוֹן וּבִירוּשָׁלַםִ *bəhar-ṣîyôn ûḇîrûšālam* and translates it as "in Jerusalem."

i. **there-will-be (an-) escape** 3rd fem. sing. Qal imperf. of היה *hyh* (see *b* above): 'to be' [Crenshaw, Keil, Dillard, Wolff; KJV, NASB, NIV, NRSV, REB].

j. **(an-) escape** פְּלֵיטָה *pəlêṭâ* [BDB p. 812], [Hol p. 292], [TWOT 1774d]: 'escape' [BDB, Hol; Crenshaw, Dillard, Wolff], 'deliverance' [BDB, Hol; KJV, NIV], 'what is spared' [Hol], 'escaped remnant' [BDB], 'remnant' [REB], 'fugitive' [Keil], 'those who escape' [NASB,

NRSV]. Allen translates this noun as a clause, "people will find security"; TEV has "some ... will escape."

k. <u>as</u> **YHWH said** כַּאֲשֶׁר *ka'ăšer* [BDB p. 455], [Hol p. 149], [TWOT 939]: 'as' [all lexica, commentators, and versions], 'according as' [BDB].

l. **as YHWH** <u>**said**</u> 3rd sing. Qal perf. of אמר *'mr* [BDB p. 55], [Hol p. 21], [TWOT 118]: 'to say' [BDB, Hol; Keil, Dillard, Wolff; KJV, NASB, NIV, NRSV, TEV], 'to promise' [Crenshaw, Allen; REB].

m. **and-among-the-**<u>**survivors**</u> **whom YHWH will-call** pl. of שָׂרִיד *śārîḏ* [BDB p. 975], [Hol p. 355], [TWOT 2285a]: 'survivor' [BDB, Hol; Crenshaw, Allen, Dillard, NASB, NIV, NRSV, REB], 'those that are left' [Keil], 'remnant' [KJV], 'those who survive' [Wolff]. TEV translates this noun as a verb: "will survive."

n. **whom YHWH** <u>**will-call**</u> sing. masc. Qal part. of קרא *qr'* (see *d* above): 'to call' [BDB, Hol; Crenshaw, Keil, Allen, Dillard, Wolff; KJV, NASB, NIV, NRSV, REB], 'to choose' [TEV]. For the relative clause וּבַשְּׂרִידִים אֲשֶׁר יְהוָה קֹרֵא *ûḇaśrîḏîm 'ăšer yhwh qōrē'* TEV has "those whom I choose will survive."

QUESTION—What is the significance of כֹּל אֲשֶׁר־יִקְרָא בְּשֵׁם יְהוָה *kōl 'ăšer-yiqrā' bəšēm yhwh* 'every one who call on the name of YHWH'?

1. It means everyone who worships YHWH (cf. Gen. 4:26; 12:8) [Allen], with the connotation of reverencing YHWH in the worldly pantheistic milieu [Wolff]. This in turn implies people in covenantal relationship with YHWH, bound to him in loyalty [Crenshaw, Keil], presumably exlusively so [Stuart]. Keil, however, unlike Allen, Stuart, and Wolff, sees the reference to Zion and Jerusalem not in literal terms, but in spiritual terms: these place names stand for the center of the Kingdom of God.
2. It means everyone who sincerely asks God to be rescued from the catastrophes of which Joel writes [Bewer; Kimchi, cited by Cohen].

QUESTION—To what does the phrase כַּאֲשֶׁר אָמַר יְהוָה *ka'ăšer 'āmar yhwh* 'as YHWH has said' refer?

1. This might be a reference to the words of YHWH in 2:27 or, if Obadiah was written before Joel, it might be a reference to Obad. 17: 'on Mount Zion there will be an escape (תִּהְיֶה פְלֵיטָה *tihyeh pəlêṭâ*)' [Crenshaw]. Bewer has no doubt that this passage is a reference to Obadiah.
2. This is a reference to Isa. 4:3: "and it shall be that he who is left in Zion and he who is left in Jerusalem will be said to be holy (קָדוֹשׁ יֵאָמֶר לוֹ *qāḏôš yē'āmer lô*), everyone who is written for life (כָּל־הַכָּתוּב לַחַיִּים *kol-hākkāṯûḇ laḥayyîm*) in Jerusalem" [nineteenth-century Jewish commentator Malbim, cited by Cohen]. This passage occurs in a context of the messianic restoration of Israel.
3. This phrase shows that the present passage is tied to text material available to Joel and that the content does not originate with him; for this passage treats the theme of escape for Israel in the manner of

Psalms 46, 48, and 76, of Isa. 28:16 and 14:32, and of Obad. 17 [Keil, Wolff].

QUESTION—What is the textual status of וּבַשְּׂרִידִים אֲשֶׁר יְהוָה קֹרֵא *ûḇaśrîḏîm ʾăšer yhwh qōrēʾ* 'and among the survivors whom YHWH will call'?

The Masoretic textual tradition is firm; it is also supported by the Greek versions of Aquila and Theodotion (see "TEXT" above). However, the fact that this phrase follows the speech margin כַּאֲשֶׁר אָמַר יְהוָה *kaʾăšēr ʾāmar yhwh* 'as YHWH has said' makes it appear that it might have been added at a later date. The various senses understood by various ancient versions suggest that the phrase's status is in fact uncertain [Wolff].

QUESTION—Who are the referents in the phrase וּבַשְּׂרִידִים אֲשֶׁר יְהוָה קֹרֵא *ûḇaśrîḏîm ʾăšer yhwh qōrēʾ* 'and among the survivors whom YHWH will call'?

1. The referents are probably the Israelites who are in Jerusalem, the same who are his subject matter from the start of the book. However, it is not their taking refuge in Jerusalem which counts, but the fact that YHWH has called them and that they have responded to him; thus, these are they who correspond to the Israelites mentioned in 3:1–2. These will indeed find refuge in Jerusalem with YHWH [Wolff]. Similarly, Malbim regards these survivors as the Israelites who have escaped YHWH's condemnation [cited by Cohen]. Bewer, Stuart, and Wolff regard this expression as having the same referent as the first part of this verse. Wolff points out that the term שָׂרִיד *śārîḏ* 'survivor' often occurs in the OT with פְּלֵיטָה *pəlêṭâ* 'escape'. Stuart furthermore identifies these survivors as those who have returned to Jerusalem following YHWH's judgment brought upon Israel by either the Assyrians or the Babylonians.
2. The referents are YHWH's people who live in Judah but outside Jerusalem, and perhaps also those who are still in exile. This verse might refer ahead to 4:7 (3:7), where YHWH speaks of rousing his people who have been abroad in slavery as if they were asleep [Crenshaw]. This interpretation requires that one regard this phrase as a second complement to the expression "there will be an escape."
3. The referents are foreigners from every land who trust in YHWH. This view requires understanding Zion and Jerusalem in spiritual terms, rather than in physical terms [Keil].

QUESTION—What is the sense of the expression אֲשֶׁר יְהוָה קֹרֵא *ʾăšer yhwh qōrēʾ* 'whom YHWH will call'?

1. It is 'whom YHWH will call to honor' [Kimchi, cited by Cohen].
2. It includes the sense of 'to invite' [eleventh-century Jewish commentator Rashi, Targum, cited by Cohen].
3. It includes the sense of 'to appoint, to choose', as in Isa. 51:2 [Wolff].

QUESTION—How is Joel 3:1–3:5 (2:28–32) used in the NT?

The following chart summarizes the use of this passage in the NT.

Joel 3:1–3:5 (2:28–32) as cited in the Pentecost sermon of Acts 2:17–21		
General theme of use	**Differences between cited passage in Acts 2 and its original form in Joel**	**Remarks**
Introduces a new era in which the Spirit will be poured out on all God's people [Wolff]. This new era is the eschatological era [Crenshaw, Keil].	Peter calls the servants God's servants (καί γε ἐπὶ τοὺς δούλους μου καὶ ἐπὶ τὰς δούλας μου), whereas "servants" and "maidser-vants" areunqualified in MT.	
	The citation does not have the last half of 3:5 (2:32), although in Acts 2:39 Peter cites part of it: ὑμῖν γάρ ἐστιν ἡ ἐπαγγελία καὶ τοῖς τέκνοις ὑμῶν καὶ πᾶσιν τοῖς εἰς μακρὰν, **ὅσους ἂν προσκαλέσηται κύριος ὁ θεὸς ἡμῶν**.	The expression ὑμῶν καὶ πᾶσιν τοῖς εἰς μακρὰν indicates that Peter intends these words for the Jews who have come from far away to Jerusalem as much as for those who inhabited Jerusalem and Judea [Allen, Crenshaw]. Keil says it shows that God's Spirit is also for the Gentiles. In the long run, all of mankind is the designated beneficiary of the promise, for only this view accords with the total Scriptural witness [Wolff].
	Joel 3:1 (2:28) begins with וְהָיָה אַחֲרֵי־כֵן *wəhāyâ ʾaḥărê-ḵēn* 'and after this'; this is changed in Peter's speech to καὶ ἔσται ἐν ταῖς ἐσχάταις ἡμέραις 'and it will be in the last days' (the LXX reads καὶ ἔσται μετὰ ταῦτα 'and it will be after these things') [Keil].	
	Peter's speech preserves the LXX's partitive expression ἐκχεῶ ἀπὸ τοῦ πνεύματός 'I will pour out of my Spirit', whereas the MT reads אֶשְׁפּוֹךְ אֶת־רוּחִי *ʾešpôḵ ʾeṯ-rûḥî* 'I will pour out my Spirit' [Dillard].	

General remarks on Acts 2 and its use of Joel 3:1–5 (2:28–32)
Peter identifies Jesus of Nazareth as the one pouring out the Holy Spirit: (τοῦτον τὸν >Ιησοῦν ἀνέστησεν ὁ θεός, οὗ πάντες ἡμεῖς ἐσμεν μάρτυρες· τῇ δεξιᾷ οὖν τοῦ θεοῦ ὑψωθεὶς, τήν τε ἐπαγγελίαν τοῦ πνεύματος τοῦ ἁγίου λαβὼν παρὰ τοῦ πατρὸς, ἐξέχεεν τοῦτο ὃ ὑμεῖς [καὶ] βλέπετε καὶ ἀκούετε) [Crenshaw, Keil].
Peter considers the name of Jesus to be the same as the name of YHWH (καὶ ἔσται πᾶς ὃς ἂν ἐπικαλέσηται τὸ ὄνομα κυρίου σωθήσεται, Acts 2:21) [Dillard].

Citation of Joel 3:5a in Rom. 10:13 πᾶς γὰρ ὃς ἂν ἐπικαλέσηται τὸ ὄνομα κυρίου σωθήσεται
Paul does not restrict the reference to Jews, for the preceding context destroys any distinction between Jew and non-Jew as far as the possibility of salvation is concerned (οὐ γάρ ἐστιν διαστολὴ >Ιουδαίου τε καὶ Ἕλληνος, ὁ γὰρ αὐτὸς κύριος πάντων, πλουτῶν εἰς πάντας τοὺς ἐπικαλουμένους αὐτόν). Paul clearly takes 'all' in Joel 3:5 (2:32) as a universal [Crenshaw, Dillard, Wolff].

QUESTION—What was the fulfillment of 3:1–3:5 (2:28–2:32)?

1. Certain ancient Christian commentators posited various events in OT times as the fulfillment of this passage, for example, the Babylonian conquest of Jerusalem or attacks upon the Jews newly returned from the Babylonian exile [Keil].
2. Whatever the fulfillment of this passage, the Acts 2 Pentecost event was not it; Luke compares this event to the Joel passage but does not see it as its fulfillment [so dispensationalist A. C. Gaebelein, *The Acts of the Apostles: An Exposition* (New York: Our Hope, 1912), cited by Treier].
3. The Acts 2 outpouring of the Holy Spirit was the complete fulfillment of this passage. This is the position of most of the church fathers and early Lutheran theologians [Keil], and this appears to be John Stott's position [J. R. W. Stott, *The Message of Acts* (Downers Grove: InterVarsity, 1990), cited by Treier].
4. The Pentecost outpouring only began the fulfillment, which continues today. Keil gives the following reasons for this view:
   (a) The introductory phrase אַחֲרֵי־כֵן *ʾaḥărê-ḵēn* 'after this' refers in Joel's immediate context back to 2:23, but Peter interprets it as indicating the era of the Messiah, the time period in which the Kingdom of God is advancing to completion, for this is what is always meant by the expression ἐν ταῖς ἐσχάταις ἡμέραις 'in the last days'.
   (b) Peter saw that the promise of God's grace in Christ was open, not only to all Jews, but also to all Gentiles who were called by God (καὶ πᾶσιν τοῖς εἰς μακρὰν, ὅσους ἂν προσκαλέσηται κύριος ὁ θεὸς ἡμῶν, Acts 2:39). This indicates a long period in which God's grace would call and save.

(c) The cosmic events involving the heavenly bodies and the appearance of blood, fire, and columns of smoke are to be associated with destructive warfare which will plague the nations from Joel's time until the full realization of the Kingdom of God.

5. While Joel 3:1–3:5 (2:28–2:32) has only one fulfillment, this fulfillment is perceived from the different perspectives of Joel, Peter, and Luke. Treier supports this view as follows:

(a) Joel sees in 2:18–27 the promise that YHWH will bring material prosperity back to Judah; similarly, he sees in 3:1–3:5 (2:28–2:32) the promise of an indeterminately later ("after this") spiritual prosperity for his people ("all flesh" referring to all classes of Israelites, even the underprivileged). The cosmic signs in this passage are to be associated with YHWH's apocalyptic judgment upon the other nations, but his faithful people ("everyone who calls on the name of YHWH") will be spared this judgment.

(b) Peter structures his Acts 2 sermon around Joel 3:1–3:5 (2:28–2:32) in such a way as not to alter Joel's purpose. Peter has three main points: (i) He explains the Pentecost outpouring of the Spirit by identifying Joel's אַחֲרֵי־כֵן *ʾaḥărê-ḵēn* 'after this' with his own day. He changes *ʾaḥărê-ḵēn* to ἐν ταῖς ἐσχάταις ἡμέραις (ἀλλὰ τοῦτό ἐστιν τὸ εἰρημένον διὰ τοῦ προφήτου >Ιωήλ ...Καὶ ἔσται ἐν ταῖς ἐσχάταις ἡμέραις 'this is what was spoken of ... and it will be in the last day'). (ii) He bases this identification on the events surrounding Jesus Christ. (iii) He implies in Acts 2:22 that the miraculous signs performed by Jesus have the same function as the cosmic signs foretold in Joel 3:3–4 (2:30–31). In fact, when citing the LXX of Joel 3:3 (2:30), Peter adds the term σημεῖα 'signs' (for the LXX itself corresponds very closely to the MT: καὶ δώσω τέρατα ἐν τῷ οὐρανῷ καὶ ἐπὶ τῆς γῆς). This term then leads into the Acts 2:22 discussion of the miraculous δυνάμεσι καὶ τέρασι καὶ σημείοις performed by Jesus. These signs speak of coming judgment and correspond in function to the cosmic signs of Joel 3:3–4 (2:30–31): as Jesus' miraculous signs are to inspire repentance and belief in him, so the cosmic signs foretold in Joel 3:3–4 (2:30–31) are to inspire repentance, even though they are presumably considered to lie in the future as harbingers of the day of the Lord.

(c) Luke presents in Acts the *eschaton*, the end-times, which is associated with the Spirit's outpouring, as in Joel. The *eschaton* is characterized by an increasingly enlarging program of divine redemption. In Acts 2, Peter may well have understood with Joel that "all flesh" was limited to Israelites and proselytes; but Luke's entire account in Acts presents an ever-widening understanding of "all flesh," including the Samaritans (Acts 8) and then the Gentiles in the region of Israel (Acts 10) with the reason for their inclusion

(Acts 11), standing in opposition to the Judaizers within the early church (Acts 15).

DISCOURSE UNIT: 4:1–21 (3:1–21) [Allen, Stuart, Wolff]. Allen gives the topic as “the judgment of the nations”; Wolff, as “the judgment on the enemies of God’s people.” Stuart is similar to Wolff. This discourse unit comprises Oracle 2 of Part 2 in Wendland’s analysis.

Comments on this discourse unit. The first part of this unit, 4:1–8 (3:1–8), has the form of an ancient lawsuit against covenant breakers, with a summons to judgment, the rehearsal of the accusations, a cross-examination, and the pronouncement of a verdict, which ends with the promise of warfare against the guilty parties [Dillard].

This discourse unit is thematically very different from the preceding one, 2:18–3:5 (2:18–32). That unit took the form of an oracle responding to a cry for help, the cry implicit in 2:12–17. In this new discourse unit, however, YHWH reveals himself, building on the recognition formula in 2:27 and leading ultimately to another one in 4:17 (3:17) [Wolff].

QUESTION—How integral to this section are its various parts?

1. This unit contains two insertions, leaving as text original to this chapter only 4:1–3 (3:1–3), 4:9–14 (3:9–14), and 4:15–17 (3:15–17) [Wolff].
   (a) The first insertion consists of 4:4–8 (3:4–8). There are some devices which attempt to produce cohesion between this insertion and the surrounding passages, but they are few. They include the introductory link וְגַם *wəḡam* in 4:4 (3:4). There are, on the other hand, many features of 4:4–8 (3:4–8), which mark this passage as having been inserted into the text at a later date. Some of these differences are as follows: This section specifically addresses the Phoenician cities of Tyre and Sidon and the region of Philistia whereas “all nations” are addressed in 4:2, 9, 11, and 12 (3:2, 9, 11, and 12). This section also has expressions found nowhere else in the book: בְּנֵי יְהוּדָה *bənê yəhûḏâ* ‘the sons of Judah’ and בְּנֵי יְרוּשָׁלָֽם *bənê yərûšālāim* ‘the sons of Jerusalem’, the exception being in 4:19 (3:19), which is itself another addition. Moreover, this insertion has no language describing Judah or anything in her as belonging to YHWH, whereas in 4:2–3 (3:2–3), we find עַמִּי *ʿammî* ‘my people’ (twice), נַחֲלָתִי *naḥălāṯî* ‘my heritage’, and אַרְצִי *ʾarṣî* ‘my land’. The style of 4:4–8 (3:4–8) is different as well—there are longer sentences and more subordinate constructions. Finally, there is a very close association in the thought pattern between 4:1–3 (3:1–3) and 4:9–17 (3:9–17) [Wolff]. Crenshaw is less definite than Wolff, but agrees that 4:4–8 (3:4–8) might be a later insertion. As opposed to the generality of “all nations” elsewhere, here two peoples, the Phoenicians and the Philistines, are named as

proximate causes of suffering inflicted on YHWH's people, and two others, the Ionians and the Sabeans, as distant causes [Crenshaw]. In 4:4–8 (3:4–8), the principle of "an eye for an eye" is stressed, whereas the rest of the book features YHWH's warfare against the nations in the Valley of Jehoshaphat. In addition, the book generally presents eschatological or even ahistorical elements which transcend specific historical periods. In 4:4–8 (3:4–8), however, the focus is on punishment which is liable to fall in a historical period. In addition, some of this passage's vocabulary is rather unique to it: בֵּן *bēn* 'son' appears instead of יֶלֶד *yeled*; גְּמוּל *gəmûl* 'recompense' and גמל *gml* 'to requite' are also unique to the passage [Dillard].

(b) The second insertion is the concluding passage, 4:18–21 (3:18–21). The introductory linking formula (וְהָיָה בַיּוֹם הַהוּא *wəhāyâ bayyôm hahûʾ* 'and it shall be in those days') is atypical for the rest of the book. Considerations about the content of this section also lead to the conclusion that one is dealing here with an addition: Egypt and Edom are mentioned specifically, as opposed to a general invocation of all nations in most of the book. Moreover, 4:21 (3:21) seems to draw on 4:17 (3:17): וַיהוָה שֹׁכֵן בְּצִיּוֹן *wayhwh šōkēn bəṣiyyôn* 'YHWH dwells on Mount Zion' in 4:21 (3:21) has a resemblance to וִידַעְתֶּם כִּי אֲנִי יְהוָה אֱלֹהֵיכֶם שֹׁכֵן בְּצִיּוֹן הַר־קָדְשִׁי *wîdaʿtem kî ʾănî yhwh ʾĕlōhêkem šōkēn bəṣiyyôn har-qodšî* 'and you shall know that I, YHWH, am your God, who dwell on Zion, my holy mountain' in 4:17 (3:17). However, this second insertion cannot come from the first insertion's source, for both content and style are quite different. The second insertion could very well come from Joel himself, as much of the language is the same as most of the book [Wolff].

2. Although there are clear thematic subsections to this discourse unit, certain factors militate against the claim that 4:1–21 (3:1–21) includes separate oracles: (a) the fact that prophets commonly inveighed against specific nations; (b) the fact that 4:4–8 (3:4–8) fits the style of an ancient covenant lawsuit; (c) the possibility that 4:4–8 is an exposition of 4:2–3 (3:2–3), in that it details specific charges against Tyre, Sidon, and Philistia, in the place of earlier generalities against unnamed nations [Dillard]. Some have pointed to the switch from poetry to prose in 4:4–8 and to the switch back to poetry in 4:9 (3:9), but other prophetic literature features similar switches (see Amos 7) [Stuart].

DISCOURSE UNIT: 4:1–11 (3:1–11) [Wendland]. This unit comprises Stanza C´; the topic is "Yahweh will gather all nations for judgment."

DISCOURSE UNIT: 4:1–3 (3:1–3) [Cohen, Crenshaw]. Cohen calls the topic "God's assize"; Crenshaw, "YHWH's reasons for judging the nations."

4:1 (3:1)

For[a] behold[b] in- those[c] -days[d] and-at- that[e] -time[f]

(MT1) when[g] I-will-bring-back[h] (the-)captivity(-of)[i] Judah and-Jerusalem,

(MT2) when[g] I-will-restore[h] (the-)fortunes(-of)[I] Judah and-Jerusalem,

INTERTEXTUAL REFERENCE—The time expression in this verse is found elsewhere only in Jer. 50:4, 20, which is also in a context of the restoration of Jerusalem, and in Jer. 33:15 (see third "QUESTION" below) [Crenshaw, Stuart, Wendland, Wolff].

TEXT–The MT reads אָשֵׁוּב *ʾāšēwb̲*, a Qal imperfect form; however, the *Qərê* (a marginal reading designed by the Masoretes to be read in place of what was written in the text) is אָשִׁיב *ʾāšîb̲*, a Hiphil imperfect form that means 'I will bring back'. This reading comes from the Masoretes' difficulty in assigning a transitive sense to the Qal of שׁוּב *šûb̲* 'to return'. The Targum Jonathan to the Prophets interprets the expression as 'when I return the captivity', thus assigning the sense of the phrase to a specific idea contained within a more general possible sense of "when I restore the fortunes"; the LXX has a sense similar to that of the Targum Jonathan [Wolff].

LEXICON—a. **<u>for</u> behold in-those-days and-at-that-time** כִּי *kî* particle [BDB p. 471], [Hol p. 155], [TWOT 976]: 'for' [all commentators and versions except Stuart, Wolff, NIV, REB, TEV]. The expression כִּי הִנֵּה *kî hinnēh* is translated "indeed it shall be so!" [Wolff], "indeed" [Stuart], not explicit [NIV, REB, TEV].

b. **for <u>behold</u>** הִנֵּה *hinnēh* [BDB p. 243], [Hol p. 82], [TWOT 510a]: 'behold' [BDB, Hol; Bewer, Dillard, Keil; KJV, NASB], 'take note' [Allen], not explicit [Crenshaw; NIV, NRSV, REB, TEV]. *Hinnēh* signals prominence of an idea or event [Keil].

c. **in- <u>those</u> -days** pl. of הוּא *hûʾ* [BDB p. 214], [Hol p. 77], [TWOT 480]: 'those' [BDB, Hol; Allen, Bewer, Crenshaw, Dillard, Keil, Stuart, Wolff; KJV, NASB, NIV, NRSV]. *Hēmmâ*, a personal pronoun, functions here as a demonstrative adjective [Hol].

d. **in- those <u>-days</u>** pl. of יוֹם *yôm* [BDB p. 398], [Hol p. 130], [TWOT 852]: 'day' [all lexica, commentators, and versions except TEV], not explicit [TEV].

e. **and-at- <u>that</u> -time** fem. of הוּא *hûʾ* (see above): 'that' [BDB, Hol; Allen, Bewer, Crenshaw, Dillard, Keil, Stuart, Wolff; KJV, NASB, NIV, NRSV, REB, TEV]. *Hûʾ*, a personal pronoun, functions here as a demonstrative adjective [Hol].

f. **and-at- that <u>-time</u>** עֵת *ʿēt̲* [BDB p. 773], [Hol p. 286], [TWOT 1650b]: 'time' [all lexica, commentators, and versions except Hol]. Holladay says that *ʿēt̲* can denote either duration or a point in time.

g. **(MT1) <u>when</u> I-will-bring-back** אֲשֶׁר *ʾăšer* [BDB p. 81], [Hol p. 30], [TWOT 184]: 'when' [Allen, Bewer, Crenshaw, Dillard, Keil, Stuart, Wolff; KJV, NASB, NIV, NRSV, REB], not explicit [TEV].

h. **(MT1) when <u>I-will-bring-back</u>** 1st sing. Qal imperf. of שׁוּב *šûḇ* [BDB p. 996], [Hol p. 362], [TWOT 2340]: 'to bring back' [BDB, Hol], 'to lead back' [Hol], 'to turn' [Keil], 'to bring again' [KJV], 'to reverse' [Allen]. Many translate the phrase אֲשֶׁר אָשֵׁוב אֶת־שְׁבוּת *ʾăšer ʾāšēwḇ ʾeṯ-šəḇûṯ* similarly: 'when I (will) restore the fortune(s)' [Bewer, Crenshaw, Dillard, Stuart, Wolff; NASB, NIV, NRSV]. Cohen regards the phrase as an idiom with this meaning. Allen and REB have "reverse the fortunes." TEV has "restore the prosperity."

i. **(the-)<u>captivity(-of)</u> Judah and-Jerusalem** constr. of שְׁבוּת *šəḇûṯ* [BDB p. 986], [Hol p. 358], [TWOT 2311d]: 'captivity' [Keil; KJV], 'imprisonment' [Hol]. The primary sense of *šəḇûṯ* is 'captivity', but it has the more general force of 'fortunes' in the expression הֵשִׁיב שְׁבוּת *hēšîḇ šəḇûṯ* (lit., 'to turn the captivity'). BDB has "to restore the fortunes." While *hēšîḇ šəḇûṯ* does indeed include the liberation of Jewish prisoners, its meaning is broader: a complete restoration of Israel's well-being [Keil].

QUESTION—To what does the introductory כִּי *kî* particle refer?

1. It refers back to 3:1 (2:28) [Dillard].
2. It refers back to the reference to the day of YHWH in 3:4 (2:31), yielding the idea that on the day that YHWH executes his judgment, only those who call on him will be saved, for he will bring all the nations opposed to him to judgment in the Valley of Jehoshaphat [Keil].
3. In an immediate sense, it refers back to 3:5 (2:32).If the faithful in Judah will be saved, then that implies that YHWH will do away with their enemies so that his people may enjoy security [Crenshaw, Wolff]. Crenshaw considers that in a larger sense *kî* links the passage it introduces to the preceding section, 3:1–5 (2:28–32): YHWH's faithful people, who have been given direct access to him by the power of the Spirit with which they will be endowed, will have nothing to fear from the judgment YHWH will inflict upon all the nations. Wolff sees *kî* here as providing a continuation of 2:19–3:5 (2:19–32) in that this conjunction introduces a further set of oracles that respond to the people's cry for help implicit in 2:12–17.
4. It is an intensifying particle, 'indeed', following on the heels of 3:5 (2:32): the safety given to YHWH's people in 3:5 is intensified by the presentation of the judgment to come upon the hostile nations [Stuart].

QUESTION—What is the function of הִנֵּה *hinnēh* in this verse?

1. Here it marks, as it normally does, prominence of the event that it introduces [Keil].
2. Here it marks change of topic: from the safety that YHWH's faithful people will gain to the justice he will mete out to her enemies [Crenshaw].

QUESTION—What does the temporal reference בַּיָּמִים הָהֵמָּה וּבָעֵת הַהִיא *bayyomîm hāhēmmâ ûḇāʿēṯ hahîʾ* 'in those days and at that time' signify?

This unusually lengthy formula is found elsewhere in only two passages: (1) Jer. 33:15, where it is in the context of the coming Messiah's rendering justice among God's people, and (2) Jer. 50:4, 20, in the larger context of YHWH's punishing Babylon and the more immediate context of Judah's repentance and forgiveness at YHWH's hands. The two parts of this phrase are probably synonymous, lending prominence to the following passage; it is possible, however, that the second part ('at that time') might be treating as punctiliar a time duration implied by the first part [Crenshaw]. Thus Joel adopts both the phrase and the general theme of Israel's restoration from Jeremiah [Stuart, Wolff].

QUESTION—To what time does the temporal reference refer?

It refers to the time described in 3:1 (2:28), when YHWH shall pour out his Spirit; contemporaneously in this verse, it refers to the restoration of Judah's fortunes [Keil, Wolff].

QUESTION—What is the meaning of שְׁבוּת *šəḇûṯ* and of the expression אָשׁוּב אֶת־שְׁבוּת *ʾāšēwḇ ʾeṯ-šəḇûṯ* ?

1. The primary sense of *šəḇûṯ* is 'captivity' (from שׁבה *šḇh* 'to capture'), but a second, more general sense is 'fortunes', which is conveyed in the expression הֵשִׁיב שְׁבוּת *hēšîḇ šəḇûṯ*, literally, 'to turn the fortunes' [BDB; Keil].
2. *Šəḇûṯ* is a cognate accusative of שׁוּב *šûḇ* 'to return' [Mitchell J. Dahood, *Psalms* III. Anchor Bible, 1970; cited in TWOT 2311]. The expression *hēšîḇ šəḇûṯ*, according to this interpretation is 'to turn the turning', that is, 'to restore one to well-being, to turn one's fortunes'.
3. Some contexts in the OT seem to indicate the first option, while others indicate the second; here, however, the sense appears ambiguous. Joel does indeed speak of a certain captivity in the following verses. But the linking formula that introduces 4:1 (3:1) seems to speak of reversal of the general misfortune so prominent in Joel 1–3 [Crenshaw, Dillard].

4:2 (3:2)

and[a]-I-will-gather[b] all the-nations[c]

and-I-will-bring-them[d] to[e] (the-)valley[f](-of) Jehoshaphat and-I-will-enter-into-judgment[g] against-them there[h]

because-of[i] my-people[j] and-my-possession[k] Israel which they-scattered[l] among[m]-the-nations

and- they-divided-up[n] -my-land.[o]

LEXICON—a. **and-I-will-gather all the-nations** -וְ *wə- waw* of the attached weqatal verb form [BDB p. 251], [Hol p. 84], [TWOT 519]: 'then' [Bewer, Wolff], 'also' [KJV], no explicit translation [Allen, Dillard, Crenshaw, Keil, Stuart; NASB, NIV, NRSV, REB, TEV].

b. **I-will-gather all the-nations** 1st sing. Piel weqatal verb form of קבץ *qḇṣ* [BDB p. 867], [Hol p. 312], [TWOT 1983]: 'to gather together' [Hol; Keil; REB], 'to bring together' [Allen], 'to gather' [BDB; Bewer, Crenshaw, Dillard, Stuart, Wolff; KJV, NASB, NIV, NRSV, TEV].

c. **all the-nations** pl. of גּוֹי *gôy* [BDB p. 156], [Hol p. 57], [TWOT 326e]: 'nation' [all lexica, commentators, and versions].

d. **and-I-will-bring-them to (the-)valley(-of) Jehoshaphat** 1st sing. Hiphil perf. of ירד *yrd* [BDB p. 432], [Hol p. 143], [TWOT 909]: 'to bring down' [BDB, Hol; Bewer, Dillard, Keil, Stuart; KJV, NASB, NIV, NRSV], 'to take down' [Allen], 'to bring' [TEV], 'to make descend' [Crenshaw], 'to lead down' [Wolff; REB].

e. **to (the-)valley(-of) Jehoshaphat** אֶל *ʾel* [BDB p. 39], [Hol p. 16], [TWOT 91]: 'to' [all lexica, commentators, and versions except Keil and KJV], 'into' [Keil; KJV].

f. **(the-)valley(-of) Jehoshaphat** עֵמֶק *ʿēmeq* [BDB p. 771], [Hol p. 277], [TWOT 1644a]: 'valley' [BDB, Hol; Allen, Bewer, Crenshaw, Dillard, Keil, Stuart, Wolff; KJV, NASB, NIV, NRSV, REB, TEV], 'plain' [Hol].

g. **and-I-will-enter-into-judgment against-them there** 1st sing. Niphal weqatal verb form of שׁפט *šp̄ṭ* [BDB p. 1047], [Hol p. 380], [TWOT 2443]: 'to enter in/into judgment' [Bewer, Stuart, Wolff; NASB, NIV, NRSV], 'to go to court' [Hol], 'to plead' [Hol; KJV], 'to seek one's claim' [Hol], 'to execute judgment' [Crenshaw], 'to enter litigation' [Dillard], 'to contend' [Keil], 'to enter into controversy' [BDB], 'to bring to judgment' [REB], 'to judge' [TEV], 'to put on trial' [Allen]. The word עִמָּם *ʿimmām* that follows *šp̄ṭ* in the Hebrew text is generally translated "with them" or "against them," depending on the translation of *šp̄ṭ*.

h. **there** שָׁם *šām* [BDB p. 1027], [Hol p. 374], [TWOT 2404]: 'there' (locative) [BDB, Hol; Allen, Bewer, Dillard, Keil, Stuart, Wolff; KJV, NASB, NIV, NRSV, REB, TEV], 'where' (locative relative pronoun) [Crenshaw].

i. **because-of my-people and-my-possession Israel** עַל *ʿal* [BDB p. 752], [Hol p. 272], [TWOT 1624p): 'because of' [Crenshaw, Bewer], 'with regard to' [Hol], 'concerning' [BDB, Hol; Dillard, Keil; NIV], 'on account of' [Wolff; NRSV], 'for' [Allen; KJV, TEV], 'on behalf of' [Stuart; NASB, REB].

j. **my-people** constr. of עָם *ʿām* [BDB p. 766], [Hol p. 275], [TWOT 1640a]: 'people' [all lexica, commentators, and versions]. The word *ʿām* refers to an entire people and stresses their ethnic unity [Hol]. REB conflates עַמִּי *ʿammî* 'my people' and נַחֲלָתִי *naḥălāṯî* 'my inheritance' and translates this as 'my own people'.

k. **and-my-possession Israel** constr. of נַחֲלָה *naḥălâ* [BDB p. 635], [Hol p. 234], [TWOT 1342a]: 'possession' [Allen, Stuart, Wolff], 'hereditary possession' [Hol], 'heritage' [Hol; Bewer; KJV, NRSV], 'inheritance' [Crenshaw, Dillard, Keil; NASB, NIV]. As frequently happens in the later and postexilic prophets, the term "Israel" here refers, not to the defunct northern kingdom, but to the southern kingdom of Judah [Dillard]. It is, however, possible that Joel means the northern kingdom also, which had fallen to the Assyrians [Crenshaw].

l. **which <u>they-scattered</u> among-the-nations** 3rd pl. Piel perf. of פזר *pzr* [BDB p. 808], [Hol p. 290], [TWOT 1755]: 'to scatter' [BDB, Hol; Allen, Bewer, Dillard, Keil, Stuart, Wolff; KJV, NASB, NIV, NRSV, REB, TEV], 'to disperse' [Hol; Crenshaw]. Compare שֶׂה פְזוּרָה יִשְׂרָאֵל *śeh pəzûrâ yiśrāʾēl* 'Israel is a scattered flock' in Jer. 50:17.

m. **<u>among</u>-the-nations** -בְּ *bə-* [BDB p. 88], [Hol p. 32], [TWOT 193]: 'among' [Allen, Bewer, Crenshaw, Dillard, Keil, Stuart, Wolff; KJV, NIV, NASB, NRSV, REB].

n. **and- <u>they-divided-up</u> -my-land** 3rd pl. Piel perf. of חלק *ḥlq* [BDB p. 328], [Hol p. 107], [TWOT 669]: 'to divide' [BDB, Hol; Bewer, Dillard, Keil; NRSV, TEV], 'to divide up' [Stuart, Wolff; NASB, NIV], 'to apportion' [BDB; Crenshaw], 'to part' [KJV], 'to share out' [Allen; REB].

o. **my-<u>land</u>** constr. of אֶרֶץ *ʾereṣ* [BDB p. 76], [Hol p. 28], [TWOT 167]: 'land' [BDB, Hol; Bewer, Crenshaw, Dillard, Keil, Stuart, Wolff; KJV, NIV, NRSV, REB, TEV], 'territory' [BDB, Hol], 'country' [Allen]. TEV specifies that it is YHWH's land: "Israel, my land."

QUESTION—Which nations does the term כָּל־הַגּוֹיִם *kol-haggôyim* refer to?

It refers to the nations which oppressed YHWH's people, as the rest of the verse indicates [Keil]. The term כֹּל *kōl* 'all' specifies, on the face of it, all nations, just as the offense against God's people is seen as having come from all quarters under the sun [Crenshaw].

QUESTION—What is עֵמֶק יְהוֹשָׁפָט *ʿēmeq yəhôšāpāṭ* 'the Valley of Jehoshaphat'?

1. *Yəhôšāpāṭ* means 'YHWH judges'. It is a functional name, similar to עֵמֶק הֶחָרוּץ *ʿēmeq heḥārûṣ* 'the valley of the verdict' of 4:14 (3:14) [Cohen]. A major Christian tradition (starting in the fourth century A.D. [Crenshaw]) identifies it with the Kidron Valley on the eastern side of the old city of Jerusalem [Keil]. In support of this identification is the fact that the river emanating from YHWH's Temple (see 4:18 (3:18)) flows into the Kidron [Dillard]. Against this view, one notes that the Kidron is only a dry stream bed (wadi), not a valley, and certainly not large enough for an assembly place for whole nations, although Jer. 31:40 mentions the Kidron Valley as part of the area which will be strewn with the slain who have been judged by YHWH [Crenshaw, Wolff]. *Yəhôšāpāṭ* is interpreted by the Targum Jonathan as "to the plain of the judicial decision," and by Theodotion's Greek translation as εἰς τὴν χώραν τῆς κρίσεως 'into the country of judgment'. The LXX simply transliterates: εἰς τὴν κοιλάδα Ιωσαφατ [Wolff].

2. Some have identified *ʿēmeq-yəhôšāpāṭ* with the valley of 2 Chron. 20:24–26, the site of Jehoshaphat's victory over the Edomites, named the Valley of Blessing [Keil].
3. Others have identified *ʿēmeq-yəhôšāpāṭ* with the Tyropoeon Valley, a depression running through Jerusalem. *Tyropoeon* is a Greek name, deriving from a term for cheesemakers. In 4:14 (3:14) *ʿēmeq-yəhôšāpāṭ* is called עֵמֶק הֶחָרוּץ *ʿēmeq heḥārûṣ* 'the valley of the verdict'. But in 1 Sam. 17:18 there is a word for cheese which is very similar or identical to *ḥārûṣ* 'verdict': חָרִיץ *ḥārîṣ* [BDB, Hol] or חָרוּץ *ḥārûṣ* [Dillard].
4. The term *ʿēmeq-yəhôšāpāṭ* probably refers to the Hinnom Valley, which lies to the west of Jerusalem [Cohen].
5. Joel's use of *ʿēmeq-yəhôšāpāṭ* is not intended to correspond to any physical feature; it is a purely visionary element [Crenshaw]. Joel chose it, not for its geographical suitability, but for the symbolism of its name (*Yəhôšāpāṭ* means 'YHWH judges'), which fits the apocalyptic quality of the book [Allen, Wolff]. Joel conceives of the valley as near to Jerusalem, but makes nothing of that image; indeed, the view that this is a purely symbolic usage is strengthened when one notes that the term is changed to עֵמֶק הֶחָרוּץ *ʿēmeq heḥārûṣ* 'the valley of the verdict' in 4:14 (3:14) [Allen]. Stuart likewise is drawn to a symbolic view of *ʿēmeq-yəhôšāpāṭ*. Crenshaw points out that Joel stands in a strong tradition of prophesying that YHWH will execute judgment in a valley (see Isa. 10:12–14; Ezek. 38–39; Zech. 9:14–16; Zech. 12:1–9).

QUESTION—What is the nature of the assembly of nations in *ʿēmeq-yəhôšāpāṭ* 'the Valley of Jehoshaphat'?

Joel here stands in a prophetic tradition of foretelling that YHWH will gather all nations to judge them, as in Isa. 66:18, Jer. 25:31, Zeph. 3:8, and Mic. 4:12. [Crenshaw].

QUESTION—What is YHWH's purpose in assembling the nations in the Valley of Jehoshaphat?

1. He has assembled them in order to bring litigation against them, for the Niphal stem of שׁפט *špṭ* normally denotes the beginning of a judicial action, the grounds of which appear in this and following verses [Dillard].
2. He has assembled them in order to execute sentence upon them, for the Niphal perf. of שׁפט *špṭ* can mean 'to execute judgment' when accompanied by the preposition עם *ʿim* 'with' (see Ezek. 38:22, וְנִשְׁפַּטְתִּי אִתּוֹ בְּדֶבֶר וּבְדָם *wənišpaṭtî ʾittô bədeḇer ûḇədām* 'and I will execute judgment on them with plague and with blood', and also 2 Chron. 22:8).
3. He has assembled them in order to accuse them, to pronounce sentence upon them, and to execute that sentence [Wolff], in keeping with the monarch's duty to fill all of these roles.

QUESTION—When did the scattering of YHWH's people and the division of the land mentioned in this verse take place?

1. Joel can mean only the Babylonian and Roman conquests of Israel; any attacks by surrounding peoples before these conquests do not qualify as a wholesale scattering of the Jews and division of the land. It should be noted that the scattering continues to the present day [Keil, who dates the prophet Joel in the first part of the reign of Joash over Judah].
2. Joel means primarily the Babylonian conquest of Judah, but he may be thinking also of the Assyrian conquest and subsequent dispersal of the northern kingdom in 731 A.D. and 722 A.D. [Crenshaw, Wolff]. He might also have in mind various depredations committed upon occupied Israel in her weakened state by bordering ethnic groups [Stuart].

QUESTION—What is the significance of the content of 4:2b–6 (3:2b–6)?

These verses present the grounds for YHWH's action against the nations. The Philistine regions are singled out for special attention in 4:4–6 (3:4–6) [Dillard].

QUESTION—What was the reason for the gravity of the charges brought by YHWH against the nations?

It was that the nations had tried to undo the work of salvation that YHWH had wrought for the Israelites in rescuing them from slavery, in making of them a nation, and in allotting to them the land. YHWH himself had divided up the land (Josh. 13–22; Mic. 2:1–5) [Crenshaw, Dillard, Wolff]. The charges are driven home by the possessive forms in this verse: עַל־עַמִּי *ʿal-ʿammî* 'on account of **my** people', וְנַחֲלָתִי *wənaḥălāṯî* 'and [against] **my** possession', וְאֶת־אַרְצִי חִלֵּקוּ *wəʾeṯ-arṣî ḥillēqû* 'and you have divided up **my** land' [Crenshaw].

QUESTION—What is the significance of the use of the name יִשְׂרָאֵל *yiśrāʾēl* 'Israel' in this verse?

Here this term is applied mainly to Judah and Jerusalem, although it is possible that the conquest of the northern kingdom and the subsequent deportation of its survivors into the Assyrian Empire in 731 and 722 B.C. is a secondary reference.

4:3 (3:3)

And[a]-for[b] my-people[c] they-threw[d] lots,[e]
and[f]-they-gave[g] the-boy(s)[h] for[i]-prostitute(s),[j]   and-the-girl(s)[k] they-sold[l] for-wine,[m] and[n]-they-drank.[o]

LEXICON—a. <u>and</u>-**for my-people they-threw lots** -וְ *wə- waw* connective [BDB p. 251], [Hol p. 84], [TWOT 519]: 'and' [Bewer, Keil, Stuart, Wolff; KJV, REB], 'also' [NASB], not explicit [Crenshaw, Dillard; NIV, NRSV, TEV]. Allen expresses the additive relation with a new clause.

b. <u>for</u> **my-people** אֶל *ʾel* [BDB p. 39], [Hol p. 16], [TWOT 91]: 'for' [Allen, Dillard, Keil, Stuart, Wolff; KJV, NASB, NIV, NRSV], 'over'

[Crenshaw, Bewer]. TEV renders the phrase אֶל־עַמִּי *ʾel-ʿammî* 'for my people' more explicitly: "to decide who would get the captives."

c. **for my-people** constr. of עָם *ʿām* [BDB p. 766], [Hol p. 275], [TWOT 1640a]: 'people' [Hol; Allen, Bewer, Crenshaw, Dillard, Keil, Stuart, Wolff; KJV, NASB, NIV, NRSV, REB]. The word *ʿām* refers to an entire people, stressing their ethnic unity [Hol]. TEV renders עַמִּי *ʾammî* 'my people' as a people in defeat: "the captives."

d. **they-threw lots** 3rd pl. Qal perf. of ידד *ydd* [BDB p. 391], [Hol p. 128], [TWOT 845]: 'to throw' [Hol; Allen; TEV], 'to cast' [BDB; Bewer, Crenshaw, Dillard, Keil, Stuart, Wolff; KJV, NASB, NIV, NRSV]. The REB translates יַדּוּ גוֹרָל *yaddû gôrāl* 'to cast lots' as "to divide by lot."

e. **lots** גּוֹרָל *gôrāl* [BDB p. 174], [Hol p. 58], [TWOT 381a]: 'lot' [Hol; Allen, Bewer, Crenshaw, Dillard, Keil, Stuart, Wolff; KJV, NASB, NIV, NRSV, REB], 'dice' [TEV]. Casting lots was a traditional way of dividing up war booty [Dillard] and captives (see Obadiah 11; Nah. 3:10) [Crenshaw].

f. **and-they-gave the-boy(s) for-prostitute(s)** -וְ *wə- waw* of the attached wayyiqtol verb form [BDB p. 251], [Hol p. 84], [TWOT 519]: 'and' [Bewer, Wolff; KJV,NIV, NRSV], not explicit [Allen, Crenshaw, Dillard, Stuart; NASB, REB, TEV].

g. **they-gave the-boy(s)** 3rd masc. pl. Qal wayyiqtol verb form of נתן *ntn* [BDB p. 678], [Hol p. 249], [TWOT 1443]: 'to give' [Hol; Bewer, Crenshaw, Dillard, Keil, Wolff; KJV], 'to trade' [Stuart; NASB, NIV, NRSV], 'to barter' [REB], 'to sell' [Allen].

h. **they-gave the-boy(s)** יֶלֶד *yeled* [BDB p. 409], [Hol p. 135], [TWOT 867b]: 'boy' [BDB, Hol; Allen, Bewer, Crenshaw, Dillard, Keil, Stuart, Wolff; KJV, NASB, NIV, NRSV, REB, TEV], 'youth' [BDB]. The definite article prefixed to 'boy' signals the generic use, hence 'boys' (see Gesenius § 126 *m*) [Wolff].

i. **for-prostitute(s)** -בְּ *bə-* [BDB p. 88], [Hol p. 32], [TWOT 193]: 'for' [Keil, Stuart, Wolff; KJV, NASB, NIV, NRSV, REB], 'for the sake of' [Hol], 'for the use of' [Bewer], 'as/for the price for/of' [Allen, Crenshaw], 'to pay for' [TEV]. The proclitic *bə-* often introduces the price of something [Dillard]. The LXX reads ἔδωκαν τὰ παιδάρια πόρναις 'they gave the boys into prostitution'; the Vulgate is similar with *et posuerunt puerum in prostibulo* [Wolff, Dillard]. Although this interpretation is allowed by BH grammar, *bə-* probably functions here to indicate commercial exchange, since the phrase וַיִּתְּנוּ הַיֶּלֶד בַּזּוֹנָה *wayyitnû hayyeled bazzōnâ* 'and they gave boys for a harlot' parallels וְהַיַּלְדָּה מָכְרוּ בַיַּיִן *wəhayyaldâ mākərû bayyayin* 'and the girls they sold for wine' [Crenshaw, Wolff].

j. **for-prostitute(s)** זוֹנָה *zōnâ* (properly the Qal fem. part. of זנה *znh* 'to commit fornication') [BDB p. 275], [Hol p. 90], [TWOT 563]: 'prostitute' [Hol; Allen, Dillard, Stuart; NIV, NRSV, TEV], 'harlot'

[Bewer, Crenshaw, Keil, Wolff; KJV, NASB], 'whore' [REB]. The singular *zōnâ* indicates collectivity, 'prostitutes' (cf. יֶלֶד *yeled* 'boy' in *h* above) [Wolff].

k. **and-the-<u>girl(s)</u> they-sold for-wine** יַלְדָּה *yaldâ* [BDB p. 409], [Hol p. 135], [TWOT 867b]: 'girl' [BDB, Hol; Allen, Bewer, Crenshaw, Dillard, Stuart, Wolff; KJV, NASB, NIV, NRSV, REB, TEV], 'maiden' [Keil]. Y*aldâ* can denote a girl of marriageable age [BDB, Hol].

l. **they-sold** מכר *mkr* [BDB p. 569], [Hol p. 194], [TWOT 1194]: 'to sell' [BDB, Hol; Bewer, Crenshaw, Dillard, Keil, Stuart, Wolff; KJV, NASB, NIV, NRSV, REB], 'to barter' [Allen]. In its rendering of מָכְרוּ *mākərû* 'and they sold' TEV makes the destination of sale explicit: "to sell into slavery."

m. **for-<u>wine</u>** יַיִן *yayin* [BDB p. 406], [Hol p. 134], [TWOT 864]: 'wine' [Hol; Allen, Bewer, Crenshaw, Dillard, Keil, Stuart, Wolff; KJV, NASB, NIV, NRSV, REB, TEV].

n. **<u>and</u>-they-drank** -וְ *wə-* *waw* of the attached C (see *f* above): 'and' [Allen, Bewer, Crenshaw, Dillard, Keil; NRSV], not explicit [TEV], introducer of purpose (e.g., 'that they might drink') [KJV, NASB, NIV]; introducer of a relative clause (e.g., 'which they drank') [Stuart, Wolff].

o. **<u>they-drank</u>** 3rd masc. pl. Qal wayyiqtol verb form of שׁתה *šth* [BDB p. 1059], [Hol p. 385], [TWOT 2477]: 'to drink' [Hol; Allen, Bewer, Crenshaw, Dillard, Keil, Stuart, Wolff; KJV, NASB, NIV], 'to drink down' [NRSV], not explicit [TEV]. The REB renders מָכְרוּ בַיַּיִן וַיִּשְׁתּוּ *mākərû bayyayin wayyištû* 'they sold for wine and they drank' with the verb 'to drink' made into a noun: "selling for a drink of wine."

QUESTION—When did wholesale enslavement of the Jewish population occur?

It occurred in the wars fought by the Ptolemaeans and Seleucids, and again in the Jewish wars with Rome. The first such war, culminating with the capture of Jerusalem in 70 A.D., saw 97,000 Jews enslaved. Many were sold at ignominiously low prices [Keil].

DISCOURSE UNIT: 4:4–8 (3:4–8) [Cohen, Crenshaw]. Cohen has as the topic "indictment of Tyre, Zidon and Philistia"; Crenshaw, "special instances of divine recompense."

Comments on this discourse unit: Containing an indictment (4:4–6) and a sentence (4:7–8), this unit has the form of a verdict being passed upon a criminal. Moreoever, it concentrates heavily upon the concepts of buying, selling, and taking reprisals (thematic intensity), with consistent alternation between first and second persons (grammatical intensity) [Wendland].

4:4 (3:4)
(MT1) Furthermore[a] what[b] (do) you(p) (want) with-me, Tyre[c] and-Sidon[d]
(MT2) Furthermore[a] what[b] (are) you(p) to-me, Tyre[c] and-Sidon[d]
(MT3) Furthermore[a] what[b] (do) you(p) (have) against-me,Tyre[c] and-Sidon[d]
and-all (the-)districts(-of)[e] Philistia[f]?
(Are) you(p) paying-back[g] reprisals[h] against-me? (MT) And-if[i] you(p) retaliate[j] against-me, (ET) Or[i] (are) you(p) retaliating[j] against-me?
I-will- very[k] quickly[l] -bring[m] your(p)-retaliation[n] upon[o]-your(p)-head.[p]

SYNTAX—The syntactic role of וְאִם *wə'im* in (MT ~ ET) is in dispute:

Syntactic role of וְאִם *wə'im*	Followed by	Remarks
Introduces a condition: '**if** you retaliate against me'.	Crenshaw; NASB, KJV, NIV, NRSV, REB, TEV.	**Requirement**: This view must accept the MT definite article prefix *ha-*: *haggəmûl* 'the reprisal'. **Opposing view**: The nations in question have already acted against YHWH; thus the conditional 'if' is in fact moot [Wolff].
Introduces a second question: '**or** are you intending to do something against me?'	Allen, Bewer, Dillard, Keil, Stuart, Wolff. LXX reads this way.	**Requirement**: This view requires that the definite article prefix *ha-* in *haggəmûl* be changed to the interrogative particle -הֲ *hă-*. BH grammar allows אִם *'im* to introduce yes-no questions following a first question introduced by the interrogative particle *hă-*. **Support**: The poetry's parallelism is better served by a disjunctive question [Allen].

LEXICON—a. <u>**furthermore**</u> **what** וְגַם *wəḡam* [BDB p. 168], [Hol p. 61], [TWOT 361a]: 'furthermore' [Allen, Crenshaw, Dillard, Wolff], 'moreover' [Bewer; NASB], 'also' [Stuart], 'now' [NIV], 'yea' [KJV], not explicit [NRSV, REB, TEV]. Keil considers *wəḡam* as introducing a subject-focus construction: 'and ye also'. Crenshaw considers *wəḡam* as introducing the particular case of the Phoenicians and the Philistines, Israel's long-time foes, who deserve YHWH's special attention. Unlike Keil, Crenshaw views *wəḡam* as lending prominence to the entire verse, and not just to the pronoun אַתֶּם *'attem* 'you(p)'.

b. **furthermore** <u>**what**</u> מָה *mâ* [BDB p. 552], [Hol p. 183], [TWOT 1149]: 'what' [all lexica, commentators, and versions). The expression מָה־אַתֶּם לִי *mâ-'attem lî* is variously rendered: "what are you to me" [Crenshaw, Dillard; NASB, NRSV, REB], "what have you against me" [NIV], "what have ye to do with me" [KJV], "what are you trying to do to me" [TEV], "what would ye with me" [Keil], "what did you want of me" [Bewer], "what were your intentions with me" [Allen]. This question is, however, an abbreviated form of the kind of question common in legal cases: 'what have you done to me?' (cf. Judges 8:1and Mic. 6:3) [Wolff]. Cohen understands this expression to concern relationship: what relationship do you have to me? Most translations employ the English present tense; the past tense is also employed (e.g., 'what were your intentions toward me' [Stuart]).

c. **Tyre and-Sidon** צֹר *ṣōr* [BDB p. 862], [Hol p. 310], [TWOT 1965]: 'Tyre' [all lexica, commentators, and versions].

d. **Tyre and-Sidon** צִידוֹן *ṣîḏôn* [BDB p. 850], [Hol p. 305]: 'Sidon' [all lexica, commentators, and versions].

e. **and-all (the-)districts(-of) Philistia** pl. constr. of גְּלִילָה *gəlîlâ* [BDB p. 165], [Hol p. 61], [TWOT 353g]: 'district' [Hol; Allen, Bewer, Stuart, Wolff; REB], 'region' [Crenshaw, Dillard; NASB, NIV, NRSV], 'territory' [BDB], 'coast' [Keil; KJV]. TEV translates וְכֹל גְּלִילוֹת פְּלָשֶׁת *wəḵol gəlîlôṯ pəlāšeṯ* 'and all the regions of Philistia' as "and all of Philistia."

f. **Philistia** פְּלֶשֶׁת *pəlešeṯ* [BDB p. 814], [Hol p. 293]: 'territory of the Philistines' [Hol), 'Philistia' [BDB; Allen, Bewer, Crenshaw, Dillard, Keil, Stuart, Wolff; NASB, NIV, NRSV, REB, TEV], 'Palestine' [KJV].

g. **(are) you(p) paying-back reprisals against-me** masc. pl. Piel part. of שׁלם *šlm* [BDB p. 1022], [Hol p. 373], [TWOT 2401]: 'to pay back' [Allen, Crenshaw, Stuart, Wolff; NRSV, TEV], 'to repay' [Hol; Dillard, Keil; NIV], 'to requite' [BDB], 'to recompense' [BDB], 'to render' [KJV, NASB], 'to take vengeance' [REB]. The entire question, הַגְּמוּל אַתֶּם מְשַׁלְּמִים עָלָי *haggəmûl ʾattem məšalləmîm ʿālāy* 'are you offering reprisals against me?', is rendered "are/were you trying to repay me for something" [Bewer, Dillard], "are you paying me back for something" [NRSV], "do you want to pay me back" [Wolff], and, more explicitly, "are you repaying me for something I have done" [NIV] and "are you bent on taking vengeance on me" [REB]. Phoenicians and Philistines are perhaps proceeding on the lines of the *lex talionis*—an eye for an eye and a tooth for a tooth—against YHWH [Crenshaw]. The Piel stem of *šlm* denotes the action of repaying either good or ill [Hol].

h. **reprisals against-me** pl. of גְּמוּל *gəmûl* [BDB p. 168], [Hol p. 62], [TWOT 360a]: 'reprisal' [Hol], 'recompense' [BDB; Crenshaw; KJV, NASB], 'vengeance' [REB]. The singular is here considered a generic reference, which allows for a plural translation.

i. **and-if/or** וְאִם *wəʾim* [BDB p. 49], [Hol p. 19], [TWOT 111]. See the discussion under "SYNTAX" above.

j. **you(p) retaliate against-me** masc. pl. Qal part. of גמל *gml* [BDB p. 168], [Hol p. 62], [TWOT 360]: 'to render to someone' [Hol], 'to requite' [BDB], 'to pay back' [NIV, NRSV, TEV], 'to get even' [Dillard], 'to recompense' [KJV, NASB], 'to work vengeance' [Crenshaw], 'to do something' [Bewer, Stuart, Wolff], 'to do anything'

[Keil], 'to initiate an attack' [Allen]. The expression וְאִם־גֹּמְלִים אַתֶּם עָלַי *wə'im-gōməlîm 'attem ʿālay* is considered a question, 'or are you trying to get even with me', by Allen, Dillard, and Stuart; however, most (e.g., NASB and REB) read it as a condition. NASB has 'if you do recompense me'; REB has 'if you were to take vengeance'.

k. **I-will- very quickly bring** קַל *qal* [BDB p. 886], [Hol p. 319], [TWOT 2028a]: this adjective is translated as an adverb: 'quickly' [Hol; Keil, Allen, Dillard, Stuart], 'swiftly' [BDB; Bewer, Wolff; KJV, NASB, NIV, NRSV, REB]. An adjective (here *qal*) combined with an adverb of similar meaning (here מְהֵרָה *məhērâ*) signals intensification; thus for קַל מְהֵרָה *qal məhērâ*. Holladay and Crenshaw have "very quickly"; TEV, "quickly."

l. **I-will- very quickly bring** מְהֵרָה *məhērâ* [BDB p. 555], [Hol p. 185], [TWOT 1152d]: 'quickly' [BDB, Hol], 'in a hurry' [Hol], 'hastily' [BDB; Keil], 'speedily' [Bewer, Dillard, Wolff; KJV, NASB, NIV, NRSV, REB], 'rapidly' [Allen, Stuart].

m. **I-will- very quickly bring** 1st sing. Hiphil imperf. of שׁוּב *šûḇ* [BDB p. 996], [Hol p. 362], [TWOT 2340]: 'to bring back' [Hol], 'to turn back' [Keil; NRSV], 'to return' [Bewer, Dillard, Stuart; KJV, NASB, NIV], 'to make recoil' [Allen; REB], 'to repay' [Crenshaw], 'to requite' [Wolff].

n. **your(p)-retaliation upon-your(p)-head** constr. of גְּמוּל *gəmûl* (see *j* above): 'payment' [Dillard], 'recompense' [KJV, NASB]. The expression אָשִׁיב גְּמֻלְכֶם *'āšîḇ gəmulḵem* 'I will bring back your recompense' is translated "I will turn your deeds back" [NRSV], "I will return what you have done" [NIV], "I should make your deeds recoil" [REB], "I will repay your deeds" [Crenshaw], "I will return what you were doing" [Stuart], "I will requite your action" [Wolff], "I will turn back your doing" [Keil], "I will return your deed" [Bewer], "I will make your actions recoil" [Allen].

o. **upon-your(p)-head** -בְּ *bə-* [BDB p. 88], [Hol p. 32], [TWOT 193]: 'on/ upon' [all lexica, commentators, and versions except TEV], not explicit [TEV].

p. **upon-your(p)-head** constr. of רֹאשׁ *rō'š* [BDB p. 910], [Hol p. 329], [TWOT 2097]: 'head' [all lexica, commentators, and versions except TEV], not explicit [TEV].

QUESTION—What is the nature of the question וְגַם מָה־אַתֶּם לִי *wəḡam mâ-'attem lî* 'what are you to me'?

1. It is sarcastic and really embodies two ideas at once: (1) what evil have I done to you that you have attacked my people, and (2) what do you intend to do about it? It is YHWH's diagnosis of the attitude of the Phoenicians and Philistines that he has wronged them [Crenshaw].
2. It is a short form for "what have you done to me?" as in Judg. 8:1 [Wolff].

3. It is ambiguous but is clearly a challenge demanding an explanation for behavior or attitudes [Stuart].
4. It protests an implied desire of Tyre, Sidon, and Philistia to invade Israel. The question means to ask, By virtue of what supposed connection to YHWH do these nations hope to succeed to the blessings of YHWH upon the land of Israel? [Kimchi, cited by Cohen].

QUESTION—What is the significance of the reference to Tyre and Sidon?

These were two principal cities in Phoenicia. Each had at various times dominated the other, but under the Persian Empire, Tyre was the leading city [Wolff]. Phoenicia as a whole had often been a rival of Israel, although the two had sometimes acted in cooperation, as during the reigns of David and Solomon and in the northern reign of Ahab, whose wife was a Phoenician princess. See, however, the elaborate prophecy against the prince of Tyre in Ezekiel 27–28 [Crenshaw]. The Phoenicians had been seafaring traders for centuries and bore heavy responsibility for trafficking in slaves from Israel, selling them to Edom in times earlier than Amos, and in later times to Greece [Stuart].

QUESTION—What is the significance of the reference to Philistia?

Philistia, a traditional enemy of Israel, had in the time of the judges been dominated by five cities. Under the Persian Empire, however, one of the five, Gaza, was in the fore as a major commercial center, trading much with the Arabs. There is extrabiblical evidence that by the later Persian Empire, Philistia and the Phoenician cities of Tyre and Sidon were regarded as a single political entity [Wolff].

QUESTION—What is the significance of אָשִׁיב גְּמֻלְכֶם בְּרֹאשְׁכֶם *ʾāšîḇ gəmulḵem bərōʾšəḵem* 'I will bring your recompense upon your heads'?

This statement accords with the ancient belief that all misdeeds would be requited in kind by God (see Judg. 9:57, Ps. 7:17). There is a strong resemblance between Joel 4:4 (3:4) and Obadiah 15 [Crenshaw].

QUESTION—How is responsibility for offending YHWH in the passage introduced by this verse divided between the Phoenicians and the Philistines?

The Philistines looted Jerusalem and captured Judeans, while the Phoenicians bought many of the captives and resold them to the Ionians [Keil; Kimchi, cited by Cohen].

4:5 (3:5)

Because/(you(p)-)who[a] my-silver[b] and-my-gold[c] you(p)-have-taken[d] and-my-precious- good[e] -things[f] you(p)-have-carried[g] to-your(p)-palaces/temples,[h]

SYNTAX—The syntactic relationship of this verse with its neighboring verses is disputed:

Syntactic relationship of 4:5 to adjacent verses	Resulting sense	Remarks
4:5 is in apposition with בְּרֹאשְׁכֶם *bərō*ᵓ*šəḵem* 'on your heads' (4:4)	"I will return your deed on your own head (4:4), **on you who have taken my silver and my gold and carried my precious good things to your palaces**..." (4:5).	**Requirement**: 4:5 and 4:6 must be viewed as parallel relative clauses. **Function of the relative clauses**: They are the reasons for YHWH's threat in 4:4 ("I will return your deed on your own head"). **Followed by**: Bewer, Keil.
4:5 and 4:6 present the reasons for YHWH's promised action in 4:7.	"**Because you have taken my silver and gold and carried my precious good things to your palaces...**" (4:5).	**Followed by** Dillard, Crenshaw, Stuart, Wolff; KJV, NASB, NIV, NRSV, REB, TEV.

LEXICON—a. **because my-silver and-my-gold** אֲשֶׁר ᵓ*ăšer* [BDB p. 81], [Hol p. 30], [TWOT 184]: 'because' [Crenshaw, Dillard, Stuart, Wolff; KJV], 'since' [NASB], 'for' [NIV, NRSV], not explicit [Allen, REB, TEV]. The relative pronoun ᵓ*ăšer* probably indicates causation here [Crenshaw]. But note that Bewer regards ᵓ*ăšer* as a relative pronoun here.

b. **my-silver and-my-gold** constr. of כֶּסֶף *kesep̄* [BDB p. 494], [Hol p. 162], [TWOT 1015a]: 'silver' [all lexica, commentators, and versions]. The terms 'silver' and 'gold' in this verse imply objects made of silver and gold; they probably do not signify money.

c. **and-my-gold** constr. of זָהָב *zāhāḇ* [BDB p. 263], [Hol p. 87], [TWOT 529a]: 'gold' [all lexica, commentators, and versions].

d. **you(p)-have-taken** 2nd masc. pl. Qal perf. of לקח *lqḥ* [BDB p. 542], [Hol p. 178], [TWOT 1124]: 'to take' [Hol; Allen, Crenshaw, Dillard, Keil, Stuart, Wolff; KJV, NASB, NIV, NRSV, REB, TEV], 'to seize' [Hol].

e. **and-my-precious- good -things** pl. of טוֹב *ṭôḇ* [BDB p. 373], [Hol p. 122], [TWOT 793]: 'good' [Hol], 'goodly' [KJV].

f. **and-my-precious- good -things** pl. constr. of מַחְמָד *maḥmāḏ* [BDB p. 326], [Hol p. 190], [TWOT 673d]: 'precious things' [BDB], 'something precious' [Hol], 'pleasant thing' [KJV]. The meaning of וּמַחֲמַדַּי הַטֹּבִים *ûmaḥămadday haṭṭōḇîm* is variously given as 'my precious treasures' [NASB], 'my finest treasures' [Allen; NIV], 'my fine treasures' [Stuart], 'my rich treasures' [NRSV, TEV], 'my costly treasures' [REB], 'my goodly treasures' [Dillard, Wolff], 'my priceless commodities' [Crenshaw], 'my best jewels' [Keil]. Cohen regards this expression as perhaps indicating the Temple utensils, but Crenshaw views it as implying objects made of valued material other than silver and gold, mentioned above.

g. <u>you(p)-have-carried</u> **to-your(p)-palaces/temples** 2nd masc. pl. Hiphil perf. of בּוֹא *bôʾ* [BDB p. 97], [Hol p. 34], [TWOT 212]: 'to carry' [Hol; Dillard, Wolff; KJV, NRSV, TEV], 'to carry off' [NIV, REB], 'to carry home' [Allen], 'to bring' [Hol; Crenshaw, Keil, Stuart; NASB],

h. **to-your(p)-<u>palaces</u>/<u>temples</u>** pl. constr. of הֵיכָל *hêḵāl* [BDB p. 228], [Hol p. 79], [TWOT 493]: 'palace' [Hol; Crenshaw, Wolff], 'temple' [Hol; Allen, Dillard, Keil, Stuart; KJV, NASB, NIV, NRSV, REB, TEV]. *Hêḵāl*, a word borrowed from Akkadian [Crenshaw], is here ambiguous and can legitimately be translated either 'palace' or 'temple' [Dillard]; it probably means both in this context [Keil]. However, the possessive suffix 'your' with *hêḵāl* tends to favor the meaning 'palaces', as one would otherwise look for an expression such as 'the temples of your gods' [Crenshaw, Wolff].

QUESTION—What is the discourse function of the relative pronoun אֲשֶׁר *ʾăšer* in this passage?

It is generally understood to indicate causation here. Cohen and Crenshaw, however, take it cataphorically as pointing ahead to the main thought conveyed in 4:7 (3:7): because the nations in question took YHWH's treasures (4:5) and sold his people as slaves (4:6), he will rouse his dispersed people and will pay back those offending nations (4:7).

QUESTION—What treasures are indicated by the expressions כַּסְפִּי וּזְהָבִי *kaspî ûzəhāḇî* 'my silver and my gold' and מַחֲמַדַּי הַטֹּבִים *maḥămadday haṭōḇîm* 'my precious things'?

1. Probably general booty of Philistine raiding parties is meant, and not Temple treasures (although מַחְמָד *maḥmāḏ* appears in connection with the Temple in 2 Chron. 36:19), for the Philistines are not recorded as having invaded Jerusalem or the Temple [Dillard, Wolff]. YHWH is specifically called the owner of all precious metals in Hag. 2:8 ("to me the silver and to me the gold"), just as all other good things come from him as well. The expression *maḥămadday haṭōḇîm* 'my precious things' implies that more than precious metals have been taken [Crenshaw, Wolff].
2. Probably booty taken from both Temple and private houses is meant. Since הֵיכָל *hêḵāl* can mean either 'temple' or 'palace', it probably means both here. Joel certainly was thinking of the incursion of the Philistines and Arabians during Jehoram's reign (2 Chron. 21:17) [Keil, Stuart].

4:6 (3:6)

And[a]-(the-)sons(-of)[b] Judah and-(the-)sons(-of) Jerusalem you(p)-have-sold[c] to-(the-)sons(-of) the-Greeks[d]
in-order-to[e] remove-them-far[f] from[g] their-homeland.[h]

LEXICON—a. **<u>and</u>-(the-)sons(-of) Judah** -וְ *wə- waw* connective [BDB p. 251], [Hol p. 84], [TWOT 519]: 'and' [Keil, Stuart, Wolff; NASB], 'also' [KJV], not explicit [Allen, Crenshaw, Dillard; NIV, NRSV, REB, TEV].

b. **(the-)sons(-of) Judah** pl. constr. of בֵּן *bēn* [BDB p. 119], [Hol p. 42], [TWOT 254]: 'son' [BDB, Hol; Dillard, Keil, Wolff; NASB], 'children' [BDB, Hol; KJV], 'people' [NIV, NRSV, REB, TEV]. The expression בְּנֵי יְהוּדָה *bənê yəhûḏâ* is translated "the young people of Judah" by Allen, and "the Judeans" by Stuart. The corresponding expression which follows in the Hebrew is translated "Jerusalemites" by Stuart. Crenshaw sees these two expressions as denoting both males and females. Wolff considers their sense restricted to males.

c. **you(p)-have-sold to-(the-)sons(-of) the-Greeks** 2nd masc. pl. Qal perf. of מכר *mkr* [BDB p. 569], [Hol p. 194], [TWOT 1194]: 'to sell' [all lexica, commentators, and versions].

d. **to-(the-)sons(-of) the-Greeks** pl. of יָוָן *yāwān* [BDB p. 402], [Hol p. 131], [TWOT 855]: 'Greek' [Hol; Allen, Dillard, Stuart, Wolff; NASB, NIV, NRSV, REB, TEV], 'Ionians' [BDB; Crenshaw], 'Javan' [Keil], 'Grecians' [KJV]. The term הַיְּוָנִים *hayyəwānîm* designates much more than merely inhabitants of Greece, for there were many Greeks also in Asia Minor [Crenshaw], especially along the western coast with its many Ionian colonies. Many Aegean islands were also filled with Ionian settlements of prominent merchants; these, of all the Greeks, were the best known to the Jews. For this reason, the term *yāwān*, borrowed from Ἴωνες 'the Ionians', came to signify in BH the Greeks in general [Bewer].

e. **in-order-to remove- them -far from their-homeland** לְמַעַן *ləmaᶜan* [BDB p. 775], [Hol p. 207], [TWOT 1650g]: all commentaries and versions except BDB, Hol, and REB, and TEV express purpose here (e.g., 'in order that'). REB and TEV have 'and'. *Ləmaᶜan* is properly composed of מַעַן *maᶜan* 'purpose, intent' and the proclitic -לְ *lə-* [BDB, Hol]. The order of the two clauses in this verse, as well as the relation between them signaled by *ləmaᶜan*, has been changed by TEV: "you have taken the people ... far from their own country and sold them to the Greeks."

f. **in-order-to remove-them-far** Hiphil infin. constr. of רחק *rḥq* [BDB p. 934], [Hol p. 338], [TWOT 2151]: 'to remove far' [Keil; KJV; NASB, NRSV, REB], 'to move someone far away' [Hol], 'to remove' [BDB; Wolff], 'to put far away' [BDB], 'to thrust' [Crenshaw], 'to be able to remove far' [Dillard], 'to send far' [NIV], 'to take far' [Allen; TEV], 'to get far away' [Stuart].

g. **from their-homeland** מֵעַל *mēᶜal* [BDB p. 758], [Hol p. 272]: 'from' [Allen, Dillard, Keil, Stuart, Wolff; KJV, NASB, NIV, NRSV, REB, TEV], 'beyond' [Crenshaw].

h. **from their-homeland** constr. of גְּבוּל *gəḇûl* [BDB p. 147], [Hol p. 53], [TWOT 307a]: 'homeland' [Wolff; NIV], 'territory' [BDB, Hol;

Allen, Stuart; NASB], 'border' [Crenshaw, Dillard, Keil; KJV, NRSV], 'frontier' [REB], 'country' [TEV].

QUESTION—What is the relation of the expression בְּנֵי יְהוּדָה *bənê yəhûdâ* 'the sons of Judah' to the following expression, וּבְנֵי יְרוּשָׁלָם *ûbənê yərûšālām* 'the sons of Jerusalem'?

It is a general-specific relation: Jerusalemites were also inhabitants of Judah. The two expressions together mean all Judeans [Crenshaw].

QUESTION—Where else in the OT are the Philistines and the Phoenicians rebuked for having enslaved Israelites?

In Amos 1:6–9 [Dillard], where the Tyrians are accused of breaking a covenant with YHWH's people by selling Israelite slaves to Edom [Crenshaw].

QUESTION—What does this reference to Greeks buying slaves imply about the Book of Joel?

This reference most likely indicates a postexilic date for the Book of Joel, but such an indication is not completely certain, for there are eighth-century-B.C. references to the Greeks in trade with the Phoenicians [Dillard]. Moreover, Joel might well have had more than merely one event or historical period in mind [Crenshaw].

4:7 (3:7)

Behold[a]-me about-to-rouse[b]-them from the-place[c] (to) which[d] you(p)-have-sold[e] them there,[f]
and[g]-I-will-return[h] your(p)-reprisal[i] upon-your(p)-heads.[j]

LEXICON—a. **behold-me** הִנֵּה *hinnēh* [BDB p. 243], [Hol p. 82], [TWOT 510a]: 'behold' [BDB, Hol; Dillard, Keil; KJV, NASB], 'look' [Crenshaw], 'see' [NIV], 'but now' [NRSV], 'but' [REB], 'now' [TEV], 'well' [Stuart], not explicit [Wolff].

b. **about-to-rouse-them** masc. sing. Hiphil part. of עור *ʿôr* [BDB p. 734], [Hol p. 268], [TWOT 1587]: 'to rouse/arouse' [BDB, Hol; Crenshaw, Dillard, Stuart; NASB, NIV, NRSV, REB], 'to stir up' [BDB, Hol], 'to set in motion' [Hol], 'to raise out' [KJV], 'to order out' [Hol], 'to waken' [Keil], 'to bring out' [TEV], 'to summon' [Hol]. Some add to the idea of compulsion a verbal complement such as 'I will arouse them to leave that place' [Dillard] or 'to make them set out from the place' [Wolff; NRSV, REB]. Some employ a modality of imminent future such as 'I am going to arouse them' [Allen; NASB, NIV, TEV], based on the fact that in BH a participle preceded by *hinnēh* indicates imminent action. Allen adds to this a modality of potentiality: "I am soon going to enable them to leave." Most others employ the normal English future tense. The Hiphil of *ʿôr* can mean 'to set in motion, to activate' [Wolff].

c. **from the-place** מָקוֹם *māqôm* [BDB p. 879], [Hol p. 212], [TWOT 1999h]: 'place' [BDB, Hol; Allen, Crenshaw, Dillard, Keil, Stuart, Wolff; KJV, NASB, NIV, NRSV, REB, TEV].

d. **(to) which you(p)-have-sold them there** אֲשֶׁר *ʾăšer* [BDB p. 81], [Hol p. 30], [TWOT 184]: 'which' [Allen, Crenshaw, Stuart; NIV, NRSV, REB, TEV], 'whither' [Keil; KJV], 'where' [NASB].

e. **you(p)-have-sold them there** 2nd masc. pl. Qal perf. of מכר *mkr* [BDB p. 569], [Hol p. 194], [TWOT 1194]: 'to sell' [all lexica, commentators, and versions except REB], 'to be sold' [REB].

f. **there** שָׁמָּה *šammâ* [BDB p. 1027], [Hol p. 374]: 'there' [BDB, Hol], not explicit [Crenshaw, Keil, Allen, Dillard, Stuart, Wolff; KJV, NASB, NIV, NRSV, REB, TEV]. This location word refers to the lands of the Greeks [Crenshaw].

g. **and-I-will-return your(p)-reprisal** -וְ *wə-* *waw* of the attached weqatal verb form [BDB p. 251], [Hol p. 84], [TWOT 519]: 'and' [Crenshaw, Dillard, Keil, Stuart, Wolff; KJV, NASB, NIV], 'and also' [Allen]. TEV and REB express the additive relation with a new clause or sentence.

h. **I-will-return your(p)-reprisal** 1st sing. Hiphil weqatal verb form of שׁוב *šûḇ* [BDB p. 996], [Hol p. 362], [TWOT 2340]: 'to return' [BDB, Hol; Stuart; KJV, NASB, NIV], 'to turn' [NRSV]. For the expression וַהֲשִׁבֹתִי גְמֻלְכֶם *wahăšiḇōṯî gəmulḵem* 'and I will return your reprisal' Crenshaw has "and I will repay your deeds"; Keil has "I turn back your doing"; Dillard, "and I will bring your deeds"; Wolff, "and I will requite your action"; NIV, "I will return what you have done"; NRSV, "and I will turn your deeds back"; Allen, also REB, "I shall make your actions/deeds recoil"; TEV, "I will do to you what you have done to them."

i. **your(p)-reprisal** constr. of גְּמוּל *gəmûl* [BDB p. 168], [Hol p. 62], [TWOT 360a]: 'reprisal' [Hol], 'recompense' [BDBP; KJV, NASB].

j. **upon-your(p)-heads** constr. of רֹאשׁ *rōʾš* [BDB p. 910], [Hol p. 329], [TWOT 2097]: 'head' [all lexica, commentators, and versions]. The singular is considered a generic reference here, hence the plural translation.

QUESTION—What does this verse imply about YHWH?

It implies that he is no territorial deity, bound to the region where he is honored, as was often assumed in the polytheistic milieu of ancient peoples. On the contrary, he can exert power far away from Judah. Isaiah 13:17 is like this verse both in language and in idea [Crenshaw].

QUESTION—What does Joel imply about the Jewish slaves in far-off lands?

In saying that YHWH will rouse the Jewish slaves Joel implies that the Jews themselves will become the ones through whom YHWH will punish the guilty nations, as is explained in the following verse [Crenshaw].

QUESTION—What principle is followed in this verse?

The principle followd is *lex talionis*—"an eye for an eye and a tooth for a tooth" (Exod. 21:24; Lev. 24:18, 20; Deut. 19:21). It is invoked against those who have oppressed YHWH's people, for it is YHWH himself who has been offended; he considers that the crimes committed against his people have been done also against himself (4:4 (3:4)). YHWH is the defender of the widows, the fatherless, and the indigent, but he is also the defender of his own people when they are oppressed (Prov. 22:22–23; 23:11) [Crenshaw, Dillard]. YHWH promises to punish the offending nations in a manner exactly matching their offenses against his covenant people [Wendland].

4:8 (3:8)
And[a]-I-will-sell[b] your(p)-sons[c] and-your(p)-daughters[d], (MT1) into[e-1]-(the-)hand(-of)[f] Judah, (MT2) by[e-2]-(the-)hand(-of)[f] Judah
(MT) and[g]-they-will-sell-them to[h]-(the-)Sabeans,[i]
(ET) and[g]-they-will-sell-them into[h]-captivity,[i] (MT1) to[j] (a-)people[k] far-away,[l] (MT2) (who will sell them) to[j] (a-)people[k] far-away,[l]
for[m] YHWH has-spoken.[n]

TEXT—Stuart proposes an emendation to the MT:

MT	Remarks
לִשְׁבָאִים *lišḇāʾîm* 'to the Sabeans'	**Followed by:** Wolff. **Supported by**: Targum Jonathan to the Prophets and the Greek translations of Aquila, Symmachus, and Theodotion [Wolff]. **Argument for:** The difficulty of two co-referent expressions in the same phrase may be solved by treating the second expression as appositive to the first [Wolff].
Proposed emendation לַשְּׁבִי *laššəḇî* 'into captivity'	**Proposed by**: Stuart. **Supported by**: LXX, εἰς αἰχμαλωσίαν 'into captivity'. **Argument for**: It would be difficult to have two co-referent expressions in the phrase, one introduced by the proclitic -לְ *lə-* 'to' and the other introduced by the preposition אֶל *ʾel* 'to' [Stuart].

LEXICON—a. **and-I-will-sell** -וְ *wə- waw* of the attached weqatal verb form [BDB p. 251], [Hol p. 84], [TWOT 519]: 'and' [Keil, Wolff; KJV], 'also' [NASB], not explicit [Crenshaw]. Allen, Dillard, Stuart, NIV, NRSV, and TEV express the additive relation with a new clause or sentence. REB translates the clause introduced by *wə-* instrumentally, "by selling."

b. **I-will-sell** 1st sing. Qal weqatal verb form of מכר *mḵr* [BDB p. 569], [Hol p. 194], [TWOT 1194]: 'to sell' [all lexica, commentators, and versions except TEV]. TEV includes an idea of permission: "I will let your sons and daughters be sold to the people of Judah."

c. **your(p)-sons** pl. constr. of בֵּן *bēn* [BDB p. 119], [Hol p. 42], [TWOT 254]: 'son' [Hol; Allen, Crenshaw, Dillard, Keil, Stuart, Wolff; KJV, NASB, NIV, NRSV, REB, TEV].

d. **and-your(p)-daughters** pl. constr. of בַּת *bat* [BDB p. 123], [Hol p. 51], [TWOT 254b]: 'daughter' [Hol; Allen, Crenshaw, Dillard, Keil, Stuart, Wolff; KJV, NASB, NIV, NRSV, REB, TEV].

e-1. **into-(the-)hand(-of) Judah** -בְּ *bə-* [BDB p. 88], [Hol p. 32], [TWOT 193]: 'into' [Cohen, Keil; KJV, NASB, NRSV], 'to' [NIV, REB, TEV], 'into the possession of' [Allen]. The LXX has εἰς χεῖρας υἱῶν Ιουδα 'into the hands of the sons of Judah', based on understanding the proclitic *bə-* as destination. Alternatively, the expression בְּיַד *bəyad* can be taken to mean e-2. **by-(the-)hand(-of) Judah** -בְּ *bə-* (see above): 'by (the) agency of' [Crenshaw, Wolff], 'by means of' [Dillard], 'by' [Stuart]. *Bəyad* 'by the hand of' usually expresses instrument; destination is normally expressed by -לְ *lə-* [Wolff].

f. **(the-)hand(-of) Judah** constr. of יָד *yād* [BDB p. 388], [Hol p. 127], [TWOT 844]: 'hand' [Keil; KJV, NASB, NRSV].

g. **and-they-will-sell-them to-(the-)Sabeans** -וְ *wə- waw* of the attached weqatal verb form [BDB p. 251], [Hol p. 84], [TWOT 519]: 'and' [Allen, Crenshaw, Dillard, Keil, Wolff; KJV, NASB, NIV, NRSV]. Stuart and TEV express the additive relation with a new clause or sentence.

h. **to-(the-)Sabeans** -לְ *lə-* [BDB p. 510], [Hol p. 167], [TWOT 1063]: 'to' [Allen, Crenshaw, Dillard, Keil, Wolff; KJV, NASB, NIV, NRSV, REB, TEV], 'into' [Stuart].

i. **(the-)Sabeans** pl. of שְׁבָא *šəḇāʾ* [BDB p. 985], [Hol p. 357]: 'Sabean' [Allen, Crenshaw, Dillard, Keil, Wolff; KJV, NASB, NIV, NRSV, REB, TEV], 'captivity' [Stuart], 'Sheba (name of people and person') [Hol].

j. **to (a-)people far-away** אֶל *ʾel* [BDB p. 39], [Hol p. 16], [TWOT 91]: 'to' [Crenshaw, Dillard, Keil, Stuart, Wolff; KJV, NASB, NRSV], not explicit [Allen; REB, TEV].

k. **(a-)people** גּוֹי *gôy* [BDB p. 156], [Hol p. 57], [TWOT 326e]: 'people' [Keil; KJV], not explicit [TEV], 'nation' [Allen, Crenshaw, Dillard, Stuart; NASB, NIV, NRSV].

l. **far-away** רָחוֹק *rāḥôq* [BDB p. 935], [Hol p.), 'far away' [Stuart; NIV, NRSV], [TWOT 2151b]: 'distant' [BDB; Allen, Crenshaw, Dillard; NASB, REB], 'far' [BDB], 'far off' [Keil; KJV, TEV].

m. **for YHWH has-spoken** כִּי *kî* particle [BDB p. 471], [Hol p. 155], [TWOT 976]: 'for' [Crenshaw, Dillard, Keil, Stuart, Wolff; KJV, NASB, NRSV], 'so', [Allen], not explicit [NIV, REB, TEV].

n. **has-spoken** 3rd sing. Piel perf. of דבר *dḇr* [BDB p. 180], [Hol p. 66], [TWOT 399]: 'to speak' [Hol; Allen, Crenshaw, Dillard, Keil, Stuart, Wolff; KJV, NASB, NIV, NRSV, TEV]. In the REB the idea of speaking is nominalized: "Those are the LORD's words." TEV renders the third person as first person to accord with the direct speech of this passage: "I, the LORD, have spoken."

QUESTION—When was this threatened punishment against the Philistines and the Phoenicians realized?

1. It was carried out when Alexander the Great conquered Tyre and sold 30,000 people into slavery, according to Arrian in *Anabasis*; he also caused the people of Gaza to be enslaved, in which commerce Jewish slave merchants probably participated [Dillard]. Even before that, in 343 B.C., Artaxerxes III Ochus conquered and enslaved Sidon [Wolff].
2. It was certainly carried out by Alexander the Great but was fulfilled before that by King Uzziah (2 Chron. 26:6–7) and King Hezekiah (2 Kings 18:8) [Keil]. This view requires, of course, that Joel be considered as pre-exilic.
3. Jewish traffic in Phoenician or Philistine slaves is undocumented in history [Stuart].

QUESTION—Who were the שְׁבָאִים *šəḇāʾîm* 'Sabeans'?

This people of Saba or Sheba, a land far from Israel (in southwestern Arabia according to Bewer, southeastern Arabia according to Crenshaw), were known for their commerce (Job 6:19; Jer. 6:20; Ezek. 27:22–23). Their queen visited Solomon, bringing many trade articles with her as gifts (see 1 Kings 10:1–2) [Crenshaw].

QUESTION—What is the relationship between the referents in the phrases לִשְׁבָאִים *lišḇāʾîm* 'to the Sabeans' and אֶל־גּוֹי רָחוֹק *ʾel-gôy rāḥôq* 'to a distant nation'?

1. The second phrase represents still another destination for the slaves, the place to which they would be sold by the mercantile Sabeans [Bewer, Keil].
2. The second phrase is in apposition to the first, indicating that the Sabeans were distant from Judah [Cohen, Crenshaw, Dillard, Wolff; KJV]. Sheba is called a distant land in Jer. 6:20 [Crenshaw]. Wolff regards the phrase *ʾel-gôy rāḥôq* 'to a distant nation' as a scribal explanatory gloss for 'Sabeans'.

QUESTION—What is the role of the expression כִּי יְהוָה דִּבֵּר *kî yhwh dibbēr* 'for YHWH has spoken'?

1. This expression occurs often in prophetic literature to emphasize or guarantee that the reported speech has indeed come from YHWH [Crenshaw, Stuart].
2. This expression serves to mark the end of the 4:4–8 (3:4–8) section [Wendland], which was inserted into the text later [Wolff].

QUESTION—What is the import of this verse?

Other OT passages present the idea of evil recoiling upon its perpetrators. Joel, however, develops this concept in two ways: YHWH is named the one who will bring evil back upon its authors, and his covenant community is named as the means of his action [Wolff]. The contrast in this strophe between the selling off of YHWH's people in 4:6 (3:6) and the selling off of the people of Tyre and Sidon in 4:8 (3:8) is very marked [Wendland].

DISCOURSE UNIT: 4:9–17 (3:9–17) [Cohen]. The topic is "God's day of retribution."

DISCOURSE UNIT: 4:9–16 (3:9–16) [Crenshaw]. The topic is "YHWH's judgment against the nations."
Comments on this discourse unit: The unit resumes the 4:1–3 (3:1–3) theme, that of YHWH's coming judgment upon the nations in general [Crenshaw].

4:9 (3:9)
Proclaim(p)[a] this[b] to[c]-the-nations[d]: prepare-(a)holy(p)[e] war[f]; rouse(p)[g] the-warriors[h]; let-them-advance[i] (and) attack[j] all-(the-)men(-of)[k] the-war.[l]

LEXICON—a. **proclaim(p) this** masc. pl. Qal imper. of קרא *qr*ʾ [BDB p. 894], [Hol p. 323], [TWOT 2063]: 'to proclaim' [Hol; Crenshaw, Keil, Stuart, Wolff], 'to cry aloud' [Dillard], 'to make a proclamation' [Allen].

b. **proclaim(p) this** fem. of זֶה *zeh* [BDB p. 260], [Hol p. 86], [TWOT 528]: 'this' [BDB, Hol; Allen, Crenshaw, Dillard, Keil, Stuart, Wolff].

c. **to-the-nations** -בְּ *bə-* [BDB p. 88], [Hol p. 32], [TWOT 193]: 'among' [BDB, Hol; Allen, Crenshaw, Dillard, Keil, Stuart, Wolff].

d. **the-nations** pl. of גּוֹי *gôy* [BDB p. 156], [Hol p. 57], [TWOT 326e]: 'nation' [all lexica, commentators, and versions].

e. **prepare-(a)holy(p) war** masc. pl. Qal imper. of קדשׁ *qdš* [BDB p. 872], [Hol p. 313], [TWOT): 'to sanctify' [Crenshaw, Dillard, Keil], 'to establish' [Hol]. Wolff translates קַדְּשׁוּ מִלְחָמָה *qaddšû milḥāmâ* 'sanctify a war' as "prepare for a holy war." Allen translates it similarly.

f. **war** מִלְחָמָה *milḥāmâ* [BDB p. 536], [Hol p. 197], [TWOT 1104c]: 'war' [BDB, Hol; Dillard, Keil, Wolff], 'battle' [Crenshaw].

g. **rouse(p) the-warriors** masc. pl. Hiphil imper. of עור *ʿôr* [BDB p. 734], [Hol p. 268], [TWOT 1587]: 'to arouse/rouse' [Crenshaw, Wolff], 'to summon' [Hol], 'to stir up' [Hol; Dillard], 'to set in motion' [Hol], 'to awaken' [Keil], 'to alert' [Allen].

h. **the-warriors** pl. of גִּבּוֹר *gibbôr* [BDB 150], [Hol p. 53], [TWOT 310b]: 'warrior' [Hol; Dillard, Wolff], 'hero' [Keil], 'mighty one' [Crenshaw], 'soldier' [Allen]. Traditionally, *gibbôr* signified an unusually strong and successful warrior, as in the heroic age of ancient Israel when the people celebrated their champions of battle. In 1 and 2 Chronicles, however, the word comes to mean warrior in general [TWOT]. If הַגִּבּוֹרִים *haggibbôrîm* is viewed here as unusually strong warriors or as seasoned warriors in contrast to other soldiers, then כֹּל אַנְשֵׁי הַמִּלְחָמָה *kol* ʾ*anšê hammilḥāmâ* 'all the men of war' would function as an expansion of thought to embrace all other possible soldiers. But if *haggibbôrîm* is viewed as warriors in general, then the following expression, *kol ʾanšê hammilḥāmâ*, must function as a synonym or a near synonym.

i. **let-them-advance (and) attack** 3rd masc. pl. Qal jussive of נגשׁ *ngš* [BDB p. 620], [Hol p. 227], [TWOT 1297]: 'to advance' [Allen], 'to approach' [Hol], 'to draw near' [Crenshaw, Keil, Wolff], 'to come near' [Dillard]. The implied object of this verb is probably 'the field of battle' [Crenshaw].

j. **(and) attack** 3rd masc. pl. Qal jussive of עלה *ʿlh* [BDB p. 748], [Hol p. 273], [TWOT 1624]: 'to go up' [Hol; Crenshaw, Dillard], 'to come up' [Keil, Wolff]. Holladay considers that *ʿlh* functions here as a technical term for the assembling of armies. Wolff points out that *ʿlh* often means to climb toward Jerusalem in order to attack her, as in Ezek. 38:9, 11, 16, 18 [also Keil]. Allen accepts *ʿlh* here in the technical military sense, 'to attack', considering that the parallelism of this verse to 1:6 precludes any but the military understanding of *ʿlh*. The absence of a *waw* connective in the expression יִגְּשׁוּ יַעֲלוּ *yiggəšî yaʿălû* 'let them advance and attack' suggests haste in the commands and disorder in the troops' compliance with them. The absence of any complement (advance where? attack what?) suggests an obvious answer, which is that the troops should advance and attack to their own doom [Crenshaw].

k. **all-(the-)men(-of) the-war** pl. constr. of אִישׁ *ʾîš* [BDB p. 35], [Hol p. 13], [TWOT 83a]: 'man' [all lexica, commentators, and versions except those that translate the larger phrase]. For the phrase אַנְשֵׁי הַמִּלְחָמָה *ʾanšê hammilḥāmâ* Dillard, Keil, and Wolff have "men of war," Crenshaw has "warrior," and Allen has "troops." *All-(the-)men(-of) the-war* is the subject of the two verbs, and the order here of the verbs and the subject is normal and unmarked for Hebrew.

l. **the-war** מִלְחָמָה *milḥāmâ* (see *f* above): 'war' [BDB, Hol]. The definite article is often used in Hebrew with a generic reference.

QUESTION—Who is the speaker, and who are the addressees, of the command קִרְאוּ־זֹאת בַגּוֹיִם *qirʾû-zōʾṯ baggôyim* 'proclaim this to the nations'?

1. The speaker might be the prophet, who is relaying YHWH's commands to unknown addressees [Wolff].
2. The speaker is probably YHWH, and the addressees are probably his heavenly servitors, whom he charges with the task of mustering an army in order to lead it to destruction [Allen, Crenshaw, Keil].

QUESTION—What is the meaning of קַדְּשׁוּ מִלְחָמָה *qaḏšû milḥāmâ* 'prepare a holy war'?

This language arises from Israel's ancient view that her wars were sacred endeavors dedicated to YHWH through sacrifice, fasting, and other ceremonial preparation [Allen, Crenshaw, Dillard, Keil, Wolff]; in such preparation, Israel's leaders asked for YHWH's will concerning their going to war [Crenshaw]. Crenshaw regards this concept as inapplicable here in the context of the muster of the nations' armies, except perhaps in an ironic way. Cohen, however, considers this a reference to the custom widespread in ancient times of offering sacrifices in preparing for war. The English versions generally translate along the lines of 'prepare for war', with no explicit indication of Israel's traditional holy war ideology. While armies traditionally are mustered in order to win victories, it becomes clear as this passage continues that the prophecy is ironic; it stands in the tradition of Isa. 8:9–10; Jer. 46:3–6, 9–10; and Ezekiel 38–39. (Note that Ezek. 38:17 itself draws on earlier prophetic activity.) Here, as in these other passages, the nations' armies are mustered to go to judgment and destruction [Wolff], for the aim of holy wars in Israel's history was to completely destroy YHWH's enemies [Stuart]. For this reason, Allen sees the phrase *qaḏšû milḥāmâ* 'prepare for a holy war' as ironic: the nations are told to prepare for war in the very same terms that YHWH had so often in the past led his covenant community to war.

QUESTION—What activities are envisioned in this verse for the divine messengers of YHWH?

They are to muster the armies (קִרְאוּ *qirʾû* 'proclaim'), provide for all the preparations of war (קַדְּשׁוּ מִלְחָמָה *qaḏšû milḥāmâ* 'sanctify a war'), and get the troops in a ready frame of mind for the coming fight (הָעִירוּ הַגִּבּוֹרִים *hāʿîrû haggəbbôrîm* 'arouse the soldiers') [Crenshaw].

QUESTION—What concept of war lies behind the phrase קַדְּשׁוּ מִלְחָמָה *qaḏšû milḥāmâ* 'prepare for a holy war'?

In Israel's view of YHWH, she acknowledged that he as sovereign had all the powers that earthly monarchs possessed, including those of being an advocate for the disadvantaged, a prosecutor, and a judge empowered to carry out any judicial sentence he might impose upon convicted offenders. As a judge, YHWH was expected to arbitrate along just principles. So, for example, when Jehoshaphat prays in time of public crisis before the Temple (2 Chronicles 20), he does not base his appeal to YHWH upon any idea that as Israel's God he would act blindly on her behalf, for it was recognized that Israel's God could act against her if she so deserved. Jehoshaphat instead puts forward two other claims: (1) that Israel has title to her land upon the best possible authority, that of YHWH himself and his action for Israel in the past; and (2) that the present attack upon Israel is unwarranted, because the Israel of the Exodus had not molested the neighboring nations of Ammon, Moab, and Mount Seir.

The Israelites saw warfare as one of YHWH's means of punishing peoples whom he had convicted of serious offenses. Not every war was so viewed, for unjust war was also possible. But warfare took its place alongside epidemics, drought, and famine as another means of YHWH's punishment. In Joel 4:9–13 (3:9–13), the prophet looks to the future and sees the nations mobilized at YHWH's command for war against Israel; the outcome is fore-ordained and represents YHWH's punishment upon the nations [Good].

4:10 (3:10)

Beat(p)[a] your(p)-plowshares[b] into[c]-swords[d] and-your(p)-vine-knives[e] into-lances;[f]
let- the weakling[g] -say[h] I (am) (a-)warrior.[i]

INTERTEXTUAL REFERENCE—Joel spectacularly reverses the wording of Isa. 2:4 and of Mic. 4:3, portending universal war instead of peace [Crenshaw, Wendland, Wolff].

LEXICON—a. **beat(p) your(p)-plowshares** masc. pl. Qal imper. of כתת *ktt* [BDB p. 510], [Hol p. 167], [TWOT 1062]: 'to beat' [BDB; Allen, Bewer, Crenshaw, Dillard, Stuart, Wolff; KJV, NASB, NIV, NRSV, REB], 'to beat fine, to pound up' [Hol], 'to hammer' [BDB; TEV], 'to forge' [Keil].

b. **your(p)-plowshares** pl. constr. of אֵת *ʾēṯ* [BDB p. 88], [Hol p. 31], [TWOT 192a]: 'plowshare' [BDB, Hol; Bewer, Stuart, Wolff; KJV, NASB, NIV, NRSV], 'mattock' [Hol; REB], 'plowtip' [Crenshaw], 'coulter' [Keil], 'plow' [Dillard], 'points of plows' [TEV], 'hoe' [Allen]. The word *ʾēṯ* signifies 'a cutting instrument of iron' [BDB] or, more precisely, probably a hand tool such as a hoe or adze, or even a kind of pruning knife, but almost certainly not a plowshare [Dillard]. Crenshaw views *ʾēṯ* as denoting the iron tip of a wooden plow.

c. **into-swords** -לְ *lə-* [BDB p. 510], [Hol p. 167], [TWOT 1063]: 'into' [all lexica, commentators, and versions]. The proclitic *lə-* functions here as a complementizer denoting destination of transformation.

d. **into-swords** pl. of חֶרֶב *ḥereḇ* [BDB p. 352], [Hol p. 115], [TWOT 732a]: 'sword' [all lexica, commentators, and versions].

e. **and-your(p)-vine-knives into-lances** pl. constr. of מַזְמֵרָה *mazmērâ* [BDB p. 275], [Hol p. 189], [TWOT 559c]: 'vine knife' [Hol], 'pruning knife' [BDB; Crenshaw, Stuart, Wolff; REB, TEV], 'pruning hook' [Bewer, Dillard; KJV, NASB, NIV, NRSV], 'pruning tool' [Allen], 'vine sickle' [Keil].

f. **into-lances** pl. of רֹמַח *rōmaḥ* [BDB p. 942], [Hol p. 340], [TWOT 2172]: 'lance' [BDB, Hol; Bewer, Wolff], 'spear' [Allen, Crenshaw, Dillard, Keil, Stuart; KJV, NASB, NIV, NRSV, REB, TEV]. *Rōmaḥ* denotes a spear with a long shaft [Hol]. This term is different from חֲנִית *ḥănîṯ* 'spear', which is used in Isa. 2:4 and Mic. 4:3; it might therefore be asked why Joel, who is undoubtedly consciously reversing the language of these other two prophets, does not use the same term [Crenshaw].

g. **let- the weakling -say** חַלָּשׁ *ḥallāš* [BDB p. 325], [Hol p. 107], [TWOT 671a]: 'weakling' [Hol; Allen, Bewer, Crenshaw, Stuart; NIV, NRSV, REB], 'weak one' [Keil], 'the one who is weak' [Dillard], although *ḥallāš* is properly an adjective, 'weak' [BDB; Wolff; KJV, NASB, TEV].

h. **let- the weakling -say** 3rd masc. sing. Qal jussive or imperf. of אמר *ʾmr* [BDB p. 55], [Hol p. 21], [TWOT 118]: 'to say' [Hol; Bewer, Dillard, Keil, Stuart, Wolff; KJV, NASB, NIV, NRSV, REB], 'to boast' [Crenshaw], 'to think' [Allen]. Most commentators and versions translate with a kind of third person command: "let ... say." Stuart has a phrase of obligation, "the weakling must say..."; the REB has a kind of concession, "let even the weakling say...."

i. **I (am) (a-)warrior** גִּבּוֹר *gibbôr* [BDB p. 150], [Hol p. 53], [TWOT 310b]: 'warrior' [Hol; Crenshaw, Dillard, Wolff; NRSV], 'strong, valiant man' [BDB], 'strong' [Bewer, Cohen; KJV, NIV, REB], 'hero' [Keil], 'soldier' [Stuart], 'mighty man' [NASB], 'fighter' [Allen]. TEV translates the phrase יֹאמַר גִּבּוֹר אָנִי *yōmar gibbôr ʾānî* as "even the weak must fight." The LXX has ἰσχύω ἐγώ 'I am strong'.

QUESTION—What custom lies behind the exhortation in this verse?

In societies with little or no standing armies, such as in pre-monarchical Israel, it was quite feasible and often necessary for cultivators to turn their bronze or iron farming implements into weapons, as in 1 Sam. 13:20–21. Standing armies of later periods had their armories and therefore stayed in better readiness for combat. But total war might still require the conversion of all suitable farm tools into weapons [Allen, Cohen, Dillard].

QUESTION—What is the rhetorical nature of this verse?

1. This verse is full of irony. Standing so consciously in the prophetic traditions as he does, the prophet is surely aware that he is reversing the messianic kingdom's peaceful proclamation in the following verses:

> He [YHWH] will judge between the nations and will settle disputes for many peoples. They will beat their swords into plowshares and their spears into pruning hooks. Nation will not take up sword against nation, nor will they train for war anymore. (Isa. 2:4 NIV)
>
> He [YHWH] will judge between many peoples and will settle disputes for strong nations far and wide. They will beat their swords into plowshares and their spears into pruning hooks. Nation will not take up sword against nation, nor will they train for war anymore. (Mic. 4:3 NIV)

These prophecies foretell that the nations would come to Jerusalem seeking life and peace from YHWH, but Joel turns the prophecies around [Wolff (a)], summoning the nations in a most ironic way to be judged, condemned, and punished by YHWH. The nations think that they are going to war, and they are indeed to prepare for war, but it will be to no avail. The nations' preparations may give an illusion of security, but their weapons will not stand against YHWH's anger. This theme relates to a larger and very prominent OT theme of the futility of depending upon weapons for victory: it is YHWH who will put an end to the weapons and bring lasting peace—a feature of the Messianic age [Crenshaw, Wolff (a)].

2. While Joel has certainly reversed Isaiah and Micah's words, this passage does not constitute a reversal of the earlier prophets' proclamation. Late prophets such as Joel foresaw a universal cataclysm before the inauguration of the messianic reign. It is to this catastrophe of universal war that 3:10 speaks [Mariottini].

QUESTION—What is the nature of the expression הַחַלָּשׁ יֹאמַר גִּבּוֹר אָנִי *haḥallāš yōmar gibbôr ʾānî* 'let the weakling say, I am a warrior'?

This phrase is actually a figure of speech. Whereas it appears to be literal, aimed at causing the reluctant among the enemy to *say* something (i.e., to say that they will fight in the coming battle), it is actually meant to cause them to *do* something (i.e., to fight). In addition, it is ironic in nature: In contrast to Deut. 20:5–-9, which stipulates that only volunteers need fight in wars, this phrase seeks to ensure that none of the enemy populations will be exempt from the coming judgment of YHWH upon them in battle [Stuart].

QUESTION—What is the concrete sense of this expression?

1. This expression (taking גִּבּוֹר *gibbôr* to mean 'mighty warrior') commands all the enemy troops to boast of their prowess in a vain buildup before their final doom. In the light of Jer. 48:14, which presents a similar boast, and of Zech. 12:8, which presents YHWH's promise of help for those who know their weakness, Joel's command is highly ironical. The irony grows with the realization that this is the only instance of the use in Joel of the first person singular pronoun אָנִי *ʾānî* apart from YHWH's own self-revelations, as in 4:17 (3:17); in other words, the enemy soldiers blasphemously appropriate language that has been reserved for YHWH alone [Crenshaw, Wolff].
2. The expression is not a command to boast, but is rather an imperative to all the enemy, even the non-combatants, to join, however reluctantly, the soldiers' ranks [Stuart].
3. The expression is meant to arouse enthusiasm for war in the whole of the enemy population [Keil].

4:11 (3:11)

(ET₁) Wake-up(p)[a-1]/ (ET₂) Hurry(p)[a-2] and-come(p),[b] all nations,[c] from-round-about,[d] (MT) and-gather[e]; (ET) and-gather[e] there[h];

(MT) bring-down,[f-1] YHWH, your(s)-warriors[g] to-that-place[h] (ET₁) let the-frightened-man[f-2] become (a-)warrior.[g] (ET₂) that- YHWH -may-shatter[f-3] your(s)-warriors.[g]

TEXT—The MT reading of עוּשׁוּ *ʿûšû* is disputed:

Reading	Remarks
MT: עוּשׁוּ *ʿûšû* 'to lend aid' [BDB]	**Followed by**: no commentator consulted. Keil accepts this reading, but treats this verb as the same as חוּשׁ *ḥûš* 'hurry'. **Difficulty:** *ʿûšû* is a hapax legomenon.
Proposed emendation: חוּשׁוּ *ḥûšû* 'hurry'	**Followed by**: Crenshaw, Dillard, Keil, Stuart; NASB, NIV, NRSV, TEV.
Proposed emendation: עוּרוּ *ʿûrû* 'wake up'	**Proposed by:** BHS editor. **Followed by**: Cohen; KJV. **Supported by**: Targum. **Argument against:** The reading has no textual support.

TEXT—The MT reading of הַנְחַת יְהוָה גִּבּוֹרֶיךָ *hanḥaṯ yhwh gibbôrêḵā* 'bring down, YHWH, your warriors' is disputed.

Reading	Remarks
MT: הַנְחַת יְהוָה גִּבּוֹרֶיךָ *hanḥaṯ yhwh gibbôrêḵā* 'bring down, YHWH, your warriors'	**Followed by**: Cohen, Crenshaw, Dillard, Keil; NASB, NIV, NRSV, REB, TEV. **Argument for**: This can be seen as a reasonable aside, interrupting the flow of thought between this verse and the next [Cohen, Dillard].
Proposed emendation: הַנִּחַת יְהִי גִּבּוֹר *hanniḥaṯ yəhî gibbôr* 'let him who is frightened become a soldier'.	**Followed by:** Allen, Bewer, Stuart. **Supported by:** LXX, ὁ πραΰς ἔστω μαχητής 'let the weakling become a soldier'. **Argument for**: The verb *yəhî* 'let become' probably was corrupted to *yhwh*.
Proposed emendation: וְיָחֵת יְהוָה גִּבּוֹרֶיךָ *wəyāḥēṯ yhwh gibbôrêḵā*' 'and YHWH will shatter your warriors'.	**Followed by:** Wolff. **Supported by:** Targum Jonathan to the Prophets. **Supported by:** Vulgate *ibi occumbere faciet Dominus robustos tuos*. **Argument for**: MT הַנְחַת *hanḥaṯ* 'bring down' was probably a misreading of an original וְיָחֵת *wəyāḥēṯ* 'and he will shatter' (from חתת *ḥtt* 'to be shattered') [Wolff].

SYNTAX—The grouping of שָׁמָּה *šāmmâ* 'there' with surrounding words is disputed.

Grouping of *šāmmâ* 'there'	Remarks
MT: "... come, all nations, from round about and gather. **There** (***šāmmâ***) bring down, YHWH, your warriors."	**Followed by:** Keil; KJV. **Condition:** This grouping of *šāmmâ* is possible only if one accepts the MT reading of 'let them come' or 'bring down' [Wolff].
Proposed emendation: "... come, all nations, from round about and gather (or, let them gather) **there**. Let the frightened man become a warrior (or, That YHWH may shatter your warriors)."	**Followed by:** Crenshaw, Dillard, Stuart, Wolff; NIV, NRSV, REB, TEV. **Supported by:** LXX.

LEXICON—a-1. **<u>Wake-up(p)</u>** (עוּרוּ *ʿûrû*) masc. pl. Qal imper. of עור *ʿôr* [BDB p. 734], [Hol p. 268], [TWOT 1587]: 'to be awake' [Hol], 'to rouse oneself' [BDB], 'to awake' [BDB]. Bewer translates this as "for the nations shall be roused." The MT reads עוּשׁוּ *ʿûšû* a hapax legomenon considered by BDB to mean 'to lend aid'.

a-2. **<u>Hurry(p)</u>** (חוּשׁוּ *ḥûšû*) masc. pl. Qal imper. of חוּשׁ *ḥûš* [BDB p. 301], [Hol p. 98], TWOT 631]: 'to hurry' [Hol; Allen, Crenshaw, Dillard, Stuart, Wolff; TEV], 'to make haste' [BDB], 'to hasten' [Keil; NASB], 'to haste' [Cohen], not explicit [REB]. NIV and NRSV translate this verb as an adverb, "quickly."

b. **and-<u>come</u>(p)** masc. pl. Qal imper. of בּוֹא *bôʾ* [BDB p. 97], [Hol p. 34], [TWOT 212]: 'to come' [all lexica, commentators, and versions except REB], 'to muster' [REB].

c. **all <u>nations</u>** pl. of גּוֹי *gôy* [BDB p. 156], [Hol p. 57], [TWOT 326e]: 'nation' [all lexica, commentators, and versions except KJV], 'heathen' [KJV].

d. **<u>from-round-about</u>** סָבִיב *sāḇîḇ* [BDB p. 686], [Hol p. 252], [TWOT 1456b]: 'round about' [BDB; Dillard, Keil; KJV, REB], 'all around' [Hol; Allen; NRSV], 'from every side' [NIV]. Properly a noun, *sāḇîḇ* denotes 'circuit' [BDB]. Crenshaw, NASB, and TEV translate the word מִסָּבִיב *missāḇîḇ* 'from all around' as an adjective: "surrounding."

e. **and-<u>gather(p)</u>** 3rd pl. masc. Niphal perf. of קבץ *qḇṣ* [BDB p. 867], [Hol p. 312], [TWOT 1983]: 'to gather' [BDB, Hol; Allen, Crenshaw, Dillard; KJV, NASB, NRSV, REB, TEV], 'to assemble' [BDB, Hol; Keil; NIV]. The word וְנִקְבָּצוּ *wəniqbāṣû* is translated as an imperative by Crenshaw, Keil, Stuart, Wolff, KJV, NASB, NIV, NRSV, and TEV. It is translated as a third person expression by Allen, Dillard, and REB (e.g., "let them gather").

f-1. **<u>bring-down(sg)</u>** masc. sing. Hiphil imper. of נחת *nḥt* [BDB p. 639], [Hol p. 235], [TWOT 1351]: 'to bring down' [BDB; Dillard; NASB, NIV, NRSV], 'to send down' [Crenshaw; REB, TEV], 'to march down' [Hol], 'to lead down' [Hol], 'to cause to come down' [KJV]. Keil translates the phrase שָׁמָּה הַנְחַת יְהוָה גִּבּוֹרֶיךָ *šāmmâ hanḥaṯ yhwh gibbôrêḵā* as "let thy heroes come down thither, O Jehovah." TEV amplifies the verb: "send down ... your army ... to attack them."

f-2. **let the-<u>frightened</u>-man** masc. sing. Niphal part. of חתת *ḥtt* [BDB p. 369], [Hol p. 121], [TWOT 784]: 'to be frightened' [Stuart], 'to be terrified' [Hol]. Bewer translates this participle as a noun: "coward." Allen has "timid man."

f-3. **<u>that</u>- YHWH -<u>may-shatter</u> your(sg)-warriors** 3rd masc. sing. Hiphil imperf. of חתת *ḥtt* (see *f-2* above): 'to shatter' [Wolff].

g. **your(sg)-<u>warriors</u>** pl. constr. of גִּבּוֹר *gibbôr* [BDB p. 150], [Hol p. 53], [TWOT 310b]: 'warrior' [Hol; Dillard; NIV, NRSV], 'strong, valiant man' [BDB], 'mighty one' [Crenshaw; KJV, NASB], 'hero'

[Bewer, Keil, Allen], 'champion' [REB], 'army' [TEV]. The singular 'warrior' is here understood as a generic reference, which allows for a plural translation.

h. **there/to-that-place** שָׁמָּה *šāmmâ*, variant of שָׁם *šām* [BDB p. 1027], [Hol p. 374], [TWOT 2404]: 'there' [BDB, Hol; Allen, Bewer, Stuart], 'to that place' [Cohen, Keil].

QUESTION—If the reading וְנִקְבָּצוּ שָׁמָּה *wəniqbāṣû šāmmâ* 'and gather there' is accepted, what is the referential nature of the local term *šāmmâ* 'there'?

1. The reference is exophoric: the speaker is pointing—with his hand or finger—to the place he means for the armies to gather [Allen].
2. The reference is cataphoric: *šāmmâ* refers ahead to a place which will be specified in the next verse, the Valley of Jehoshaphat [Cohen, Crenshaw, Stuart, Wolff].

QUESTION—What is the cause of this projected battle?

The cause is YHWH's judgment. In the battle and its outcome reside both his judgment and his execution of sentence upon his enemies (see the discussion of the holy war in 4:9). The nations are drawn irresistibly by YHWH to their own doom, as is explicit in the following verse—a doom that constitutes the climactic theme of the entire book [Allen, Stuart].

4:12 (3:12)

Let- the-nations[a] -be-set-in-motion(p)[b] and-let-them-advance(p)[c] to-(the) valley(-of)[d] Jehoshaphat,[e]
for[f] there I-will-sit[g] to-judge[h] all-the-nations from-round-about.

LEXICON—a. **the-nations** pl. of גּוֹי *gôy* [BDB p. 156], [Hol p. 57], [TWOT 326e]: 'nation' [all lexica, commentators, and versions except KJV],'heathen' [KJV].

b. **let- the-nations -be-set-in-motion(p)** 3rd masc. pl. Niphal imperf. or jussive of עור *ʿôr* [BDB p. 734], [Hol p. 268], [TWOT 1587]: 'to be set in motion' [Hol], 'to rouse oneself' [Crenshaw; NRSV], 'to be roused' [Bewer, Stuart; NASB, NIV], 'to rise up' [Keil], 'to stir' [Dillard], 'to set out' [Wolff], 'to get ready' [TEV], 'to be awakened' [KJV], 'to hear the call to arms' [REB], 'to be alerted to advance' [Allen]. The root meaning of *ʿôr* is 'to awaken'. Bewer translates this verb with a future expression ("the nations shall be roused"). It is also translated as a desire or command, such as "let the nations rouse themselves" [Allen, Crenshaw] or "the nations are to rise up" [Keil, also Dillard, Stuart, Wolff; TEV].

c. **and-let-them-advance(p)** 3rd masc. pl. Niphal imperf. or jussive of עלה *ʿlh* [BDB p. 748], [Hol p. 273], [TWOT 1624]: 'to advance' [NIV], 'to go up' [Hol], 'to come up' [Crenshaw, Dillard, Wolff; KJV, NASB, NRSV], 'to come' [Keil; TEV], 'to march' [Bewer; REB], 'to advance for attack' [Stuart]. Bewer translates this verb with a future expression. Crenshaw, Dillard, Keil, Stuart, and Wolff translate it as a jussive.

d. **to-(the)valley(-of) Jehoshaphat** constr. of עֵמֶק *ᶜēmeq* [BDB p. 771], [Hol p. 277], [TWOT 1644a]: 'valley' [all lexica, commentators, and versions].

e. **Jehoshaphat** יְהוֹשָׁפָט *yəhôšāpāṭ* [BDB p. 221], [Hol p. 130]: 'Jehoshaphat' [all lexica, commentators, and versions except TEV], 'judgment' [TEV]. See the discussion of *yəhôšāpāṭ* under 4:2 (3:2).

f. **for there I-will-sit to-judge** כִּי *kî* particle [BDB p. 471], [Hol p. 155], [TWOT 976]: 'for' [Allen, Crenshaw, Bewer, Dillard, Keil, Stuart, Wolff; KJV, NASB, NIV, NRSV], not explicit [REB, TEV].

g. **I-will-sit** 1st sing. Qal imperf. of ישׁב *yšḇ* [BDB p. 442], [Hol p. 146], [TWOT 922]: 'to sit' [all lexica, commentators, and versions except Stuart], 'to sit down' [Stuart]. This verb, far from signaling a relaxed position on YHWH's part, denotes his acting in royal authority [Stuart], assuming the position of a judge [Dillard].

h. **to-judge** Qal infin. of שׁפט *špṭ* [BDB p. 1047], [Hol p. 380], [TWOT 2443]: 'to judge' [Hol; Keil, Stuart, Wolff; KJV, NASB, NIV, NRSV, TEV], 'to punish' [Hol]. The word לִשְׁפֹּט *lišpōṭ* is translated as "in judgment" [Allen, Bewer, Crenshaw, REB], "to render judgment" [Dillard]. Wolff views the force of *špṭ* here as 'to condemn', as in 1 Sam. 3:13. In reality, the verb signifies here the consideration of evidence, the rendering of a verdict, and the carrying out of the sentence [Allen].

QUESTION—What OT theme does Joel take up here?

Here Joel takes up the theme of YHWH's victory over his enemies who have attacked Jerusalem, as in Psalms 46 and 76, Isa. 9:5, and Hos. 2:18. An apocalyptic cast is given the theme in Zechariah 12 and 14. YHWH's judgment of the nations as presented in this verse is the very climax of the entire book. These nations who have attacked Jerusalem are brought back before her in order that YHWH may pass sentence on them [Allen].

4:13 (3:13)

Swing(p)[a] (the-)sickle,[b] for[c] (the-)harvest[d] is-ripe[e];
go(p)[f] tread(p)(grapes in the winepress),[g-1] / go(p) descend,[g-2] for[h] (the-) winepress[i] is-full,[j]
(the-)wine-vats[k] have-overflowed,[l] for[m] great[n] (is) their-wickedness.[o]

INTERTEXTUAL REFERENCE—Joel here takes the great OT theme of harvest, which in earlier prophetic literature (Isa. 17:4–6; Hos. 6:11) was a figure of YHWH's judgment of his covenant people, and turns it into a figure of judgment upon the nations who are against YHWH [Wendland].

TEXT—The verb רְדוּ *rəḏû* is taken by most to represent the root רדה *rḏh* 'to tread grapes'. It is, however, understood by KJV as representing the root ירד *yrḏ* 'to descend, to go down'.

LEXICON—a. **swing(p) (the-)sickle** masc. pl. imper. of שׁלח *šlḥ* [BDB p. 1018], [Hol p. 371], [TWOT 2394]: 'to swing' [Dillard; NIV], 'to put forth' [Hol; Crenshaw], 'to put in' [Cohen], 'to stretch out' [BDB], 'to give free play to' [Hol], 'to send' [Hol; Wolff], 'to put in' [Keil; KJV, NASB, NRSV], 'to wield' [Allen; REB], 'to let loose' [Stuart]. The metaphor relating to grain that is implicit in שִׁלְחוּ מַגָּל כִּי בָשַׁל קָצִיר *šilḥû maggāl kî bāšal qāṣîr* 'swing the sickle, for the harvest is ripe' is translated as a simile by TEV: "cut them down like grain at harvest time."

b. **(the-)sickle** מַגָּל *maggāl* [BDB p. 618], [Hol p. 182], [TWOT 1292a]: 'sickle' [all lexica, commentaries, and versions except REB], 'knife' [REB].

c. **for (the-)harvest is-ripe** כִּי *kî* particle [BDB p. 471], [Hol p. 155], [TWOT 976]: 'for' [all lexica, commentaries, and versions except Allen]. Allen expresses a reason relationship with a new clause introduced by no conjunction: "wield the sickle: the harvest is ripe."

d. **(the-)harvest** קָצִיר *qāṣîr* [BDB p. 894], [Hol p. 322], [TWOT 2062a]: 'harvest' [BDB; Allen, Crenshaw, Dillard, Keil, Stuart, Wolff; KJV, NASB, NIV, NRSV, REB], 'time of harvest' [BDB], 'activity of grain harvest' [Hol].

e. **is-ripe** 3rd masc. sing. Qal perf. of בשל *bšl* [BDB p. 143], [Hol p. 51], [TWOT 292]: 'to be ripe [Allen, Crenshaw, Dillard, Keil, Stuart, Wolff; KJV, NASB, NIV, NRSV, REB], 'to grow ripe' [BDB], 'to ripen' [Hol]. Wolff considers the primary sense of *bšl* to be 'to boil'; Keil regards the primary sense of *bšl* to be 'to ripen'; the grain harvest is thereby suggested.

f. **go(p) tread(p) (grapes in the winepress)** masc. pl. imper. of בוא *bô'* [BDB p. 97], [Hol p. 34], [TWOT 212]: 'to go' [BDB], 'to go out' [Crenshaw], 'to go in' [Hol; NRSV], 'to get in' [Allen], 'to come' [BDB; Dillard, Keil, Stuart, Wolff; KJV, NASB, NIV, REB]. In the expression בֹּאוּ רְדוּ כִּי־מָלְאָה גַּת הֵשִׁיקוּ הַיְקָבִים *bō'û rədû kî-mal'â gat hēšîqû hayqābîm*, the metaphor is translated as a simile by TEV: "crush them as grapes are crushed in a full wine press until the wine runs over."

g-1. **tread(p) (grapes in the winepress)** masc. pl. imper. of רדה *rdh* [Hol p. 333], [TWOT 2121]: 'tread' [Hol; Crenshaw, Dillard, Keil, Stuart, Wolff; NASB, NRSV]. Some commentators and versions supply the implicit complement of the verb: "to trample the grapes" [NIV], "to tread the grapes" [Allen; REB]. *Rdh* denotes specifically to tread grapes in a winepress [Hol; Cohen], but its root meaning appears to be 'to rule over' [Hol].

g-2. **go(p) descend** masc. pl. imper. of root ירד *yrd* [BDB p. 432], [Hol p. 143], [TWOT 909]: 'to get down' [KJV], 'to descend' [BDB], 'to go down' [Hol].

h. **for (the-)winepress is-full** כִּי *kî* particle (see *c* above): 'for' [all lexica, commentaries, and versions except Allen]. Allen expresses a reason relationship with a new clause introduced by no conjunction.

i. **(the-)winepress** גַּת *gat* [BDB p. 178], [Hol p. 65], [TWOT 841a]: 'winepress' [BDB, Hol; Cohen, Crenshaw, Dillard, Keil, Stuart, Wolff; NASB, NIV, NRSV, REB], 'press' [Allen; KJV]. *Gat* denotes a basin in which grapes were pressed out underfoot and from which the juice flowed into a lower basin.

j. **is-full** 3rd fem. sing. Qal perf. of מלא *mlʾ* [BDB p. 569], [Hol p. 195], [TWOT 1195]: 'to be full' [BDB, Hol; Allen, Cohen, Crenshaw, Dillard, Keil, Stuart, Wolff; KJV, NASB, NIV, NRSV, REB], 'to fill' [BDB].

k. **(the-)wine-vats have-overflowed** pl. of יֶקֶב *yeqeb* [BDB p. 428], [Hol p. 141], [TWOT 900a]: 'wine vat' [BDB, Hol], 'fats' [KJV], 'vat' [Allen, Crenshaw, Dillard, Keil, Stuart, Wolff; NASB, NIV, NRSV, REB]. *Yeqeb* usually refers to a basin hollowed out of rock and situated lower than the winepress for receiving the juice trodden out of the grapes in the upper basin. Sometimes, however, *yeqeb* refers to the winepress itself [BDB].

l. **have-overflowed** 3rd masc. pl. Hiphil perf. of שׁוּק *šûq* [BDB p. 1003]. [Hol p. 365], [TWOT 2351]: 'to overflow' [BDB, Hol; Allen, Crenshaw, Dillard, Keil, Stuart, Wolff; KJV, NASB, NIV, NRSV]. REB translates הֵשִׁיקוּ *hēšîqû* as an imperative: "empty."

m. **for great (is) their-wickedness** כִּי *kî* particle (see *c* above): 'for' [Crenshaw, Dillard, Keil, Stuart, Wolff; KJV, NASB, NRSV, REB], not explicit [TEV]. Allen and NIV have 'so', producing an exclamatory clause: "so great."

n. **great (is) their-wickedness** fem. sing. of רַב *rab* [BDB p. 912], [Hol p. 330], [TWOT 2099a]: 'great' [BDB, Hol; Allen, Dillard, Keil, Stuart, Wolff; KJV, NASB, NIV, NRSV], 'copious' [Crenshaw]. *Rab* denotes great in extent or quantity [BDB, Hol]. REB translates the clause כִּי רַבָּה רָעָתָם *kî rabbâ rāʿātām* as "for they are full to the brim"; TEV translates it as "they are very wicked."

o. **their-wickedness** constr. of רעה *rāʿâ* [BDB p. 949], [Hol p. 342], [TWOT 2191c]: 'wickedness' [Hol; Allen, Cohen, Dillard, Keil, Stuart, Wolff; KJV, NASB, NIV, NRSV], 'evil' [BDB, Hol], 'evil deed' [Crenshaw].

QUESTION—Who are the addressees in this verse?

The addressees are YHWH's heavenly servants, the angels [Allen, Cohen, Keil], probably acting as a great heavenly army, reminiscent of the great host which protected Elisha (2 Kings 6:17; see also Deut. 33:2) [Allen, Wolff].

QUESTION—To what agricultural products does this verse refer?

1. This verse refers to Israel's three main crops, grain, grapes, and olives; the harvest here is metaphorical for YHWH's judgment. It is possible that the exact point of similarity between judgment (see Isa. 17:4–6; 63:3; Hos. 6:11; Mic. 4:13) and harvest is the act of cutting down or trampling the crop as in the threshing of grain and the treading of

grapes. The gathering of the harvest crops symbolizes the hostile nations who have been gathered [Stuart].

2. This verse refers to the grain harvest and the grape harvest [Allen, Crenshaw, Keil]. The distinction between the two is found in Rev. 14:15, 18, where the grain harvest appears in v. 15, and the grape in v. 18 [Keil]. The word קָצִיר *qāṣîr* 'harvest' usually denotes the grain harvest [Crenshaw].
3. This verse refers to the grape harvest alone [Dillard, Wolff]. The use of the verb בשל *bšl*, whose primary sense is 'to boil', in the phrase כִּי בָשַׁל קָצִיר *kî bāšal qāṣîr* 'for the harvest is ripe' suggests that the grape harvest is in focus here [Wolf]. The verb *bšl* (but in the Hiphil stem instead of the Qal) occurs also in Gen. 40:10 in connection with the grape harvest [Dillard].

QUESTION—What is the point of similarity and the topic of the metaphor in this verse?

1. The topic of this metaphor is YHWH's punishment of the nations; the cutting (of the grapes) and the treading (the winepress) serve as the primary points of similarity, e are violent and destructive acts, just as YHWH's punishment will be. A secondary point of similarity is between pressed grape juice and blood, grape juice suggesting the shedding of blood in war (cf. Isa. 63:1–6) [Wolff].
2. This verse has two metaphors: the grain harvest and the process of wine production. The ripe grain represents the right time for YHWH to judge. The grape figure represents the vast numbers of mankind who are to be presented for judgment. The winepress represents the complete destruction YHWH will inflict upon his enemies, as in Isa. 63:3 and in Rev. 14:20 [Keil]. Allen, however, considers that the grape figure represents both the mass of mankind and the enormity of its wickedness.

QUESTION—What is the rhetorical nature of 4:12–13 (3:12–13)?

These verses are very elliptical, omitting an explicit reference to the battle between the nations and YHWH's army. The implied sequence of events is as follows: the mustering of the nations' armies; their attack on Jerusalem; the counter-attack of YHWH and his heavenly army, which is likened to the action of harvesting; and the complete destruction of the enemy, which is also couched in terms of judicial action. These events are implied again in the following verses, 4:14–16 (3:14–16) [Allen].

QUESTION—What is the nature of the wickedness referred to in the clause כִּי רַבָּה רָעָתָם *kî rabbâ rāʿāṯām* 'for their wickedness is great'?

It is the wickedness of the nations that have opposed Israel [Kimchi, cited by Cohen].

4:14 (3:14)

Tumult,[a] tumult in-(the-)valley(-of)[b] the-verdict,[c]
for[d] near[e] (is) (the-)day(-of) YHWH in-(the-)valley(-of) the-verdict.

LEXICON—a. **tumult** pl. of הָמוֹן *hāmôn* [BDB p. 242], [Hol p. 81], [TWOT 505a]: 'tumult' [Crenshaw, Keil, Wolff], 'crowd' [BDB, Hol], 'agitation' [Hol], 'turmoil' [Hol], 'roar' [BDB], 'multitude' [Cohen; KJV, NASB, NRSV], 'noisy throng' [REB], 'noisy crowd' [Allen], 'thousands' [TEV], 'horde' [Dillard], 'mêlée' [Stuart]. Bewer translates the expression הֲמוֹנִים הֲמוֹנִים *hămônîm hămônîm* dynamically as "multitudes roar." The repetition of the term *hămônîm* is meant to increase its intensity [Allen, Cohen, Keil]. Dillard sees it as denoting either vast numbers of people ("hordes") or the sound and confusion of a great battle ("tumult"). The Vulgate opts for the former with its rendering *populi*, as does Aquila's Greek translation with συναγωγαί and Theodotion's with πλῆθη. The LXX opts for the latter interpretation with ἦχοι [Dillard]. Bewer sees *hămônîm hămônîm* as denoting the noise of war.

b. **in-(the-)valley(-of) the-verdict** עֵמֶק *ᶜēmeq* [BDB p. 771], [Hol p. 277], [TWOT 1644a]: 'valley' [all lexica, commentators, and versions].

c. **the-verdict** חָרוּץ *ḥārûṣ* [BDB p. 358], [Hol p. 116], [TWOT 752a]: 'verdict' [Allen, Dillard, Stuart], 'strict decision' [BDB], 'decision' [Hol; Crenshaw, Keil, Wolff; KJV, NASB, NRSV, REB], 'judgment' [TEV]. *Ḥārûṣ* comes from the verb root חרץ *ḥrṣ* 'to cut' [BDB], the same as the root of the word חָרִיץ *ḥārîṣ* [BDB p. 358], [Hol p. 116], [TWOT 752c]: 'cheese' [BDB, Hol]. The expression חֲרִצֵי הֶחָלָב *ḥăriṣê heḥālāḇ,* literally 'cuttings of milk', means 'cheeses' [BDB] (see the discussion under 4:2). The noun חָרוּץ *ḥārûṣ* 'sledge for threshing' (an instrument with sharp, cutting teeth, as in Amos 1:3) also comes from *ḥrṣ* 'to cut' and is a homonym with *ḥārûṣ* 'decision, verdict'. Thus it is possible that the expression בְּעֵמֶק הֶחָרוּץ *bəᶜēmeq heḥārûṣ* in fact carries a double meaning, 'in the valley of the verdict' and 'in the valley of threshing' [Allen, Cohen, Crenshaw]. Keil, however, sees the expression *bəᶜēmeq heḥārûṣ* not as word play on two homonyms, but rather as intensifying the literal meaning of 'Valley of Jehoshaphat'.

d. **for near (is) (the-)day(-of) YHWH** כִּי *kî* particle [BDB p. 471], [Hol p. 155], [TWOT 976]: 'for' [Crenshaw, Dillard, Keil, Stuart, Wolff; KJV, NASB, NRSV], 'because' [Allen], not explicit [REB].

e. **near** קָרוֹב *qārôḇ* [BDB p. 898], [Hol p. 325], [TWOT 2065d]: 'near' [BDB, Hol; Crenshaw, Dillard, Keil, Stuart, Wolff; KJV, NASB, NRSV], 'imminent' [Hol], 'at hand' [REB], 'soon to come' [Allen]. TEV translates the adjective *qārôḇ* as a verb phrase: "will soon come."

QUESTION—What link is there between Joel's use of הֲמוֹנִים *hămônîm* 'multitudes, tumult, mêlée' and its use in other prophetic material?

This passage is similar to Isa. 13:4 (NIV):

Listen, a noise [קוֹל הָמוֹן *qôl hāmôn*] on the mountains,
like that of a great multitude!
Listen, an uproar among the kingdoms,
like nations massing together;
[YHWH of hosts] is mustering an army for war.

It is also similar to Isa. 17:12 (NIV):

Oh, the raging of many nations [הֲמוֹן עַמִּים רַבִּים *hămôn ᶜammîm rabbîm*]—
they rage like the raging sea!
Oh, the uproar of the peoples—
they roar like the roaring of great waters!

Both of these passages occur in the context of YHWH's bringing judgment in warfare upon hostile nations. The context of Isa. 13:4 speaks of the emerging Persian Empire's multiethnic army that would destroy Babylon. The context of Isa. 17:12 speaks of the Assyrian army attacking Judah: Isaiah foretells their unexpected defeat [Allen, Crenshaw]. Whereas the language of Isa. 13:6 was used in Joel 1:15 as a threat against YHWH's covenant community, the language of military defeat and destruction is now used by Joel against the hostile nations [Allen].

QUESTION—What is the sense of הֲמוֹנִים הֲמוֹנִים בְּעֵמֶק הֶחָרוּץ *hămônîm hămônîm bəᶜēmeq heḥārûṣ*, the opening passage of this verse?

1. It refers to a scene of battle, and *hămônîm* should be translated on the order of *mêlée* to give the idea of the sound of combat [Crenshaw, Stuart].
2. It refers to the noise of the vast crowds of humanity entering the valley of the verdict [Keil].

QUESTION—What is the significance of the expression בְּעֵמֶק הֶחָרוּץ *bəᶜēmeq heḥārûṣ* 'in the valley of the verdict'?

The referent of this expression is the same as עֵמֶק יְהוֹשָׁפָט *ᶜēmeq yəhôšāpāṭ* 'the Valley of Jehoshaphat' in 4:2. The different name in 4:14 emphasizes that the valley functions as the final judgment place of YHWH upon the peoples [Allen, Cohen, Crenshaw, Dillard, Wolff]. While this passage has been a favorite of many evangelists appealing to their audiences to make a decision for Christ, the context clearly shows a multitude of nations gathered, not to decide anything, but rather to hear and receive YHWH's verdict about them—they have no more opportunity for decision making [Dillard].

QUESTION—What is the main point of this verse?

It is that these events begin the day of YHWH, which had been averted from coming upon Israel (1:15; 2:1, 11) and is instead coming upon all the other nations. This view is supported by the fact that the cosmic upheavals portrayed in 2:10b, in the context of YHWH's threatened judgment upon Jerusalem, are repeated in the new context of 4:15 (3:15), and the language of 2:10a is repeated in 4:16 (3:16) [Wolff]. Bewer, however, sees a contradiction in the passage, for if war is going on between the nations and YHWH's heavenly armies, his day can hardly be said to be only imminent or near.

4:15 (3:15)

Sun[a] and-moon[b] have-become-dark,[c] and[d]-stars[e] have-withdrawn[f] their-shining.[g]

TEXT—This verse is the same as 2:10b and expresses the same thought as 3:4a (2:31a) [Crenshaw, Stuart].

LEXICON—a. **Sun and-moon** שֶׁמֶשׁ *šemeš* [BDB p. 1039], [Hol p. 378], [TWOT 2417a]: 'sun' [all lexica, commentators, and versions].

b. **and-moon** יָרֵחַ *yārēaḥ* [BDB p. 437], [Hol p. 144], [TWOT 913a]: 'moon' [all lexica, commentators, and versions]. This noun appears especially in OT poetry [BDB].

c. **have-become-dark** 3rd masc. pl. Qal perf. of קדר *qḏr* [BDB p. 871], [Hol p. 313], [TWOT 1989]: 'to become dark' [Crenshaw], 'to be dark' [BDB], 'to grow dark' [Hol; Allen, Dillard; NASB, TEV], 'to be darkened' [KJV, NIV, NRSV, REB], 'to darken' [Stuart], 'to become black' [Cohen, Keil]. The English present perfect tense is used by Crenshaw and Keil; the present tense is used by Allen, Dillard, NASB, NRSV, REB, and TEV; the future tense is used by KJV and NIV.

d. **and-stars have-withdrawn their-shining** -וְ *wə- waw* connective [BDB p. 251], [Hol p. 84], [TWOT 519]: 'and' [Allen, Dillard, Keil; KJV, NASB, NIV, NRSV, REB, TEV]. Crenshaw and Stuart express the additive relation with a new clause.

e. **stars** pl. of כּוֹכָב *kôḵāḇ* [BDB p. 456], [Hol p. 152], [TWOT 942a]: 'star' [all lexica, commentators, and versions].

f. **have-withdrawn** 3rd masc. pl. Qal perf. of אסף *ʾsp̄* [BDB p. 62], [Hol p. 23], [TWOT 140]: 'to withdraw' [Keil; KJV, NRSV], 'to draw back' [Hol], 'to lose' [NASB], 'to withhold' [Crenshaw; REB], 'to recall' [Dillard]. The English present perfect tense is used by Crenshaw and Keil; the present tense is used by Allen, Dillard, NASB, NIV, NRSV, REB, and TEV; the future tense is used by KJV. TEV and NIV translate אָסְפוּ נָגְהָם *ʾāsəp̄û nōḡhām* 'they have withdrawn their shining' as "no longer shine." Allen has "stop shining"; Stuart is similar.

g. **their-shining** constr. of נֹגַהּ *nōḡah* [BDB p. 618], [Hol p. 226], [TWOT 1290a]: 'shining' [Hol; Keil, Stuart; KJV, NRSV], 'gleam' [Hol], 'brightness' [BDB; NASB], 'light' [Dillard; REB], 'splendor' [Crenshaw].

QUESTION—What is the sense of this verse?

The moon and stars usually stand in parallel construction to the sun in OT poetry; therefore, the sense of the verse is not that day and night both become dark, but rather that the day of the verdict is very dark [Stuart]. The heavenly bodies become dark, not because of any thick stormclouds gathered over the earth, but because their very shining fails [Keil].

QUESTION—What is the further significance of this verse?

It is that the phenomenon of time, part of creation's fabric, is unraveling in the face of YHWH's final judgment [Dillard, Keil]. The fading of the heavenly bodies and the earth's quaking (in 4:16) are standard prophetic signs of the arrival of the day of YHWH [Stuart]. Such fading and quaking portend the return of creation to primeval chaos, as in Ps. 46:4(3) and Ps. 77:18, which will usher in YHWH's final judgment [Dillard, citing Brevard S. Childs, "The Enemy from the North and the Chaos Tradition," *Journal of Biblical Literature* 78 (1959)]. Joel's language appears in the NT in Rev. 14:15, 18, 20 and in Mark 4:29 [Allen]. The eleventh-century Jewish commentator Rashi understood the sun's darkening as a divine device to counter those who worshiped the sun [cited by Cohen].

4:16 (3:16)

Then[a]-YHWH roars[b] from[c]-Zion,[d] and[e]-from-Jerusalem he-lifts-up[f] his-voice,[g]
and[h]- (the-)heavens[i] and- (the)earth[j] -quake,[k]
but[l]-YHWH (is/will be) (a)refuge[m] for[n]-his-people,[o] and-(a)fortress[p] for-(the-)sons(-of)[q] Israel.

INTERTEXTUAL REFERENCE—Joel evokes, if he does not quote directly, Amos 1:2: "YHWH roars from Zion and lifts up his voice from Jerusalem." The difference is that in Amos this line introduces coming judgment upon YHWH's people, whereas in Joel it introduces an assurance of coming security and blessing for them [Wendland].

LEXICON—a. <u>then</u>**-YHWH roars from-Zion** -וְ *wə- waw* connective [BDB p. 251], [Hol p. 84], [TWOT 519]: 'then' [Crenshaw], 'and' [Keil; NASB], 'also' [KJV]. Dillard, Stuart, NIV, NRSV, REB, and TEV express the additive relation with a new clause or sentence. Crenshaw has "then," expressing a consecutive temporal relationship. Allen expresses a circumstantial relation with "as," and Wolff with "while." In the Hebrew text "YHWH" is emphasized by virtue of the inversion in this clause of the normal word order [Crenshaw].

b. <u>**roars**</u> 3rd masc. sing. Qal imperf. of שׁאג *šʾg* [BDB p. 980], [Hol p. 356], [TWOT 2300]: 'to roar' [BDB, Hol; Allen, Crenshaw, Dillard, Keil, Stuart, Wolff; KJV, NASB, NIV, NRSV, REB, TEV]. The English present tense is used by Crenshaw, Keil, Allen, Dillard, Wolff, NASB, NRSV, REB, and TEV; the future tense is used by KJV and NIV.

c. <u>**from**</u>**-Zion** מִן *min* [BDB p. 577], [Hol p. 200], [TWOT 1212]: 'from' [Crenshaw, Allen, Dillard, Stuart, Wolff; NASB, NIV, NRSV, REB, TEV], 'out of' [Keil; KJV].

d. <u>**Zion**</u> צִיּוֹן *ṣiyyôn* [BDB p. 851], [Hol p. 306], [TWOT 1910]: 'Zion' [all lexica, commentators, and versions except TEV], 'Mount Zion' [TEV].

e. **<u>and</u>-from-Jerusalem he-lifts-up his-voice** -וְ *wə-* *waw* connective (see *a* above): 'and' [Allen, Keil, Wolff; KJV, NASB, NIV, NRSV, REB]. Crenshaw, Dillard, Stuart, and TEV express the additive relation with a new clause or sentence.

f. **<u>he-lifts-up</u> his-voice** 3rd masc. sing. Qal imperf. of נתן *nt̲n* [BDB p. 678], [Hol p. 249], [TWOT 1443]—with the complement of "voice" in *g* below: 'to lift up one's voice' [Hol], 'to raise one's voice' [Dillard, Stuart, Wolff], 'to utter one's voice' [Crenshaw; KJV, NASB, NRSV], 'to thunder' [Allen, Keil; NIV, REB]. The primary sense of *nt̲n* is 'to give'. TEV makes קוֹל *qôl* 'voice' the subject: "his voice thunders."

g. **his-<u>voice</u>** constr. of קוֹל *qôl* [BDB p. 876], [Hol p. 315], [TWOT 1998a]: 'voice' [Hol; Crenshaw, Dillard, Stuart, Wolff; KJV, NASB, NRSV, TEV].

h. **<u>and</u>- (the-)heavens and- (the)earth -quake** -וְ *wə-* *waw* connective (see *a* above): 'and' [Allen, Dillard, Keil; KJV, NASB, NRSV]. NIV expresses the additive relation with a new clause, Crenshaw with a verb phrase (no conjunction). Stuart, Wolff, and REB have "so that," expressing a result relation.

i. **(the-)<u>heavens</u>** שָׁמַיִם *šāmayim* [BDB p. 1029], [Hol p. 375], [TWOT 2407a]: 'heavens' [Hol; Dillard, Wolff; KJV, NASB, NRSV], 'heaven' [Hol; Crenshaw, Keil; REB], 'sky' [Hol; Allen, Stuart; NIV, TEV].

j. **and- (the)<u>earth</u> -quake** אֶרֶץ *ʾereṣ* [BDB p. 76], [Hol p. 28], [TWOT 167]: 'earth' [Allen, Crenshaw, Dillard, Keil, Stuart, Wolff; KJV, NASB, NIV, NRSV, REB, TEV], 'ground' [Hol].

k. **<u>quake</u>** 3rd pl. Qal perf. of רעשׁ *rʿš* [BDB p. 950], [Hol p. 344], [TWOT 2195]: 'to quake' [Hol; Keil, Wolff], 'to shake' [Hol; Dillard, Stuart; KJV, NRSV], 'to tremble' [Crenshaw; NASB, NIV, TEV], 'to vibrate' [Allen], 'to shudder' [REB]. See the discussion of רעשׁ *rʿš* 'to shake' under 2:10.

l. **<u>but</u>-YHWH (is/will be) (a)refuge for-his-people** -וְ *wə-* *waw* connective (see *a* above): 'but' [Allen, Crenshaw, Keil, Stuart, Wolff; KJV, NASB, NIV, NRSV, REB, TEV]. Dillard expresses the additive relation with a new clause.

m. **(a)<u>refuge</u>** מַחֲסֶה *maḥăsẹ* [BDB p. 340], [Hol p. 191], [TWOT 700b]: 'refuge' [BDB, Hol; Crenshaw, Keil, Stuart, Wolff; NASB, NIV, NRSV, REB], 'shelter' [BDB; Allen], 'hope' [KJV]. TEV conflates and translates *but-YHWH (is/will be)(a)refuge for-his-people, and-(a)fortress for-(the-)sons(-of) Israel* as "but he will defend his people."

n. **<u>for</u>-his-people** -לְ *lə-* [BDB p. 510], [Hol p. 167], [TWOT 1063]: 'for' [Allen, Crenshaw, Dillard, Stuart, Wolff; NASB, NIV, NRSV, REB], 'to' [Keil], 'of' [KJV]. The proclitic *lə-* expresses a benefactive relation here, the so-called dative of advantage [Hol].

o. **his-<u>people</u>** constr. of עָם *ʿām* [BDB p. 766], [Hol p. 275], [TWOT 1640a]: 'people' [Hol; Allen, Crenshaw, Dillard, Keil, Stuart, Wolff;

KJV, NASB, NIV, NRSV, REB]. The word *ʿām* refers to an entire people and stresses their ethnic unity [Hol].

p. **and-(a)fortress for-(the-)sons(-of) Israel** מָעוֹז *māʿôz* [BDB p. 731], [Hol p. 205], [TWOT 1578a]: 'fortress' [TWOT; Crenshaw], 'refuge' [BDB], 'stronghold' [Allen, Dillard, Keil, Stuart, Wolff; NASB, NIV, NRSV], 'strength' [KJV], 'defense' [REB]. The primary sense of *māʿôz* is 'mountain stronghold', 'place of safety' [Hol], or 'fortress' [TWOT], but here the word is used figuratively of YHWH.

q. **(the-)sons(-of)** pl. constr. of בֵּן *bēn* [BDB p. 119], [Hol p. 42], [TWOT 254]: 'son' [BDB, Hol; Keil, Wolff; NASB]. The phrase בְּנֵי יִשְׂרָאֵל *bənê-yiśrāʾēl* is translated as "Israelites" [Allen, Crenshaw, Stuart], "children of Israel" [Dillard, KJV], "people of Israel" [NIV, NRSV], "Israel" [REB]. This phrase, as in 2:27 and 4:2 (3:2), refers not to the defunct northern kingdom, but to YHWH's covenant community, centered in Jerusalem [Crenshaw].

QUESTION—What is the literary source for this verse?

It may well be that Joel is citing Amos 1:2 here [Allen, Wolff].

QUESTION—What is the function of the reference to YHWH's thunderous voice in OT prophetic literature?

It signals that YHWH in the midst of battle is triumphing over his enemies, as in 1 Sam. 2:10, 7:10, and Jer. 25:30 [Bewer, Stuart].

QUESTION—What is the significance of the expression יְהוָה מִצִּיּוֹן יִשְׁאָג *yhwh miṣṣiyyôn yišʾāg* 'YHWH roars from Zion'?

Amos 1:2 uses this expression to announce to the northern kingdom that YHWH has revealed himself in Jerusalem and that the religious worship of the northern kingdom is illegitimate [Allen, Stuart]. Joel uses YHWH's roar of triumph, together with the shaking of the cosmos, as the sole but nevertheless sufficient indication in this passage that he actually does render his judgment in battle against the hostile nations, destroying them once for all—not, in fact, by means of his own armies, but simply by the roar of command [Bewer]. Joel also uses this expression to comfort the covenant people: YHWH is in their midst and is defeating their enemies for all time [Allen]. Crenshaw sees in this expression an implication that YHWH not only roars at his enemies, but also charges forth from Jerusalem like an angry lion, leading his forces against them.

QUESTION—What is the relationship between the first two clauses of this verse: וַיהוה מִצִּיּוֹן יִשְׁאָג *wayhwh miṣṣiyyôn yišʾāg* 'and YHWH roars from Zion' and וּמִירוּשָׁלַם יִתֵּן קוֹלוֹ *ûmîrûšālaim yittēn qôlô* 'and from Jerusalem he lifts up his voice'?

These two clauses stand in synonymous parallelism with each other [Crenshaw].

QUESTION—What is the function of the *waw* connective in the phrase וַיהוה מַחֲסֶה לְעַמּוֹ *wayhwh maḥăsê̩ ləᶜammô* 'but YHWH will be a refuge for his people'?

It introduces the contrasting role which YHWH will play for his covenant community, that of a protector instead of a condemning executioner [all commentators]. Joel uses language from the Psalms (e.g., Psalms 14, 27, 46, 60, and 142), in which are found the words *maḥăsê̩* 'refuge' and its shorter version מַחְסֶה *maḥsê̩* and מָעוֹז *māyôz* 'fortress', as well as Nah. 1:7 and Isa. 25:4 [Crenshaw].

QUESTION—What poetic device does Joel employ in 4:12–16?

He employs two images which seem concretely opposed to each other: that of YHWH sitting as a judge in the Valley of the Verdict, and that of YHWH roaring against his enemies and charging forth from Jerusalem against them. The medium of poetry is certainly elastic enough to admit multiple images, as in Isa. 52:12, in which YHWH will be for the returning Judeans both their leader and their rearguard [Crenshaw].

DISCOURSE UNIT: 4:17–21 (3:17–21) [Crenshaw]. The topic is "Judah's security is assured."

4:17 (3:17)

Then[a]-you(p)-will-know[b] that[c] I (am) YHWH your(p)-God,[d] (I who) live[e] on[f]-Zion, (the-)mountain(-of)[g] my-holiness,[h]
and[i]- Jerusalem -will-become[j] (a)holy-thing,[k] and-foreigners[l] will- never-again[m] -pass-through[n]-her.

SYNTAX—The syntactic function of יְהוָה אֱלֹהֵיכֶם *yhwh ᵓĕlōhêḵem* is disputed:

Syntactic function of phrase	Resulting sense	Followed by
It is part of a predication with אֲנִי *ᵓănî* 'I'.	"I am YHWH your God" or "I YHWH am your God; I dwell on Zion...."	Allen, Dillard, Keil, Wolff; KJV, NASB, REB, TEV
It is in apposition to "I."	"I YHWH your God dwell on Zion...."	Crenshaw, Keil, Stuart; NIV, NRSV

LEXICON—a. <u>then</u>-you(p)-will-know -וְ *wə- waw* of the attached wayyiqtol verb form [BDB p. 251], [Hol p. 84], [TWOT 519]: 'then' [Crenshaw; NASB, NIV, TEV], 'and' [Dillard, Keil, Wolff], 'so' [KJV, NRSV], 'thus' [REB]. Stuart expresses the additive relation with a new clause (no conjunction).

b. <u>you(p)-will-know</u> 2nd masc. pl. Qal perf. of ידע *yḏᶜ* [BDB p. 393], [Hol p. 128], [TWOT 848]: 'to know' [all lexica, commentators, and versions except Keil], 'to perceive' [Keil].

c. **<u>that</u> I (am) YHWH your(p)-God** כִּי *kî* particle [BDB p. 471], [Hol p. 155], [TWOT 976]: 'that' [all lexica, commentators, and versions].

d. **your(p)-<u>God</u>** constr. of אֱלֹהִים *ʾĕlōhîm* [BDB p. 43], [Hol p. 16], [TWOT 93c]: "God' [all lexica, commentators, and versions].

e. **(I who) <u>live</u> on-Zion** masc. sing. Qal part. of שׁכן *škn* [BDB p. 1015], [Hol p. 369], [TWOT 2387]: 'to live' [Hol; TEV], 'to inhabit' [Hol], 'to dwell' [BDB; Crenshaw, Dillard, Keil, Stuart; KJV, NASB, NIV, NRSV, REB], 'to abide' [BDB]. Allen translates this verb as a noun plus verb phrase: "whose home is in Zion." *Škn* and ישׁב *yšb* 'to dwell, inhabit' are sometimes used synonymously in the OT, but often with an apparent difference in their usage: *yšb* seems to denote the state of permanent dwelling, as of one among his people, or of God in heaven, as in Ps. 2:4. In this latter case, there is a connotation of loftiness and majesty. *Škn*, on the other hand, connotes an intimate presence [TWOT].

f. **<u>on</u>-Zion** -בְּ *bə-* [BDB p. 88], [Hol p. 32], [TWOT 193]: 'on' [Dillard, Stuart, Wolff; TEV], 'in' [Allen, Crenshaw; KJV, NASB, NIV, NRSV, REB], 'upon' [Keil].

g. **(the-)<u>mountain(-of)</u> my-holiness** constr. of הַר *har* [BDB p. 249], [Hol p. 83], [TWOT 517a]: 'mountain' [all lexica, commentators, and versions except NIV and TEV], 'hill' [NIV, TEV].

h. **my-<u>holiness</u>** constr. of קֹדֶשׁ *qōdeš* [BDB p. 871], [Hol p. 314], [TWOT 1990a]: 'holiness' [Hol]. Some translate this noun as an adjective: "sacred," [Allen, Crenshaw, TEV], "holy" [Dillard, Keil, Stuart, Wolff, KJV, NIV, NASB, REB]. *Qōdeš* here probably denotes YHWH's essential divine quality, which is worthy of all honor and respect.

i. **<u>and</u>- Jerusalem -will-become (a)holy-thing** -וְ *wə- waw* of the attached wayyiqtol verb form (see *a* above): 'and' [Allen, Crenshaw, Keil, Wolff; NRSV], 'then' [KJV], 'so' [NASB]. Dillard, Stuart, NIV, REB, and TEV express the additive relation with a new clause or sentence.

j. **<u>will-become</u>** 3rd fem sing. Qal *waw*-consecutive perf. of היה *hyh* [BDB p. 224], [Hol p. 78], [TWOT 491]: 'to become' [BDB, Hol], 'to be' [Crenshaw, Dillard, Keil, Stuart, Wolff; KJV, NASB, NIV, NRSV, REB, TEV], 'to be made' [Allen].

k. **(a)<u>holy-thing</u>** קֹדֶשׁ *qōdeš* (see *h* above): 'holy thing' [Hol], 'place of holiness' [Crenshaw], 'sanctuary' [Keil, Wolff]. Some translate this noun as an adjective: "sacrosanct" [Allen]; "holy" [Dillard; KJV, NASB, NIV, NRSV, REB]. Others have a noun phrase: "holy place" [Stuart], "sacred city" [TEV]. *Qōdeš* here probably denotes the quality of something which has been transformed by its association with God [Hol]. That is to say, while Jerusalem's complete acceptability to YHWH is included in the sense, this is secondary to the fact that she belongs entirely to YHWH; she is his "sanctuary" [Wolff]. Crenshaw takes a different view, seeing as the primary sense of *qōḏeš* here the city's freedom from anyone who would degrade its acceptability to YHWH.

l. **and-foreigners will- never-again -pass-through-her** pl. of זָר *zār* [BDB p. 266], [Hol p. 91], [TWOT 541]: 'foreign' [BDB, Hol], 'strange' [Hol]; 'foreigner' [Crenshaw, Dillard, Stuart; NIV, REB, TEV], 'stranger' [Keil, Wolff; KJV, NASB, NRSV], 'alien' [Allen]. In both BDB and TWOT, *zār* is treated as a Qal part. of זוּר *zûr* 'to be a stranger'.

m. **never-again** עוֹד *ʿôḏ* [BDB p. 728], [Hol p. 267], [TWOT 1576]: (with the negation לֹא *lōʾ*) 'never again' [Allen, Dillard, Wolff; NIV, NRSV, REB, TEV], 'no more' [BDB, Hol; NASB], 'no longer' [Crenshaw], 'any more' [Keil; KJV], 'not again' [Stuart].

n. **will- never-again -pass-through-her** 3rd masc. pl. Qal imperf. of עבר *ʿḇr* [BDB p. 716], [Hol p. 263], [TWOT 1556]: 'to pass through' [BDB, Hol; Allen, Cohen, Keil, Wolff; KJV, NASB, NRSV], 'to go through' [Hol], 'to traverse' [Crenshaw], 'to travel through' [Stuart], 'to violate' [Dillard], 'to invade' [NIV], 'to set foot' [Bewer; REB], 'to conquer' [TEV].

QUESTION—What rhetorical functions does this verse have?

This verse is an oracle assuring the Israelites that they will recognize YHWH for who he actually is, the covenant Protector-God of Israel [Wolff].

QUESTION—What prophetic echoes are raised by שֹׁכֵן בְּצִיּוֹן הַר־קָדְשִׁי *šōḵēn bəṣiyyôn har-qoḏšî* 'dwelling on Zion my holy mountain'? (Literally this is, perhaps, 'on Zion, the mountain of my sanctuary'.)

This phrase is most reminiscent of Isa. 8:18: 'YHWH of hosts, who dwells (הַשֹּׁכֵן *haššōḵēn*) on Mount Zion'; Joel's phrase 'on the mountain of my sanctuary' reflects the religious language of his later day. It also resembles Zech. 8:3: 'thus says YHWH, I will return to Zion and will live (וְשָׁכַנְתִּי *wəšāḵantî*) in the midst of Jerusalem.' In contrast to this image of YHWH dwelling among his people, Joel speaks of him as a sovereign in his palace [Wolff].

QUESTION—What ancient associations are raised by the expression *šōḵēn bəṣiyyôn har-qoḏšî* 'dwelling on Zion my holy mountain'

Ethnic groups in ancient times often identified some particular mountain as the residence of a particular god. For example, Mount Saphon in Phoenicia was considered the residence of Baal. The true divine residence, however, will be Mount Zion in Jerusalem [Allen].

QUESTION—What is the sense of the verb עבר *ʿḇr* as used in this verse?

1. It means 'to inhabit' or even 'to visit'; YHWH promises that no unacceptable person will ever inhabit Jerusalem again, as in Isa. 35:8 [Allen, Crenshaw, Keil]. This theme is found also in Isa. 52:1 and Zech. 14:21, where the ban is applied to merchants ('Canaanites'); the ban is extended also to any item unacceptable to YHWH (Zech. 14:21)

[Wolff]. A similar promise (adopting the reading of the *Qərê*) is found in Nah. 2:1 (1:15): worthless people will never again be allowed to roam the city [Crenshaw]. Crenshaw sees irony in the use of *ʿḇr* here: the noun and adjective עִבְרִי *ʿiḇrî* 'Hebrew' comes from this verb; Jerusalem will become fully Hebrew as intended by YHWH when all foreigners and unclean objects are permanently excluded from her.

2. It means 'to invade', that is, to pass through in triumphant conquest [Bewer, Dillard, Stuart; NIV, TEV].

DISCOURSE UNIT: 4:18–21 (3:18–21) [Cohen]. The topic is "God's award."

4:18 (3:18)

And[a]-it-will-come-about[b] in- that -day[c]
the-mountains[d] will-drip[e] (with) new-wine,[f] and[g]-the-hills[h] will-flow[i] (with) milk,[j]
and[k]-all (the)ravines(-of)[l] Judah will-flow (with) water,[m]
and[n]-(a)spring[o] from-(the-)house(-of)[p] YHWH will-go-forth[q] and[r]-will-water[s] (the-)valley(-of)[t] Shittim/the-acacias.[u]

INTERTEXTUAL REFERENCE—Colon α is an allusion to Amos 9:13 [Cohen, Crenshaw]. Colon ε gives precision in this verse to Zechariah's mention of living water (Zech. 13:1; 14:8; see also Ezek. 47:1) [Wendland].

LEXICON—a. **and-it-will-come-about in- that -day** -וְ *wə- waw* of the attached weqatal verb form [BDB p. 251], [Hol p. 84], [TWOT 519]: 'and' [Dillard, Keil, Wolff; KJV, NASB]. Allen, Crenshaw, Stuart, NIV, NRSV, REB, and TEV do not translate the expression וְהָיָה *wəhāyâ* 'and it will be' explicitly.

b. **it-will-come-about** 3rd masc. sing. Qal weqatal verb form of היה *hyh* [BDB p. 224], [Hol p. 78], [TWOT 491]: 'to come about' [NASB], 'to come to pass' [Dillard, Keil, Wolff; KJV]. The temporal expression וְהָיָה בַּיּוֹם הַהוּא *wəhāyâ bayyôm hahûʾ* 'and it will be in that day' is often used in eschatological material, especially to link two passages together (e.g., see Isa. 7:18, 24:21, Jer. 4:9, and especially Zechariah 12–14 and Ezekiel 38–39, where this formula accompanies content that is very similar in some respects to Joel's). Variants of this expression are also used in eschatological passages, as in 4:1 (3:1) [Crenshaw]. Wolff regards this formula as introducing 4:18–21, which in his view is a later addition to Joel, the formula itself being foreign to Joel.

c. **in- that -day** יוֹם *yôm* [BDB p. 398], [Hol p. 130], [TWOT 852]: 'day' [all lexica, commentators, and versions except REB, Stuart, and TEV]. REB translates בַּיּוֹם הַהוּא *bayyôm hahûʾ* 'in that day' as "when that day comes"; Stuart has "at that time," as does TEV.

d. **the-<u>mountains</u> will-drip (with) new-wine** pl. of הַר *har* [BDB p. 249], [Hol p. 83], [TWOT 517a]: 'mountain' [all lexica, commentators, and versions].

e. **<u>will-drip</u>** 3rd masc. pl. Qal imperf. of נטף *nṭp̄* [BDB p. 642], [Hol p. 236], [TWOT 1355]: 'to drip' [BDB, Hol; Crenshaw, Dillard, Stuart, Wolff; NASB, NIV, NRSV], 'to drop' [BDB], 'to drop down' [KJV], 'to trickle down' [Keil], 'to flow with' [Allen], 'to run with' [REB]. TEV translates the figurative expression *the-mountains will-drip (with)new-wine* concretely as "the mountains will be covered with vineyards."

f. **(with) <u>new-wine</u>** עָסִיס *ʿāsîs* [BDB p. 779], [Hol p. 279], [TWOT 1660a]: 'new wine' [Keil; KJV, NIV, REB], 'sweet wine' [BDB; Allen, Crenshaw; NASB, NRSV], 'must' [Dillard], 'grape juice' [Hol; Stuart], 'juice' [Wolff]. BDB and Holladay consider that *ʿāsîs* denotes newly pressed, unfermented grape juice. TWOT, however, views some OT contexts of the word as requiring a sense of fermented juice, namely, wine, as in 1:5 and Isa. 49:26. Even the traditional gloss of 'sweet wine' might erroneously give today's reader the impression of wine in which the process of fermentation has been arrested prematurely, leaving some unfermented sugar. This differs from ancient "sweet wine," which seems to have been very strongly alcoholic (cf. γλεῦκος in Acts 2:13). Song of Songs 8:2 refers to *ʿāsîs* as pomegranate juice, which usage may represent the primary, generic sense of *ʿāsîs* or an extended sense.

g. **<u>and</u>-the-hills will-flow (with) milk** -וְ *wə-* *waw* connective [BDB p. 251], [Hol p. 84], [TWOT 519]: 'and' [Allen, Keil, Wolff; KJV, NASB, NIV, REB, TEV]. Crenshaw, Dillard, Stuart, and NRSV express the additive relation with a new clause or sentence.

h. **the-<u>hills</u>** pl. of גִּבְעָה *giḇʿâ* [BDB p. 148], [Hol p. 54], [TWOT 309a]: 'hill' [BDB, Hol; Allen, Crenshaw, Dillard, Keil, Stuart, Wolff; KJV, NASB, NIV, NRSV, REB, TEV]. *Giḇʿâ* denotes an elevation lower than a mountain [BDB]. TEV translates the figurative *and-the-hills will-flow (with)milk* nonfiguratively: "and cattle will be found on every hill."

i. **<u>will-flow</u>** 3rd fem. pl. Qal imperf. of הלך *hlḵ* [BDB p. 229], [Hol p. 79], [TWOT 498]: 'to flow with' [Hol; Dillard, Keil, Wolff; KJV, NASB, NIV, NRSV, REB], 'to course with' [Crenshaw], 'to run with' [Allen, Stuart]. The primary sense of *hlḵ* is 'to go'.

j. **(with) <u>milk</u>** חָלָב *ḥālāḇ* [BDB p. 316], [Hol p. 104], [TWOT 650a]: 'milk' [all lexica, commentators, and versions]. *Ḥālāḇ* has a range of senses: 'milk, sour milk, cheese' [TWOT].

k. **<u>and</u>-all (the)ravines(-of) Judah will-flow (with) water** -וְ *wə-* *waw* connective (see *g* above): 'and' [Allen, Crenshaw, Dillard, Keil, Stuart, Wolff; KJV, NASB, NRSV]. NASB, REB, and TEV express the additive relation with a new clause (no conjunction).

l. **(the)ravines(-of) Judah** constr. pl. of אָפִיק *ʾāp̄îq* [BDB p. 67], [Hol p. 25], [TWOT 149a]: 'ravine' [BDB; Stuart; NASB], 'brook' [Keil; NASB], 'stream channel' [Hol], 'stream bed' [BDB; Dillard; NRSV], 'river bed' [Allen], 'river' [KJV], 'channel' [Crenshaw; REB], 'torrent' [BDB; Wolff]. The word *ʾāp̄îq* denotes the principal watercourse of a valley [Hol]. TEV translates *and-all(the)ravines(-of) Judah will-flow (with) water* as "there will be plenty of water for all of Judah." Bewer understands this as promising an abundance of water for all time, even though the streams would normally be filled with water only in the rainy season.

m. **(with) water** מַיִם *mayim* [BDB p. 565], [Hol p. 193], [TWOT 1188]: 'water' [all lexica, commentators, and versions].

n. **and-(a)spring from-(the-)house(-of) YHWH will-go-forth** -וְ *wə-waw* connective (see *g* above): 'and' [Keil; KJV, NASB]. Crenshaw, Dillard, and TEV express this as an appositive relation with a new clause (no conjunction). Wolff has "for," introducing an amplifying or causal relation. Allen, Stuart, NRSV, and REB express it as an additive relation with a new clause or sentence.

o. **(a)spring** מַעְיָן *maʿyān* [BDB p. 745], [Hol p. 206], [TWOT 1613a]: 'spring' [BDB, Hol; Allen; NASB], 'fountain' [Dillard, Keil, Stuart, Wolff; KJV, NIV, NRSV, REB]. Crenshaw and TEV express the idea of a spring as the source of water; Crenshaw has "a stream rushing from YHWH's house." *Maʿyān* is not to be confused with words signifying a well or cistern [TWOT].

p. **from-(the-)house(-of) YHWH** constr. of בַּיִת *bayiṯ* [BDB p. 108], [Hol p. 38], [TWOT 241]: 'house' [BDB, Hol; Crenshaw, Keil, Stuart, Wolff; KJV, NASB, NIV, NRSV, REB], 'temple' [Allen, Dillard; TEV].

q. **will-go-forth** 3rd masc. sing. Qal imperf. of יצא *yṣʾ* [BDB p. 422], [Hol p. 139], [TWOT 893]: 'to go forth' [Hol], 'to go out' [BDB; NASB], 'to come out' [BDB; Stuart], 'to come forth' [KJV, NRSV], 'to rush' [Crenshaw], 'to issue' [Allen, Keil, Dillard], 'to flow' [Wolff; NASB, TEV], 'to spring' [REB].

r. **and-will-water (the-)valley(-of) Shittim/the-acacias** -וְ *wə- waw* of the attached weqatal verb form (see *g* above): 'and' [Dillard, Keil, Stuart, Wolff; KJV, NIV, NRSV, REB, TEV]. Allen and Crenshaw express a descriptive relation with a new clause (no conjunction). NASB expresses a purpose relation: "[in order] to water the valley…."

s. **and-will-water** 3rd masc. sing. Hiphil weqatal verb form of שקה *šqh* [BDB p. 1052], [Hol p. 382], [TWOT 2452]: 'to water' [Hol; Allen, Crenshaw, Dillard, Keil, Stuart, Wolff; KJV, NASB, NIV, NRSV, REB, TEV], 'to irrigate' [BDB], The primary sense of *šqh* is 'to give to drink' [BDB].

t. **(the-)valley(-of) Shittim/the-acacias** נַחַל *naḥal* [BDB p. 636], [Hol p. 233], [TWOT 1343a]: 'valley' [Crenshaw, Dillard, Keil, Wolff;

KJV, NASB, NIV, TEV], 'gorge' [Allen], 'stream bed' [Hol; Stuart], 'stream' [Hol], 'wadi' [BDB; NRSV, REB], 'torrent' [BDB]. *Naḥal* can denote either a wadi (i.e., a dry stream bed which fills only after rainfall) or a perennial stream or small river [Hol]. Many commentators opt for the former.

u. **Shittim/the-acacias** שִׁטִּים *šiṭṭim* [BDB p. 1008], [Hol p. 367]: 'Shittim' [Cohen, Crenshaw; KJV, NASB, NRSV, REB], 'acacia' [Allen, Dillard, Keil, Stuart, Wolff; NIV, TEV].

QUESTION—What is the referent of בַּיּוֹם הַהוּא *bayyôm hahûʾ* 'in that day'?

1. It is the day that YHWH executes his judgment upon the nations [Cohen].
2. It is the period following YHWH's execution of his judgment upon the nations [Dillard, Keil].

QUESTION—What is the literary background of the phrase יִטְּפוּ הֶהָרִים עָסִיס *yiṭṭəpû hehārîm ʿāsîs* 'the mountains will drip with sweet wine'?

This and the phrase that follows it are reminiscent of Amos 9:13: "and the mountains will drip with sweet wine (*ʿāsîs*), and all the hills will flow (*wəhiṭṭîpû*) with it." Amos's language suggests a lavish outpour of wine down the hills, while Joel is rather more restrained. Images of God blessing the land so that it produces its bounty in lavish quantities are seen throughout the OT (e.g., Exod. 3:8; Job 29:6) [Cohen, Crenshaw]. The fulfillment of this promise will remedy the lack of wine bemoaned in 1:5 [Crenshaw, Dillard]. Joel substitutes חָלָב *ḥālāḇ* 'milk' for Amos's second (and anaphorical) reference to wine, perhaps in order to have a triad of elements (wine, milk, water), or perhaps in allusion to Canaan as described in Exod. 3:8 [Wendland].

QUESTION—What is the sense of וְהַגְּבָעוֹת תֵּלַכְנָה חָלָב *wəhaggəḇāʿôṯ tēlaḵnâ ḥālāḇ* 'and the hills will flow with milk'?

1. It is probably that the pastures will have plenty of grass, which will enable the cows to produce much milk [Allen, Crenshaw].
2. The milk represents all products of animal husbandry, just as the sweet wine represents the products of all crops and plants [Dillard].

QUESTION—What is the sense of וְכָל־אֲפִיקֵי יְהוּדָה יֵלְכוּ מָיִם *wəḵol-ʾăpîqê yəhûḏâ yēləḵû māyim* 'and all the ravines of Judah will flow with water'?

It is that water will be permanently abundant in Judah, a promise implying coming prosperity to the often water-starved farmers. Thus the conditions of drought depicted in Joel 1–2 will be reversed [Bewer, Dillard, Stuart, Wolff]. This reversal will be superabundant and for all time, belonging, in fact, to the apocalyptic vision of a restored Judah and a restored paradise [Bewer, Wolff].

QUESTION—What is the literary background of the second half of v. 18 with its images of a spring gushing forth from the Temple and watering the Valley of the Acacias?

1. The background appears to be Ezek. 47:1–12 and Zech. 13:1 and 14:3–9. However, there is a difference in how Ezekiel and Zechariah treat the spring. Ezekiel connects the spring to resulting fertility in the land and in the Dead Sea, while Zechariah connects it to a great earthquake which marks the eschatological war against YHWH's enemies. Joel combines both treatments, for he speaks of the spring in the passage following the war against the nations, relating it, as Ezekiel does, to a renewal of the land and its fertility. The theme of the spring is found elsewhere in the OT, for example, Pss. 36:9(8), 46:5(4), 87:7, and Isa. 8:6 and 33:21. Ultimately, Joel implies a further theme, that of the restoration of a Paradise which gives birth to a river, as in Gen. 2:10 [Dillard]. Ancient Near Eastern tradition also featured rivers flowing from the residences of deity, as is attested by both Ugaritic and Akkadian texts [Allen].
2. The background is Ezek. 47:1–12, but not Zech. 14:3–9, for Joel knows nothing of a division in the stream coming from the Temple into a western and eastern half. This fact promotes the inference that Joel 4:18–21 (3:18–21) is older than Zechariah 14. Moreover, Joel's expression נַחַל הַשִּׁטִּים *naḥal haššiṭṭim* 'the valley of Shittim (or of the acacias)' is entirely independent of Ezekiel and Zechariah [Bewer, Wolff].

QUESTION—What is the referent of נַחַל הַשִּׁטִּים *naḥal haššiṭṭim* 'the valley of Shittim (or of the acacias)'?

1. This expression refers to the valley of the Jordan just above the river's entrance into the Dead Sea, where the ground is barren. Since the acacia grows in very dry areas, Joel chose the designation *šiṭṭim* to indicate aridness [Cohen, Keil].
2. The referent is not known. The final camp of the Israelites in their desert wandering, named *Šiṭṭim* (Num. 25:1), does not seem a suitable referent, for the wadi or stream referred to by Joel would have to cross the Jordan River [Bewer, Crenshaw]. The referent is probably only symbolic, not meant to be geographically located [Allen, Wolff].
2. The referent might be the Kidron Valley. If the Kidron is indeed the concrete referent of "the Valley of Jehoshaphat" and "the Valley of the Verdict," then "the Valley of the Acacias" might be yet a third designation of the same place. Acacias grow in the Kidron Valley, but there is also another factor favoring this possibility: the theme of a spring issuing from the Temple reminds one of Ezek. 47:1–12, which features a stream flowing from the Temple down through the Kidron Valley and into the Dead Sea. Joel's apparent dependence on Zech. 13:1 and Zech. 14:3–9 leads to the same possibility [Bewer, Dillard].

4:19 (3:19)

Egypt will-become[a] (a-)desolation,[b] and[c]-Edom will-become (a-)wilderness (-of)[d] desolation
because-of[e]-(the-)violence(done-to)[f] (the-)sons(-of)[g] Judah, because[h] they-shed[i] innocent[j] blood[k] in-their-land.[l]

LEXICON—a. **Egypt will-become** 3rd fem. sing. Qal imperf. of היה *hyh* [BDB p. 224], [Hol p. 78], [TWOT 491]: 'to become' [BDB, Hol; Allen, Crenshaw, Dillard, Keil, Stuart, Wolff; NASB, NRSV, REB, TEV], 'to be' [KJV]. NIV translates מִצְרַיִם לִשְׁמָמָה תִהְיֶה *miṣrayim lišmāmâ ṯihyeh* 'Egypt will become a desolation' as "Egypt will be desolate."

b. **(a-)desolation** שְׁמָמָה *šəmāmâ* [BDB p. 1031], [Hol p. 376], [TWOT 2409b]: 'desolation' [Hol; Allen, Keil, Stuart, Wolff; KJV, NRSV, REB], 'devastation' [BDB], 'waste' [BDB; Crenshaw; NASB], 'desolate waste' [Dillard], 'desert' [TEV]. *Šəmāmâ* denotes an area which because of its ruin and solitude invokes horror or terror [Hol]. The proclitic -לְ *lə-* serves as a complementizing particle with the verb היה *hyh* 'to become' [BDB, Hol].

c. **and-Edom will-become** -וְ *wə- waw* connective [BDB p. 251], [Hol p. 84], [TWOT 519]: 'and' [all commentators and versions except Allen, Crenshaw, Stuart, NIV]. Allen, Crenshaw, Stuart, and NIV signal the additive relation with a new clause.

d. **(a-)wilderness(-of) desolation** constr. of מִדְבָּר *miḏbār* [BDB p. 184], [Hol p. 182], [TWOT 399l): 'wilderness' [BDB, Hol], 'desert' [Hol]. The expression מִדְבַּר שְׁמָמָה *miḏbar šəmāmâ* is translated "desolate heath" [Allen], "desolate steppe" [Crenshaw], "desolate wilderness" [Dillard, Stuart; KJV, NASB, NRSV], "barren waste" [Keil], "desert waste" [NIV], "desolate waste" [REB], "ruined waste" [TEV], "wilderness of desolation" [Wolff]. *Miḏbār* denotes an uncultivated area [Hol], an uninhabited area [BDB]. It is a key word for Ezekiel, who uses it especially in the context of divine punishment coming upon Edom and Egypt [Allen, Wolff]. For Joel it is also a key word: it describes in Joel 2 the plight of Judah during her economic crisis and in 4:19 the punishment coming upon Egypt and Edom [Crenshaw].

e. **because-of** מִן *min* [BDB p. 577], [Hol p. 200], [TWOT 1212]: 'because of' [Allen, Crenshaw, Dillard, Stuart; NASB, NIV, NRSV, REB], 'for' [Keil, Wolff; KJV]. The preposition *min* here designates cause [Hol, BDB].

f. **(the-)violence(done-to) (the-)sons(-of) Judah** constr. of חָמָס *ḥāmas* [BDB p. 329], [Hol p. 109], [TWOT 678a]: 'violence' [BDB, Hol; Crenshaw, Dillard, Stuart, Wolff; KJV, NASB, NIV, NRSV, REB], 'wrong' [BDB, Hol], 'sin' [Keil], 'violent treatment' [Allen]. TEV translates this noun as a verb, "to attack."

g. **(the-)sons(-of) Judah** pl. constr. of בֵּן *bēn* [BDB p. 119], [Hol p. 42], [TWOT 254]: 'son' [BDB, Hol; Keil, Wolff; NASB], 'child' [KJV]. The phrase בְּנֵי יְהוּדָה *bənê yəhûḏâ* 'sons of Judah' is translated as "Judeans" [Allen, Stuart], "people of Judah" [NIV, NRSV], "Judah" [REB], "land of Judah" [TEV]. The construct relationship between חָמָס *ḥāmas* 'violence' and *bənê yəhûḏâ* 'sons of Judah' is treated in various ways: the entire phrase *mēḥămas bənê yəhûḏâ* is rendered as "because of their violent treatment of Judeans" [Allen], "because of violence against Judeans" [Crenshaw; KJV is similar], "because of the violence done to the sons of Judah" [Dillard; Wolff, NASB, NIV, NRSV, and REB are similar], "for the sins upon the sons of Judah" [Keil], "because of their violence to the Judeans" [Stuart]. In any case, the expression *bənê yəhûḏâ* 'sons of Judah' is widely understood here as designating the destination of *ḥāmas* 'violence'.

h. **because** אֲשֶׁר *ʾăšer* [BDB p. 81], [Hol p. 30], [TWOT 184]. The relative pronoun *ʾăšer* functions here as a conjunction introducing cause [Hol, BDB]. Dillard translates *ʾăšer* as a conjunction introducing a reason, "because they shed" (KJV is similar); Keil, as a conjunction introducing an explication of the previous phrase, "that they have shed." Allen and Crenshaw translate like Keil.

i. **they-shed innocent blood in-their-land** 3rd masc. pl. Qal perf. of שׁפך *špḵ* [BDB p. 1049], [Hol p. 381], [TWOT 2444]: 'to shed' [BDB; Keil, Stuart, Wolff; KJV, NASB, NIV, NRSV, REB], 'to pour out' [Hol], 'to spill' [Hol; Allen, Crenshaw]. The English past tense is employed by Keil: 'they have shed'. The English present tense is employed by Dillard: 'they shed'. TEV treats the phrase אֲשֶׁר־שָׁפְכוּ דָם־נָקִיא *ʾăšer-šāp̄əḵû ḏām-nāqîʾ* 'because they shed innocent blood' as figurative and translates it nonfiguratively as "because ... they killed innocent people...."

j. **innocent blood** נָקִיא *nāqîʾ* [BDB p. 667], [Hol p. 245], [TWOT 1412b]: 'innocent' [BDB, Hol; Allen, Crenshaw, Dillard, Keil, Stuart, Wolff; KJV, NASB, NIV, NRSV, REB, TEV], 'free from guilt' [BDB]. The primary sense of *nāqîʾ* is 'empty, free of anything'. In this case, it means 'free from guilt' [BDB].

k. **innocent blood** דָם *dām* [BDB p. 196], [Hol p. 71], [TWOT 436]: 'blood' [BDB, Hol; Allen, Crenshaw, Dillard, Keil, Stuart, Wolff; KJV, NASB, NIV, NRSV, REB].

l. **in-their-land** constr. of אֶרֶץ *ʾereṣ* [BDB p. 76], [Hol p. 28], [TWOT 167]: 'land' [BDB, Hol; Crenshaw, Dillard, Keil, Stuart, Wolff; KJV, NASB, NIV, NRSV, REB], 'territory' [BDB, Hol], 'country' [BDB; Allen], not explicit [TEV].

QUESTION—What is the referent of אַרְצָם *ʾarṣām* 'their land'?

1. It is the land of the Egyptians and the Edomites. Joel alludes to mistreatment of Judean slaves in these lands going back in time as far as the experience of Jacob's descendants in Egypt, and more recently in Edom

when this country rebelled against Judah's domination (see Amos 1:11) [Keil].

2. It is the land of the Judeans [Bewer, Stuart, Wolff; Allen, Crenshaw and Dillard also lean toward this view]. NASB, NIV, NRSV, REB, and TEV translate so as to make clear that they support this view.

QUESTION—If אַרְצָם *ʾarṣām* 'their land' is understood as referring to the land of the Israelites, to what wrongs would Joel be alluding to in this verse?

1. If one assigns an early date to Joel, then the prophet would probably be understood as referring to Egypt's attack against King Rehoboam of Judah (1 Kings 14:25–26) [Cohen].
2. If one assigns a late date to Joel, then the prophet could be understood as referring to Egypt's invasion of Judah in 609 B.C. (2 Kings 23:29–36) and the killing of King Josiah (the "innocent blood"). Joel might be alluding to the Edomites' violence against Judah spoken of in Obadiah 9–14 (Edom and Judah typified the two brothers Esau and Jacob). Edomites had raided Judah and had profited from the Babylonian attack against Jerusalem ca. 587 B.C. [Cohen, Crenshaw, Dillard, Wolff]. Bewer regards this passage as referring to the destruction of Jerusalem in 586 B.C.
3. The twelfth-century Jewish commentator Kimchi regarded "Egypt" as referring to the Arabs, whose forebearer was Ishmael, and "Edom" as referring to Rome [cited by Cohen].

4:20 (3:20)

But[a]-Judah[b] will-be-inhabited[c] forever,[d] and[e]-Jerusalem to-generations[f] and-generations.

SYNTAX—The single verb *will-be-inhabited* applies to both parts of this verse, the parts being in synonymous parallelism with each other [Crenshaw].

LEXICON—a. **<u>but</u>-Judah will-be-inhabited forever** -וְ *wə- waw* connective [BDB p. 251], [Hol p. 84], [TWOT 519]: 'but' [Allen, Dillard, Keil, Wolff; KJV, NASB, NRSV, REB, TEV]; not explicit [Crenshaw, Stuart; NIV]. The *waw* connective is here viewed as indicating contrast between the lot of Egypt and Edom and that of Judah [Cohen].

b. **<u>Judah</u>** יְהוּדָה *yəhûḏâ* [BDB p. 397], [Hol p. 130], [TWOT 850c]: 'Judah' [all commentators and versions]. The prominence lent to *yəhûḏâ* by the abnormal word order is recognized and translated by Keil as "but Judah, it will dwell for ever."

c. **<u>will-be-inhabited</u>** 3rd fem. sing. Qal imperf. of ישׁב *yšḇ* [BDB p. 442], [Hol p. 146], [TWOT 922]: 'to be inhabited' [Hol; Crenshaw, Dillard, Wolff; NASB, NIV, NRSV, REB, TEV], 'to abide' [BDB], 'to endure' [BDB], 'to dwell' [Keil; KJV], 'to be settled' [Stuart]. Allen translates this verb with a phrase: "to lack inhabitants." In this context, *yšḇ* 'to be inhabited', while of course indicating the opposite of the depopulated wilderness which Egypt and Edom are to become, implies also a population living in joyous freedom, which the presence of YHWH would suggest [Wolff].

d. <u>**forever**</u> עוֹלָם *ᶜôlām* [BDB p. 761], [Hol p. 267], [TWOT 1631a]. The expression לְעוֹלָם *ləᶜôlām* is translated "forever" [Hol; Dillard, Keil, Stuart, Wolff; KJV, NASB, NIV, NRSV, REB], "for all time" [Hol], "from now on" [Crenshaw]. The primary sense of *ᶜôlām* is 'long time, constancy' [Hol]. TEV conflates the two time expressions in this verse, *ləᶜôlām* 'forever' and לְדוֹר וָדוֹר *ləḏôr wāḏôr* 'to generations and generations', and translates them as "forever."

e. **<u>and</u>-Jerusalem to-generations and-generations** וְ- *wə- waw* connective [BDB p. 251], [Hol p. 84], [TWOT 519]: 'and' [Dillard, Keil, Stuart, Wolff; KJV, NASB, NIV, NRSV], 'nor' [Allen]. Crenshaw and REB express the additive relation with a new clause or sentence (no conjunction). TEV conflates the two clauses of this verse into one.

f. **to-<u>generations</u> and-<u>generations</u>** דּוֹר *dôr* [BDB p. 189], [Hol p. 69], [TWOT 418b]. The primary sense of *dôr* is 'generation' [Hol]. The meaning of the expression לְדוֹר וָדוֹר *ləḏôr wāḏôr* is '(from) generation to generation' [Hol; Keil, Stuart, Wolff; KJV], 'for generations to come' [Allen], 'for untold generations' [Crenshaw], 'to/for/through all generations' [Dillard; NASB, NIV, NRSV], 'for generation after generation' [REB].

QUESTION—What is the theme of this verse?

It is that the future of Judah will be made secure for all time, YHWH having revealed himself as the ruler of all and as present in Jerusalem [Allen, Crenshaw, Dillard, Keil].

4:21 (3:21)

(MT1) And[a]-I-will-declare-innocent[b-1] their-blood,[c] (which) I-had-not -declared-innocent (before);

(MT2) And[a]-I-will-expiate[b-1] their-blood,[c] (which) I-had-not -expiated (before);

(MT3) And[a]-I-will-avenge[b-2] their-blood[c]; (which) I-had-not -avenged (till now);

(ET1) And[a]-I-declare-innocent[b-1] their-blood[c]; indeed, I-declare (it)

(ET2) And[a]-I-will-pour-out[b-1] their-blood[c]; indeed, I-will-pour-out (it)

(ET3) And[a]-shall-I-declare-innocent[b-1] their-blood[c]? I-shall-not-declare-innocent (their-blood);

and[d]-YHWH dwells/will-dwell[e] on[f]-Zion.[g]

TEXT AND SYNTAX—Many solutions to the difficulties of this verse have been proposed. Charted here are two which propose to preserve the MT and three which propose to emend it.

<table>
<tr><th colspan="2">Preserving the Masoretic Text</th></tr>
<tr><th colspan="2">Views of the syntax of bicolon α–β while preserving the MT</th></tr>
<tr><td colspan="2">1. Understand MT as two declarative clauses: an independent clause followed by a dependent clause [Bewer, Cohen, Driver, Keil, Wolff; KJV, Vulgate]. See MT$_1$, MT$_2$, and MT$_3$.</td></tr>
<tr><th>Views of lexical items</th><th></th></tr>
<tr><td>Understand דָּמָם dāmām 'their-blood' as referring to the death of Jewish slaves in the lands of Egypt and Edom [Cohen—see MT$_1$], or the death of Jews in general at the Gentiles' hands [Keil—see MT$_2$].

—OR—</td><td>Sense: "I will declare the Jews to have died innocently at the hands of the Gentiles."
Implication: People had regarded these Jews as guilty before YHWH, since he had not avenged their deaths. But their innocence will be demonstrated when YHWH avenges their deaths. He will do so, for he promised Abraham that his descendants will not be mistreated with impunity (Gen. 12:3) [Cohen, following the thirteenth-century Jewish commentator Isaiah de Trani].
Lexical support: This view accepts the traditional interpretation of the verb נקה nqh as 'to declare to be innocent'. The LXX's καὶ οὐ μὴ ἀθῳώσω 'and I will not leave unpunished' suggests this view of nqh [Wolff].</td></tr>
<tr><td>Understand dāmām 'their-blood' as referring to the violence committed by the Jews [Wolff]. See MT$_1$.</td><td>Sense: "I will declare the Jews innocent of having shed blood."
Implication: YHWH had held these Jews guilty, threatening them with judgment in Joel 1–2. But the coming of the "day of YHWH" reverses this judgment in 4:21 (3:21): instead of the Jews, it is Egypt and Edom which will suffer permanent judgment for their violence against Judah [Wolff].
Argument against: Nowhere does Joel unambiguously refer to the Judeans' bloodguilt [Allen].</td></tr>
<tr><td>Understand נקה nqh not as the traditional 'to declare to be innocent', but as 'to cleanse' or 'to expiate' [Keil; KJV, Vulgate]. See MT$_2$.</td><td>Sense: "I will make the Gentiles suffer for, and thereby pay the debt of, their guilt for having shed Jewish blood."
Implication: Joel is summing up the effect of YHWH's judgment upon the Gentiles: their punishment will expiate the guilt they have incurred in harming YHWH's covenant people (dāmām 'their-blood' signifies the Gentiles' guilt in shedding Jewish blood) [Keil].
Argument against: Allen argues that nqh cannot be taken to denote 'to cleanse' or 'to expiate'.</td></tr>
</table>

2. Understand the first two words of MT as a question and the third and fourth words as its response [Allen, Dillard, Stuart, following a proposal of H. Steiner]. See ET2.	**Sense**: "Shall I declare these Gentiles innocent of murdering Jews? I shall not declare them innocent." **Resemblance to Jer. 25:29:** 'And you, will you indeed go unpunished (הִנָּקֵה תִנָּקוּ *hinnāqēh tinnāqû*)? You will not go unpunished (לֹא תִנָּקוּ *lôᵓ tinnāqû*).' The same syntax and the same verb (*nqh*) are used here. **Argument for:** A yes-no question in BH does not usually feature the interrogative particle -הֲ *hă-* if the clause begins with a conjunction, as in this case (see Gesenius §150a) [Allen, Dillard, Stuart].

<table>
<tr><th colspan="2">Emending the MT</th></tr>
<tr><th colspan="2">Views of emending the MT</th></tr>
<tr><td colspan="2">1. Emend the negation לֹא lôᵓ 'not' to the emphatic לְ lameḏ. See ET1.</td></tr>
<tr><th>Views of lexical items</th><th></th></tr>
<tr><td>Understand dāmām 'their-blood' as referring to the violence committed by the Jews.
At the same time, understand נקה nqh as the traditional 'to declare to be innocent'.
—OR—</td><td>Sense: "I will pronounce the Jews guiltless for having killed Gentiles; indeed, I pronounce it."
Implication: YHWH will forgive the Judeans for shedding Gentiles' blood, bloodshed which he formerly had not forgiven. Dāmām 'their-blood' here signifies the Jews' action of killing Gentiles.
Argument against: Nowhere does Joel unambiguously refer to bloodguilt of the Judeans [Allen].</td></tr>
<tr><td>Understand דָּמָם dāmām 'their-blood' as referring to the death of Jewish slaves in the lands of Egypt and Edom or the death of Jews in general at the Gentiles' hands
At the same time, understand נקה nqh as 'to pour out' [Ahlström, Driver].</td><td>Sense: "I will pour out the blood of the Gentiles; indeed, I will pout it out." [Ahlström, Joel and the Temple Cult of Jerusalem, Supplement to Vetus Tetamentum 21 (Leiden: Brill, 1971), cited by Dillard].</td></tr>
<tr><td colspan="2">2. Emend the verb נקה nqh in both occurrences to נקם nqm 'to avenge'. See MT3.</td></tr>
<tr><td></td><td>Sense: "And I shall avenge the Jews' death, which I have not till now avenged."
Supported by: LXX reads καὶ ἐκδικήσω τὸ αἷμα αὐτῶν καὶ οὐ μὴ ἀθῳώσω, understanding ἐκδικήσω as 'I will avenge' [Bewer].
Argument against: LXX's witness cannot be relied upon in Joel 4:21 (3:21), for in Zech. 5:3 LXX mistranslates נקה nqh with ἐκδικέω 'to avenge', although nqh has the force of 'to be banished' there [Allen].</td></tr>
<tr><td colspan="2">3. Change the order of verses to the following:
4:19 (3:19); 4:21a (3:21a); 4:20 (3:20); 4:21b (3:21b) [Bewer, Crenshaw; NEB].</td></tr>
</table>

Resulting arrangement:

Egypt will become a waste, Edom a ruin; because of violence done to Judeans, the spilling of innocent blood in their land (4:19)
I shall avenge their blood, yet unavenged (4:21a)
Judah will be inhabited from now on,
Jerusalem for untold generations (4:20)
And YHWH will dwell in Zion (4:21b)

Advantages:

(1) In this rearrangement, the sense of the much-disputed *dāmām* becomes clear: it refers to the deaths of Judeans at the hands of surrounding hostile nations.
(2) The thematic expressions of dwelling and habitation become consolidated.
(3) The transition from YHWH's speaking to the prophet's speaking becomes smoother [Bewer, Crenshaw; NEB].

LEXICON—a. **and-** -וְ *wə- waw* connective [BDB p. 251], [Hol p. 84], [TWOT 519]: 'and [Allen, Keil, Wolff; NASB], 'for' [KJV]. Crenshaw, Dillard, Stuart, NIV, NRSV, REB, and TEV express the additive relation with a new clause or sentence.

b-1. **I-will-declare-innocent their-blood** 1st sing. Piel perf. of נקה *nqh* [BDB p. 667], [Hol p. 245], [TWOT 1412]: 'to declare innocent' [Hol], 'to hold as innocent' [Cohen], 'to leave unpunished' [BDB; Allen, Stuart], 'to let go unpunished' [Dillard], 'to expiate' [Keil], 'to declare exempt from punishment' [Wolff], 'to cleanse' [KJV], 'to pardon' [NIV].

b-2. **I-will-avenge their-blood** 1st sing. Piel perf. of נקם *nqm* [BDB p. 667], [Hol p. 245], [TWOT 1413]: 'to avenge' [Hol; Crenshaw; NASB, NRSV, REB, TEV]. The NRSV adopts different senses for its two readings of *nqm* in this verse, as is evident in its translation: "I will avenge their blood, and I will not clear the guilty." TEV does the same: "I will avenge those who were killed; I will not spare the guilty." By contrast, NASB keeps the same sense: "And I will avenge their blood which I have not avenged."

c. **their-blood** דָּם *dām* [BDB p. 196], [Hol p. 71], [TWOT 436]: 'blood' [BDB, Hol; Crenshaw, Keil, Wolff; KJV, NASB, NRSV, REB], 'blood shed by violence' [Hol], 'bloodshed' [Allen, Stuart], 'bloodguilt' [Dillard; NIV]. TEV translates this noun with a clause: "those who were killed."

d. **and-YHWH dwells/will-dwell on-Zion** -וְ *wə- waw* connective (see *a* above): 'and' [Crenshaw, Keil; TEV], 'for' [Dillard; KJV, NASB, NRSV, REB], 'since' [Keil], not explicit [Stuart; NIV]. Allen has "as surely as Yahweh has his home in Zion." Cohen is similar.

e. **YHWH dwells/will-dwell** masc. sing. Qal part. of שׁכן *šḵn* [BDB p. 1015], [Hol p. 369], [TWOT 2387]: 'to dwell' [BDB; Crenshaw, Dillard, Keil, Stuart, Wolff; KJV, NASB, NIV, NRSV, REB], 'to inhabit' [Hol], 'to have one's home' [Allen], 'to live' [TEV]. Most commentators and versions employ the English present tense here. The

REB and TEV use the future tense: REB has "and the Lord will dwell in Zion." Wendland regards the force to be "YHWH still dwells in Zion."

f. **on-Zion** -בְּ *bə-* [BDB p. 88], [Hol p. 32], [TWOT 193]: 'on' [Wolff; TEV], 'upon' [Keil], 'in' [Allen, Crenshaw, Dillard, Stuart; KJV, NIV, NASB, NRSV, REB].

g. **on-Zion** צִיּוֹן *ṣiyyôn* [BDB p. 851], [Hol p. 306], [TWOT 1910]: 'Zion' [all commentators and versions except TEV], 'Mount Zion' [TEV].

QUESTION—What is the significance of Joel's ending with the declaration of colon β that YHWH dwells on Mount Zion?

YHWH's residence on Mount Zion in the midst of his people is a prominent OT theme. This theme became central to Israel's hope for eternal peace and prosperity. See, for example, Ps. 9:11–12 and Ezek. 48:35 'and the name of the city from that time on will be YHWH is there (יְהוָה שָׁמָּה *yhwh šāmmâ*)', with which Ezekiel ends on the same note as Joel [Cohen, Crenshaw]. It is thus fitting that Joel should close with the same ringing affirmation [Cohen, Stuart]. Colon β, in fact, expresses the main theme of the book [Wendland].

QUESTION—What application to the Christian church does Joel 4 (3) have?

1. Christians await the day of YHWH as much as Joel did (Acts 17:31; 1 Thess. 5:2). On that day YHWH will show to all the world that the Christians have been right to trust him, and he will end all opposition among the nations to his universal and eternal rule (Rev. 20:7–15), which rule he will effect from the holy city (cf. 'the New Jerusalem' of Rev. 21:1–3), the source of life to all the world (Rev. 22:1–2 and Ezekiel 47) [Dillard, Stuart, Wolff]. Even those Christians who have suffered much abuse or death at the hands of the world will finally be avenged (cf. Rev. 6:10) [Allen].
2. The events portrayed in this chapter will have no earthly fulfillment; instead, Mount Zion and Jerusalem are symbols of God's eternal presence with his glorified church. Similarly, Egypt and Edom symbolize the hostile nations of the world, which God will entirely overcome. One is obliged to read this chapter as symbolic because (a) it would be impossible for the nations to gather in the Valley of Jehoshaphat, which is a small part of the Kidron Valley, and (b) the imagery of 4:18 (3:18) as well as the corresponding passages of Zech. 14:6–8 and Ezek. 47:1–12 is too fantastical to be understood literally [Keil].

APPENDIX 1: Recursive Structures in Joel[23]

It is important to note recursive structures in Joel for at least two reasons: (1) The recursive features often allow the translator to see patterns in thematic cohesion, textual constituent bounding, and textual prominence in Joel. (2) Once the effects of the recursion have been noted, the translator should strive for the same effects by employing strategies belonging to the target language.

These strategies might well include similar kinds of recursion. For example, semantic recursion, which features the repetition of an idea but typically without the same vocabulary, might be considered a "loose" recursion, as in Joel 1:5:

> RECURSION$_{\text{semantic}}$—The conclusions of Strophes 1–4 all feature language denoting drought and disaster for the farmers, an example of epiphora.

Translators should not find this sort of recursion difficult to replicate.

Lexical recursion, which features the repetition of the same lexical items (with or without repetition of the same propositions) can be considered a "tighter" kind of recursion. Consider the example noted under Joel 1:16:

> RECURSION$_{\text{lexical}}$—The verb כרת *kr<u>t</u>* 'to cut off' occurs in 1:5, 1:9, and again here in colon β to stress the land's complete ruin [Wendland, Wolff]. It would be desirable to translate the three occurrences of *kr<u>t</u>* with the same verb, if possible, in order to maintain the correspondence and the resulting lexical cohesion.

The phonologico-morphological repetition of lexical affixes would appear to be very language-specific, as can be seen in Joel 1:13–14:

> RECURSION$_{\text{morphological}}$—A sequence of nine plural imperatives ending in *û* gives cohesion and a sense of urgency to 1:13–14 [Wendland]. If this morphological feature can be replicated in the target language, it might be desirable, depending upon the effect of such recursion in the target language.

It could be very difficult to replicate this sort of recursion in another language; and even if it could be done, the effect upon the readers might be very unexpected and undesirable.

---

[23] The material in Appendix 1 is drawn from Wendland.

1:2

Listen-to this, (you) the-elders, and-hear (this), all (you) dwellers(-in) the-land.

Did- this –happen in-your(p)-days or in-(the-)days(-of) your(p)-forefathers?

(1) RECURSION$_{lexical}$—The beginnings of each strophe of this stanza feature recursive material which forms an anaphora, a type of recursion in which similar or identical textual material or patterns characterize the beginnings of different discourse units. Each strophe of Stanza A begins with commands addressed to a different class of persons among the Jews; each strophe also contains the reason for the command, often introduced by the conjunction כִּי *kî*. The effect is one of increasing intensity and emotion. It is very important that the command–reason relation in each strophe of this stanza be made explicit in translation.

(2) RECURSION$_{lexical}$—Bicolon α–β of this verse and bicolon γ–δ of 1:14 form an inclusio, a type of recursion which marks the boundaries of a discourse unit, in this case Stanza A. The key words of this inclusio are זְקֵנִים *zəqēnîm* 'priests' and כֹּל יוֹשְׁבֵי הָאָרֶץ *kol yôšəḇê hāʾareṣ* 'all the habitants of the land'. It often happens that an inclusio begins just after the start of a discourse unit or ends just before the unit's conclusion, in which case the excluded textual material is usually considered to be very prominent. Such is the case with bicolon ε–ζ of 1:14.

(3) RECURSION$_{lexical}$—The material in 1:2–3 and 2:1–2 forms an anaphora characterizing the beginnings of Stanza A and Stanza C, as follows:

Anaphora between Stanza A and Stanza C

a Hear (this), all (you) dwellers(-in) the-land **1:2–3**

b Did- this -happen in-your(p)-days or in-(the-)days(-of) your(p) fathers?

c Relate it to-your(p)-children, and-your(p)-children (should relate it) to-their-children, and- their-children to- (the-)generation following

a´ Let- all (the-)inhabitants(-of) the-land tremble **2:1–2**

b´ for (the-)day(-of) YHWH is-coming

c´ such-as has- not (before) -happened from the-far-past and-after-it not continuing to (the-)years(-of) generations(s) and-generation(s)

The point of this anaphora is to contrast the times ("days") of Joel's audience: even though they have suffered terrible ravages from the locusts he is about to describe, the experience of these locust attacks will be insignificant compared to the coming day of YHWH, the subject of 2:1–2. The recursive material in this anaphora consists, not of repeated verses or clauses, but of repeated ideas and expressions.

(4) RECURSION$_{\text{lexical}}$—The theme of יוֹם־יְהוָה *yôm-yhwh* 'the day of YHWH' is foreshadowed in this verse: however memorable and unique the plague of locusts Joel is about to describe, the coming day of YHWH will be more so. Adding this foreshadowing to Joel's references to the day of YHWH gives the following scheme of recursion:

Recursion in Joel alluding to or referring to the Day of YHWH

Did- this –happen in-your(p)-days or in-(the)-days(-of) your(p)-fathers? [*reference to a plague of locusts foreshadowing the day of YHWH*]	**1:2**
Alas for-the-day, for near (is) (the-)day(-of) YHWH, and-as-(the)violence (that it is) from Shaddai it-will-come.	**1:15**
For (the-)day(-of) YHWH is-coming, for (it is) near.	**2:1**
Surely/For great (is) (the-)day(-of) YHWH and fearful (its-)power, and-who (can-)endure-it?	**2:11**
The-sun shall-be-turned into-darkness and-the-moon (shall-be-turned) to-blood, before the- day(-of) YHWH comes	**3:4**

In all of these references, "the day of YHWH" is treated consistently as a day of suffering and judgment brought upon the nations. Moreover, the recursion of the theme of the day of YHWH across a range of varied material, treated as it is similarly in each instance, exhibits a great deal of prominence in the book.

1:5

Wake-up, (you) drunkards, and-weep, and-howl, all (you) drinkers (-of) wine,
because-of (the-)new-wine for it-has-been-cut-off from-your(p)-mouth.

(1) RECURSION$_{\text{lexical}}$—See Recursion 1 under 1:2 in Appendix 1 for a comment on the anaphora between 1:2 and 1:5.

(2) RECURSION$_{lexical}$—The verb כרת *kr<u>t</u>* 'to cut off' occurs in colon γ and again in 1:9 and 1:16 to stress the land's complete ruin [Wolff]. If the same verb in translation could appear in all three of these verses, so much the better.

(3) RECURSION$_{semantic}$—The conclusions of Strophes 1–4 all feature language denoting drought and disaster for the farmers. This is an example of epiphora (i.e., recurring material characterizing the ends of two discourse units).

1:6

For (a-)nation has-come against my-land, powerful and-not numbered,
its-teeth (the-)teeth(-of) (a-)lion and-(the-)fangs(-of) (a-)lioness (are) to-it.

RECURSION$_{lexical}$—The double description of lions' teeth comprises a recursion signifying the intense ferocity and strength of a lion.

1:8

Lament like-(a-)virgin clad-in sackcloth for (a-)husband(-of) her-youth.

RECURSION$_{lexical}$—See Recursion 1 under 1:2 for a comment on the anaphora between 1:2, 1:5, and 1:8.

1:9

(Grain-)offerings and-drink-offerings have-been-cut-off from-(the-) house(-of) YHWH,
and- the-priests have-mourned, (the-)ministers(-of) YHWH.

RECURSION$_{lexical}$—The verb כרת *kr<u>t</u>* 'to cut off', first met in 1:5, recurs here in colon α and again in 1:16 to stress the land's complete ruin [Wolff].

RECURSION$_{lexical}$—Colon β of this verse recurs as colon ε of 1:13 (Strophe 5), with a slightly different wording, and again in 1:14 (Strophe 5), but in the sense of 'to, or toward, the house of God'. This last occurrence closes the sequence of recursion.

Recursion of 1:9 β in later verses

a	from-(the-)house(-of) YHWH	**1:9**
a′	from (the-)house(-of) your(p)-God	**1:13**
a″	(to) (the-)house(-of) YHWH your(p)-God	**1:14**

1:11

Be-ashamed/wilt (you-)serfs; howl, (you-)wine-growers, over-(the-)wheat and-over-(the-)barley, for (the-)grain-harvest(-of) (the-)fields is-ruined.

(1) RECURSION$_{\text{lexical}}$—See Recursion 1 under 1:2 for a comment on the anaphora between 1:2, 1:5, 1:8, and 1:11.

(2) RECURSION$_{\text{semantic}}$—This strophe features parallelism in alternating associations of concepts:

Parallelism characterizing Stanza A, Strophe 4

a	Be-ashamed / wilt, (you-)serfs;	**1:11**
b	howl, (you-)wine-growers,	
a´	over-(the-)wheat and-over-(the-)barley, for (the-)grain-harvest(-of) (the-)field(s) is-ruined.	
b´	The-vine(s) have-withered and-the-fig-tree(s) are-ready-to-fall, (the-)pomegranate(s), even (the-)date-palm(s) and-(the-)apple-tree(s), all (the-)trees(-of) the-field have-dried-up	**1:12**

(3) RECURSION$_{\text{semantic}}$—A series of recursions characterizes the ends or near ends of Stanzas A, D, and A´, thus setting up an epiphora in which occurs semantic reversal. That is, the theme progresses from shame to no shame:1:13

Ephiphora among ends of Stanzas A, D, and A´

a	Be-ashamed / wilt, (you-)serfs; howl, (you-)wine-growers	**1:11**
b	and-do- not –hand-over your(s)-possession to-mockery	**2:17**
c	and- my-people will- not -be-ashamed (again) for-all-time	**2:27**

1:13

Put-on-sackcloth and-lament, (you(p)) the-priests, wail, (you(p)) servants(-of)(the-)altar.

Go-in(p) (and) spend-the-night in-sackcloth, servants(-of) my-God,

for withheld- from (the-)house(-of) your(p)-God (-have-been) offerings and-drink-offerings.

(1) RECURSION$_{morphological}$—A sequence of nine plural imperatives ending in *û* gives cohesion and a sense of urgency to 1:13–14 [Wendland]. If this morphological feature can be replicated in the target language, it might be desirable, depending upon the effect of such recursion in the target language.

(2) RECURSION$_{lexical}$—The bicolon α–β of this verse (in the last strophe of Stanza A) forms an epiphora with cola α–γ of 2:17 (the last verse of Stanza D). In addition, most of the textual material of Strophe 5 of Stanza A "decompacts" and recurs—both in thematic and grammatical ways—in all of Stanza D, and, what is more, in a highly structured fashion, as shown here:

Epiphora between ends of Stanza A and Stanza D, with other material of Stanza A, Strophe 5, recurring in Stanza D

Strophe 5 of Stanza A

a	Lament, (you(p)) the-priests, wail, (you(p)) servants(-of) (the-)altar	**1:13a**
b	For withheld- from (the-)house(-of) your(p)-God (have-been) offering(s) and-drink-offering(s)	**1:13b**
c	Announce-(a)-holy fast, call (a-)solemn-assembly, gather (the-)elders, all inhabitants(-of) the-land,	**1:14a**
d	(to) (the-)house(-of) YHWH your(p)-God, and-call-for-help to YHWH.	**1:14b**

Stanza D

d´	return/turn to-me with-all your(p)-heart and-with-fasting and-with-weeping and-with-rites-of-mourning. And-tear your(p)-heart(s) and-not (only) your(p)-garment(s), and-turn/return to-YHWH your(p)-God	**2:12–13a**
b´	Who (is) (the-)one-knowing (whether) he-will-turn and-relent and-leave behind-him blessing, sacrifice and-drink-offering for-YHWH our-God?	**2:14**
c´	announce-(a)-holy fast, call (a-)solemn-assembly. Gather (the-) people, announce-(a)-sacred assembly, gather (the-) elders, gather (the-)children and-those-who-suck (the-)breasts,	**2:15–16**
a´	let- the-priests -weep, (the-)ministers(-of) YHWH	**2:17**

A chiasmus results among the four outer elements of the structure:

a	d´
d	a´

Within this outer structure is an inner parallelism among the other elements:

b	b´
c	c´

Syntactically, this complex structure is held together by a recurring imperative–reason sequence in most of the elements. Joel's purpose is to stress the call to turn to YHWH and to stress the necessity of turning to him completely and genuinely.

(3) RECURSION$_{\text{lexical}}$—See Recursion 1 under 1:2 for a comment on the anaphora between 1:2, 1:5, 1:8, and 1:11.

1:14

Announce-a-holy fast, call (a-)solemn-assembly,
gather (the-)elders, all inhabitants(-of) the-land,
(to) (the-)house(-of) YHWH your(p)-God, and-call-for-help to YHWH.

(1) RECURSION$_{\text{lexical}}$—The inclusio between bicolon α–β of 1:2 and bicolon γ–δ of this verse excludes bicolon ε–ζ, which in turn signals an emotive climax.

(2) RECURSION$_{\text{lexical}}$—An epiphora exists between this verse and 1:16:

	Epiphora between Stanza A and Stanza B, Strophe 1	
a	(to) (the-)house(-of) YHWH your(p)-God	**1:14** **end of Stanza A, Strophe 5**
b	from (the-)house(-of) our-God	**1:16**

(3) RECURSION$_{\text{lexical}}$—Material in bicola γ–δ and ε–ζ of this verse forms with material in 1:19–20 an epiphora, in which recurring material characterizes the ends of two or more discourse units—in this case the ends of Stanzas A and B.

In this epiphora, *a´* represents an intensification of *a*. In 1:14, all the inhabitants of the land are to gather to cry out to God for help, while in 1:20, even the wild animals are looking to God as well. Elements *b* and *b´* present a contrast between the Temple, which ought to be the safest of places, with the uninhabited reaches of Judea, which have been subject to destruction.

Epiphora between Stanzas A and B

a gather (the-)elders, all inhabitants(-of) the-land **1:14**

b (to) (the-)house(-of) YHWH your(p)-God, and-call-for-help to YHWH

b´ To-you, YHWH, I-call, for fire has-burned (the-)pastures (-of)(the)wilderness **1:19–20**

a´ Indeed, (the-)beasts(-of) (the-)field(s) pant for-you, ... and-fire has-burned (the-)pastures(-of) the-wilderness

1:15
Alas for-the-day,
for near (is) (the-)day(-of) YHWH, and-as-(the)violence (that it is) from Shaddai it-will-come.

RECURSION$_{\text{lexical}}$—Cola α and β of this verse and cola γ and δ of 2:1 form an anaphora; this recursive material characterizes the beginnings of Stanzas B and C. The recursive elements are as follows:

Anaphora between Stanzas B and C

a Alas for-the-day **1:15 beginning of Stanza B**

b for near (is) (the-)day(-of) YHWH

a´ Let- all (the-)inhabitants(-of) the-land -tremble **2:1 beginning of Stanza C**

b´ for (the-)day(-of) YHWH is-coming, for (it is) near

1:16
Have-not before our-eyes food been-removed,
(and-)from (the-)house(-of) our-God joy and-rejoicing?

RECURSION$_{\text{lexical}}$—The verb כרת *krṯ* ‘to cut off’ occurs in 1:5, 1:9, and again here in colon β to stress the land’s complete ruin [Wendland, Wolff]. It would be desirable to translate the three occurrences of *krṯ* with the same verb, if possible, in order to maintain the correspondence and the resulting lexical cohesion.

1:17
(The-) seeds have-withered under their-clods/shovels,
(the-)storehouses have-been-deserted, (the-)granaries have-been-laid-in-ruins, for (the-)grain has-dried-up.

RECURSION$_{\text{lexical}}$—This verse features introverted recursion.

Introversion characterizing 1:17

a (the-)seeds have-withered

b (the-)storehouses have-been-deserted

b´ (the-)granaries have-been-laid-in-ruins

a´ for (the-)grain has-dried-up

RECURSION$_{\text{lexical}}$—A small inclusio is formed by the occurrence of the verb שׁמם *šmm* 'to be deserted, desolate' in this verse and again in 1:18, marking the two verses of Strophe 2 of Stanza B. This analysis depends upon reading the verb *šmm* in 1:18.

1:18
How (the-)cattle groan; (the-)herds(-of) cattle wander-in-agitation/weep,
for there-is-no pasturage for-them; indeed,(the-)flocks(-of) the-sheep-and-goats have-suffered-punishment / have-been-deserted.

RECURSION$_{\text{lexical}}$—The theme of animals' suffering in this verse occurs also in 1:20, creating an epiphora from Strophe 2 to Strophe 3.

1:19
To-you, YHWH, I-call,
for fire has-burned (the-)pastures(-of) (the-)wilderness,
and-flames have-scorched all (the-)trees(-of) (the-)fields.

(1) RECURSION$_{\text{lexical}}$—Strophe 3 is demarcated by an inclusio. Excluded from this inclusio is colon α of 1:19, which is the most prominent line in this strophe.

Inclusio demarcating Stanza B, Strophe 3

	to-you, YHWH, I-call	**1:19 α** **excluded, highlighted text**
a	for fire has-burned (the-)pastures(-of) (the-)wilderness	**1:19 β–γ**
a´	and-fire has-burned (the-)pastures(-of) (the-)wilderness	**1:20 ε–ζ**

(2) RECURSION$_{lexical}$—This strophe is characterized by a complex parallelism. The reversed positions of *c´* and *b´* may close the strophe on a heightened note of catastrophe. The entire recursive structure, in effect, signals intense disaster.

Parallelism characterizing Stanza B, Strophe 3

a	to-you, YHWH, I-call	**1:19**
b	for fire has-burned (the-)pastures(-of) (the-)wilderness	
c	and-flame(s) have-scorched all (the-)trees(-of) (the-)field(s)	
a´	indeed, (the-)beasts(-of) (the-)field(s) pant for-you	**1:20**
c´	for they-have-dried-up, (the-)streams(-of) water,	
b´	and-fire has-burned (the-)pastures(-of) (the-)wilderness	

DISCOURSE UNIT: 2:1–11 [Cohen, Crenshaw]. Cohen gives as the topic "The invasion of the Locusts"; Crenshaw, "YHWH's efficient army." This discourse unit comprises Stanza C in Wendland's analysis.

RECURSION$_{lexical}$—Stanza C (2:1–11) is characterized by an inversion extending over the whole of the discourse unit, as follows:

Thematic inversion characterizing Stanza C

a	the imminence of the day of YHWH	**2:1–2a**
b	the great army of locusts	**2:2b**
c	the destruction caused by the army: on the earth	**2:3**
d	the army described: its movement	**2:4–5**
e	the terror caused by the army	**2:6**
d´	the army described: its movement	**2:7–9**
c´	the destruction caused by the army: above the earth	**2:10**
b´	the great army of YHWH	**2:11a**
a´	the greatness of the coming day of YHWH	**2:11b**

The tension mounts through Stanza C as the military language piles up and as the invaders actually reach and penetrate Jerusalem. Nature joins the disaster as heavenly bodies fail. Finally, YHWH reveals himself, and the climax of the discourse unit is expressed in the final question of 2:11b: וּמִי יְכִילֶנּוּ *ûmî yəḵîlennû and-who (can-)endure-it?*. This question then leads into the next discourse unit, Stanza D, and YHWH's invitation to turn to him.

2:1

Blow (a-)ram's-horn on-Zion, and-sound-an-alarm on-(the-)mountain(-of) my-holiness.

Let- all (the-)inhabitants(-of) the-land -tremble/ All (the-)inhabitants (-of) the-landwill-tremble, for (the-)day(-of) YHWH is-coming, for (it is) near.

(1) RECURSION$_{\text{lexical}}$—Elements of 2:1–2 form a very extended inclusio with elements in 2:10–11, thus demarcating the boundaries of Stanza C. These elements fall into an irregular interlocking scheme, as shown below:

	2:1–2	2:10–11	
a	Blow (a-)ram's-horn on-Zion, and-sound-an-alarm…	Before-it (the-)earth quakes, (the-)heavens tremble	**b**′
b	Let- all (the-)inhabitants(-of) the-land -tremble	(the-)sun and-(the-)moon grow-dark, and-(the-)stars draw-back their-luster	**d**′
c	for (the-)day(-of) YHWH is-coming, for (it is) near	And-YHWH utters his-voice	**a**′
d	(A-)day(-of) darkness and-gloom, (a-)day(-of) cloud-masses and-gloom…	before his-army, for great (is) (the-)power(-of) his-army…	**e**′
e	(is/comes)(a-)people numerous and-vast	For great (is) (the-)day(-of) YHWH	**c**′
		and fearful (its-)power, and-who (can-)endure-it?	**b**″

One simple aspect of this complex inclusio is the recurring theme of the day of YHWH in the first and last verses of Stanza C. Colon δ of 2:1 reads כִּי־בָא יוֹם־יְהוָה כִּי קָרוֹב *kî-ḇāʾ yôm-yhwh kî qārôḇ* 'for the day of YHWH is coming; indeed, it is near'. Cola ε–ζ of 2:11 reads כִּי־גָדוֹל יוֹם־יְהוָה וְנוֹרָא מְאֹד וּמִי יְכִילֶנּוּ *kî-gāḏôl yôm-yhwh wənôrāʾ məʾōḏ ûmî yəḵîlennû* 'for great is the day of YHWH and fearful its power, and who can endure it?'.

(2) RECURSION$_{\text{lexical}}$—Synonymous parallelism is exhibited in bicolon α–β and again in colon δ. Care should be taken that these expressions be understood as synonymous in translation.

(3) RECURSION$_{\text{morphological}}$—The repetition of plural imperative forms (with their constant *û* endings) lends cohesion and urgency to this verse.

2:2

(A-)day(-of) darkness and-gloom, (a-)day(-of) cloud-masses and-gloom;
(MT) like dawn being-spread over-the-mountains,
(ET) like blackness being-spread over-the-mountains,
(is/comes)(a-)people numerous and-vast,
such-as has- not -happened from-the-far-past,
and-after-it not continuing to (the-)years(-of) generations and-generations.

(1) RECURSION$_{\text{lexical}}$—Synonymous parallelism is exhibited in bicolon α–β. The effect is one of intensity.

(2) RECURSION$_{\text{semantic}}$—A recursion of concepts characterizes the near end of Strophe 1 (2:2) and the near end of Strophe 2 (2:5), forming an epiphora:

Epiphora between Stanza C, Strophes 1 and 2

a	(a-)people numerous and-vast	**2:2**
b	like (a-)mighty -people prepared-for battle	**2:5**

(3) RECURSION lexical—An irregular but complex recursive structure spans the boundary of Strophe 1–Strophe 2, forming a kind of anadiplosis (recursion across a discourse unit boundary):

Recursion spanning Stanza C, Strophes 1–2

a	such-as has- not -happened from-the-far-past	**2:2**
a´	and-after-it not continuing to (the-)years(-of) generation(s) and-generation(s)	
b	before-it fire burns	**2:3**
c	and-after-it flame(s) scorch	
b´	like (the-)Garden(-of) Eden (is) the-land before-it	
c´	and-after-it (a-)wilderness(-of) desolation	
	and- there-is -absolutely nothing/no one spared from-it/of-it	**excluded, highlighted text**

Cola ε–θ of 2:2 are structured in a parallel couplet, a/a´; this parallelism is to emphasize the contrast between the present event and past or future event. In 2:3 is a more complex parallel structure, b/c // b´/c´; again, the aim is to emphasize a contrast—that between the prosperous first state of the land and the land's ruin following the catastrophic invasion. The excluded material is very prominent, as it expresses the final result of the invasion. Viewed as a whole, this recursive structure is irregular in pattern, but through it runs the repeated motif וְאַחֲרָיו *wəʾaḥărâw* 'and after it' and the concept of an anterior quality, whether temporal or spatial, expressed by מִן־הָעוֹלָם *min-hāʿôlām* 'from the far past' and לְפָנָיו *ləpānâw* 'before it'. Note that the nature of the contrasted anterior and posterior qualities varies through the passage: it is temporal in 2:2, spatial in 2:3 cola α–β, and qualitative in 2:3 cola γ–δ.

2:3

Before-it fire burns, and-after-it flames scorch.
Like (the-)Garden(-of) Eden (is) the-land before-it, and-after-it (a-) wilderness(-of) desolation
and- there-is-absolutely nothing/no one spared from-it/of-it.

(1) RECURSION$_{\text{lexical}}$—Bicolon α–β exhibits antithetic parallelism.

(2) RECURSION$_{\text{lexical}}$—The opening expression in colon α (*ləp̄ānâw* 'before it') recurs as the opening expression of Strophe 4 (2:10); the opening expression of Strophe 3 (2:6) is similar (*mippānâw* 'before it'). These expressions constitute an anaphora, whose role is to help build up the tension of this stanza.

Recursion of (*ləp̄ānâw*) and (*mippānâw*)

a	before-it (*ləp̄ānâw*)	**2:3**
b	before-it (*mippānâw*)	**2:6**
c	before-it (*ləp̄ānâw*)	**2:10**

(3) RECURSION$_{\text{semantic}}$—This strophe is demarcated by an inclusio, producing excluded, highlighted material:

Inclusio characterizing Stanza C, Strophe 2

a	before-it fire burns, and-after-it flame(s) scorch	**2:3**
b	like-(the-)sound(-of) (a-)flame(-of) fire devouring stubble	**2:5**
	like (a-) mighty -people prepared-for battle	**excluded, highlighted text**

2:4

As-(the-)appearance(-of) horses (is) their-appearance, and-as-horsemen so they-run.

RECURSION$_{\text{lexical}}$—Joel 2:4–5 exhibits a complex kind of recursion featuring both comparative and additive relations.

2:7
Like valiant-men they-run, like men(-of) war they-scale (the-) wall, (each) man goes in-his-paths, (MT) and- they-do- -not -abandon their-path. (ET1) and- they-do- -not bend-aside their-path. (ET2) and- they-do- -not -turn-aside their-path.

RECURSION$_{lexical}$—Joel 2:7–9 features linear recursion with an embedded chiasm (signaled in bold). This recursion characterizes most of Strophe 3.

Linear recursion covering most of Stanza C, Strophe 3

a	they-run	**2:7**
b	they-scale	
c	**goes**	
d	**and- they-do- -not -abandon**	
d´	**one does- not -crowd**	**2:8**
c´	**goes**	
a´	they-run	**2:9**
b´	they-go-up	

(2) RECURSION$_{morphological}$—This same recursion features morphological recursion as well, which includes the *û/ûn* verb ending, providing additional cohesion to 2:7–9.

2:9
Against-the-city they-rush, upon-the-wall they-run; into-the-houses they-go-up,
through-the-windows they-go as-(a)-thief.

RECURSION$_{semantic}$—This verse is characterized by a simple parallel recursion, each element consisting of one colon. This recursion signals the peak of a prophetic narrative. The final element, *as-(a)-thief*, is unique in the patterning, hence extremely prominent in emphasizing the sudden and brutal nature of the attack.

Parallel recursion in 2:9

a Against-the-city they-rush

b upon-the-wall they-run

c into-the-houses they-go-up

d through-the-windows they-go as-(a)-thief

unique and prominent material

2:10

Before-it (the-)earth quakes, (the-)heavens tremble;
(the-)sun and-(the-)moon grow-dark, and-(the-)stars draw-back their-light.

RECURSION$_{lexical}$—Joel 2:10–11 introduces an ensemble of extended motifs concerning cosmic signs associated with the day of YHWH in its three modes in Joel: imminent and temporal judgment upon Israel (2:10–11), messianic (3:3–5), and the eschatological, final judgment upon all nations (4:15–16). The motifs are presented in various fashions in these passages, in accordance with the themes Joel wishes to highlight. In particular, the textual material which is excluded from the recursive elements (see below) presents a question which will be answered in 3:3–5 by the excluded material in that passage, as well as in 4:15–16 by that passage's excluded material.

Extended motifs in Stanza C, Strophe 4

a Before-it (the-)earth quakes, (the-)heavens tremble **2:10**

b (the-)sun and-(the-)moon grow-dark,
and-(the-)stars draw-back their-light

c And-YHWH utters his-voice before his-army **2:11**

d for great (is) (the-)day(-of) YHWH and fearful (its-)power

and-who (can-)endure-it? **excluded, highlighted text**

2:12
Yet-even now, (the-)declaration(-of) YHWH:
return/turn to-me with-all your(p)-heart and-with-fasting and-with-weeping and-with-rites-of-mourning.

(1) RECURSION_{semantic}—Strophe 1 has the following introverted recursive structure:

Introversion characterizing Stanza D, Strophe 1

a Yet-even now, (the-)declaration(-of) YHWH: turn/return to-me with-all your(p)-heart **2:12**
imperative to return to YHWH

b and-with-fasting and-with-weeping and-with-rites(-of)mourning and-tear your(p)-heart(s) and-not (only) your(p)-garment(s)
description of repentance

c and-turn/return to-YHWH your(p)-God **2:13**
imperative to return to YHWH

b´ for-gracious and-compassionate (is) he slowness(-of) anger and-great (in) faithfulness and-relenting from the-intended-evil
description of YHWH, who receives repentance

a´ Who (is) (the-)one-knowing (whether) he-will-turn and-relent and-leave behind-him blessing, sacrifice and-drink-offering for-YHWH our-God **2:14**

(2) RECURSION_{semantic}—Stanza D is demarcated by an inclusio having to do with weeping:

Inclusio characterizing Stanza D

a and-with-fasting and-with-weeping and-with-rites-of-mourning **2:12**

a´ between the-porch and- the-altar let-them-weep **2:17**

2:13

And-tear your(p)-hearts and-not (only) your(p)-garments,
and-turn/return to-YHWH your(p)-God, or gracious and-compassionate (is) he,
slowness(-of) anger and-great (in) faithfulness and-relenting from the-intended-evil.

RECURSION$_{\text{lexical}}$—The description of YHWH, *for gracious and-compassionate ... and-relenting from the-intended-evil*, amounts to recursive description of a single one of his qualities. The effect is to stress his abundant love in response to the question "who can endure it?" that concludes 2:11.

2:14

Who (is) (the-)one-knowing (whether) he-will-turn and-relent and-leave after-him blessing,
sacrifice and-drink-offering for-YHWH our-God?

RECURSION$_{\text{lexical}}$—The element אֱלֹהֵיכֶם *ʾĕlōhêḵem* 'your God' recurs nearly exactly in 2:17 as אֱלֹהֵיהֶם *ʾĕlōhêhem* in אַיֵּה אֱלֹהֵיהֶם *ʾayyēh ʾĕlōhêhem* 'where is their God?', a taunt. This creates an epiphora between Strophes 1 and 3.

2:15

Blow (a-)ram's-horn on-Zion,
announce-(a)-holy fast, call (a-)solemn-assembly.

RECURSION$_{\text{morphological}}$—The sevenfold repetition in this strophe of the plural imperative (with the constant *û* ending) lends it cohesion and a sense of urgency.

2:17

Between the-porch and-the-altar let- the-priests -weep,
(the-)ministers(-of) YHWH, and-let-them-say, YHWH, look-compassionately upon your(s)-people,
and-do- not -hand-over your(s)-possession to-mockery, (MT) that (the-) nations should-rule over-them; (ET) to-scoffing among-them (the-)nations;
why should-they-say among-the-peoples, where (is) their-God?

(1) RECURSION$_{\text{lexical}}$—Elements from 2:17, which closes Part 1 of Joel, recur in 2:27, which closes the first stanza of Part 2, and again in 4:21, which concludes Part 2 of Joel, thus forming an epiphora as follows (the essential recurring concepts are italicized and underlined). The recurring theme of shame is signaled by "disgrace" and "be ashamed." The recurring theme of the question of YHWH's power or perhaps of his existence is signaled by *where (is) their-God?*, *I (am) in-(the-)midst(-of) Israel*, and *YHWH dwells/will-dwell on-Zion*. The recurring theme of the people of Israel is signaled by a variety of concepts: "people," "inheritance," and "their blood." Note

that the analysis of this last recurrence ("their blood") argues for understanding colon α of 4:21 as referring to the Jews (see TEXT AND SYNTAX in the discussion of 4:21).

Epiphora among Part 1, Stanza A´, and Part 2 of Joel

a	and-let-them-say, YHWH, look-compassionately upon your(s)-people, and-do not -hand-over your(s)-possession to-mockery	**2:17**
b	why should-they-say among-the-peoples, *where (is) their-God*?	
b´	And-you(p)-will-know that *I (am) in-(the-)midst(-of) Israel*	**2:27**
a´	I (am) YHWH your(p)-God, and-there-is-no other, and- my-people will- -not -be-ashamed (again) for-all-time	
a″	And-I-declare-innocent their-blood / And-I-will-avenge their-blood	**4:21**
b″	*and-YHWH dwells / will-dwell on-Zion*	

(2) RECURSION$_{semantic}$—Three elements recur on either side of the boundary between 2:17 and 2:18, creating a constellation of anadiplosis (i.e., recursion across a discourse unit boundary). These verses straddle the boundary of Part 1 and Part 2 of the book. This recursion prominently marks the discourse unit boundary between Parts 1 and 2. The people's turning to YHWH is strongly implied, and YHWH is shown to answer the people in their own terms.

Anadiplosis between Part 1 and Part 2 of Joel

YHWH, look-compassionately upon your(s)-people (*ᶜām*) **2:17**

and-do not -hand-over your(s)-possession to-mockery (*ḥerpâ*)

to-scoffing among-them (the-)nations (*gôyim*)

why should-they-say among-the-peoples (*ᶜammîm*)

YHWH...he-took-compassion on his-people (*ᶜām*) **2:18–19**

And- YHWH -answered and-said to-his-people (*ᶜām*)

and-I-will- not -make you(p) any-longer (a-)disgrace (*ḥerpâ*) among-the-nations (*gôyim*)

DISCOURSE UNIT: 2:18–27

(1) RECURSION$_{\text{thematic}}$—Stanza A´ is characterized by an *a–b–a´* structure. Between the two halves of the introverted and extended inclusio structure diagrammed above lies 2:21–24, which comprises Strophe 2 and furnishes the *b* element in the stanza:

Structure of Stanza A´

a	YHWH will drive out Israel's enemies	**Strophe 1** **(2:18–20)**
b	YHWH's blessings will come (depicted in agricultural terms)	**Strophe 2** **(2:21–24)**
a´	YHWH will drive out Israel's enemies	**Strophe 3** **(2:25–27)**

Stanzas A´ and B´ comprise a very extended progression of the outpouring theme. They make reference first to physical things relating to harvest, then to the emotions of joy and thankfulness on the part of YHWH's people, and finally to YHWH's spirit and the accompanying spiritual blessings.

2:19

And- YHWH -answered and-said to-his-people, behold-me about-to-send to-you(p)
the-grain and-the-wine and-the-oil, and-you(p)-will-be-satisfied with-it,
and-I-will- not -make you(p) any-longer (a-)disgrace among-the-nations.

RECURSIONlexical—Stanzas A´ and B´ are spanned by an inclusio:

Inclusio spanning Stanzas A´ and B´

	Then- YHWH -was-zealous for-his-land, and-he-took-compassion on his-people	**2:18** **excluded, highlighted text**
a	And- YHWH -answered and-said	**2:19**
a´	as YHWH said	**3:5 (2:32)**

Verse 2:18 is left excluded and very prominent.

2:20

And-the-northerner I-will-remove from-you(p),
and-I-will-drive-it to (a-)land (a-)dry-country and-(a-)sinister-desolation,
its-front-end into the- eastern -sea and-its-rear into the- western -sea.
And- its-stench -will-go-up and- its-foul-odor -will-go-up,
(MT) because/indeed he/it-has-done great-things
(ET) for I-have-done great-things.

RECURSIONlexical—The last colon of this verse recurs at the end of 2:21, forming an anadiplosis across the strophe boundary:

Anadiplosis between 2:20 and 2:21

a	because/indeed he/it-has-done great-things	**2:20**
a´	for YHWH has-done great-things	**2:21**

The contrast in this recursion is between negative and positive, as the first element pertains to "the northerner," whom YHWH will destroy, whereas the second pertains to the wondrous works of YHWH for his covenant people. This recursion bridges not only the strophe boundary, but also the change from direct speech of YHWH to third person commentary of the prophet.

2:21

Do- not -be-afraid(p), fields; shout-for-joy(p) and-rejoice(p),
for YHWH has-done great-things.

RECURSION$_{\text{lexical}}$—In contrast to the introverted structure which Strophes 1 and 3 exhibit together (see the discussion under discourse unit 2:18–27), Strophe 2 features a complex parallelism based on thematic elements, as shown below:

Thematic parallelism in Stanza A´, Strophe 2

a Do- not -be-afraid(p), field(s) **2:21**
command not to fear

b shout-for-joy(p) and-be-rejoice(p)
command to rejoice

c for YHWH has-done great-things
reason for command

a´ Do- not -be-afraid(p), beasts(-of) field(s) **2:22**
command not to fear

d for (the-)pastures(-of) (the-)wilderness
have-become-green, for (the-)tree(s) have-yielded
their-fruit, (the-)fig-trees and-the-vine(s) have-given
their-strength
result

b´ And-sons(-of) Zion, rejoice(p) and-be-glad(p) in-YHWH **2:23**
your(p)-God
command to rejoice

c´ for he-has-given to-you(p) the-early-rain for-righteousness,
and-he-has-brought-down to-you(p) shower(s),
(the-)early-rain and-(the-)late-rain,
(as) in-the-former-times
reason for command

d´ And- the-threshing-floors(-of) grain **2:24**
-will-be-full, and- the-wine-vats -will-overflow
(with) new-wine and-olive-oil
result

In this recursive form, two sets of four parallel elements (*a*, *b*, *c*, *d* // *a´* , *b´* , *c´*, *d´*) are overlapped, so that *a´* occurs before *d*. Particularly strong cohesion is thus produced, and the final result in *d´* is highlighted.

2:25

And-I-will-repay to-you(p) the-years/two-fold which/that-which the-locusts have-eaten,
the-creeping-locusts and-the-young-locusts and-the-flying-locusts, my-great army which I-sent against-you(p).

RECURSION_{lexical}—The verb אכל *ʾkl* 'to eat', applied here to locusts, recurs in 2:26 and is there applied to YHWH's addressees, in this way heightening the contrast between disaster and restoration [Wolff]. A translator would do well to replicate this recursion, if at all possible.

2:26

And-you(p)-will-eat in-plenty and-be-satisfied, and-you(p)-will-praise (the-)name(-of) YHWH your(p)-God,
who has-worked wonderfully for-you(p), and- my-people will- not -be-ashamed (again)-for-all-time.

RECURSION_{lexical}—The linear recursion shown below gives cohesion to 2:26–27; it also serves to end stanza A′ on one of the book's principal themes [Wendland].

Recursion in 2:26–27

a and-you(p)-will-praise (the-)name(-of) YHWH your(p)-God **2:26**
result

b who has-worked wonderfully for-you(p)
result

c and- my-people will- not -be-ashamed (again)-for-all-time
implication

a′ And-you(p)-will-know that I (am)...YHWH your(p)-God **2:27**
result

b′ and-there-is-no other
reason

c′ and- my-people -will- not -be-ashamed (again) for-all-time
implication

2:27
And-you(p)-will-know that I (am) in-(the-)midst(-of) Israel;
I (am) YHWH your(p)-God, and-there-is-no other, and- my-people will- -not -be-ashamed (again)-for-all-time.

RECURSION$_{\text{lexical}}$—Elements of 2:27 (final verse of Stanza A´) recur as an epiphora in 3:5 (final verse of Stanza B´), in 4:17 (the end of Stanza D´, Strophe 2), and in 4:21 (the final verse of Stanza D´ and of the book), as displayed below. In this interlacing of themes, Joel responds powerfully to the disdain thrown at YHWH's people in 2:17.

Epiphora extending from 2:27 to later verses

And-you(p)-will-know that I (am) in-(the-)midst(-of) Israel	**2:27**
I (am) YHWH your(p)-God, and-there-is-no other	
For on-(the-)mountain(-of) Zion and-in-Jerusalem there-will-be escape as YHWH said	**3:5**
And-you(p)-will-know that I (am) YHWH your(p)-God, (I who) live on-Zion, (the-)mountain(-of) my-holiness	**4:17**
and-foreigners will- never-again -pass-through-her	
and-YHWH dwells / will-dwell on-Zion	**4:21**

3:1 (2:28)
And-it-will-happen after-this,
I-will-pour-out my-spirit upon-all-flesh, and- your(p)-sons and your(p)-daughters -will-prophesy;
your(p)-old-men will-dream dreams; your(p)-young-men will-see visions.

(1) RECURSION$_{\text{lexical}}$—The time expressions in 3:1–2 form a small inclusio with אַחֲרֵי־כֵן *ʾaḥărê-kēn* 'after this' (3:1) and בַּיָּמִים הָהֵמָּה *bayyāmîm hāhēmmâ* 'in those days' (3:2). The recurrence marks the peak of the strophe, which consists of *and-even upon-the-servants and-upon the-maidservants in-those-days*.

(2) RECURSION$_{\text{lexical}}$—The first half of colon β (*I-will-pour-out my-spirit*) forms an inclusio with colon γ of 3:2 (*I-will-pour-out my-spirit*), which demarcates in a general way this strophe, and which also serves to bring into cohesion the references to diverse groups of people.

(3) RECURSION$_{lexical}$—Recursion of the prophetic formula in colon α sets up an anaphora with later verses. All of these formulas provide a very prominent opening to their respective units of discourse:

Anaphora between 3:1 and later verses

a	And-it-will-happen after-this	**3:1 (2:28)** **start of Stanza B´ Strophe 1**
b	And-it-will-be	**3:5 (2:32)** **start of Stanza B´ Strophe 3**
c	in-those-days and-at-that-time	**4:1 (3:1]** **start of Stanza C´ Strophe 1**
d	And-it-will-come-about in- that -day	**4:18 (3:18)** **start of Stanza D´ Strophe 3**

3:3 (2:30)
And-I-will-place signs in-the-heavens and-on-the-earth, blood and-fire and-billows(-of) smoke.

RECURSION$_{lexical}$—Joel 3:3–5 contains an important ensemble of elements in recursion which were first met in 2:10–12. Here they are found in the following scheme:

Recursion in Stanza B´, Strophes 2 and 3

a	And-I-will-place signs in-the-heavens and-on-the-earth, blood and-fire and-billows(-of) smoke	**3:3**
b	The-sun shall-be-turned to-darkness and-the-moon (shall be turned) to-blood	**3:4**
d	before (the-)day(-of) YHWH comes -great and-the-fearful (day)	
	<u>And-it-will-be (that) everyone who calls on-(the-)name(-of) YHWH will-escape</u>	**excluded, highlighted text**
c	for on-(the-)mountain(-of) Zion and-in-Jerusalem there-will-be escape...	**3:5**
	<u>and-among-the-survivors whom YHWH will-call</u>	**excluded, highlighted text**

3:4 (2:31)

The-sun shall-be-turned to-darkness and-the-moon (shall-be-turned) to-blood,

before the- day(-of) YHWH comes -great and-the-fearful (day).

RECURSION$_{lexical}$—Recursion of the day of YHWH theme sets up an epiphora between the 2:11, the end of Stanza C, and 3:4 (2:31), which is very close to the end of Stanza B´. The placement of this epiphora leaves 3:5 (2:32) very prominent (the last verse of Stanza B´).

Epiphora characterizing the ends of Stanza C and B´

a	for great (is) (the-)day(-of) YHWH and fearful (its-)power, and-who (can-)endure it?	**2:11**
a´	before (the-)day(-of) YHWH comes the-great and-the-fearful (day)	**3:4**

3:5 (2:32)

And-it-will-be (that) everyone who calls on-(the-)name(-of) YHWH will-escape,

for on-(the-)mountain(-of) Zion and-in-Jerusalem there-will-be escape as YHWH said,

and-among-the-survivors whom YHWH will-call.

RECURSION$_{lexical}$—This verse is structured around an inversion of lexical items, as follows:

Inversion marking Stanza B´, Strophe 2 (3:3–4)

a	And-I-will-place signs in-the-heavens *heavenly signs*	**3:3**
b	and-on-the-earth *earthly signs*	
b´	blood and-fire and-billows(-of) smoke *earthly signs*	
a´	The-sun shall-be-turned to-darkness and-the-moon (shall be turned) to-blood *heavenly signs*	**3:4**
	before (the-)day(-of) YHWH comes the-great and-the-fearful (day)	**excluded, high-lighted text**

Inversion characterizing 3:5 (2:32)

a everyone who calls

b on-(the-)name(-of) YHWH

c will-escape

c´ there-will-be escape

b´ as YHWH said

a´ whom YHWH will-call

(2) RECURSION$_{\text{lexical}}$—Material from colon γ recurs in 4:8 (3:8), creating an epiphora, as the two occurrences mark the end of discourse units:

Epiphora marking the ends of two discourse units

a	as YHWH said (*kaʾăšer ʾāmar yhwh*)	**3:5 (2:32)** **(last verse of Stanza B´)**
a´	for YHWH has-spoken (*kî yhwh dibbēr*)	**4:8** **(Last verse of Stanza C´, Strophe 2)**

(3) RECURSION$_{\text{lexical}}$—The pairing of צִיּוֹן *ṣiyyôn* 'Zion' and יְרוּשָׁלַםִ *yərûšālaim* 'Jerusalem' represents a recursion which occurs also in 4:16–17 and in a reversed fashion in 4:20–21. The two terms are, for all practical purposes, synonymous in these contexts. Care should be taken that a translation present them as such. The two terms paired together present Jerusalem as the abode of YHWH and as therefore the refuge of his covenant people.

DISCOURSE UNIT: 4:1–11 (3:1–11).

RECURSION$_{thematic}$—Stanza C′, like Stanza A, has an *a–b–a′* structure:

Structure of Stanza C′

a	YHWH will judge all nations	**Strophe 1** **4:1–3 (3:1–3)**
b	Tyre, Sidon, and Philistia are singled out for comment	**Strophe 2** **4:4–8 (3:4–8)**
a′	YHWH will judge all nations	**Strophe 3** **4:9–11 (3:9–11)**

4:1 (3:1)

For behold in-those-days and-at-that-time
(MT$_1$) when I-will-bring-back(the-)captivity(-of) Judah and-Jerusalem,
(MT$_2$) when I-will-restore (the-)fortunes(-of) Judah and-Jerusalem,

RECURSION$_{semantic}$—This strophe is characterized by repeated reference, both nominal and pronominal, to various groups of people: 'Judah and Jerusalem', 'all the nations', 'them', 'them', 'my people', 'my possession Israel', 'they', 'the nations', 'they', 'my people', 'they', 'the boy', 'the girl, 'prostitute' (feminine), 'wine' (masculine). The last four elements here are the most prominent, as they break with the established pattern in this recursion of plural and mass nouns, and as they set up a grammatical chiasm of gender ('boy'/ feminine noun ('prostitute') // 'girl' / masculine noun ('wine')). The effect of this prominence is to emphasize in the most telling way possible that YHWH will take full retribution against his enemies.

4:2 (3:2)

and-I-will-gather all the-nations
and-I-will-bring-them to (the-)valley (of) Jehoshaphat and-I-will-enter-into-judgment against-them there because-of my-people and-my-possession Israel which they-scattered among-the-nations
and- they-divided-up -my-land.

RECURSION$_{lexical}$—A complex recursive ensemble consisting of an inclusio combined with anaphora and anadiplosis occurs in 4:2–12 (3:2–12). The inclusio (see the following display) spans most of Stanza C′. It excludes and leaves as prominent 4:1 (3:1)—which consists of a stylized introduction to the salvation oracle of Stanza C′—and the final part of 4:11 (3:11), which is the prophet's aside, *bring-down, YHWH, your-warriors*.

	Inclusio characterizing Stanza C´	
a	and-I-will-gather all the-nations and-I-will-bring-them to (the-)valley(-of) Jehoshaphat	**4:2**
b	and-I-will-enter-into-judgment against-them there	
a´	Wake-up(p) / Hurry(p) and-come(p), all nations, from-round-about,	**4:11**
b´	and-gather there	

The anadiplosis is the recursive material marking the boundary between Stanzas C´ and D´: *a´–b´* characterizes 4:11 and *a˝–b˝* characterizes 4:12. The effect of this device is to highlight the discourse unit boundary, as well as the excluded material of 4:12 (*all-the-nations from-round-about*), thus reinforcing the theme of the universality of YHWH's judgment presented in *a* and *a´*.

DISCOURSE UNIT: 4:4–8 (3:4–8). The thematic structure of this strophe falls into a kind of parallelism.

	Thematic structure of Stanza C´, Strophe 2	
a	I-will- very quickly -bring your(p)-retaliation upon-your(p)-head	**4:4 (3:4)**
b	you(p)-have-sold	**4:6 (3:6)**
a´	And-I-will-return your(p)-reprisal upon-your(p)-head(s)	**4:7 (3:7)**
b´	And-I-will-sell	**4:8 (3:8)**

4:9 (3:9)
Proclaim(p) this to-the-nations: prepare(p)-for-(a)holy war; rouse the-warriors; let-them-advance (and) attack, all-(the-)men(-of) the-war.

RECURSION$_{\text{lexical}}$—An additional anadiplosis occurs in this strophe (4:9–11) and 4:12 (the first verse of Stanza D´). Joel creates an irregular but compelling semantic web out of the themes of war and divine judgment with the message that YHWH's judgment will come upon all nations in the midst of their attack upon Jerusalem. Recurring concepts in 4:9–12 are:

גּוֹי *gôy*	'nation'	**4:9, 11, 12**
מִלְחָמָה *milḥāmâ*	'war'	**4:9 (twice)**
הָעִירוּ הַגִּבּוֹרִים *hāʿîrû haggibbôrîm* הַנְחַת יְהוָה גִּבּוֹרֶיךָ *hanḥat yhwh gəbbôrêkā*	'rouse the mighty warriors, bring down your warriors, YHWH'	**4:9, 4:11**
עלה *ʿlh* / עוּשׁ *ʿûš*	'to advance' / 'to hurry'	**4:9, 4:11**
מִסָּבִיב *missābîb*	'from around about'	**4:11, 12**
שָׁמָּה *šāmmâ* / שָׁם *šām*	'there'	**4:11, 4:12**
יְהוֹשָׁפָט *yəhôšāpāṭ*	'YHWH judges'	**4:12**
שׁפט *špṭ*	'to judge'	

RECURSION$_{\text{morphological}}$—The ninefold repetition of the plural imperative (with the constant *û* ending) in this strophe lends it cohesion and a sense of urgency.

4:11 (3:11)

(ET$_1$) Wake-up(p) (ET$_2$) Hurry(p) and-come(p), all nations, from-round-about, (MT) and-gather; (ET) and-gather^e there;
(MT) bring-down, YHWH, your(sg)-warriors to-that-place (ET$_1$) let the-frightened-man become (a-)warrior. (ET$_2$) that- YHWH -may-shatter your(sg)-warriors.

RECURSION$_{\text{lexical}}$—See 4:2 (3:2) in this appendix for the discussion of the inclusio that spans most of Stanza C′. The textual material not included by this inclusio is 4:1 (consisting of a stylized introduction to the salvation oracle of Stanza C′) and the final part of 4:11 (the prophet's aside, *bring-down, YHWH, your-warriors*).

4:12 (3:12)

Let-the-nations be-set-in-motion(p) and-let-them-advance(p) to-(the-)valley(-of) Jehoshaphat,
for there I-will-sit to-judge all-the-nations from-round-about.

RECURSION$_{\text{lexical}}$—A tightly woven but irregular scheme of recursion of certain lexical items and themes relates this verse to the last strophe of stanza C′, a recurrence phenomenon which by virtue of the crossing of a discourse unit boundary (in this case a stanza boundary) is termed anadiplosis. The implicated theme is YHWH's judgment coming upon all nations in the midst of their military attack upon Jerusalem, with special emphasis on the phrase אֶת־כָּל־הַגּוֹיִם מִסָּבִיב *ʾeṯ-kol-haggôyim missāḇîḇ* 'all nations round about', this phrase being excluded from the inclusio of 4:1–12 (see the discussion under 4:2 in this appendix).

RECURSION$_{\text{morphological}}$—The fivefold repetition of the plural imperative and jussive (with the constant *û* ending) in 4:12–13 (3:12–13) lends this strophe cohesion and a sense of urgency.

RECURSION$_{\text{thematic}}$—This strophe has a general *a–b–a′* structure, as follows:

Structure of Stanza D´, Strophe 1

a **a** Let-the-nations be-set-in-motion(p) and-let-them-advance(p) α **4:12**

b to-(the-)valley(-of)Jehoshaphat, β

b´ for (*kî*) there I-will-sit to-judge γ

a´ all-the-nations from-round-about δ

b **c** Swing(p) (the-)sickle, α **4:13**

d for (*kî*) (the-)harvest is-ripe; β

c´ go(p) tread(p)(grapes in the winepress) γ

d´ for (*kî*) (the-)winepress is-full, δ

c″ (the-)wine-vats have-overflowed, ε

d″ for (*kî*) great (is) their-wickedness ζ

a´ **a″** Tumult, tumult α **4:14**

b″ in-(the-)valley(-of) the-verdict, β

e for (*kî*) near (is) (the-)day(-of) YHWH γ

b‴ in-(the-)valley(-of) the-verdict δ

The internal structure of this recursion is finely patterned. In both 4:12 and 4:14, a locative expression occurs in colon β and a *kî*-clause in colon γ. Many of the concepts of 4:12 recur in 4:14; in fact, the latter verse reads as a continuation of the former, with the only new element in 4:14 being colon γ, which in turn expresses precisely the main theme of this strophe. Verse 13 functions as an interruption to v. 12, having its own structure, with every second colon consisting of a *kî*-clause. The lines of 4:13 in Hebrew are two-foot lines, lending themselves to describing rapid action, which stands in contrast to the two surrounding verses. The intricately structured recursion of this strophe signals the high point of this apocalyptic episode.

4:15 (3:15)
Sun and-moon have-grown-dark, and-stars have-withdrawn their-shining.

RECURSION$_{lexical}$—Joel 4:15–16 (3:15–16) contains an important ensemble of elements in recursion, which elements were seen earlier in 2:10–12 and 3:3–5 (2:30–32). Here they are found in the following scheme:

Recurring elements in Stanza D´, Strophe 2

b	Sun and-moon have-become-dark, and-stars have-withdrawn their-shining	**4:15 (3:15)**
c	Then-YHWH roars from-Zion, and-from-Jerusalem he-lifts-up his-voice	**4:16 (3:16)**
a	and- (the-)heavens and-(the-)earth -quake	
	but-YHWH (is/will be) (a)refuge for-his-people, and-(a)fortress for-(the-)sons(-of) Israel.	**excluded, high-lighted text**

Element *a* is shifted back to a less prominent position, but its position highlights the new material of colon γ in 4:16 (3:16), which shares the same theme as the highlighted material from 2:10–12 and 3:3–5 (2:30–32) [Wolff].

4:16 (3:16)
Then-YHWH roars from-Zion, and-from-Jerusalem he-lifts-up his-voice,
and- (the-)heavens and-(the)earth -quake,
but-YHWH (is/will be) (a)refuge for-his-people, and-(a)fortress for-(the-)sons(-of) Israel.

RECURSION$_{lexical}$—See the comments under 3:5 in this appendix on the recursion of the terms "Zion" and "Jerusalem."

4:17 (3:17)
Then-you(p)-will-know that I (am) YHWH your(p)-God, (I who) live on-Zion, (the-)mountain(-of) my-holiness,
and- Jerusalem -will-become (a)holy-thing, and-foreigners will- never-again -pass-through-her.

RECURSION$_{thematic}$—See 2:27 in this appendix for a display of the epiphora marking 2:27, 3:5 (2:32), 4:17 (3:17), and 4:21 (3:21). The element *and-foreigners will- never-again -pass-through-her* of 4:17 (3:17) is prominently highlighted vis-à-vis the structure of the epiphora, providing very strong closure to Strophe 2.

4:18 (3:18)

And-it-will-be in- that -day
the-mountains will-drip (with) new-wine, and-the-hills will-flow (with) milk,
and-all (the)ravines(-of) Judah will-flow (with) water,
and-(a)spring from-(the-)house(-of) YHWH will-go-forth and-will-water (the-)valley(-of) Shittim/the-acacias.

RECURSION$_{lexical}$—See Recursion 3 (lexical) in 3:1 (2:28) for a display of the anaphora involving this verse.

4:20 (3:20)

But-Judah will-be-inhabited forever, and-Jerusalem to-generations and-generations.

RECURSION$_{lexical}$—See 3:5 in this appendix for comments on the recursion of the terms "Zion" and "Jerusalem" in 4:20–21.

4:21 (3:21)

(MT$_1$) And-I-will-declare-innocent their-blood, (which) I-had- not -declared-innocent (before);
(MT$_2$) And-I-will-expiate their-blood, (which) I-had- not -expiated (before);
(MT$_3$) And-I-will-avenge their-blood; (which) I-had- not -avenged (till now);
(ET$_1$) And-I-declare-innocent their-blood; indeed, I-declare (it)
(ET$_2$) And-I-will-pour-out their-blood; indeed, I-will-pour-out (it)
(ET$_3$) And-shall-I-declare-innocent their-blood? I-shall-not-declare-innocent (their-blood);
and-YHWH dwells/will-dwell on-Zion.

RECURSION$_{lexical}$—See Recursion in 2:27 for a display of an epiphora involving colon β. This theme is seen by now to be the main theme of the book.

APPENDIX 2: Wendland's Organization of the Book of Joel

Part 1	**Oracle 1**	Stanza A		
1:2–2:17	1:2–20	1:2–14	Strophe 1	1:2–4
			Strophe 2	1:5–7
			Strophe 3	1:8–10
			Strophe 4	1:11–12
			Strophe 5	1:13–14 peak of Stanza A
		Stanza B		
		1:15–20	Strophe 1	:15–16
			Strophe 2	1:17–18
			Strophe 3	1:19–20
	Oracle 2	Stanza C		
	2:1–17	2:1–11	Strophe 1	2:1–2
			Strophe 2	2:3–5
			Strophe 3	2:6–9
			Strophe 4	2:10–11
		Stanza D		
		2:12–17	Strophe 1	2:12–14
			Strophe 2	2:15–16
			Strophe 3	2:17
Part 2	**Oracle 1**	Stanza A´		
	2:18–3:5	2:18–27		
	(2:32)		Strophe 1	2:18–20
			Strophe 2	2:21–24
			Strophe 3	2:25–27
		Stanza B´		
		3:1–5		
		(2:28–32)	Strophe 1	3:1–2 (2:28–29)
			Strophe 2	3:3–4 (2:30–31)
			Strophe 3	3:5 (2:32) very prominent because of an epiphora between 2:11 and 3:4 (2:30) and because of shift in speaker
	Oracle 2	Stanza C´		
	4:1–21	4:1–11		
	(3:1–21)	(3:1–11)	Strophe 1	4:1–3 (3:1–3)
			Strophe 2	4:4–8 (3:4–8)
			Strophe 3	4:9–11 (3:9–11)
		Stanza D´		
		4:12–21		
		(3:12–21)	Strophe 1	4:12–14 (3:12–14)
			Strophe 2	4:15–17 (3:15–17)
			Strophe 3	4:18–21 (3:18–21)

Index